I0821268

"In a world of constant challenge of Christianity's intellectual integrity, Lohfink highlights that the Christian faith is not outdated or just a leftover after the European Enlightenment. In his broad scope of topics, he demonstrates not only his expertise as a biblical scholar; in a highly personal voice, he also presents his own spirituality in deep attachment to his academic profession. Following Lohfink's thoughts, we can recognize that there is no stalemate between Christian faith and reason. Even further, by joining Lohfink's adventure of faith, we can see this undertaking as deeply fulfilling."

—Florian Klug, lecturer at Julius-Maximilians-Universität Würzburg, Germany and the University of Vienna, Austria

"A surprising valedictory offering from the late renowned New Testament scholar Gerhard Lohfink. His insightful (and at times moving) interpretations of Scripture show how the ideals of human dignity, freedom, equality, and tolerance, often equated with the Enlightenment's emphasis on reason alone and critique of traditional religion, are rooted in the Jewish and early Christian scriptural traditions and continue to animate contemporary life. While a few debatable notions are here, Lohfink's cornucopia of on-target arguments reveal the deep connections between faith and reason—a very positive Roman Catholic take on how divine revelation and human experience are mutually supportive and provide our current complex situation with reasons for hope."

—Anthony J. Godzieba, professor emeritus of fundamental and systematic theology, Villanova University

Gerhard Lohfink

The Light of Faith and Reason

Israel, Jesus, and the Enlightenment

Translated by

Linda M. Maloney

LITURGICAL PRESS
Collegeville, Minnesota

litpress.org

Cover art: *Moon and Stars* by Br. Martin Erspamer, a monk of Saint Meinrad Archabbey

Unless otherwise noted, Scripture quotations are taken from the New Revised Standard Version Updated Edition. Copyright © 2021 National Council of Churches of Christ in the United States of America. Used by permission. All rights reserved worldwide.

Gerhard Lohfink, *Im Ringen um die Vernunft. Reden über Israel, die Kirche und die Europäische Aufklärung* © 2016 Verlag Herder GmbH, Freiburg im Breisgau.

© 2026 by Order of Saint Benedict, Collegeville, Minnesota. All rights reserved. No part of this book may be used or reproduced in any manner whatsoever, except brief quotations in reviews, without written permission of Liturgical Press, Saint John's Abbey, PO Box 7500, Collegeville, MN 56321-7500. Printed in the United States of America.

ISBN 979-8-4008-0114-3 979-8-4008-0115-0 (e-book)

A Cataloging-in-Publication record is available for this book from the Library of Congress.

In memory of Marianne and Margarete

We freely admit that we are trying to free the idea of Enlightenment from the exclusive claims of an 18th-century historical and philosophical movement and to trace it back to its biblical roots.

—Eckhard Nordhofen
"Biblische Aufklärung—die Entdeckung einer Tradition," in *Biblische Aufklärung—die Entdeckung einer Tradition*, ed. Martin Frühauf and Werner Löser (Frankfurt: Josef Knecht, 2005), 9–24, at 11. Trans. LMM.

Faith is not fearful of reason; on the contrary, it seeks and trusts reason.

—Pope Francis
Evangelii Gaudium 242.

Contents

Preface

The word "enlightenment" has acquired a new tone. The "dialectic of enlightenment," which also encompassed its demonic aspect,[1] has almost been forgotten. The European Enlightenment has acquired a new dignity; it has emerged as an almost mythic reality with a positively numinous character.

The reason for this is clear enough: it is the stunned, often speechless reaction of the West to the barbarity of Islamist violence. When human rights are trampled underfoot there is a justified appeal to the achievements of the European Enlightenment, and that appeal is often associated with a hope that, as the church had to accept and adopt the Enlightenment, so Islam should be open to it as well.

What is so profoundly irritating about such comparisons is that all too often the Enlightenment is presented as something far superior to Christianity, entirely the product of the self-sufficient, autonomous reason of modern humanity, which at last is employing its understanding and bringing light to the world.

To continue the "light" metaphor: what Germans call "Aufklärung"[2] is "Enlightenment" in English, "(Siècle des) Lumières" in French, and "Illuminismo" in Italian. But many centuries earlier the church had called the sacrament of baptism by which one became a Christian *illuminatio*, "enlightenment," meaning not only illumination by the divine Spirit but at the same time entry into the long history of enlightenment that began with Abraham and was perfected in Jesus.

The history of the European Enlightenment did not begin in the eighteenth century of the Common Era. It originated in Greece (something no one doubts) and in the stories about Abraham and about

[1] Max Horkheimer and Theodor W. Adorno, *Dialectic of Enlightenment*, trans. John Cumming (New York: Herder & Herder, 1972).

[2] Literally "clarification."—Trans. LMM.

Israel's exodus from Egypt (something many do not know or refuse to accept).

This book is intended to illustrate the extent to which the Hebrew Bible already served the cause of enlightenment and how that work of illumination was continued and deepened through Jesus and the church. The first ten chapters are primarily dedicated to that end. Each of the remaining chapters then treats the rational character of faith, even if their subjects are not primarily the Jewish and Christian history of enlightenment.

In general these chapters are based on lectures I have given in recent years. I have made no attempt to disguise their oral character. It is my hope that they do nothing to deny the mystery of faith and yet serve to illuminate its rationality.

The book is dedicated to the memory of my two sisters: Marianne, at the age of fourteen, was a victim of the terror of World War II, and Margarete, aged seven, was run over by a streetcar in Frankfurt.

†Gerhard Lohfink
Munich
1 January 2016

Abbreviations

AAS	*Acta Apostolicae Sedis*
ABG	Arbeiten zur Bibel und ihrer Geschichte
ACJD	Abhandlungen zum christlich-jüdischen Dialog
AUS	American University Studies
AV	Authorized Version ("King James")
BK	*Bibel und Kirche*
BK	Biblischer Kommentar
BKAT	Biblischer Kommentar, Altes Testament
BWANT	Beiträge zur Wissenschaft des Neuen Testaments
BZ	*Biblische Zeitschrift*
BZAW	Beihefte zur Zeitschrift für die alttestamentliche Wissenschaft
BZNW	Beihefte zur Zeitschrift für die neutestamentliche Wissenschaft
CiG	*Christ in der Gegenwart*
CSEL	Corpus Scriptorum Ecclesiasticorum Latinorum
EHS.T	Europäische Hochschulschriften.Theologie
EKKNT	Evangelisch-katholischer Kommentar zum Neuen Testament
ETL	*Ephemerides Theologicae Lovanienses*
EvTh	*Evangelische Theologie*
FAZ	*Frankfurter Allgemeine Zeitung*
FB	Forschung zur Bibel

FRLANT	Forschungen zur Religion und Literatur des Alten und Neuen Testaments
FTS	Frankfurter theologische studien
HBS	Herders biblische Studien
HThKNT	Herders Theologischer Kommentar zum Neuen Testament
IECOT	International Exegetical Commentary on the Old Testament
IKaZ	*Internationale katholische Zeitschrift*
JBT	Jahrbuch für biblische Theologie
KEK	Kritisch-exegetische Kommentar über das Neue Testament (Meyer-Kommentar)
LD	Lectio Divina
LXX	Septuagint
MGH DD	Die Urkünden der Karolinger
MThSt	Münchener Theologische Studien
NAB	New American Bible
NABRE	New American Bible, Revised Edition
NEB	Neue Echter Bibel
NRSV	New Revised Standard Version
NRSVue	New Revised Standard Version, Updated Edition
NTOA	Novum Testamentum et Orbis Antiquus
ÖBS	Österreichische biblische Studien
OTL	Old Testament Library
QD	Quaestiones Disputatae
SANT	Studien zum Alten und Neuen Testament
SBAB	Stuttgarter biblische Aufsatzbände
SBS	Stuttgarter Bibelstudien
TDNT	*Theological Dictionary of the New Testament*
ThPQ	*Theologisch-praktische Quartalschrift*
ThQ	*Theologische Quartalschrift*

TRE	*Theologische Realenzyklopädie*
TTS	Tübinger theologische Studien
UTB	Uni-Taschenbücher
WA	Weimarer Ausgabe (Martin Luther, *Works*)
WMANT	Wissenschaftliche Monographien zum Alten und Neuen Testament
WUNT	Wissenschaftliche Untersuchungen zum Neuen Testament
ZTK	*Zeitschrift für Theologie und Kirche*

1

Is the Church Required to Undergo Enlightenment?

When I studied theology in the 1950s I heard almost nothing about the subject of "Islam." Even in lectures on church history it was only a marginal topic. But that was true not only of theology. In the world of the media as well, the subject of Islam hardly appeared, and the word "Islamism" in its current sense did not even exist.

That all changed at one stroke in September 1972. The Summer Olympics were being held in Munich that year, and on September 5 eight members of the Palestinian freedom movement "Black September" broke into the Olympic housing where the Israeli team were quartered and took eleven Israeli athletes hostage. By evening the hostages were all dead.

Twenty-nine years later, on September 11, 2001, the towers of the World Trade Center in New York crumbled. The images still spring to mind in an instant. On that day a total of about three thousand people fell victim to Islamist terrorism.

Since then the themes of "Islam" and "Islamism" have become familiar topics in mass media. Again and again we hear the questions: How will Islam develop? Will it gradually assume an enlightened form—an "Islam of peace" that repudiates religiously motivated wars, rejects the identification of state and religion, and respects the rights of individuals and peoples? Or will the contrary be the case: Will Islam drift even more strongly in the direction we see today in the "Islamist states" in Iraq, Syria, northern Nigeria, and recently in Europe as well, in the most repulsive forms?

That is one of the major and still altogether open questions of our time. It worries all of us, and the mass media as well. And precisely in this context we more and more often encounter a strange comparison between the church and Islam.

The church, it is said, has been literally forced, in these last three hundred years, to accept reason. It simply could not escape the world-altering results of the European Enlightenment. Freedom, equality, sisterhood and brotherhood, human dignity, tolerance, the separation of church and state—the church had to learn all those (and the learning process is by no means complete). It simply had to accept the great achievements of modernity. In the end it has given in to the new values, though with much moaning and groaning.

Hopefully, it is then said, Islam will also come gradually to accept the major values of the Enlightenment, just as the church had to, so that one day it will no longer permit any kind of Islamist terrorism. At the Frankfurt Römerberg Debates in 2015 (which bore the title "Islam: Partner or Opponent of Our Civil Society?") the long-time North Africa correspondent of the German press corps, Samuel Schirmbeck, put it this way: "Unlike Christianity, Islam has not succeeded in bringing its God under control."[1]

In all this the European Enlightenment appears as a near-mythical element with a numinous character and quasi-religious value—one that stands far above Christianity, having arisen entirely out of the self-aware, autonomous reason of modern people, who have at last made use of their power of understanding and brought light to a world that, however, is still repeatedly threatened by the darkness of religious superstition and Christian intolerance.

Let me here quote from two letters from readers—representative of many other voices—that were published in the *Frankfurter Allgemeine Zeitung* (*FAZ*). They make it clear how "enlightenment" is set in opposition to Christianity. Here is an excerpt from the first one:[2]

> Enlightenment is not at home in Christianity or any other religion; if it functions at all it is over and beyond religion, undermining religious certainties of every sort. . . . Christian and enlightenment worldviews are not identical. . . . Intellectual honesty is not primarily a mental

[1] Cf. Inga K. Trauthig, "Seinen Gott muss man in Schach halten können. Das Heilige und die Gewalt. Die Frankfurter Römerberggespräche fragen nach der Rolle des Islams," *FAZ* 97/12 (April 27, 2015).

[2] Letter to the editor, *FAZ* 179/6 (May 8, 2014).

> attitude that is characteristically Christian or Muslim or based on any other religion; rather, it is constitutive of enlightenment. . . . Please, let us not participate in betraying our infinitely precious cultural heritage, which lies beyond all religions!

A second letter reads in part:[3]

> As an agnostic, perhaps already part of a majority here in the West, I postulate that, for me, religions and ideologies are the same. . . . No religion/ideology has so many human lives on its conscience as Christianity. I need not add up all the victims of crusades and witch-burnings, together with all the pre-Napoleonic wars, to arrive at a mortality rate the Islamic State, Al Qaeda, and Boko Haram could not even nibble at.
>
> The good and praiseworthy social values of the enlightened West owe no more than limited thanks to Christian foundations. . . . A little love of neighbor, of course. But otherwise: freedom, equality, brotherhood are more to be found in the works of Locke, Hobbes, and Montesquieu—and there is no danger that they will be suspected of receiving royalties from the Vatican.

One thing that strikes me about these and similar voices is that Christianity and Islam are bundled together in the same sack: that of violent, unenlightened, ideology-soaked "religion." The difference between Christianity and Islam is said to be only that the church, under duress, has learned something, but supposedly the true values of the Enlightenment did not come from the church; they are the fruit of the autonomous reason of intellectually honest Europeans.

I can understand that construct of history—certainly I can understand it in light of inhumane Islamic terror as well as hideous Christian violence and oppression in previous centuries. Still, such a construction of history is questionable, for it fails to recognize the profound difference between Christianity and Islam. To take just one point: the New Testament demands absolute nonviolence on the part of the church. Whenever Christians have gone against that demand they have acted contrary to the Sermon on the Mount and against Jesus.

But above all we have to ask: where do the great ideas of the European Enlightenment come from? Did Israel and the church really play no part in them? Did the church have to accept the Enlightenment

[3] Letter to the editor, *FAZ* 23/6 (January 28, 2015).

"from outside" as something altogether foreign to it—or did the Enlightenment (even though it was not always aware of it) draw to an astonishing degree on Jewish-Christian tradition?

What follows is about precisely that question. I will simply address the primary words that appear again and again in this context: freedom, equality, sisterhood/brotherhood, human dignity, tolerance, and separation of church and state.

Let me say from the outset, to avoid a possible misunderstanding: I am not saying that the church has learned nothing from the European Enlightenment, was not inspired or stimulated by it, was not startled out of its rigidity, inertia, and forgetfulness of tradition.

I am certainly not saying that. Israel and the church have always needed impulses from without, foreign prophets, often even profound historical forces. Instead, what I assert is that freedom, equality, sisterhood and brotherhood, human dignity, tolerance, and separation of church and state were not things foreign to the church that it needed to receive as if via an intravenous infusion from outside. To the contrary: all of them rested for ages in its own tradition, arose out of its inherent origins and experiences, and even played a decisive role in the origins of the European Enlightenment.

But enough with the preliminaries! Let's get to the point!

Freedom

There have been many, many liberation movements in human history, even as early as the major cultures of Mesopotamia and the Nile region. But there is one symbol of freedom that has been hugely consequential for subsequent history: the liberation of Israel from Egypt.

I am not concerned here with the question of what actually happened at the Sea of Reeds in about 1250 BCE. There are certainly historical facts underlying the great narrative in the book of Exodus, but they are not of interest at this point. What concerns me is what is said about that great event, and indeed in such a way that it was able to become the model for later stories of liberation.

The book of Exodus does indeed tell a story of liberation: how an entire people is led out of oppression, bondage, and inhuman enslavement into freedom. This is not about a political revolution. The Israelites did not take power in Egypt or overthrow the rule of the pharaoh. Their story of liberation consists in an exodus: they flee from the land of their oppressors. They go out— and enter into a new land.

That makes it clear that this is about a new society. It is not just a matter of being politically free but of beginning something unique: a new social order. It is radically different. This new thing could not have been attained merely by improvement of Israel's social situation in Egypt. Hence the exodus. Hence the new land. The land is a symbol of the other new thing: the new society that will now begin.

God gives the social order for this new thing from Sinai. It is based no longer on force but on freedom; it is voluntary. Hence Israel may no longer serve the gods of the nations, which make people unfree; it may assume only the yoke of YHWH, the God of its freedom. Hence at a later time, with the building of the tabernacle, the sanctuary that gives the new thing a center and becomes symbolic of the new creation, it is repeatedly emphasized that all Israelites contribute, freely and without compulsion, to that sanctuary, working to establish it.[4]

Thus rescue from the power of an oppressive state is only part of the exodus. What follows is equally important: a new, free society no longer based on force. We can see that the biblical story of the exodus establishes a long arc: from deliverance out of enslavement to construction of a new society. That arc was always recalled when the story of Israel's exodus was told. And Israel's exodus from Egypt was told countless times. It was and is celebrated by Jews every year on the evening of the Seder. It was and is told and celebrated by Christians at the Easter Vigil. The continued telling of the exodus story played an extraordinary role in Europe (and beyond), establishing an archetypical model transparent to every present time, wherever and whenever oppression and violence have appeared.[5] Jan Assmann rightly said:

> To write the reception history of the book of Exodus is . . . an impossible undertaking: its influence has been immeasurably vast, its impact all but ubiquitous.[6]

For example: the exodus story had its effect on the English revolution under Oliver Cromwell (1599–1658) as he sought to transform

[4] The repeated formulas for this willingness include "whoever is of a generous heart" or "everyone whose heart was stirred and everyone whose spirit was willing," "all . . . whose hearts made them willing." Cf. Exod 35:5, 21, 22, 29, 31; 36:2, 5, 7.

[5] Jan Assmann, *The Invention of Religion: Faith and Covenant in the Book of Exodus*, trans. Robert Savage (Princeton, NJ: Princeton University Press, 2018), 167. But see also esp. the study by Michael Walzer, *Exodus and Revolution* (New York: Basic Books, 1995).

[6] Assmann, *Invention of Religion*, 1.

England into a republic. It influenced the English Separatists and Puritans who emigrated to North America, where they played an essential role in the creation of American democracy. Both Cromwell and the Pilgrims explicitly appealed to the Old Testament exodus; it was their stimulating model.

Thomas Paine (1737–1809), one of the significant "founding spirits" of the United States, in his famous pamphlet *Common Sense* denigrated George III, the king of England from whose rule the American settlers had to win their freedom, as "the English Pharaoh." The pamphlet played an utterly decisive role in the American Revolution.[7]

Later American freedom movements would also have been inconceivable without the typology of the exodus story. Think only of the spirituals sung again and again by the enslaved African Americans, such as "When Israel was in Egypt's land . . . Let my people go!"

Equality

Thus a new social order was instituted at Sinai. But let us look more closely, for something extraordinary happened in the process, something that, according to the Egyptologist Jan Assmann, brought an incomparably new element into the world at that time.[8] The book of Exodus gathers at Sinai all those who came out of Egypt: the whole nation. And it is at Sinai, on the "day of the assembly" (Deut 9:10), that this people truly became Israel. That is, they became a people whose true identity is not ultimately constituted by biological descent, not by a common language, not by territorial identity, not even by a central government, but solely by God's decree, what the Bible calls the "covenant" with God. The essence of that covenant is the Torah, the new social order God gives.

Now for what is crucial: this social order must be freely accepted by all the people; otherwise the covenant will not exist. That is why Moses goes up the mountain, descends, and goes up again to bring Israel's assent (Exod 19:3, 7-8). And that is why the whole people speak as one and declare: "Everything that the Lord has spoken we

[7] Thomas Paine, *Common Sense* (New York: Dover Publications, 1997), 26. The pamphlet almost instantly achieved a huge circulation; its influence on the struggle for independence cannot be overestimated.

[8] Cf. Assmann, *Invention of Religion*, 32–34, 138–39, 167–70.

will do" (Exod 19:8; 24:7; cf. Deut 5:27). That is also why the book of Deuteronomy commands that all Israel must come together every seventh year—"men, women, and children, as well as the aliens residing in your towns"—so that the social order from Sinai may be renewed again and again by all (Deut 31:10-13).

Here, therefore, a whole nation affirms its basic law solemnly and in freedom, by acclamation. Note: women and men, all Israel. If that does not depict the crucial basic element of every democracy, then I do not know what democracy can mean. But we should not regard the assembly and the acclamation on Sinai as a matter of course! Here in Germany, in fact, we cannot assent directly to the constitution of the Republic.[9] Let me emphasize once more that I am not interested in the question of what happened or did not happen at Sinai. I am concerned with the texts from Exodus that tell of a contractual event, one that was unique in the ancient world in this form and has had enormous consequences.

Some authors believe that the covenant theology of the Old Testament was the conscious or unconscious model for the principle of the social contract as developed by Thomas Hobbes, John Locke, and Jean-Jacques Rousseau.[10] But I need to describe that more specifically. The theory of the "social contract" is, as we know, based on a fiction that could be described as follows: the multitude of individuals, by their own will, submit to an order of law that in part restricts their rights as those are surrendered to the state. In return, however, this legal arrangement secures peace within society. No longer is it the case that individuals must create their own law, by force if necessary. The state now has monopoly control, but because of that it is also obligated to secure the rights of individuals. All individuals agree to this fictive contract that, in fact, is the basis for the state. Thus when

[9] The constitution of the Federal Republic of Germany was created by a "Parliamentary Council," approved by the Allies, and then adopted by elected representatives of the German states. Similarly, the US Constitution was created by representatives of the states and is amended by Congress with the assent of state legislatures.

[10] Cf., e.g., Rolf Schieder, ed., *Die Gewalt des Einen Gottes: die Monotheismus-debatte zwischen Jan Assmann, Micha Brumlik, Rolf Schieder, Peter Sloterdijk und anderen* (Berlin: Berlin University Press, 2014), 27: "The Exodus story [has] become a master-narrative of modern ideas of constitutional democracy. The covenant theology created at Sinai has been the blueprint for modern social contracts." Also important is Walzer, *Exodus and Revolution*, 83–98.

constitutional scholars liken the event at Sinai to the "social contract" of the European Enlightenment the point of comparison is the agreement of all Israel to its social order.

The "equality" of all the people, its women and men, is based on this free and forthright agreement. But what does this *égalité*, this equality, mean in detail? Much could be quoted from Torah at this point, but I do not want to lose myself in fine points. Let me point directly to a single text. Leviticus 19:33-34 reads: "When an alien resides with you in your land, you shall not oppress the alien. The alien who resides with you shall be to you as the native-born among you; you shall love the alien as yourself, for you were aliens in the land of Egypt: I am the LORD your God."

If, according to Torah, Israel itself is to treat foreigners in the land thus, in solidarity and brotherhood/sisterhood, as though they were members of their own families (which is what "as yourself" means), then obviously the same is true for all the women and men of their own people (cf. Lev 19:18). Israel's Torah prescribes not only freedom but equality.

However, Torah is being realistic here. It is aware that poverty and inequality can arise again and again (cf. Deut 15:4, 11), but it contains a wide variety of ordinances for eliminating the scandal of poverty and leveling inequality. So did the European Enlightenment or the French Revolution invent *égalité*? The only answer is: no! Israel's Torah always advocated for the equality of all. Certainly it fought with the means and opportunities of its own time, but fight it did—to such an extent that in every seventh year all debts were to be forgiven in order that poverty and debt slavery might be eliminated (cf. esp. Deut 15:1-3). The law of forgiveness of debts in the sabbatical year sought to create in Israel an egalitarian society wherein the constraints produced by social dependency that arise over and over could be destroyed, again and again, at a minimum every seven years.[11]

[11] For the whole question cf. Georg Braulik, *Deuteronomium 1–16:17*, NEB (Würzburg: Echter Verlag, 1986), 111–12; also his "Eine Gesellschaft ohne Arme. Das altorientalische Armenethos und die biblische Vision," *IKaZ* 44 (2015): 563–76; Frank Crüsemann, *The Torah: Theology and Social History of Old Testament Law*, trans. Allan W. Mahnke (Minneapolis: Fortress, 1996), esp. "The Forgiveness of Debts in the Sabbath Year," 226–33; Norbert Lohfink, "Das deuteronomische Gesetz in der Endgestalt—Entwurf einer Gesellschaft ohne marginale Gruppen," in *Studien zum Deuteronomium und zur deuteronomischen Literatur*, vol. 3, SBAB 20 (Stuttgart: Katholisches Bibelwerk, 1995), 205–18

Sisterhood and Brotherhood

At the center of Torah stand the familiar words: "You shall love your neighbor as yourself" (Lev 19:18). "As yourself" is not meant to refer to modern self-esteem; it is about one's own family, one's own clan. The love commandment says: The solidarity and care that are due to one's own "self," that is, one's own family, must be extended to all Israel and even to foreigners in the land. All the members of the people of God are to be treated as one would treat sisters and brothers in one's own family.

It follows, appropriately, that all those in Israel may address one another as "brother" or "sister." The book of Deuteronomy then drew the natural consequences. Again and again we encounter the "sibling" address there;[12] in fact, it lends a unique coloring to the whole deuteronomistic historical work.[13] There is no comparable frequency of sibling address for members of the people of God anywhere else in the Old Testament.[14] Elsewhere in the ancient Near East, apart from the Old Testament, we encounter the sibling-address style from time to time, but only in the language of royal courts, between one ruler and another or between court officials. Never is it used for all the members of a people.

What is important in our context is this: the language used in the book of Deuteronomy produced an extraordinary historical effect: in the speeches in Acts, Peter addresses his Jewish audience as "brothers [and sisters],"[15] and Paul does the same;[16] Christians are shown interacting with each other as a community of siblings.[17] Examples of this kind of intimate address within the Christian community are

[12] For "brother" language in the book of Deuteronomy cf. Lothar Perlitt, "'Ein einzig Volk von Brüdern.' Zur deuteronomischen Herkunft der biblischen Bezeichnung 'Bruder,'" in *Kirche. Festschrift für Günther Bornkamm zum 75. Geburtstag*, ed. Dieter Lührmann and Georg Strecker (Tübingen: Mohr, 1980), 27–52.

[13] Cf. Deut 15:2, 3, 7, 9, 11, 12; 17:15, 20; 18:2, 7; 19:18, 19; 20:8; 22:2, 3; 24:7, 14; 25:11. NRSVue translates with nongendered language, often "member of your community."

[14] The closest comparison would be parts of the Holiness Code in Lev 19:17; 25:25, 35, 36, 39, 49.

[15] Acts 2:29; 3:17.

[16] Cf. Acts 13:26, 38; 22:1, 5; 28:17.

[17] See Acts 1:15, 16; 6:3; 9:17, 30; 10:23; 11:1, 12, 29; 12:17; 13:15; 14:2; 15:1, 3, 7, 13, 22, 23, 32, 33, 36, 40; 16:2, 40; 17:6, 10, 14; 18:18, 27; 21:7, 17, 20; 22:13; 23:1, 5, 6; 28:14. The texts show that "the brothers [and sisters]," like "the disciples," is stereotypical language for the Christian community.

especially frequent in Paul's letters, and the use of "sister" appears also.[18] Naturally, the New Testament was stylistically influential in this regard. In the churches, whether in local communities, especially Protestant ones, or in Christian communities and orders, the address "sister" or "brother" has frequently been used; often it is simply a matter of course.

Consequently we need not spend a lot of time puzzling about where the French Revolution got its *fraternité* slogan. In fact: during the Revolution itself the word *fraternité* was not nearly as popular as *liberté* and *égalité*; after all, people knew where it came from. In fact, it was a French archbishop, François Fénelon (1651–1715), who first used the triad "freedom, equality, and brotherhood." That, again, makes it clear what sources the French Revolution really drew on. Of course it did not refer directly to church language. *Liberté* and *égalité* had already become powerful and arousing words in many tractates published before the revolution.[19] The language of the lodges of Freemasons would also have played a role.[20] The question is merely: what was the ultimate basis of the three concepts?

Obviously what interests me here is not mere words; they alone would prove very little. It is a question of the reality that underlies the words, and therefore it is appropriate to take at least a brief glance at the letter to Philemon, that little-known but highly revealing Pauline letter. It shows that an enslaved man named Onesimus had run away from the wealthy Christian Philemon. He had fled to Paul, who at the time was in prison, and Onesimus had entrusted himself to Paul. Paul won him over to the Christian faith, baptized him, and now sends him back to his master along with a very heartfelt letter. In the letter Paul asks Philemon to forgive his servant Onesimus and from now on to treat him as his "beloved brother" (Phlm 16).

This event is revealing in a number of ways. For example: the church at that time had not abolished the ancient system of enslavement, and in the first century such a thing was impossible anyway.

[18] Rom 16:1; 1 Cor 7:15; 9:5; Phlm 2. Cf. Jas 2:15. Twenty-first century usage interprets ἀδελφοί as "brothers and sisters" or simply "brothers" according to context.

[19] This is especially well described by Artur Greive, "Die Entstehung der französischen Revolutionsparole *Liberté, Egalité, Fraternité*," *Deutsche Vierteljahresschrift für Literaturwissenschaft und Geistesgeschichte* 43 (1969): 726–51.

[20] Greive, "Die Entstehung," 749.

But it had subverted that institution. If an enslaved person, female or male, asked for baptism, then she or he from that point on took part in Christian worship and was there addressed as "sister" or "brother." Obviously that had enormous consequences for the social position of such persons within the broad family of Christians. Here, as in many other cases, a silent revolution was taking place. The social institution could not, for the moment, be changed, but it was undermined.

Let me draw a first conclusion: freedom, equality, and fraternity were the great mottoes of the French Revolution. Those words—and the reality behind them—were not invented by the members of the Enlightenment. Their principal source is the Jewish-Christian tradition.[21]

Human Dignity

From the twentieth century onward the idea of human dignity has appeared in the constitutions of any number of nations. As is well known, the beginning of the fundamental law of the Federal Republic of Germany reads "Human dignity shall be inviolable" (art. 1, par. 1).

If we pursue the question of when the idea of human dignity first[22] appears in a constitutional text we discover the preamble to the Irish constitution of 1937, which reads:

> In the Name of the Most Holy Trinity, from Whom is all authority and to Whom, as our final end, all actions both of men and States must be referred,
> We, the people of Éire . . . seeking to promote the common good, with due observance of Prudence, Justice and Charity, so that the dignity and freedom of the individual may be assured, true social order attained, the unity of our country restored, and concord established with other nations,

[21] Certainly this is not to deny the role of Greek and Roman philosophy, above all that of the Stoa. [Neither there nor in the ideology of the French Revolution was there a concept of "sorority," but in that respect Christianity was—at first—different, as the cited texts show.—Trans.]

[22] The source question is addressed also by the Weimar Constitution of 1919 and the Constitution of Portugal, 1933. However, the Weimar document speaks only of "humane conditions of existence for all" (art. 151), and the Portuguese Constitution refers to "humanity" (art. 6.3).

Do hereby adopt, enact, and give to ourselves this Constitution.[23]

Naturally, the idea of human rights and dignity itself is much older. We find it already in the work of the Renaissance philosopher Pico della Mirandola (1463–1494), from whom we have the famous "Oration on Human Dignity."[24] He begins the text with an interpretation of Genesis 1: God created the human being only after making the plants and animals. Why? Humans are different from all other beings in that they are not predetermined. They are not bound to a place. They can discover and shape everything. They can choose freely. Therein lies their dignity and worth. Therein are they the "image" of God, says della Mirandola.

The philosopher thus anchors human dignity in the Old Testament text: "God created humans in [God's] image, in the image of God he created them" (Gen 1:27). That statement was, in fact, the basic text that argued for human dignity throughout many Christian centuries. Even if the word "dignity" or "worth" was not always present, the thing itself had no better foundation anywhere in the world than in this biblical text.

Naturally one can dig deeper theologically and ultimately establish human dignity in the fact that in Jesus God became human and thus gave human beings the highest possible honor and glory. But even then we are still moving within the aura of Genesis 1:27, because the New Testament understands Jesus Christ as the new, eschatological Adam.[25]

Thus the idea of human dignity that achieved such prominence and value in the twentieth century that it appears in national constitutions and is the very essence of the European Enlightenment was not invented in the seventeenth or eighteenth century. It is much, much older. It is rooted in Genesis 1, in the text about the human as the image of God. That text has been cited again and again since the time of the great theologian Irenaeus (second century CE), whenever there was need to give a reason why humans should be respected. Most important for our question, certainly, is the church's liturgy. As

[23] *Constitution of Ireland*, Preamble. Available at https://www.irishstatutebook.ie/eli/cons/en/html.

[24] Pico della Mirandola, *Oratio de hominis dignitate*, published posthumously, 1496.

[25] Cf. Rom 5:12-21; 1 Cor 15:21-22, 45.

early as the sixth century the Western church prayed this collect on Christmas Day:

> O God, who wonderfully created the dignity of human nature and still more wonderfully restored it, grant, we pray, that we may share in the divinity of Christ, who humbled himself to share in our humanity.[26]

The standard reference works always cite the Roman politician and philosopher Cicero (106–43 BCE) in connection with the idea of human dignity. He does, in fact, speak in his work "On the State" about the *dignitas*, the dignity, of the human being,[27] and he does so in the context of his discussion of the best constitution. According to Cicero democracy cannot be the best constitutional form because in that system "dignity" belongs equally to all citizens, without regard to rank. We can see from this surprising assertion that for Cicero human dignity is relative. A highly placed personage who has acquired honor and respect has more dignity than a simple citizen.

It is true that Cicero goes deeper in his work "On Duty." Human dignity, he writes, lies in the fact that the human is distinct from animals. But here again dignity is relativized: people who live only out of greed and lust make themselves so like animals that they lose their dignity.[28] Thus one can minimize one's dignity or increase it.

Of course it is a good thing that even Cicero spoke about human dignity, but the problem with his concept cries to heaven, for if a human can lose her or his dignity, then a criminal has certainly lost it and others may do with him or her as they will, since such a one no longer has any rights.

Here the Jewish-Christian tradition begins at a much more profound level in its concept of human dignity. According to Genesis 1:27 the human being is the image of God. That is: God has created the human as a "thou," as a "companion," so that one may enter into conversation with God. That is our ultimate dignity, and this dignity is inviolable and cannot be lost.

[26] *Leonianum* (second half of the sixth century CE). The collect, somewhat modified, is still in use today in some churches: for example, *The Book of Common Prayer* (ECUSA) prescribes it for the second Sunday after Christmas.

[27] Cf. Cicero, *De re publica* 1.43.

[28] Cf. Cicero, *De officiis* 1.42.

Tolerance

As regards freedom, equality, sisterhood/brotherhood, and the idea of human dignity we have repeatedly encountered Jewish-Christian tradition, but that seems to change when we approach the idea of tolerance. Have Christians not shown despicable intolerance when they forcibly missionized whole tribes, hauled people before the Inquisition, burned heretics, and conducted bloody wars of religion in Europe—and, above all, when they have persecuted their Jewish sisters and brothers?

Where was tolerance then? Did not the European Enlightenment here, at last, put an end to the dreadful impulses of the baptized? Does not the church need to learn something here—indeed, something essential that was previously altogether unknown to it? Here, at least, does it not need to see reason? Before I attempt an answer let me say as clearly as possible:

Every kind of forced missionizing was a crime. The persecution of heretics by the church and their being handed over to secular courts to be executed was a crime. The wars of religion in Europe, initiated by the baptized, were criminal. The slandering, ghettoizing, marking, persecution, and murder of countless Jews throughout the centuries by Christians was a long series of crimes.

I say that in advance, before I utter a word about the history of the idea of tolerance. Here, however, we need to examine the matter more closely and make some distinctions.

First, an observation about language:[29] "Tolerance" comes from Latin *tolerare*, which means "bear with," "endure," "put up with." In classic Latin literature it refers to the acceptance of injustice, torture, and violence, or enduring hunger, pain, and danger. Accordingly, in antiquity the noun *tolerantia* represented the endurance of all want and every evil that can befall a human being.

It was only due to the Christian theology of the early centuries CE that the concept acquired a new meaning. Now it ascended far above the mere endurance of the blows of fate: *tolerantia* for the first time began to refer to a social virtue: right behavior toward others, namely,

[29] For the linguistic observations that follow let me refer to Arnold Angenendt, *Toleranz und Gewalt. Das Christentum zwischen Bibel und Schwert* (Münster: Aschendorff, 2007), 233, with references to the relevant recent literature.

that as a Christian one has patience with fellow human beings, bears with those who are troublesome, lovingly draws a veil over others' failings.

Thus the idea of tolerance as we use it today derives from its Christian expansion—in fact, its transformation of an ancient idea. That change did not happen by accident; it arose out of congregational "encouragement," as we find it often in the New Testament letters:

> [Love] bears all things, believes all things, hopes all things, endures all things. (1 Cor 13:7)
> [Walk] with all humility and gentleness, with patience, bearing with one another in love. (Eph 4:2)
> Bear with one another and, if anyone has a complaint against another, forgive each other. (Col 3:13)

The Christian notion of tolerance also has another root, however: the word of Jesus himself. Three Gospel texts in particular rooted themselves deeply in the memory of the early church.

Luke 9:51-56 tells how, when Jesus and his disciples found no lodging in a Samaritan village, James and John turned to Jesus and asked: "do you want us to command fire to come down from heaven and consume them?"

> But [Jesus] turned and rebuked them. (v. 55)

Some manuscripts have Jesus continue:

> You know not what spirit is speaking from within you. The Son of Man has not come to destroy people but to save them.

This expansion of the text was derived from Luke 19:10 ("For the Son of Man came to seek out and to save the lost"), and it was certainly appropriate. The parable of the weeds in the wheat in Matthew (Matt 13:24-30, 36-43), however, played a still greater role in shaping the concept of tolerance in the first Christian centuries. The weeds among the wheat must not be uprooted; they must remain until the harvest. Then God alone will judge, not human beings. The church at that time saw in this parable a direct response to the question of how to deal with heretics within. The answer was: "Let the weeds and the wheat grow until the harvest!"

Augustine (354–430) formulated a principle based on the parable of the weeds in the wheat: the church "bears with what it cannot correct [*tolerat, quos corrigere non potest*]."[30] He also wrote: "Love sinners, not as sinners but as people."[31]

The third text that played an important role in the early church was, of course, the one about love of enemies, and the reason for it:

> [God] makes his sun rise on the evil and on the good and sends rain on the righteous and on the unrighteous. (Matt 5:45)

These texts, together with Jesus' absolute renunciation of violence, dug themselves deeply into the awareness of the early church and made it impossible to persecute heretics and have them executed by the state. The only thing that could be done was to excommunicate heretics: that is, they were excluded from the communities because of the damage they did.

There was, however, another reason why the church was imbued with the idea of tolerance: it was itself repeatedly persecuted by the Roman state for three centuries; of course it wanted tolerance to be shown toward its communities! Tertullian, writing about the persecution of Christians in his *Ad Scapulam*, said:

> It is a fundamental human right, a privilege of nature, that every man should worship according to his own convictions. . . . It is assuredly no part of religion to compel religion—to which free-will and not force should lead us.[32]

Lactantius wrote in a similar vein in his *Epitome of the Divine Institutes*:[33]

[30] Augustine, *Epistola* 93, 9.34, CSEL 34.2.

[31] Augustine, *Sermones de vetere testamente* (*Tractatus de Esau et Iacob*) 4.20. Translation in *The Works of Saint Augustine: A Translation for the 21st Century*, III, *Sermons*, vol. 1: *Sermons 1–19*, trans. Edmund Hill (Brooklyn: New City Press, 1990), 196. Later, in the wake of his experiences with the Donatists, Augustine took a more restricted view. Now he called for "a defense [by the state] against violent provocations as well as a beneficent promotion of the true religion." Thus Angenendt, *Toleranz*, 237–38. In the same context, however, he still rejected torture and execution.

[32] Tertullian, *Ad Scapulam* 2.2. Translation at https://www.newadvent.org/fathers/0305.htm.

[33] Lactantius, *Epitome of the Divine Institutes*, 54. Translation at https://www.newadvent.org/fathers/0702.htm.

> [Religion] is a matter which is voluntary above all others, nor can necessity be imposed upon any, so as to worship what [one] does not wish to worship.

Regrettably, the church very quickly abandoned those fundamental insights. The period when Christians were persecuted had scarcely ended and the church joined itself to the Roman state when Christians began to persecute Jews—first of all by destroying their synagogues. The following case is well documented: In the year 388 Christians in Callinicon on the Euphrates, urged on by their bishop, torched a Jewish synagogue. When Emperor Theodosius I, then resident in Milan, ordered that the synagogue be rebuilt at the expense of the perpetrators, Ambrose, bishop of Milan, forced him to annul the edict. Under Theodosius II the burning of synagogues became so frequent that most of that emperor's edicts were about protection of Jewish synagogues and private homes.[34] All this casts a shadow on the church that had gained its freedom as well as on some of its bishops, its theologians, and its understanding of Israel.

Things were different as regards the church's internal dealings with heretics. We must acknowledge that at least in the Western church in the first thousand years—with a single exception—no heretic was handed over to state authority and executed.[35] That one exception was the Spanish layman Priscillian (b. ca. 340), who led a radical life according to the gospel and gathered many followers. He was accused of heresy, and in the year 385 his church opponents brought an action against him at the imperial court in Trier. He was condemned and executed. Still, at the time a number of bishops, together with Pope Siricius, raised a sharp protest against the act. Martin of Tours, disgusted at the event, severed eucharistic communion with the bishops who had brought about Priscillian's execution. For me personally this attitude of St. Martin is more significant and important than the division of his cloak, because with his protest against the execution of Priscillian he was much closer to Jesus and the Gospels than in his sharing of his coat with the poor.

[34] Cf. Peter Schäfer, *The History of the Jews in the Greco-Roman World*, trans. David Chowcat (London: Routledge, 2003), 187–88.

[35] Apart from Priscillian, however, there is no historical attestation of such an event that is completely certain. Here I am following Arnold Angenendt, *Toleranz*, 250–54.

Regrettably, the Western Church did not sustain its tolerance of heretics beyond those thousand years. Even earlier, episodes of forced Christianization (for example, of the Saxons by Charlemagne) bore no relation to Christian tolerance.[36] And after the millennium, so far as heretics were concerned, there gradually developed "a veritable wave of persecutions, now employing sword and fire."[37]

I cannot enter into a discussion of the reasons for all these forms of crass intolerance. Probably a major factor was that, in the second half of the fourth century, Christianity had become an "imperial church," and as such it was far too closely integrated into the structures and interests of the *imperium*. For example, the execution of heretics began on a broad basis at the beginning of the thirteenth century with the movement against the Cathari, who had established a counter-church especially in southern France but also in upper Italy. Dominic, commissioned by the pope to "convert" the Cathari, believed that the main reason for the continual rise of new heresies was the secularization of the church. Hence one should persuade the heretics—and this should be done through the example of one's own apostolic life and the power of the gospel. But the church had no time for such a work of persuasion. It was much too solidly embedded in the politics of the European powers: for example, the French feudal lords and the king of France, Philip II (1165–1223). As a result, a crusade against the Cathari was carried out between 1209 and 1229, by military means, bringing their territories in southern France under the rule of the French crown.

Here, then, the church's profound involvement in state structures was its undoing. A second and related cause was that the memory of Jesus' absolute renunciation of violence was more and more overlaid and glossed by texts from the Old Testament that demanded the

[36] Here, certainly, we must be careful with our concepts and judgments. Cf. Angenendt, *Toleranz*, 391–94. In antiquity as well as in the Middle Ages every member of a community or association was obligated to participate in the religion of that community. On the other hand, the Jews were already an exception in the Roman imperial period, and during the time of persecution the Christians were demanding that the Roman state tolerate their own belief. Cf. the text of Tertullian, *Ad Scapulam* 2.2, cited above. Had the Christians remained faithful to their own principles, therefore, they could certainly have recognized the injustice of any kind of religious compulsion.

[37] Angenendt, *Toleranz*, 252.

extirpation of everything in Israel that was wicked and contrary to the will of God. Thus, for example, the Deuteronomic collection of laws required the destruction of all cultic sites in the land that were dedicated to heathen gods (Deut 12:2-3) and that Israelites who served other gods must be executed (Deut 13:7-12; 17:2-7).

Evidently the fusion of the church with political structures contributed heavily to the legitimation of violence with the aid of Old Testament texts. But whatever reasoning was involved, from the time of Charlemagne's politics of expansion and then of the battle against the Cathari the church showed fewer and fewer traces of the tolerance practiced in the early centuries. The intolerance and violence that found a place in the church over such a long period of time did extreme damage to its credibility, and that damage continues today.

The Catholic Church, however, was able to repent. That is signaled primarily, on the part of the official church, by the Declaration on Religious Freedom issued by Vatican II. The fact of a radical repentance by a worldwide community of faith is exciting in every aspect, and it should not be minimized. The European Enlightenment certainly aided the church in arriving at that repentance, but ultimately it was made possible by a renewed awareness and acceptance of the New Testament and Jesus' absolute nonviolence. In the end it was also able to arrive at a new awareness of its own first centuries, during which the church itself was persecuted. With regard to the whole question one must not forget that at one time the idea of tolerance played a role in shaping the church and was part of its practice for a long period.

Separation of Church and State

In its beginnings the church itself called for and lived tolerance, but it did not maintain that stance. The situation as regards the separation of church and state was similar and yet different. Here again the medieval view of the Old Testament was too one-sided and much too simplistic. The great King David was enthusiastically admired as the model for all Christian kings anointed by the church: the result was a kind of "theocratic state." The fact that in Torah, the five "books of Moses," the king plays virtually no role, and where one appears the royal rights and privileges are highly restricted—this was something the Middle Ages simply could not accept. We may say, without exaggeration, that in the Torah the king makes only a marginal appearance, and there he is drastically relativized in comparison to other ancient Near Eastern kings.

According to Deuteronomy 17:16 a king in Israel "must not . . . return the people to Egypt." That is: sovereign power within the people of God must be utterly different from every kind of state power that was common among the peoples of the time. In Deuteronomy 17 the king is installed by the people[38] and thus does not belong to the dynasty of the gods, as was otherwise the case everywhere in the ancient Near East. The king appointed by the people may not "[exalt] himself [= lift up his heart] above other members of the community" or "[turn] aside from the commandment, either to the right or to the left" (Deut 17:20).

That, however, means that Torah is the "constitution" of the people of God to which the king must submit. Hence in chapters 16–19 the book of Deuteronomy also prescribes a division of powers: judges, priests, prophets, and king each have separate functions within the people of God. The judges, priests, and prophets are not chosen by the king, and the king is neither the supreme judge (as elsewhere in the ancient Near East) nor the highest priest, nor the supreme commander of the armed forces. In essence the king is a "model Israelite." The division of powers—perhaps the elementary structural characteristic of European civilization—was thus not invented by Calvin or John Locke or Montesquieu.[39] It already exists in the book of Deuteronomy.[40]

The First Book of Samuel, in fact, goes far beyond this desacralization and demythicization of the king: it depicts the establishment of kingship in Israel as an evil that the people have desired for themselves in order to be "like other nations."[41] First Samuel 8:11-20

[38] See Deut 17:15. That need not mean that every king must be chosen by the people or the elders. An inherited monarchy is probably implied (cf. Deut 17:20), but it must be established by the people to begin with.

[39] Cf. Eckhard Nordhofen, "Biblische Aufklärung," 20: "The initial impulse, before the separation of legislative, judicial, and executive [powers], was apparently the idea of the *disempowerment* of the supreme earthly authorities by God."

[40] See, in detail, Norbert Lohfink, *Great Themes from the Old Testament*, trans. Ronald Walls (Chicago: Franciscan Herald Press, 1981), 55–76; also Georg Braulik, *Deuteronomium II, 16,18–34,12*, NEB (Würzburg: Echter Verlag, 1992), 126–51.

[41] See esp. 1 Sam 8:5, 7, 11-18, 20; cf. Deut 17:14.

describes, with unbelievable clarity, how the king whom Israel desires for itself will exploit and enslave the people.

But as I have already said, the medieval church was evidently unable to accept this wholesale questioning of state structures in the Old Testament's "deuteronomistic redaction." It preferred, instead, the way the great King David was supposed to have prayed in Psalm 144:

> Blessed be the Lord, my rock,
> who trains my hands for war and my fingers for battle, . . .
> who subdues the peoples under me. (Ps 144:1-2)

Or they enjoyed reading what David is said to pronounce as a royal principle in Psalm 101:

> No one who practices deceit
> shall remain in my house;
> no one who utters lies
> shall continue in my presence.
> Morning by morning I will destroy
> all the wicked in the land,
> cutting off all evildoers
> from the city of the Lord. (Ps 101:7-8)

This style of Bible reading then matched very well with the campaigns of Otto the Great (912–973) against the Slavs in central Germany or, later, the forced conversions carried out by the Teutonic Knights in Prussia and the Baltic region. The empire was expanded—supposedly following the Old Testament model—by means of the sword and was then forcibly missionized. Other Old Testament texts (including other psalms) that contradicted this were ignored.

The same deaf ear was turned to New Testament voices. It is true that the New Testament does not oppose the state; on the contrary: taxes must be paid, state authority respected, prayers must be offered for the emperor and his officials.[42] That corresponds exactly to Jesus' saying: "Give to Caesar the things that are Caesar's" (Mark 12:17). But Jesus adds: "and [give] to God the things that are God's." That obviously means more than daily prayer and keeping the commandments.

[42] Rom 13:1-7; 1 Tim 2:1-3; Titus 3:1-2; 1 Pet 2:13-14.

Everything Jesus says is connected to the reign of God, which is the center of his preaching, and that reign of God is not somewhere in cloud-cuckoo-land. It is actively creating a unique people for itself.[43]

Basically, Jesus is here continuing—though with eschatological intensity—what Judaism had been living in its synagogal communities since the Babylonian exile: that Israel is not a state; it is a people in the midst of other peoples. Jesus wants a people of God that gives to the emperor, as the embodiment of state sovereignty, what belongs to the emperor but reserves for God the crucial thing, in the form of the way of life of the people of God: doing God's will. That is already a "separation of church and state" in an unequivocal, indeed a radical, form.

The early church practiced that separation for over three hundred years, acknowledging the authority of the Roman state as a sovereign power whose duty was to provide for peace and the securing of the people's rights, and to which one must therefore pay taxes and to which obedience was owed. But the Christians of the first three centuries did not acknowledge the divine aura that increasingly surrounded the Roman emperor and therefore the Roman state. They emphasized that the church is a *politeuma*, a citizen community of a special kind (Phil 3:20), structured quite differently from the state. How else should we understand Tertullian's outrageous statement: "Nor is there anything more entirely foreign to us than affairs of state."[44]

Assuredly not all Christians at that time would have agreed with this statement—but it was possible to say it! Ultimately it was based on the awareness that Christian communities constituted a separate "people" or "nation." Thus the separation of church and state was not only expressed quite clearly: it was reality.

The utter change that came about with the elevation of Christianity to the status of Roman state religion in the year 380 corresponds to the burial of the church's notion of tolerance we spoke of previously. For the ancient state it was a matter of course that religion and state are united; still more, religion and cult secured the existence of the state. That position could not be shed like a garment. At the moment when the church became the imperial religion, the ancient ideas were

[43] For more detail see Gerhard Lohfink, *Jesus of Nazareth: What He Wanted, Who He Was*, trans. Linda M. Maloney (Collegeville, MN: Liturgical Press, 2012), 39–85.

[44] Tertullian, *Apology* 38.3: *nec ulla magis res aliena quam publica.*

again in force. While the church was never equivalent with the state, it was in bed with it. The two had become "one flesh."

Nevertheless, spousal conflict between church and state arose very quickly in the West. Prominent representatives of the conflict were Athanasius (298–373), Hilary of Poitiers (ca. 315–367), Ambrose (339–397), John Chrysostom (ca. 344–407), and Pope Gelasius I (d. ca. 496). They stressed that the church would not interfere in the exercise of state power, but the state must not meddle in the spiritual affairs of the church. The long conflict escalated in the Investiture Controversy (1076–1122). Arnd Uhle, professor of political science and constitutional theory, writes of the whole development:

> [The Investiture Controversy] has rightly been called a revolution by many, because as a result, in the western hemisphere, a complete unity of secular and spiritual power in Christendom was rejected, thus creating an altogether indispensable basis for the rise of the free constitutional state.[45]

I cannot describe the century-long wrangle over this matter. The result was that the Western church, in contrast to the Eastern, developed the profound difference between church and state to a greater and greater degree. We can forgive it for thus contributing to making a church-state inconsequential, since ultimately that very lack of consequence served to bring about the church's freedom from the state.

Therefore I can end this part of my remarks with the assertion that the church was not unprepared for the European Enlightenment's demand for the separation of church and state. There were indeed groups within it that could not free themselves from the idea of a sacral state, but in principle the church, in its battle to achieve independence from the state, had long since laid the ground for church-state separation—even though it was still very far from the Jewish and early Christian insight that the church was a "people among the peoples." Essentially, many Christians have never yet understood what "people of God" means from that point of view.

[45] Arnd Uhle, "Unser Lebenselixier. Ursprung und Zukunft des freiheitlichen Verfassungsstaates und der westlichen Moderne: Das Christentum," *FAZ* 299/7 (December 24, 2015).—Trans.

One thing, however, is certain: the church in the era of the Enlightenment did not have to learn for the first time why the separation of church and state makes sense—and is, indeed, necessary. It bore that knowledge within its own tradition, however suppressed and buried it had so often been.

Second Scholasticism: Avant Garde of the Enlightenment

First, a brief look backward: the preceding six sections have shown that the major concepts of the European Enlightenment were already present in the Jewish-Christian tradition; indeed, in many cases they were first developed within it. Even if at a later date they were sometimes buried, still they were present; they could be dug up and revitalized.

To this point, however, we have left open the question of whether the elements of enlightenment that already existed in Jewish-Christian tradition were also handed on to the European Enlightenment. To put it another way: was the Enlightenment of the seventeenth and eighteenth centuries a glowing star that emerged entirely from the reason and self-awareness of Europeans marching into a new era, or was it only a newly emerging flower on a tree with deep roots, one that had already bloomed often and was still rich with sap?

Of course, every proponent of the Enlightenment will admit that the roots of enlightened thought go deep—to the pre-Socratics, Plato, Aristotle, Cicero, Marcus Tullius Varro, and many others—but the Jewish-Christian tradition is then often politely ignored. Likewise frequently overlooked is the Spanish theology of the sixteenth century, sometimes called "Spanish Late Scholasticism."[46] Not a word is said about it; only specialists study it. It is not acknowledged that in sixteenth-century Spain there were as many as twenty universities, five other institutes of learning, and any number of *studia generalia* belonging to the various orders. Even in theological encyclopedias the words "Spanish Late Scholasticism" are mostly absent, and it is

[46] Sometimes, instead of "Spanish Late Scholasticism," scholars speak of "Iberian Late Scholasticism" or simply "Baroque Scholasticism." The term "Second Scholasticism," derived from Spanish usage, is most commonly used today.

generally unknown to many of those who despise Christianity. At least a few words about it are called for here.[47]

Spanish Late Scholasticism, like all Scholasticism of the high Middle Ages, referred back to the great philosophers of antiquity, especially Aristotle, but it was more involved with Sacred Scripture and Jewish-Christian tradition. From the beginning of the Modern Era, however, especially after the discovery and colonization of the Americas and the flowering of international economies, Christian theology addressed some entirely new questions. For example: How do economies function? Which elements of the economy are permissible, and which are not? Above all there was the question: Are the indigenous peoples of the Americas full-fledged human beings? And if so, how should they be treated? Is it right to simply take away their lands? May they be stripped of their "superstitions" and "atrocities" by the use of force and violence? May they be compelled to accept baptism?

On the basis of these and similar problems the question of human rights reappeared in a new and elementary form. Is there such a thing as an irrevocable human dignity, a right to freedom and self-determination—even for the native peoples of the Americas? What about the rights of a whole nation? Where do the rights of the powerful come from? Who bestowed them? Finally, what about rights among the people themselves?

Such questions were now being asked everywhere in Europe. The issue of "natural rights," already treated in antiquity, was taken up anew. The question was especially urgent in Spain, because Spain was making conquests throughout the world—and its rulers were Christians who certainly asked themselves what they might and might not do.

Spanish Late Scholasticism arose out of that constellation and was the work mainly of members of religious orders, especially Dominicans and Jesuits. They were primarily located in the Spanish universities, especially Alcalá, Valladolid, and Salamanca. Of course I cannot list all the great lights of Spanish Late Scholasticism; I will mention only the Dominicans Francisco de Vitoria (ca. 1483–1546), Domingo de Soto (1494–1560), and Melchior Cano (1509–1560) and the Jesuits

[47] For an overview of Second Scholasticism see esp. *Vivarium* 33/1 (1995), with the Introduction by E. J. Ashworth.

Luis de Molina (1535–1600), Gabriel Vásquez (1549–1604), and above all Francisco Suárez (1548–1617), the most famous of them all.

Those named above and many others adapted medieval Scholasticism—especially that of Thomas Aquinas—to the changed situation and developed it further. In the process they also ventured into entirely new fields. I will list only a few selected positions advocated by Spanish Late Scholasticism. They were not accepted unanimously by all its representatives, but these positions were stated and upheld—even against government opposition—and they opened the path to the European Enlightenment.

1. The aboriginal peoples of the Americas are not inferior half-humans. They have the same irrevocable human dignity as Europeans, because before God all humans are equal. Natural law applies to all. Therefore, for example, the property and lands of the Indios in South and Central America may not be claimed and seized by the Christians. Political interference in the territories of the Indios or Indians is only valid if the latter are in agreement with it.

2. All human beings are free. Therefore the indigenous peoples of the Americas have the right to defend themselves against forced missionization. Certainly they may not interfere with a nonviolent preaching of the gospel, but in any case a possible rejection of Christianity by indigenous societies does not justify making war against them—still less do indigenous customs and usages that appear to be contrary to natural law.

3. The human being is a person and is free, because she or he is made in the image of God. Therefore enslavement is immoral.

4. The citizens of every land have a fundamental right to resist an unjust and exploitative government. There is even a right to revolution, because every regime is obligated to support human rights.

5. People entrust their rights to the current government because, for the sake of good order in the land, there must be a government. But the people themselves are the true sovereign.

6. Certainly it is God's will that every land should have a government, but it is not God who installs a ruler or a government.

That is done by the community itself. The citizens bestow political power on their rulers.

7. Earthly and spiritual powers must be strictly distinguished and kept separate. The emperor is not master of the world, nor is the pope. Instead, the peoples themselves, of their own accord, constitute free and natural societies. That means, for example, that the emperor cannot depose indigenous rulers; also, the pope has authority only in spiritual matters and cannot impose Catholic rulers on newly discovered lands.[48]
8. Not only is there natural law applying to all humanity; there is also positive law among nations. All peoples have equal rights and are bound by mutual legal relationships that must not be applied by force; they must be supported by treaties.
9. Individual states or commonwealths are sovereign, but they must not be closed off from one another. Throughout the world there must be freedom to travel, to trade, and to settle.
10. None but "just wars" are permitted, and those are allowed only in the most extreme circumstances; the civilian population must not be attacked in the course of such wars.

This brief sketch must suffice here. It shows that Spanish Late Scholasticism touched on all the great themes of the European Enlightenment: human rights, political and religious freedom, private property, tolerance, equality, national sovereignty, the rights of nations and peoples, and in principle even the construction of the social contract.

Recent scholarship in particular has accorded more and more recognition to the extraordinary achievement of these scholars among the Spanish Dominicans and Jesuits. Their positions were not unknown after them, either. Hugo Grotius, Alberico Gentili, Samuel Pufendorf, and many other European advocates of natural rights quoted them repeatedly.[49] It was only in the eighteenth century that

[48] Pope Alexander VI, for example, attempted just that. He issued a bull, *Inter caetera*, dividing ownership of the New World between Spain and Portugal. A number of theologians who were part of Spanish Late Scholasticism disputed the idea that the pope had that power.

[49] For the influence of Suárez, for example, cf. J. P. Sommerville, "Suárez," *TRE* 32:290–93, at 292.

they were apparently forgotten. We must assume, however, that their insights continued to have influence, even if no individual names were attached to them. After all, in the eighteenth century an appeal to Catholic theologians was not always opportune. The twentieth century then rediscovered them and saw them as a European avant-garde. They have come to be regarded by genuine scholars as the founders of the modern rights of nations. Even among economic historians today the School of Salamanca are regarded as the "'founders' of scientific economics."[50]

The Purification of Faith

At the outset I posed a question: must the church be compelled to accept reason (i.e., enlightenment)? My answer was in the affirmative: indeed, the church is required to say yes to it, as also to other positive forces—I would mention only humanism, the Reformation, the growth of the natural sciences. All those were beneficial, even healthful requirements imposed on the church. It may be that the growth of Islam was another of those cataclysmic-healing forces encountered by Christianity.

I do not think there is any need for a long discussion about whether there were such external forces; there certainly were, and the church will continue to need them. The effect of those forces is, however, quite another question. I said at the beginning of this essay that freedom, equality, sisterhood/brotherhood, human rights, tolerance, and separation of church and state were not unfamiliar to the church, so that they had to be imposed on it by force. No, all those things had long rested within its own tradition. They did not have to be added; they had to be reawakened.

This is precisely the point at which the problem lies for anyone who is not thoroughly familiar with biblical tradition and the church's theology. I will use an example to clarify it: on September 16, 2010, Ernst-Wolfgang Böckenförde wrote an important essay in the *Frankfurter Allgemeine Zeitung* titled "The Purification of Faith."[51] He

[50] See Joseph Schumpeter, *History of Economic Analysis* (New York: Oxford, 1954), 97.

[51] E.-W. Böckenförde, "Die Reinigung des Glaubens," *FAZ* 215/32 (September 16, 2010).

wanted to show that the content of faith must itself be accommodated to "the insights of the current era that are regarded as reasonable." As a concrete example in support of his thesis he points to *Dignitatis Humanae*, the Declaration on Religious Freedom of the Second Vatican Council. He shows that here the Roman Catholic Church—after many directives to the contrary—finally declares that human persons have a right to religious freedom and that such freedom is grounded in the dignity of the human person. He then continues:

> How could this Copernican revolution happen in the Catholic Church in light of the long tradition of contrary declarations by the church's teaching office, not least those of nineteenth-century popes? What is in evidence here is a process of change in church positions and teachings that is founded on faith, and so faith itself is grounded in reason. In retrospect this change appears as a reflective purification of faith itself through reason. But what reason? Not just any reason, but that of the Enlightenment, whose insights have an abiding influence here—the very reason that led to the American Declaration of Independence and the Declaration of the Rights of [Humanity] and the Citizen (1789), whose influence is apparent in Lessing's "Nathan the Wise" and found one of its great thinkers in Immanuel Kant. It was a secular, worldly reason, not theologically inspired by faith in revelation but taking leave of it.[52]

Böckenförde is quite right when he speaks of a "purification of faith" in the face of nineteenth-century church pronouncements. It was indeed a "purification," and a very profound one. When he says that here "faith itself" was changed by reason, however, he is off the mark. We have already seen that the concept of tolerance is firmly anchored in the New Testament and the early church, and tolerance and freedom of belief are inseparable. Moreover, the Second Vatican Council, in article 10 of its Declaration on Religious Freedom, rightly points out that it has always been a substantial component of Catholic faith "that [the human] response to God in faith must be free: no one therefore is to be forced to embrace the Christian faith against [one's] own will." The only possible conclusion is that here we have a concept of universal freedom of religion, even if that conclusion was

[52] Trans. LMM.

applied less and less since the Constantinian turn and was gradually transformed into its exact opposite.

In addition, article 10 of the council's declaration contains a number of scriptural references pointing to Jesus' example and that of early witnesses to Christian faith. They never forced anyone to believe, but they always hoped faith might be arrived at freely. In subsequent centuries the church became blind to religious freedom or was made blind to it. The church's faith did indeed have to be purified, but it did not need to be changed. What was needed was a renewed consciousness of its past.

Furthermore, Böckenförde is completely wrong about the roots of the European Enlightenment. I have already indicated the extent to which the freedom movement that led to the American Declaration of Independence depended on biblical texts and Christian initiatives. That really should be further developed here, but I can only give a few pointers:[53]

In the year 1895 the important constitutional historian and legal scholar Georg Jellinek published his book, *Die Erklärung der Menschen- und Bürgerrechte*.[54] It was a sensation. Jellinek asserted that the French Revolution was not the real beginning and source of the codification of human rights; rather, the French declaration of human rights was inspired and shaped by the various "Bills of Rights" in the "North American states such as Virginia, Pennsylvania, etc., which were declaring their independence in the year 1776, and in the American Declaration of Independence."[55]

But above all Jellinek emphasized that theories of natural rights alone could never have led to a solemn declaration of human rights; that required a catalyst, a concrete impulse, a social dynamic—and North American Calvinists, people concerned with their own religious freedom, were precisely that. The concrete occasion for the codification of human rights was not the French declaration, with its hostility to religion; it came from American Christians who took their

[53] Here I am following Hans Joas, "Max Weber und die Entstehung der Menschenrechte. Eine Studie über kulturelle Innovation," in Frühauf and Löser, *Biblische Aufklärung*, 65–90.

[54] Georg Jellinek, *Die Erklärung der Menschen- und Bürgerrechte. Ein Beitrag zur modernen Verfassungsgeschichte* (Leipzig: Duncker & Humblot, 1895).

[55] Cf. Joas, "Max Weber," 72. For the various "Bills of Rights" that preceded the US Declaration of Independence cf. Wolfgang Hüber, "Menschenrechte / Menschenwürde," *TRE* 22:577–602, at 582–83.

guidance from the Bible. We should add that this was true not only of Calvinists but also involved Puritans, Baptists, Congregationalists, and Quakers.

Georg Jellinek's theses opened a wide space for further research in this field. Since his time many have affirmed what he said—to the point of asserting that the Americans of the eighteenth century had drawn their Declaration from the pulpit.[56] The American ethicist and social philosopher Michael Walzer, in his book *Exodus and Revolution*, tells how, in the 1960s, he listened eagerly to a Baptist preacher in Montgomery, Alabama—a preacher who, with dramatic rhetoric, compared the then-current political struggles of African Americans in the southern United States with Israel's situation in Egypt. Walzer writes:

> The sermon struck me with especial force because I was, in 1960, a graduate student writing a dissertation on the Puritan Revolution, and I had read many sermons [from seventeenth-century England] in which the book of Exodus figured as a central text or a reiterated reference. Indeed, in a long speech opening the first session of the first elected parliament of his Protectorate, Oliver Cromwell described the Exodus as "the only parallel of God's dealing with us that I know in the world."[57]

Elsewhere Walzer writes:

> So common is the Exodus reference in the political history of the West . . . that I began to notice when it was missing—as in the years of the French Revolution, whose leading actors were resolutely hostile to Jewish as they were to Christian conceptions of history. Hostile, but not ignorant . . .[58]

The two evidently belong together: natural-rights theory in the sixteenth and seventeenth centuries, inspired also or even primarily by Late Spanish Scholasticism, and concrete freedom movements in which Puritans and other Christian groups played an important role. It is thus not correct to simply play off "secular, worldly reason" against "belief in revelation," as Böckenförde does.

[56] Cf. Joas, "Max Weber," 79.

[57] Walzer, *Exodus and Revolution*, 3–4.

[58] Walzer, *Exodus and Revolution*, 5.

I see things this way: The church is subject to a multitude of historical forces and is shoved in many directions. It is constantly tracing new paths. It has to contend with false teachers who force it to formulate its own teaching more clearly and precisely, but it also encounters prophets from outside who speak truths that alarm it. Then it wants to ignore them, not to listen to them, but it must do so because reality is dawning on it. And it bends down, tightens its backpack, discovers its ancient traditions, the treasure of reason and enlightenment it has collected since Abraham—and draws it into the light.

Admittedly, Ernst-Wolfgang Böckenförde wrote his article with reference to Islam, and the question of Islam was also the beginning of my own reflections. What will be the future of that great world religion? Will it open itself to human rights, to the separation of state and religion, and to the achievements of the Enlightenment? Do not expect a prognosis from me. I simply do not know. I am certain of only two things:

1. If Islam, as represented by its most important figures, does not open itself to human rights and freely adopted constitutions because it is convinced that the Qu'ran itself and the ruling traditions of Islam forbid such an opening, there will be dreadful consequences for the coming decades, perhaps even for centuries.

2. The question of whether Islam can open itself to the insights of enlightened reason concerns us all. By "us all" I mean above all the formerly Christian lands of the West. Only if freedom, equality, justice, and human dignity are no longer propagated among us merely as beautiful phrases but are lived convincingly will anything change in Islam. If, however, Muslim women and men experience Western society (and especially the Christians within it) as one in which there is no respect for God, no surrender to God's will, no solidarity and sisterhood/brotherhood, but only a divided and shameless society in which each seeks only the self, then nothing will change. Islam as a whole will then withdraw more firmly than ever into its own roots, harden itself, and continue to produce dreadful eruptions of Islamism—even when this clashes with the ideas of liberal-thinking Muslims.

2

The World Emptied of Its Gods

The Old Testament begins in Genesis 1:1–2:4 with God's creation of the world. The older I get, the more I am astonished by this text. It gives a formal account, with many repetitions—the sort of thing children love to hear when they are listening to a story. The numerous repetitions almost transform the narrative into a list, but by that very fact the text is extraordinarily concentrated. Nothing in it is accidental, nothing is superfluous. It wants to be attended to in every detail. The power of this text, completed some five hundred years before Christ, is evident when it is read at the liturgy of the Easter Vigil as the first of all the readings. Then it reveals itself in its full greatness and lapidary force.

> When God began to create the heavens and the earth, the earth was complete chaos, and darkness covered the face of the deep, while a wind from God swept over the face of the waters. Then God said, "Let there be light," and there was light. (Gen 1:1-3)

Obviously I cannot continue with the whole text, certainly not comment on it. For example, I cannot give a detailed explanation for why I read the first verse not as a separate sentence and thus as a title or superscription for the creation account, but rather—in a way that may be unfamiliar—as a relative clause. Thus it is not "In the beginning God created the heavens and the earth," but "When God began to create the heavens and the earth." There are serious reasons for my translation, but I cannot go into them here.[1] In this essay I want

[1] Simply in terms of the Hebrew syntax both readings are possible. What is decisive is that any number of comparable creation accounts in the ancient Near East begin

to address one particular point: namely, the radical de-divinization of the world. It proceeds throughout the whole Bible, and it is programmatically anticipated at the very beginning of the whole.

A Babylonian Version of the World's Beginning

To make this de-divinization clear in its full extent I will compare Genesis 1:1–2:4 with a text on the origins of the world from the Land Between the Rivers: *Enuma elish*, written on seven clay tablets. This Babylonian text begins very impressively:

> When on high the heaven had not [yet] been named,
> Firm ground below had not been called by name,
> Naught but primordial Apsu, their begetter,
> (And) Mummu*–Tiamat, she who bore them [the gods] all,
> Their waters [still] commingling as a single body;
> No reed hut had been matted, no marsh land had appeared,
> When no gods whatever had been brought into being,
> Uncalled [as yet] by name, their destinies [still] undetermined—
> Then it was that [the gods] were formed within [= in the womb of] them [Apsu and Tiamat].[2]

So begins the famous narrative *Enuma elish*, which was recited every year on the fourth day of the New Year festival in Babylon, in the temple of the imperial god Marduk. What is it about? In summary: Apsu is the (freshwater) primal ocean and, so to speak, the original god. Tiamat, his spouse, is the second deity of the primal ocean; she represents salt water and is depicted as a kind of sea monster. The

---

with the same sentence structure: "When this and that and the other were . . . then the following happened." Cf. the beginning of the *Enuma elish* or of the Sumerian myth, "Gilgamesh, Enkidu, and the Underworld." "When heaven was separated from earth, when earth dripped down from heaven, when the name of humanity was established," etc. Cf. also especially Gen 2:4b-5 in the Old Testament itself. [The NRSV Updated Edition (2022) now reads, "When God began to create the heavens and the earth." The NRSV itself also had a relative clause, "In the beginning when God created the heavens and the earth," but the NRSVue is identical with the author's reading. The NABRE retains the older structure of the English, but also contains "when": "In the beginning, when God . . ."—Trans.]

[2] Based on James B. Pritchard, ed., *Ancient Near Eastern Texts Relating to the Old Testament*, 3rd ed. (Princeton: Princeton University Press, 1969), 60–61.

text presumes an original situation: the fresh- and salt-water oceans still combine their waters; they are not yet separate.

Apsu and Tiamat beget whole generations of gods, but the racket these gods create with their merrymaking robs Apsu of his sleep. He decides to destroy them. This results in a battle among the gods in which Apsu is killed. Tiamat wants to avenge her spouse, but she and her helpers are also killed—by Marduk. He had been promised, in the assembly of the gods, that through victory over Tiamat he would become supreme over all the gods and be master of the whole cosmos. Marduk splits the body of Tiamat into two parts, like a gigantic oyster, and builds heaven and earth from the corpse of the dead primal goddess.

Then Ea, Marduk's father, creates human beings, using the blood of Kingu, a son of Tiamat. In fact, he creates human beings to serve the gods. The true hero of *Enuma elish*, however, is the great world orderer and ruler Marduk. The whole tale is told to glorify him.

No educated person today would think of regarding such texts about the origins of the world as absurd or bizarre. All peoples have myths (in enlightened eras also!), and there are endless variations of them. Their purpose is not only to tell about beginnings; their precise intent in doing so is to explain today's world. In the present case Marduk is to be elevated to the rank of supreme god, and with him the authority of those who represent Marduk in society is likewise elevated. *Enuma elish* ends, accordingly, with a hymnic apotheosis of Marduk in tablet 7:

> (For) his word is reliable, his command unchanged,
> No god can alter the utterance of his mouth.
> When he looks in fury, he does not relent,
> When his anger is ablaze, no god can face him.
> His mind is deep, his spirit is all-embracing.[3]

But this myth intends still more. It not only means to elevate Marduk from local city deity to god above all gods. It reflects the ecological problem in the swampy land between the Tigris and the Euphrates; indeed, its battles between the gods shed light on social power struggles and upheavals in Mesopotamia. It reflects human efforts

[3] *Enuma elish*, tablet 7, lines 151–55. From W. G. Lambert, *Babylonian Creation Myths* (Winona Lake, IN: Eisenbrauns, 2013), 133.

to secure orderly political governance, since that is all that assures the security of the universe. Finally, it shows that the whole world is divine because, after all, it was made from the body of Tiamat: the goddess of chaos was defeated and the fixed order of the world was constructed from her corpse.

Myths interpreted the world in which ancient peoples lived. They were intended to create security for the societies in which they were told, while at the same time showing the peoples that they constantly existed on the brink of chaos and for that reason needed security and balance. In terms of the imagery, the chaos-dragon Tiamat is indeed dead, but it took superhuman strength to defeat her. Thus in its own way the myth pointed to the incomprehensible and often highly dangerous forces and energies in the world. It portrayed them as divine or demonic potencies and powers. We understand the myths better today than previous generations did; after all, we know how close our world stands to the brink of the abyss.

An Enlightened Text

Despite the archaic power of these myths, the world they depict is full of demons and gods; it is filled with strife, war, and treachery and is saturated with apathy and elemental anxiety. Basically, it is a single scene of carnage. Against that religious-historical background the narrative with which the Bible begins is an unbelievably sober and enlightened text. Seven times it says that the world is good. Here there are no dynasties of gods, most certainly no creation of or by multiple deities, but only the one, unique God, of whose origins nothing is said in our text. God is simply there, and altogether as a matter of course. There is not a word about where God came from.

How can that be? A comparison with the gods in Israel's environment makes it clear: this God is in no way a description or personification of the world and its powers. This God stands over against the world as something completely different: its creator. From that perspective we can also clearly see what biblical monotheism is. It is not the reduction of the world's many gods to a single one. In that case the monotheistic God would still belong to the world. No, this God is the Wholly Other, who therefore is one, precisely because this God is not world.

At this point a side glance at Greece is helpful. Around the year 700 BCE there lived in Boeotia the great poet Hesiod. One of his major works, the *Theogony*, describes the origins of the gods and the world in more than a thousand hexameters. Thus theogony (origin of the gods) is likewise cosmogony (origin of the world). In Hesiod's work, which collected and rearranged the ancient myths, the origin of the world and the gods was like this: At the beginning of the cosmos there was chaos, which here again is the primeval deity. From the chaos come five other primeval gods: namely, Gaia (earth), Tartarus (underworld), Eros (love), Erebus (darkness), and Nux (night). Gaia gives birth to Uranus (heaven), Uranus begets the Titans, and one of the Titans is Chronos, who begets Zeus.

As we can see, here as in Mesopotamia the primary power at work in the beginning is that of chaos. Other primitive forces flow from it, including the productive and ever-fruitful earth and then, above all, Eros. Finally, out of these primeval powers come the dynasties of the gods that, as in Mesopotamia, sometimes work together and sometimes engage in deadly strife with one another: for example, Chronos the Titan castrates his father Uranus with a sharp sickle.

Obviously all these primeval forces and gods are worldly powers, of which the Greeks made use and which they revered but also feared: Eros, fertility, night, water, ocean, air, grain, wine, war, peace, wisdom, fate, death. In the strata of Greek experience of the world there was no phenomenon that was not embodied in a god. Even envy became a separate deity as Phthonos. For that very reason the gods of Greece, like all the gods of the nations, were worldly elements and powers. For the same reason cosmology and theogony were interwoven, and the totality of what is in the world is divine. Even the pre-Socratic Thales of Miletus (d. ca. 546 BCE), who was one of those who no longer simply repeated myths but was a philosopher seeking the world's *logos*, would say: "Everything is full of gods."[4]

Genesis 1:1–2:4 stands over against this world of gods; the difference could not be more radical. God is not the world, and the world is not God, nor is it divine. Therefore it is created. It is not begotten of God; it is not an emanation, something that flows from God; it is not something that emerges from chaos; it is not a transformation of eternal original matter: it is creation. To mark the distance from all the creation myths of the nations the Old Testament uses a word it

[4] Aristotle, *De anima* 405a 20-22.

reserves exclusively for the divine act of creation: *bara*ʾ. Alongside the word "make" (*ʿāśâ*, Gen 1:7, 16, 25, 26, 31; 2:2a, 2b, 3), *bara*ʾ appears in the creation account in Genesis 1:1–2:4 no fewer than seven times, always in a place of prominence (1:1, 21, 27a, 27b, 27c; 2:3, 4a).

Add to this that creation happens through word alone. God speaks, and God's word becomes reality (Gen 1:3, 6, 9, 11, 14, 20, 24, 26). It is true that we cannot regard "creation by word alone" as a distinctive mark of Israel that is excluded from the creation myths of other peoples. There were texts in Egypt that also spoke of creation by the word of a god. But Israel did not simply adopt such theological ideas; it followed them to their logical conclusion.

Still, the difference does not lie solely in creation by word alone. In this creation account God acts with absolute sovereignty in everything, not only speaking the creative word but acting continually and without interruption. God not only says "Let there be light," but separates the light from the darkness and then calls the light "day" and the darkness "night." We should know that in the ancient Near East naming was itself a creative act and also the prerogative of a sovereign. By calling the darkness "night," God asserts a claim on it, thus removing everything demonic from it. Therefore (at least here in Genesis 1) God does not carry on a battle against numinous powers but acts as absolute Sovereign.

This calm, certain, and sovereign action is all the more remarkable since the author of Genesis 1:1–2:4 is deeply familiar with ideas about the world emerging from chaos or arising from a battle with it. The statement in verse 2, that the earth was still "complete chaos"[5] (Heb. *tōhû wābōhû*) echoes the ideas in ancient Near Eastern cosmogonies. Likewise the primal flood (the deep, Heb. *tehôm*) in the same verse—does it have something to do with Tiamat from the *Enuma elish*? The words *tehôm* and Tiamat (*tihâmat*) are etymologically related, and many Hebrew Bible scholars see a genuine connection here. At any rate, the matter is completely clear in Genesis 2:4a, where the narrator concludes the creation account by writing: "These are the generations of the heavens and the earth when they were created."

The word for "generations" in Hebrew is *tôledôt*, and "generations" or "begettings" is its literal meaning. As we have seen, the world's

[5] NRSVue; NRSV, "a formless void"; NABRE, "without form or shape."

origins in ancient Near Eastern and Greek myths consist primarily of generating or begetting: chaos brings forth primal gods; they in turn beget new generations of gods; gods beget humans—ancient mythology is fascinated with generating. The fact that the narrator of Genesis 1 does not wait until later in the great story to use this word, in the genealogical lists (cf. esp. Gen 5), but employs it already here, at the end of the creation story, shows a significant familiarity with the ancient creation myths of the nations.

But look what the Genesis narrator did with it! The creation that here arises from the mere word of the true God is absolutely de-divinized. The primal flood has nothing more to do with the gods of chaos; it becomes an ocean (Gen 1:10) that links the lands together, and it becomes the lifegiving water that is collected above the firmament or the groundwater that is held in the depths of the earth (Gen 1:6-7).

The arc of the heavens, which Marduk built in Babylon out of half of the necrotic body of Tiamat, is now a shimmering fabric and nothing more. God fastens the heavenly bodies to that fabric: the sun for the day, the moon for the night, and the stars. And since the narrator knows that the sun, moon, and stars are high and supreme gods in the religions round about, they are here ruthlessly profaned as mere "lamps" that God fastens to the heavenly fabric—I almost said twists into their sockets (Gen 1:14-19).

Thus the de-divinization continues. Previously the narrator had deliberately described vegetation as coming forth from the earth. More precisely: the already-created earth was commanded to get to work on its own. In the manner of textbook biology, the narrator here distinguishes between plants that bear unhoused seed and those whose seeds are embedded in the flesh of fruits (Gen 1:11-12). The living beings are likewise catalogued as a natural scientist would do, distinguishing among the great sea mammals, fish, birds, wild animals, cattle, and creeping things. We should not conclude from these details that this is an early form of natural science. Genesis 1's interest is theological—and yet it already casts a testing and distinguishing glance at Nature, precisely because the latter must be seen appropriately and stripped of any kind of divinity.

The text then speaks, with the same admiration, about human beings. Here the word *bara'* (create) occurs no fewer than three times in a single sentence. Again a religious-historical comparison is revealing: the human being is not made from the blood of a slain god (as in *Enuma elish*), or from soil soaked with a god's blood (as in the ancient Babylonian *Atrahasis* epic); instead it is fashioned by God in God's own image (Gen 1:26-31). Above all: the human being is not created to relieve the gods of their burdens, or to serve them, to ease their daily work,[6] or to tickle their noses with the scent of thousands of burning sacrificial animals—but to have dominion over the earth (Gen 1:26, 28).

So is the human being a potentate who is allowed to make everything subject to itself? The human as ruler over the earth? Today many people who are concerned with care for the earth react against this statement with anxiety and a lot of question marks. Some have a positively allergic reaction to Genesis 1:26, 28. They denounce the Bible, saying that with such statements it is guilty of supporting the exploitation of the earth by human beings who threaten to destroy it and to exterminate indigenous peoples.

But that anger misses the mark entirely. The statements about dominion in Genesis 1:26, 28 are intended to say that God did not create human beings to be slaves of the gods, as in the religions, but in order that they might live freely and responsibly, taking charge of the earth. Freely and responsibly! That is the point. It means that the human is to act like a thoughtful shepherd who cares for the flock. After all, the text speaks primarily of ruling over the animals. Is it possible that in this way, very subtly, our text intends to say that no human shall make herself or himself ruler over other human beings?

I will return to the ecological problem at the end of this essay. Other questions need to be addressed first. Above all, at this point I need to discuss Psalm 82 because this text too, like many others in the Bible, speaks of the de-divinization of the world.[7]

A Death Sentence for the Gods

The psalm begins with an assembly of the gods; it seems as if we find ourselves inside the full-formed mythology of the ancient Near East, which often speaks of such assemblages. We may recall that

[6] See Claus Westermann, *Genesis 1–11*, trans. John J. Scullion (Minneapolis: Fortress, 1994), 221.

[7] The following interpretation follows Erich Zenger, *Psalmen. Auslegungen* 1–4, vol. 2, *Ich will die Morgenröte wecken*, 2nd ed. (Freiburg: Herder, 2006), 106–12. See also Frank-Lothar Hossfeld and Erich Zenger, *Psalms 2: A Commentary on Psalms 51–100*, trans. Linda M. Maloney, Hermeneia (Minneapolis: Fortress, 2005), 328–37.

Marduk was licensed to kill Tiamat by such an assembly. Having won the battle, he becomes lord of the earth and of all the gods.

Psalm 82 also tells of such a gathering of gods, but it only plays with it because this assembly is staged for the purpose of stripping the gods of their power. They stand before the judge, are unmasked, and are condemned to death. But really, is that only a fictional staging? In fact it is deadly serious, because what the psalm depicts is dread reality, extending even to us: the gods still have to be disempowered. They still sit inside our heads, in our hearts, in the power structures of society and in every corner of the world. But first, the psalm itself:

> God [stands] in the divine council;
> in the midst of the gods [God] holds judgment:
> "How long will you judge unjustly
> and show partiality to the wicked? *Selah*
> Give justice to the weak and the orphan;
> maintain the right of the lowly and the destitute.
> Rescue the weak and the needy;
> deliver them from the hand of the wicked."
> They have neither knowledge nor understanding;
> they walk around in darkness;
> all the foundations of the earth are shaken.
> I say,[8] "You are gods,
> children of the Most High, all of you;
> nevertheless, you shall die like mortals
> and fall like any prince."
> Rise up, O God, judge the earth,
> for all the nations belong to you!

The psalm has three parts: first, God stands up in the assembly of the gods (vv. 1-4). God cannot remain seated because God functions as accuser and judge, and the trial scene will take on dramatic form. The accusation reads: the assembled gods do not do their duty, which is to save from their misery the poor, the little ones, the weak, and those without rights. We may interpret this: the powerful of the

[8] "I say" (NRSVue; AV, "I have said"; NABRE, "I declare") plays on the idea formulated in Deut 32:8-9 that when God divided humanity each god received a people, together with its territory. Israel was reserved as God's own possession. That order is now repealed. The gods have allowed their portions to come to ruin.

world, who are supposed to see to equity and justice in it, are leaving the poor in misery, and yet they celebrate their power as divine and so legitimate their crimes against those subject to them.

The judgment is given in the second part of the psalm (vv. 5-7): the powerful are enduringly blind and without insight. They lead their lives in darkness, and they leave the world in darkness. They live in chaos, and chaos emerges from them. Therefore the foundations of the world shake, though it is meant to be a just and orderly world. The sentence on them can only be death: "you shall die like mortals." We can see from this statement that the psalm is about the powerful in society, the magnates in the land who let themselves be celebrated as gods and misuse their might unrestrainedly, the ones of whom Jesus would later say "those in authority over them are called benefactors" (cf. Luke 22:25). But at the same time it is about the gods of the ancient Near East. There can be no separation between human power brokers and the gods of this world. They are joined together, and in this text they are condemned to death.

The third part of the psalm is very brief: it is simply an urgent plea from the poor and oppressed that God will arise and assume the role of judge over the earth. The final statement expands the horizon. This is about the whole world; all peoples belong to the true God.

Psalm 82 is an astonishing text. What Genesis 1:1–2:4 says in veiled language and more as a hint is here expressed openly and in full clarity: the twilight of the gods, the death of the gods, the de-divinization of the world. The one who prays the psalm is standing at the origin of monotheism. At the same time, here are crucial statements about the true God: this God is absolutely not a symbol that legitimizes injustice. This is a God "for" the world, "for" righteousness, "for" the poor and defenseless. That is the criterion of this God's divinity. It is no accident that Psalm 82 is placed immediately after Psalm 81, which tells of the rescue of Israel from enslavement in Egypt and at the same time warns the people against turning to foreign gods. The battle against the gods of society is far from over.

When the World Is Emptied of Gods . . .

I have now spoken at some length about Genesis 1:1–2:4 and Psalm 82. Both are exciting texts. They signal a revolution. As a rule we do not appreciate the revolutionary nature of these texts because we no longer live in the world of antiquity and the ancient Near East. That was a world full of gods. Every land had its national god and the divine dynasty belonging to him or her, but every city had its own goddess as well, and every family had its personal protective deity. And that was not all! There were also what scholars of religion today call "specialist gods." These were goddesses or gods who were responsible for fields, houses, women's fertility, health, rain, weather, contracts, war, sickness, and even death. In this world infused with gods, to acknowledge only a single god—to appeal to that god alone and reject all other gods—was an immense breach of piety, religion, and culture. In the end such a breach had to bring people to see the world with different eyes. Here are just three examples:

> *When the world is emptied of gods, the experience of times and eras necessarily changes. History is then no longer the eternal recurrence of the same.*

If the world was created by the one God it had an initial day of creation. In that case it did not emerge from unfathomable chaos or from some eternal primal matter; it was created out of nothing (2 Macc 7:28) and so had a beginning.[9] But if it had a beginning, and if that beginning itself established time—would not the world's time also have an ending?

In that case, however, it would be impossible to think of the world any longer as moving in endless circles; it could no longer be depicted as a series of gold, silver, bronze, heroic, and iron ages as Hesiod did or, as Ovid projected, as returning from the present iron age to a golden one, or being repeatedly re-created through periodic world-conflagrations as many ancient authors proposed. Instead, time would have to be aimed like an arrow flying toward its goal, and the world would have a history. Thus eventually historical-linear thinking had to prevail and develop its whole dynamic.

Obviously this is not to say that the writing of history arose only in Israel. That would be an insult to Herodotus and Thucydides, but it would also fail to do justice to Hittite and late Babylonian

[9] That is how it had to appear to normal believers, in any case. The theological question whether God, as the metaphysical final cause, could not also create a cosmos out of nothing without a "temporal" beginning and without a "temporal" end is completely foreign to ordinary thinking, and that is all we are considering here.

historiography. The question of the de-divinization of the world that concerns us here is not primarily about unique characteristics of Israel and the church but rather the dynamic by means of which the Old Testament and then the Jewish-Christian worldview affected the history of Europe.

> *If the world is entirely emptied of gods, then necessarily all kings, rulers, and potentates of this world are de-deified along with it.*

If even the heavenly gods are stripped of their power by God and condemned to death because they oppress the poor and miserable, then with them go all the human rulers who claim divine power and pretend to be gods. There is no need for me to describe here all the titles and symbols the rulers of the ancient Near East, from Egypt to Mesopotamia, applied to themselves as sovereigns legitimated by the gods or even begotten by them. In the Old Testament those figures are de-deified along with the world. They are revealed as what they truly are.

Often their might is positively ridiculed. It begins with the Egyptian Pharaoh, as a mob of frogs hops up the palace steps and crawls into his bed (Exod 7:28), and it continues to the "requiem" for the emperor of Babylon in Isaiah 14:4-20, which is really a bitingly satirical liturgy: it describes how the emperor who has destroyed cities and made the world a desert arrives in the underworld and has to lie down on worms and cover himself with maggots while the nations at last have peace and even the cedars of Lebanon rejoice because they will no longer be cut down by the Babylonian conquerors.

One can, of course, object that there was always criticism of foreign rulers in the ancient Near East and in antiquity everywhere. That is also true. But Israel even called its own kings to account. In 1 Samuel 8 there is an enlightened and sober description of how future kings of Israel will exploit their own people, and the well-known fable of Jotham (Judg 9:7-21) caricatures the power politics of the kings with biting sarcasm; indeed, they are ridiculed. There is probably no nation that has so critically unmasked its own kings as Israel did. It is true that the divine legitimation of the house of David plays an important role, and great promises are attached to King David. But that dynasty, too, must follow God's commandments, and its crimes are mercilessly revealed (2 Sam 11).

> *If the world is cleansed of gods to its very depth and only one God remains, one who stands on the side of the poor and the disenfranchised, then suspicion and fear of the gods, or of God, can fade.*

A glance into the world of the religions shows the role played by fear: of demons, of black magic, of the evil eye, of powers to be defended against. All religions contained a multitude of apotropaic rituals and means for averting demons: making noise or spitting toward the demon, sticking out one's tongue or drawing a protective circle around oneself. Still more drastic was kindling a fire whose smoke would drive away demons and evil spirits. None of that was ironic foolishness; it was deadly serious. Amulets, tattoos, or apotropaic objects affixed to the doors of houses, such as the image of a giant eye, were widespread.

In principle, however, fear of divine envy was even more dreadful. In case of extraordinary good luck—in fact, at every brilliant success—one had to be afraid that calamity and misfortune would follow as a kind of counterblow. It was necessary to appease the gods over and over again, to placate them, to propitiate them. The Greeks, despite all the objections of their great philosophers, were particularly driven by the trauma of divine jealousy.

It is clear that the image of a god who created the world for the sake of human beings and whose essence is saving and helping would not leave room for demons and their superpowers. According to the Bible those still exist; after all, Jesus expelled demons. But they are no longer to be feared. Where there is genuine faith (and the religions do not creep back in) the demons are no longer driven away by magic and amulets but by trusting in God and God's protecting power. It is clear that here also the worldview is changed, or at least it can be. It is now a calm, fearless attitude that can view the world and its powers with a mixture of respect, curiosity, and desire for knowledge.

> *Thus when the world is de-divinized in the sense described and there is only the one Creator who has made the world, bestowed order and meaning on it, and entrusted it to human beings—then it is open to humanity and they are in a position to measure and examine the world. To put it another way: if the one God created the world and has looked at it and seen that it is good, this world must have structures and laws that are not hidden from or inaccessible*

> *to any examination by reason. From still another point of view: if God has personally worked on the world, then people may also work on it; they are positively invited to examine and shape the world. Nothing, neither gods nor demons nor one's own internal anxieties, can prevent human beings from exploring and sounding the depths of the world, studying its laws, and using the material of the world to build something new.*

It Began in Europe

With this I have arrived at what this essay is really about: the question of the incredible development of science and technology to which we are witnesses today. We have all experienced it: a digital revolution that seemed unthinkable only a few years ago. We carry all the data from our computer in a tiny stick on our keychain, and very soon there will be nano-robots circulating in our bloodstream that are able to cleanse hardened and narrowed vessels and even carry away the remnants of plaque. Within a few decades our children and grandchildren will live in a world we would not recognize.

The corresponding scientific and technical revolution is being pursued throughout the world today: in Europe, the United States, Israel, Russia, India, China, Japan—everywhere. But the Industrial Revolution that has assumed global proportions today, together with its preconditions, began in Europe. Whether one is proud of our technological advances or regards them as a catastrophe, it was in Europe that they had their beginning.

Moreover, it all began not in the eighteenth or nineteenth century, not with the technical use of the steam engine or the utilization of electricity. It did not begin with the calculator Blaise Pascal built in 1644, or with the invention of printing by Johannes Gutenberg in the fifteenth century, although that certainly introduced the "media revolution" that shapes our present world. No, none of that was the beginning of the Industrial Revolution. That started in Europe in the early Middle Ages.[10]

[10] What follows rests primarily on Rodney Stark, *The Victory of Reason* (New York: Random House, 2005); Lynn T. White Jr., "The Historical Roots of Our Ecological Crisis," *Science* 155 (1967): 1203–7; idem, "Was beschleunigte den technischen Fortschritt im westlichen Mittelalter?," *Technikgeschichte* 32 (1965): 201–20; idem, *Machina ex Deo: Essays in the Dynamism of Western Culture* (Cambridge, MA: MIT Press, 1968); idem, *Medieval Technology and Social Change* (London: Oxford, 1962) [German

It is true that water mills and windmills were not invented in the Middle Ages; they are older than that. But water mills spread in Europe beginning in the early medieval period, and in the high Middle Ages so did windmills, to a degree never before seen anywhere in the world. And with the spread of mills, especially water mills, a corresponding technique was developed whereby simple devices for grinding grain were shaped into genuine power tools for the most varied purposes. A complicated combination of axles, gears, cogwheels, and gearboxes, but above all the introduction of the camshaft, made it possible to build hammer mills, sawmills,[11] fulling mills, bark mills, and wire-drawing mills. The water mill, with its transmission technology, would have an importance for the later modern Industrial Revolution that can scarcely be imagined.

Huge bellows were employed for the smelting of metals; those were also driven by mills. Hammer mills were created for working metals, stamping mills for the pulverizing of stones containing metals, grinding mills to make knives, paper mills to mince rags and wood pulp, and even silk-spinning machines. In some regions there were so many windmills that their owners went to court over wind rights.[12] Thanks to fulling mills, a prospering cloth industry arose in England as early as the Middle Ages.

However, the pinnacle of medieval technology was the invention of the clock. Of course, there had been clocks for centuries: water clocks, for example, in which liquid dripped steadily from a vessel and its level showed when time had "run out." And obviously there had long since been sundials. But the invention of the wheel clock, which by means of "escapement" transformed traction into uniform movement, was the work of medieval tinkerers. The first mention of a wheel clock can be dated to the year 1335. Its discovery was a quantitative leap in technology because it not only made other devices possible: by enabling an exact measurement of time it opened the way to developments in other areas of research.

---

translation: *Mittelalterliche Technik und der Wandel der Gesellschaft* (Munich: H. Moos, 1968)]; Marcus Popplow, *Technik im Mittelalter* (Munich: Beck, 2010).

[11] The first water-driven sawmills are reported in the "sketchbook" or "manual" of Villard de Honnecourt, ca. 1235.

[12] The first windmill with a horizontal axle is reported in the year 1185. "In the thirteenth century 120 windmills were built in the neighborhood of Ypres alone" (White, "Was beschleunigte," 209).

I can only mention other medieval innovations in passing here. Some were new discoveries; others were inventions from foreign lands that, however, first achieved broad usage in the European Middle Ages. I would name the chimney, which made possible an effective removal of smoke; then nailed horseshoes, replacing hoof sandals or iron horse-boots; then the horse collar, with which it was at last possible to employ horses for tough field work such as the drawing of iron plows with shares and moldboards. Another innovation was the construction of large wagons for transporting burdens; these had pivoting front axles so that it was no longer necessary to heave the wagon ninety degrees in order to negotiate a crossroad, as the Romans had still done. Or think of the artful medieval cranes with block and tackle that made possible the building of the great cathedrals.[13] Above all, however, we should mention the three-field rotation of crops, which multiplied grain yields and allowed the population of Europe to grow rapidly.[14] Another invention that certainly comes from the Middle Ages was eyeglasses, which made filigree work possible.[15]

The primary locations for technical innovation in the early Middle Ages were the monasteries, which were places not only of prayer but also of work. Cloisters were often departmentalized enterprises involving agriculture, crafts, and schools. Many of them had master builders and metalworkers, developed orchards, created dyes, and copied books. The Franciscan monk Roger Bacon, in his *Opus maius* (ca. 1267), celebrated the building of "canals, conduits, bridges, hoists, ships, and the manufacture of weapons as branches of applied geometry."[16] But beyond all that, Roger Bacon was interested in producing a comprehensive synthesis of knowledge of the natural sciences and philosophy.[17]

[13] France alone saw some eighty cathedrals built between 1050 and 1350; their creation required an enormous degree of technical knowledge.

[14] In three-field rotation the cultivable land was divided into three parts: one-third was sowed with winter wheat or rye, one-third got spring seed (oats, barley, peas, lentils, or beans), and one-third remained fallow. This type of rotation appeared in Europe in the late eighth century.

[15] Eyeglasses are first mentioned in a sermon delivered in Florence in 1305.

[16] Popplow, *Technik*, 21.

[17] Cf. Christopher Dawson, *Religion and the Rise of Western Culture*, Gifford Lectures 1948–1949 (New York: Sheed and Ward, 1950), 17–18. [German translation: *Die Religion im Aufbau der abendländischen Kultur* (Düsseldorf: Schwann, 1953).]

All this means that the technical innovations of the Middle Ages were not the result only of tinkering; people were already searching for theoretical foundations. For that purpose the works of Greek thinkers, which at this period were making their way into the Latin-speaking West by way of Muslim scholars, offered rich material.

In the high Middle Ages the monasteries were supplemented by the rising cities. Here also new techniques were handed on, further developed, and communicated. Cities such as Venice, Genoa, Florence, Cologne, Ghent, Bruges, Antwerp, and Amsterdam were at the same time commercial centers that made innovation economically attractive. In this connection we should not forget the medieval universities, where knowledge was transmitted and training in rational thought was offered. Scholars were already developing methods of applying mathematical concepts to natural-scientific phenomena. Here we should mention especially the scientist and philosopher Nicole Oresme (ca. 1325–1382). Incidentally, he was also bishop of Lisieux.

The Enlightenment figures of the seventeenth and eighteenth centuries loved to paint the Middle Ages in dusky shades. They viewed those times as having been a period of indoctrination, superstition, and clerical misuse of power. In Enlightenment England they spoke of the "Dark Ages." The Oxford English Dictionary expanded the concept to include the whole of the medieval period. In Germany, correspondingly, people for a long time referred to the "finsteren Mittelalter" ("Murky Middle Ages"). Accordingly, the development of science and technology was said to have begun only in the fifteenth and sixteenth centuries. That view is outdated today. Contemporary histories of science and technology have come to see the Middle Ages in a completely different light.[18]

Why Especially in Europe?

All this, of course, raises some serious questions. I do not know whether you have ever asked yourself why the Industrial Revolution developed especially in Europe from the early Middle Ages onward, and not, for example, in India, where there are outstanding mathematicians and programmers today. Or why not in China, where the

[18] Cf. White, "Was beschleunigte," 204.

stirrup, paper, gunpowder, and the windmill were invented?[19] It cannot have been about lack of intelligence. Why not in Mali, the once-powerful empire in West Africa? Why not among the Aztecs in Mexico? Why in Europe?

Reasons for this striking phenomenon have been repeatedly proposed: Europe had better soil, the right kind of domestic animals, a temperate climate, moderate but regular precipitation, and it is uniquely endowed geographically, with islands, peninsulas, bays, mountains, plains, the Mediterranean Sea. Another proposed explanation is that, after the fall of the central Carolingian Empire, Europe was characterized by competing power centers crowded close together, and they were all driven to technical and economic developments by their competition.[20]

Still, explanations resting on Europe's different worldview are more illuminating. In Christian Europe the world was no longer a divine-numinous reality in which everything was god-filled but also dangerous; instead, it was the work of a God who acts personally in creating and has empowered human beings to know and use the world. Since, through belief in the one God, the world had been de-deified, it was available to scientific thought and creative work. Ultimately that worldview comes from the biblical tradition. In Israel, at the nodal point between Asia, Africa, and Europe, the foundation had been laid for an unfathomable development whose witnesses and participants include us all. Not only Nature but society, and not only society but also the course of history could now be radically scrutinized.

Please do not misunderstand me. Obviously Greece and Rome played significant parts in this great history of the development of European science and technology: Greece with its probing and enlightened philosophy, its historical writings, its natural science and technology; republican and imperial Rome especially with its system of laws, which formed the basis for reliable contracts and individual freedom. But medieval Islam was important as well, with its out-

[19] Popplow, *Technik*, 47–48: "In China there were already major commercial establishments involving textiles, shipbuilding, and smelting of iron with coal in the period of the Song Dynasty. Iron was even produced in quantities that were only achieved in Europe toward the end of the early modern period. Milling technology was also very advanced." In light of this finding the broader development in Europe is all the more astonishing.

[20] Cf., e.g., Popplow, *Technik*, 121.

standing scholars and technical experts who handed on an immense Greek tradition. And obviously not all the important discoveries were achieved in Europe. Significant findings had already been made in Egypt and among the Persians. None of that is debated, and it would be foolish to question it.

The issue here is by no means, in the first place, the originality of the inventions but the ground on which isolated discoveries were seized upon. This is about the force with which technology was able to establish itself, precisely in the early and high Middle Ages. It is about the hidden impetus that drove all of it forward to achieve a development that took place in Europe and nowhere else in the world. I still hold to the thesis that ultimately it was the de-divinization of the world, the enlightenment about the world that took place in Israel through a long process and continued in Christianity.

But Was the Old Polytheism Better?

Now, in conclusion, let me pose the question again: Did this Jewish-Christian emptying of the world of its gods really represent progress? Did it truly advance the world and human life, its happiness and well-being? Did it not achieve just the opposite? Hasn't the world been deprived of its magic? Hasn't it lost its mystery, its depth, its soul?

The accusation is not new. It emerges at regular intervals: as early as the Renaissance, then in the neo-classical period. It was heard in minor chords and as an impressive lament by Friedrich Schiller, especially in the first version of his poem "The Gods of Greece." In that elegy Schiller dreamt of a world saturated with gods in which, in the noble figures of the Olympians, "from heaven's heights the Gods were flowing," in which "the Gods were to humans ever closer" and "men on earth were more divine." Schiller summoned back a bright world in which cult, art, culture, and nature were a perfect unity and in which even the most serious sides of life shimmered in "the garbs of chastened humanity."[21] Martin Walser recalls these Schillerite notes when he writes in his essay "Ich vertraue. Querfeldein":

[21] Friedrich Schiller, "The Gods of Greece" (original version, 1788), trans. David B. Gosselin, available at https://www.thechainedmuse.com/post/2017/12/20/original-translation-friedrich-schillers-the-gods-of-greece.

> Almost nothing but the names of our rivers remains to recall our pre-Christian ancestors. Then there was a different god in every tree, in every spring, and in every brook. It is unimaginable that danger could ever have threatened the planet that was shielded by a multitude of gods spread over fields and forests.[22]

Leaving aside whether the facts in these pleasant texts are correct, it is still true that the Babylonian conquerors cut down the forests of Lebanon despite their multitude of gods (Isa 14:8), and in the ancient Near East it was altogether common to level the orchards of conquered lands, despite their blessed divine nature as Walser describes them, in order to inflict enduring damage (something opposed by Deut 20:19-20). It also appears from bones discovered in North America that Native Americans, despite their respect for Mother Earth, could drive a whole herd of bison over a cliff as a faster way to get meat.

Still, I have no desire to question that people in a state of nature had a rational relationship with the resources they needed to sustain life and that such a rational order had a religious basis. What I dispute is that the Bible advanced the exploitation and destruction of Nature by its de-divinization of the world. Where the world is being destroyed, where Nature is brutally exploited and crushed, it is not the spirit of the Bible that is at work but rabid greed for consumption and the unbounded misuse of power the Bible condemns from beginning to end.

It would take a long time to discuss the relationship between the Bible and Nature and the biblical love for creation. We would have to speak about how, in the second biblical creation account (Gen 2:4-25), human beings are commissioned by God to "till and keep" the earth (2:15). But above all we should talk about how, in the Bible, the whole of creation is summoned to praise God—for example, in Psalm 148:

> Praise the Lord from the heavens;
> praise him in the heights!
> Praise him, all his angels;
> praise him, all his host!

[22] Martin Walser, *Ich Vertraue. Querfeldein. Reden und Aufsätze* (Frankfurt: Suhrkamp, 2000), 18.—Trans. LMM.

Praise him, sun and moon;
    praise him, all you shining stars!
Praise him, you highest heavens
    and you waters above the heavens!
Let them praise the name of the LORD,
    for he commanded and they were created. (Ps 148:1-5)

Creation that itself lifts up praise to God because human beings look at it lovingly and make it their voice is neither drained of its magic nor incapacitated, nor is it subjected to humanity. For this it needs neither water nymphs nor river gods nor tree spirits. In the Bible the de-deified creation remains full of glory and mysterious power. What destroys our world is the human race with its arrogance, dreams of violence, and lust for power. It is not the biblical story of creation.

3

Are the Ancient Gods Returning?

A veil enhances beauty and gives the veiled object an aura of desirability. The world of the ancient religions—hard, often cruel, and quite frequently unworthy of humanity—is reappearing at the beginning of the third millennium as if covered with a shimmering veil, one that lies on the religions of the native peoples of North America as over those of Asia, on the nature religions of Africa as over those of the Celts and the German peoples.

The veil reveals just enough so that the religions stand before us in their full sensuousness, but at the same time it conceals everything revolting and hateful: the deep wrinkles, the open wounds, their unredeemed nature.

The New Image of the Religions

Surprisingly many of our contemporaries want to get back beyond Christianity. They are convinced they have discovered in the ancient religions everything they dream about and long to possess: direct contact with Nature, tolerance toward all living things, juicy eroticism, the capacity for enjoyment, a full life—and, of course, also that pinch of transcendence that is the spice of life.

That is the source of the mysterious veil that lies over the ancient religions today. The neopagans have clothed the religions in a bridal garment and at the same time have laid the church naked on the dissecting slab. It is mercilessly eyed and taken to pieces. The churches, so it is said—for example, by Martin Walser—have brought all forms of evil into the world with their rape of human nature, their intolerance, and their efforts to missionize others.[1] Walser contrasts this with what is local, natural, and native:

> Remain local. No centralist visions. Absolutely no ethic that applies to everyone. Absolutely no secularized monotheism accommodated to democracy. Instead of the upward service of faith, a capacity for enjoyment among ourselves. No matter what will become of this or that one as a result.[2]

Alongside those who fervently missionize in this style and accuse Christianity of having taught people to be unnatural there are others who at first glance seem more serious. They speak of the one great truth that is hidden from us. The truth of the divine is said to be an impenetrable mystery. All religions, obviously including Judaism and Christianity, have shed light on particular facets of this mystery. Moses, Buddha, Zarathustra, Socrates, Jesus, Muhammad, but also the ancient shamans and wise women—all of them, in different ways, lead us toward the one light that is reflected in the world in a thousand fragments. There are as many incarnations of the divine as there are religions, and therefore all religions take part in the one concealed Truth, and each of them has its weight and should be taken seriously.

Taking the Religions Seriously

I want to remain with that last statement for now. Indeed, I think the same: we should take all religions seriously. But that means we should see them as they really have been. It means we must not shape the ancient religions to fit our own desires and should not dress them in modern clothing that conceals their true form. Taking them seriously means recognizing their longings, their gropings, their seeking to acknowledge the truth they have found and let themselves be fascinated by; but it also means seeing their problems, their sicknesses, what is unredeemed and inhuman in them.

For example, we can most certainly speak of the wonderful "we" feeling within African tribal groups—but then, to be fair, we would

[1] Martin Walser, *Ich Vertraue. Querfeldein. Reden und Aufsätze* (Frankfurt: Suhrkamp, 2000), 17–19.—Trans. LMM.

[2] Walser, *Ich Vertraue*, 19.

have to expand on the elements of compulsion within African tribal cultures, the pressures that have been and still are applied by clans. Within clans, which are certainly not confined to Africa, no one had the right to make decisions as an individual and to live a unique personal life.

To take another example: we may consider whether in the context of older religions a human being was not in more profound contact with Nature and the so-called "world of the spirits" than is possible for us today—whether that was the case as regards what so many esoterics today refer to as "the cosmic whole" or "the great web." Then, however, I would have to speak about the fear of the spirits of the dead in which people lived before Israel and the church freed them from it.

In the ancient religions the dead played a role we can scarcely imagine now. They had to be buried according to a precisely defined ritual. The threnody had to be raised, memorial meals had to be celebrated, gifts had to be laid at the grave of the deceased, and one had to speak of the dead in the correct manner. Behind all that was certainly respect and care for the dead, but in the background there was always the fear that the dead might become dangerous if they were not treated rightly. "The dangerous dead" is a motif found in all ancient religions. People were constantly afraid that the dead would return as ghosts to do harm to the living.

In West Africa, among the Anyi people, the dead person was addressed in a dramatic magical incantation:

> Why have you come back?
> Why do you not rest?
> After all, we are here.
> We are here for you.
> Leave us in peace!
> You come to devour us.
> Why? Why?
> We are your children.
> Leave us in peace!
> We are here for you.
> We did not banish you.
> We did nothing bad to you.
> Why do you come to devour us?
> Why do you steal our flesh?
> Leave us in peace!
> We are here for you.

And then, in accordance with the dramaturgy of conjuring the dead, the dreadful answer is given through the mask of a dancer:

> I had my house.
> I had my farm.
> Then I had to leave.
> I had to go.
> You lied.
> You betrayed me.
> I am alone.
> I have no one.
> I had to go forth all alone.
> Now I am coming back.[3]

"Now I am coming back." Here speaks naked terror, pagan fear of the dead, the dread that they could return as ghosts, spirits, or vampires and take vengeance on the living. That fear was one reason for the lavish and expensive cults of the dead in previous millennia. There was no getting rid of the dead.

A third example. Post-Christians are ecstatic about how, for our ancestors, everything was divine: the whole world, the fields, the forests, every animal and every bush, every river and every lake, and how for that reason Nature was inviolable. Even Martin Walser invokes the ancient world of the gods and describes to his readers how a different spirit was concealed "in every tree, in every spring, and in every brook." Supposedly Nature was protected and kept whole within this "multitude of gods."[4]

The archaeological facts speak differently. Before the invention of bows and arrows it was common for our ancestors to mercilessly drive whole herds of animals over cliffs because there was no other way to hunt and kill the desired prey in large numbers. The herds of wooly mammoths in North America vanished, some twelve millennia ago, within a relatively short time. Why? Well, not long before that, as the glaciers were receding, *Homo sapiens* entered North America. For these people the broad land with its gigantic herds of animals was a richly stuffed cupboard. "Animals belong on the plate," they

[3] For this translation see also Gerhard Lohfink, *Between Heaven and Earth: New Explorations of Great Biblical Texts*, trans. Linda M. Maloney (Collegeville, MN: Liturgical Press, 2022), 195–96.

[4] Walser, *Ich Vertraue*, 18.

said then. They had no thought of protecting the animal population. Since then there have been no more mammoths in North America. Alas! It was many millennia later that, at last, the biblical creation account formulated the command that human beings should cultivate and protect the world as one would a garden (Gen 2:15).

Moreover: those who, like Martin Walser, mourn for the nymphs of the springs and the spirits of the trees should also speak of the unending hardship this world of gods imposed on people. Odysseus, returning from Troy, did have his Athena to intervene constantly in the affairs of her protegé. But at the same time he had Poseidon as his enemy, the one who could shake the earth and was the dangerous god of the ocean, who hated Odysseus implacably and repeatedly thwarted his return.

The polytheism that shines such a fascinating light for many today also meant continual worry and fear: of the gods, of dangerous spirits, of breaking a taboo, of fate—fear even in times of good fortune, because the gods were jealous and permitted no unmixed joy among mortals.

We are scarcely in a position today to recover the sensibilities of people long ago who thought they could see the face of a demon in every bush. In many religions people were surrounded by superpowerful spirits who were out to harm them. Chinese farmers in ancient times, whenever they expected a good rice harvest, commonly walked through their fields shouting, "Bad rice! Bad rice!" to deceive the evil spirits, who were supposed to be fooled into thinking that it was no use lurking there to destroy anything.

We have equally little idea of what it meant that, among the many gods, one must always summon the right one. One must know its name, call its attention to oneself, put it in a good mood, if necessary soothe it, reconcile it, bring it expensive offerings. And it was not easy to appease gods when they were annoyed and thus to restore the cosmic order. In many religions the restoration of order, or protection against enemies, required human sacrifices. Those who want to return to the basic model of the ancient religions—must they not, to be consistent, go back also to their temples, their oracles, their magic, their sacrificial cult, and their human sacrifices, such as the customs of the Aztecs or the Carthaginians that, although ritually regulated, were nothing but "human slaughterhouses," "devotional bloodlettings"?[5]

[5] See Wolfgang Sofsky, "Der Prozeß der Gewalt," lecture at the University of Erfurt, April 25, 2000, in *Gewalt—interdisziplinär*, ed. Michael Klein (Münster: LIT, 2002), 173–83, at 177.

Many religions sacrificed children, even their own, because those were the most precious, their loss the most bitter—and the bitterest sacrifices were what the gods loved best. We could list much more.

Certainly the religions must be taken seriously: their dark and their bright sides, their hateful aspects and their beauties, their follies and their wisdom. Ultimately, all religions are about the search for truth, and consequently there are always elements of truth in them. After all, the religions of the Near East and Egypt had inklings of the path by which Israel, through its religious critique of the gods of the nations, could find the true God. But we are not taking the religions seriously when we suppress their dark sides and paste together a religious world out of isolated and mismatched fragments of distant religions corresponding to our own inclinations and completely without obligation. Those who make the pagan religions into a supermarket, a self-service shop for individual tastes, are acting like late-arriving colonialists who come only to exploit, pillage, and plunder.

Not long ago posters appeared in a major city in southern Germany, advertising a coming event featuring "meditative song and dance." They read:

> This evening we will journey through ages and religions. We will meet Rama, Krishna, Buddha, and Jesus, hear the essence of their teachings, and sing their names. Circle dances from the Sufi tradition will help to draw the body into meditation as well, inducing a profound sense of peace resulting from a harmony of body and soul.

The way in which Buddha and Jesus are instrumentalized for the producers' own purposes shows that the latter have no clue about either Jesus or Buddha. Anyone who wants to grasp the "essence" of the Buddha's teaching must know that the Indian nobleman Siddhartha Gautama taught absolute detachment from things, denial of the world and of desire of any kind. Conversely, that kind of rejection of the world, for which the "thirst for life" is perverse and the person's "self" is nothing but a dangerous illusion—that kind of denial of life and its drives never existed in Judaism and therefore not in Jesus the Jew.

The Buddha demands of every individual a radical asceticism, complete poverty, renunciation of sexuality, rejection of the will—concretely, a life as a beggar monk—in order to achieve the final rebirth before sinking into Nirvana. The pseudo-Buddhist dream dancers have no thought of following that path. Hence they should be honest enough to leave Buddha out of it, to say nothing of Jesus.

We owe sincere respect to the Buddha and what he embodies, and we should take him seriously. For that very reason we dare not stir him into an innocuous religious soup that appeals to the tastes of Westerners tired of Christianity. The Buddha was in no way innocuous or noncommittal.

No religion is or was innocuous. The religions were costly. They made demands; they were dangerous. Those today who rhapsodize about the old religions, who dream of druids and shamans, who build Indian sweat houses for themselves, take part in courses on Tibetan evocation of spirits, or seek a sacramental renewal of their life-energy through *tantra* techniques should know what areas they are entering into. The ancient gods were not just empty formulas, figments of the imagination, or creatures of fantasy; they were powers, utterly real powers of this world.

For example, people have experienced again and again the immense temptation to rule over others. They could only regard the fascination of power in family, clan, and society as something divine: that is, something ultimate. So they served the power and gave it names such as Zeus, Jupiter, or Thor, and when they worshiped the supreme god they revered the power of dominance and assumed that they had the right to subjugate and mistreat others.

Similarly, human beings made all the great and fascinating realities of the world into gods and submitted to them: nature and fertility, homeland and war, ecstasy and rapture, money and science, love and hatred—even death itself. All those powers figured as gods. There were gods of death and the underworld just as there were gods of war and goddesses of love. Supposedly even "rumor" was worshiped as a god in Athens. That was not illogical: rumors have a dreadful power, and they are immortal.

There have always been powers in the world that were worshiped, and those powers were not empty names. There can be no playing with such powers. Do we really want to bring them all back as gods, that is, as the ultimate and normative, as what we serve and to which we surrender ourselves utterly? That would mean reversing a long history of enlightenment, liberation, and emancipation, a history that began primarily in Israel.

Enlightenment in Israel

Israel emptied the world of gods in a long process of critical examination of the high cultures surrounding it, a process of constant questioning and making distinctions. The Old Testament begins immediately in Genesis 1 with an outrageous series of insults directed at the gods: sun and moon, which were gods and goddesses of the highest dignity throughout the Near East, were used by the God of Israel simply as "lamps," thus utilitarian objects fastened to the firmament. In this way they were robbed of their omnipotence and their divinity by this eminently religious-critical text, and the way was prepared for later natural science, which can regard the sun and moon as material objects in the heavens. The simple statement "God made the two great lights . . . [and] set them in the dome of the sky to give light upon the earth" (Gen 1:16-17) is an act of demythologizing that possesses a vehemence we can scarcely imagine.

But the process of enlightenment in Israel extended much further. Not only the universe was demythologized; so was the state. While in the ancient Near East kingship was part of the divine order of the world and kings traced their lineage to gods, so that the state was sacrosanct and untouchable, Israel in retrospect called its whole time as a state—its royal period—into question and said: We wanted a king because we wanted to live like the other nations (cf. 1 Sam 8:5-8). But the consequence of that being-like-the-other-nations was exile. Therefore in the future no human being shall rule over us again; we will be ruled only by the Law, the Torah, and by God through the Torah—and even if there be kings among us they will be subject to the Torah in all things, and the king may never exalt himself over other members of the community (cf. Deut 17:18-20).

What I have just summarized is one of the fundamental statements of the five books of Moses, the basis for the whole Hebrew Bible. The five books (the Pentateuch) were only created after the catastrophe of the exile, and the whole composition, which already takes a retrospective view of the royal period, quite deliberately centers not on Mount Zion, the seat of the Jerusalem kings, but on Sinai as the place of the giving of the Torah. In that way the final redactors of the five books of Moses intended to say that everything that makes Israel what it is came into being not through its government and its kings, neither through David nor through Solomon. No, Israel came to be what it is through Moses, or, more precisely, through its deliverance from the theocracy of Egypt and the gift of a new social order from Sinai. Therefore the principal figure in the Torah is not the king, but Moses, and Moses is anything but a king. He is depicted as Israel's greatest prophet.

Thus the Torah shapes a contrasting image. It proposes a society that is not congruent with the state. It imagines a people of sisters and brothers in which there is only one absolute master: God. All human governance is relativized. Even the land, the territory fundamental to every state, is relativized. It is indeed promised—and emphatically so! But within the Torah it is not taken possession of. The basic text of the Torah leaves the people of God standing on the border, just outside the promised land.[6] The Jordan has not yet been crossed. Is that an accident, or is it theological genius that opens the gates to a people of God that is meant to live among other peoples—but not with an authoritarian king at its center, not with a territory it clings to, but as a people of siblings, a different kind of society?

That, however, proposes a new vision of society that is meant to have enormous historical consequences, for in this way the Law, a just social order, became the true basis of Israel—and it was a law that intends there be no poor or debased persons, no class society. The state as mythical, sacrosanct entity, the state as absolute authority, the state as untouchable god was thus disempowered and a crucial foundation was laid for the Western state governed by laws. And this touched not only state and society: the whole of human life in Israel was given a new basis through its liberation from false rulers and the world's demonic powers.

The moving story of the so-called binding of Isaac in Genesis 22 makes it clear, once and for all, that God does not desire child sacrifice. Rather, God wants our children to be able to see from our own lives how much God means to us, so that they will not run after people and things they make into idols. The story of the binding of Isaac comes from the royal period and thus was composed at least half a millennium before the day in 97 BCE when child sacrifice was

[6] See the extended discussion in Norbert Lohfink, "Death at the River Frontier: Moses' Incomplete Mission and the Contours of the Bible," in *In the Shadow of Your Wings: New Interpretations of Great Texts from the Bible*, trans. Linda M. Maloney (Collegeville, MN: Liturgical Press, 2003), 1–14.

finally abolished in Rome by a decree of the Senate. Israel's theologians had understood much earlier that for children to be slaughtered and burned in worship is absolutely against God (cf. also Deut 12:31).

Still, the Torah's critique of cultic worship is even more radical. God desires not only no child sacrifice but no sacrifice of any kind corresponding to the structure of *do ut des*: "I give to you, my God, so that you will give to me." All sacrifices in Israel were understood as grateful response to what God long ago created by the rescue from Egypt and the gift of the Torah: a free, egalitarian, and brotherly/sisterly society. Therefore in the holiest place Israel knew, namely, within the ark of the covenant, lay the tablets containing the Ten Commandments (1 Kgs 8:9): representative, so to speak, of the whole social order of the people of God. It is an unheard-of phenomenon in religious history.

The prophets of Israel worked out this social basis for worship in Israel with the greatest emphasis and unmistakably for all time. They said: God desires no sacrifices, and absolutely no worship, if Israel does not live as a just society in which the weak receive what is rightly theirs. The prophets thus emphasized a basic intention of Torah. But Torah not only opposes antisocial, inhuman, and demonizing sacrifices; it is also against pagan belief in fate, which likewise bears demonic features. The meaning of human life does not lie somewhere in the stars, says Torah; no inevitable fate looms over humans. Life is not determined by the jealousy and vengeance of gods—no, it is shaped by God's loving care and human free will. The people of God themselves determine their fate. In the grandiose finale to the whole Torah in Deuteronomy 30 we read:

> See, I have set before you today life and prosperity, death and adversity. If you obey the commandments of the LORD your God that I am commanding you today . . . then you shall live and become numerous, and the LORD your God will bless you in the land that you are entering to possess. But if your heart turns away and you do not hear but are led astray to bow down to other gods and serve them . . . you shall not live long in the land that you are crossing the Jordan to enter and possess. . . . Choose life so that you and your descendants may live. (Deut 30:15-19)

Biblical scholars call this linking of human choice and human destiny the "cause-and-effect relationship." Rightly understood, it applies today as well. Cause-and-effect equals self-determination, because it says there are no blind powers of fate. We hold our lives in our own hands. But it also means responsibility. If our German forebears had resisted Hitler's words from the beginning, many millions of people would not have been murdered or thrust into unspeakable misery. Hitler was not fated to succeed.

The Torah thus empties the world of gods; it does the same for the universe and for the state. It focuses the lamp of theological enlightenment on the sacrificial cult, and it exposes fatalism and belief in fate. Finally, it even de-demonizes the mightiest power in the world: death.

We have already spoken of the significance for the pagan religions of the reality of death. Cult of the dead, inquiring of the dead, fear of ghosts, invocation of spirits, the attempt to secure one's fate hereafter—in the pagan world death was constantly intruding on life, and it had enormous power. The people Israel was very conscious of that power, so much so that for centuries it set aside any kind of belief in an afterlife (cf. Deut 14:1). Israel focused its whole energy on the here and now. It is here, in this world, that God should be sovereign—and the place that reveals God's sovereignty is not the world of the dead but God's people, who reveal it by living as a just society. If Israel lives with such a concern for God's cause in the world it can also place itself trustingly in God's hand, in life and in death.

Thus in Israel even death was robbed of its demonic darkness and mythic power—and in just that way the reality of death can be taken seriously: much more seriously than what the religions are able to achieve with their cult of the dead.

Israel's New Experience of God

The concept of enlightenment in Israel, however, still requires definition because it would not have been possible apart from a new experience of God, the encounter with YHWH, the God who saves and frees. When Israel needed to describe its God it could only repeat, over and over again: YHWH is the one "who freed us from the slave-state Egypt."

Thus when Israel calls its God "Lord" it is referring not to some despot with a claim to have others submit but to its creator and liberator. This God snatched this people from the hands of Pharaoh, moved with them through the wilderness, sustained and fed them, and forgave their misdeeds again and again. This was no absent, rejecting, distant God. This was a God who is near, a God "who is there." Israel certainly resisted its God again and again, but it also returned to its trust in this God over and over again—and in its profession of faith it confessed with greater and greater clarity that only this one God exists and Israel must serve no other God.

Therefore we must insist that Israel's breathtaking step from many gods to one unique God was not a reduction of the number of gods. Israel's revolutionary step consisted precisely *not* in concentrating the many powers of the world in a single one. If that were true, Israel's faith would scarcely differ at all from the religions around it.

What happened in the Old Testament people of God was something fundamentally different. In a thrilling process of enlightenment Israel came to see that God is not part of the world, nor is God the foundation of the world—not even the combination of the many powers of nature and history. Instead, God stands over against the world as the Wholly Other who created the world and therefore is not world. God stands over against the nations and history, not as their true depth but as the master of history who has chosen one people out of all the others in order to make divine salvation visible and tangible in the world.

It was only on the basis of that insight that Israel was able to de-deify the world, making it empty of gods who are nothing but human projections, free from the self-created demons that constantly drive people into fear and unfreedom. This de-deification of the world was not a watering down, not a banalization of the world. On the contrary: now, for the first time, the true splendor, the true beauty that inhabits the world as God's creation was made visible.

The de-deification of the world first opened up the opportunity to properly encounter its great realities such as *eros*, community, history, and the state, and to give them a redeemed form—that is, to make all these realities what, in God's intention, they are meant to be. The de-deification of the world, for which the Jewish-Christian tradition is reproached now, robs the world of none of its depth and beauty as long as the world is understood as creation within which the reign of God is to shine forth.

In closing let us take a brief look at Jesus and then at the church.

Jesus and the Reign of God

We can be brief in our consideration of Jesus because, as a Jew, he grasped the core of Israel's faith with the sharpest precision. After all, the so-called Great Commandment, part of Israel's daily confession of faith, begins with:

> Hear, O Israel: YHWH is our God, YHWH alone. (Deut 6:4)

When Jesus made the proclamation of the *basileia tou theou*—that is, the rule or reign of God— the center of his work, he was doing nothing other than what that Great Commandment had always said and willed: Jesus made a serious statement that for Israel there is only one God and that this one God is the Lord, the only Lord—and therefore this God must have a realm in the world in which the benevolence of God's rule can become visible, tangible, and identifiable, and this space, to begin with, is nothing other than the people of God, Israel.

Essentially, then, Jesus' proclamation of the reign of God is nothing new. Israel had always confessed that God is its Lord and had long since prayed that the saving reign of God might come. What is new is that Jesus placed that confession and plea more radically in the present time than anyone in Israel had ever done before. Therefore Jesus could not hope for the coming of the reign of God—that is, the day on which it is shown that God is truly the Lord—at some time in the distant future; he could only say: It is happening today. God's desire is to begin to reign among us today. It is up to us to determine whether this new world will come. Everything depends on whether we accept it.

But Jesus not only proclaimed the reign of God, not only preached it, not only spoke words about it. He began to make a real place for the reign of God, to give it a secure location, by gathering disciples and followers around him—indeed, by not only collecting them around himself in some way or other but by gathering them at table, in order that the new reality would be made present in a lively table fellowship. That, in fact, is what is new about the New Testament: the today of the reign of God that Jesus proclaimed and the indivisible table companionship of Jesus' disciples.

Of course, the fact that this Jesus, so radically one with God's "today," with the will of the Father, exists at all: that is something new. Everything else was already prepared through the history of Israel.

We have seen that enlightenment in Israel required not only service to the one Lord, the one God; rejection of the gods was also essential. Was there anything comparable for Jesus? At first glance Jesus does not seem to speak of foreign gods: of Isis or Astarte, of Zeus or the Ba'als. He did not need to, since in his time critique of the gods had long since begun within Hellenistic culture, and in Israel itself confession of the one and only God was a matter of course.

But if we look more closely we can see that Jesus did indeed talk about false gods: the demons that bore their way into people's heads, robbing them of their freedom, becoming their masters, and making them creatures divided and torn. Jesus could speak of those powers quite clearly. For example, he could describe how one can make her or his life free for goodness and truth by cleaning and decorating one's house—the house that is one's life—and how the evil spirit one was supposedly rid of then returns and brings seven other demons with it: "they enter and live there, and the last state of that person is worse than the first" (Luke 11:24-26).

Jesus had no illusions. He was aware of the power of evil, manifested in the relentless forces of society and the instability of the human heart. But he also knew the remedy against these demons. It is complete surrender to God's cause: the undividedness, the wholeness, the "everything" of trust. Jesus spoke again and again of that wholeness; in essence, that is the subject of the whole Sermon on the Mount. "No one can serve two masters," Jesus says, "for a slave will either hate the one and love the other or be devoted to the one and despise the other. You cannot serve God and wealth" (Matt 6:24).

Thus Jesus also fights against false gods. He even meets them with the utmost seriousness because he knows that they sit in human hearts in the form of pride, jealousy, greed, and sluggishness, trying to block every attempt at discipleship and emulation of him. But that is precisely the ground on which people can also resist them: by placing their lives entirely at God's service—more precisely by surrendering themselves, in their joy at what then happens, with all that they are, their whole existence, to the new thing that is beginning with Jesus. When they do that they do not enter into a new dependency; they acquire an unexpected freedom.

So it is not only Israel but Jesus who brought enlightenment. Not only Israel but Jesus unmasked the false gods. And for him, too, it was always about only one thing: the reign of God, which is the only path to the liberation of human beings.

Enlightenment Continues in the Church

Out of all that—Israel's enlightenment, its turning away from the gods of the world, its confession of the one true God, the radical "today" of Jesus that revolutionizes everything, his circle of disciples as the visible space of the reign of God, the table fellowship he instituted, the undividedness he lived—from all that, the church arose. It is not a social lobby, not a religious umbrella organization, most certainly not a pious club or a society for moral armament. Instead, it is the place in the world where the reign of God should already be visible today, where the rule of false gods is broken, where there need be no more mortal fear, where people regard one another as sisters and brothers, and where none rule over others any longer, because God alone is sovereign.

I know: the church has repeatedly fallen far short of all that. Christians have often rejected the Old Testament. They have frequently forgotten their origins in Israel's enlightenment. They have repeatedly betrayed Jesus and the Sermon on the Mount. In every century they have crucified him anew. They have fallen back into structures and mentalities that have nothing to do with Jesus. They have allowed reflexes and rituals of the religions, formerly conquered, to creep back into their midst.

And yet because Jesus, with his death, endowed the church with that new reality it has never again been lost. The church believes that the silent revolution that began with Jesus will succeed. It believes that the desire for God and all that God wants is ultimately stronger than all the powers of evil in the world. It believes in eternal life, while knowing that everything depends on today, this history and this earth. It will never accept dubious things like the idea of reincarnation, things that cannot withstand the weight of history. With Israel, it has always maintained that there are such things as guilt, sin, and conscience, and at the same time it has always believed, together with Israel, that the human being is the image of God and has been elevated to live before the face of God. With the Jewish teachers it maintains that every person has two notes in her or his pockets: in the left pocket is a slip that reads, "You are dust," and in the right pocket another slip says, "And for your sake the world was created."

It has always treated what is within and what is without as equally important. It was never in favor of pure interiority, what is purely spiritual. Like the Torah, it knew of the "overpowering will of God for immanence" (Gerhard von Rad): that faith must shape, reconcile, liberate, and so sanctify the concrete realities of this world.

4

Freedom to Believe

The Bible has lost its good reputation in Europe. It is true that, over the centuries, rich and sensitive translations of the Bible into European languages have constantly appeared. Think what significance just Jerome's Vulgate and, before it, the Old Latin translation of the Bible had for European culture! Then there was Wulfila's Gothic translation, and the language of Luther's Bible, and, in English-speaking countries, the Authorized (King James) Version. We can scarcely estimate the extent to which the Bible's content and language have supported and advanced—indeed, have shaped—intellectual and spiritual life in Europe.

Despite that, the Bible has an unsavory reputation among many of our contemporaries; regrettably, that is true for many Christians as well. There are a number of reasons. One is a lack of understanding of the Old Testament. For Christians as well as non-Christians it has become a strange and desolate land from which—as they see it—dread shapes emerge along with incomprehensible customs, disgusting laws, inhuman cruelties, and unbearable violence.

Among the repeatedly misunderstood themes of the Old Testament is the election of Israel from among the nations. People nowadays who claim to be "chosen" must expect people to shake their heads, make fun of them, or call for a psychiatrist. What about a whole people that says it is chosen by God—aren't those the fevered dreams of a tiny nation that has been oppressed and persecuted again and again and again?

It is worthwhile taking a closer look at the subject of "election"—in terms of what the Bible says about it. We will then come across something that makes the election of Israel appear altogether different from what is casually supposed. We will encounter a classic example of enlightened reason: the human right to freedom of belief.

Not Only Jews, But Christians Too

God's desire is to have a people in the world, a precisely-defined people of God's choice, different from the other peoples. The Bible says this in countless passages or simply assumes it as a matter of course. It is not only Torah that thinks and speaks that way. So do the prophets. So does even the Old Testament wisdom literature (Wis 10:15-19, 22; Sir 24:7-12). Still more: that is how the whole of the New Testament thinks and speaks. It is true that the Egyptologist Jan Assmann has recently revived Adolf von Harnack's thesis that only the Old Testament is about the people of God. He writes:

> The New Testament is about the individual soul, which becomes the stage for the drama of salvation history, but in the Old Testament it is about the people that is in covenant with God.[1]

Evidently Assmann has never heard that Jesus' intention was precisely to gather and renew Israel, and apparently he is unfamiliar also with the similitude of the olive tree in Romans 11. In fact, the New Testament is not primarily about "God and the soul, the soul and its God"[2] but instead is about the people of God, the church, which is not a "new" people in the world,[3] God having supposedly rejected the "old" people of God. Instead, it is still the one olive tree into which the Gentiles have been grafted by the grace of God.[4] That is why Paul not only speaks of Israel's "adoption" (Rom 9:4) but can also address his Gentile Christian communities as the "elect" or "chosen" (Rom 8:33; 1 Cor 1:26-29; 1 Thess 1:4). Hence the author of

[1] Jan Assmann, "Die Fremdheit des Alten Testaments. Bemerkungen zu einer These von Notger Slenczka," *FAZ* 149, no. 3 (July 1, 2015).

[2] For this theme in Adolf von Harnack's work see Gerhard Lohfink, *Wie hat Jesus Gemeinde gewollt? Kirche im Kontrast* (Stuttgart: Katholisches Bibelwerk, 2015), 10–13, 254–55; 1st English ed.: *Jesus and Community: The Social Dimension of Christian Faith*, trans. John P. Galvin (Philadelphia: Fortress Press, 1982), 1–4, 184–85.

[3] For this subject see, recently, Tamás Czopf, *Neues Volk Gottes? Zur Geschichte und Problematik eines Syntagmas*, MThSt 78 (St. Ottilien: EOS Verlag, 2016).

[4] For a more detailed treatment see chap. 12 of this book, "Was Paul Anti-Jewish?"

1 Peter is able to take up the ancient adoption formula from Exodus 19:5-6:

> But you are a chosen people, a royal priesthood, a holy nation, God's own people, in order that you may proclaim the excellence of him who called you out of darkness into his marvelous light. Once you were not a people, but now you are God's people. (1 Pet 2:9-10)

Thus we cannot avoid the fact that the theme of "chosen people" runs through the whole Bible.[5] It refers to Israel and then to the newly gathered Israel in the church; it means Jews as well as Christians. The fatal misunderstanding that this is only about Israel and the Jews is a notion that must be abolished once and for all. Still, even then the question remains: what does the election of the people of God mean? Why must God have a special people in the world? Why, out of all the nations, does God choose a single people? Is that not an offense against all the "directives for non-discrimination" established by the European Union?

The Burden of Election

One thing is immediately clear from the biblical text: this is in no way about a preference for Israel, benefits accorded it, or any kind of special rights. On the contrary: the election is a burden. The Bible illustrates that burden with various exemplary figures such as Moses and Jeremiah.[6] Moses is chosen by God to lead the people Israel out of Egypt, but he resists. His objection: "Who am I that I should go to Pharaoh and bring the Israelites out of Egypt?" (Exod 3:11). But God encourages him, saying: "I will be with you." That promise is not persuasive, as far as Moses is concerned. He has another problem: "If I come to the Israelites and say to them, 'The God of your ancestors has sent me to you,' and they ask me, 'What is his name?' what shall I say to them?" (Exod 3:13). God also rejects this objection with a long speech, formulating the answer Moses should give. Still, Moses is not persuaded. He has a third caveat ready to hand: "But look, they

[5] For the New Testament cf. also Rom 8:33; Eph 1:4; Col 3:12; 2 Tim 2:10; Titus 1:1; 1 Pet 1:1; 2 Pet 1:10; 2 John 13.

[6] Cf. esp. Jer 20:7-18.

may not believe me or listen to me but say, 'The LORD did not appear to you' " (Exod 4:1).

God has patience with Moses, taking this objection seriously as well: God gives Moses the power to do "signs" in the presence of the Israelites. Those will convince them. But Moses stands firm. He does not want to do it. He produces yet another argument: "O my Lord, I have never been eloquent, neither in the past nor even now that you have spoken to your servant, but I am slow of speech and slow of tongue" (Exod 4:10). God addresses this problem also, pointing out to Moses that it is the Lord God who gives mortals speech. God will teach him what he is to say. But Moses still refuses; now what he says is curt and even rude: "O my Lord, please send someone else" (Exod 4:13). It is as if one of us would say, "I've had it with you! Do whatever you want!" Finally, at this point, God gets angry with Moses but still continues to invite him, giving him Aaron as his mouthpiece—and now Moses agrees and accepts his calling.

What the book of Exodus presents here is an enigmatic sort of scene. Moses is not a vacillating type, nor is he a coward. After all, he has already killed an Egyptian overseer who was beating an Israelite (Exod 2:11-12). But now he anticipates unending resistance to what he is assigned to do: not only from Pharaoh but above all from Israel itself. He knows his own incapacity to meet such resistance. The task God is setting him is beyond human strength.

That, however, is precisely the situation of the elect nation, here embodied in the figure of Moses. God proposes to place on this people a burden it cannot bear. It is supposed to be a people that lives apart from the other nations (Lev 20:24, 26). It is to be a holy people for God (Exod 19:6), utterly different from the other peoples—different in the sense that it will not defy God's order of creation but live it, from morning to night and in every sphere of human life. Israel is to live according to a social order that constantly reminds the people of its God and draws it out of its fixation on itself. That is the precise meaning of the Torah. We can understand that Israel resists its election—exactly as Moses does in the story.

Again and again the people grumble against God. The book of Exodus is full of stories of murmuring, beginning at the Sea of Reeds. The Israelites want to be left in peace. They would rather live as enslaved people in Egypt than be led out into freedom by God (Exod 14:11-12). The people grumble at Marah, on the way to Sinai (Exod

15:24). They grumble in the wilderness of Sin (Exod 16:2). The stories of grumbling continue in the book of Numbers (Num 11:1-10; 14:1-2, 11, 27, 36; 16:13; 17:6; 20:2-13; 21:4-5).

A great many other texts in the Bible reveal similar attitudes.[7] The book of Isaiah describes Israel as "obstinate," "treacherous," and "a rebel from birth" (Isa 48:4, 8). In the book of Ezekiel we find a long retrospect beginning with Israel's election in Egypt and extending to the time of the exile (Ezek 20). God personally recapitulates this long road, station by station, and says again and again "but they rebelled against me" (Ezek 20:8, 13, 21; cf. 20:16, 24, 28, 38). Israel wants to be "like the other nations" (Ezek 20:32; cf. 1 Sam 8:5, 20), and therefore it will be cast by God "into the wilderness of the peoples" (Ezek 20:35): that is, into the Diaspora. From beginning to end, its whole history is portrayed as one of unwillingness, of hard-heartedness, and of rising up against God. It is true that the people of God are led out of Egypt, yet part of its heart remains there. God has to educate this people through a long and tedious effort. God "not only has to bring Israel out of Egypt, but Egypt out of Israel."[8]

Moreover, the grumbling against God in the Bible is by no means limited to the time of the Old Testament. It continues in the church. Again and again the New Testament authors warn their communities against it (cf. John 6:43; Acts 6:1; 1 Cor 10:1-6, 10; Phil 2:14; 1 Pet 4:9). All this shows that the election of the people of God is not a perquisite and not any kind of preferential treatment. It is a burden that is hard to bear.

Why Israel in Particular?

Why does God lay this burden on Israel? Is it an especially great nation or a people of strong faith? Or does it have some other kind of advantages that recommend it to God? All those things are categorically denied in the Old Testament. The book of Deuteronomy pays particular attention to such ideas, and yet God says there:

> . . . you are a people holy to the LORD your God; the LORD your God has chosen you out of all the peoples on earth to be his people, his trea-

[7] Especially Pss 78 and 106, as well as the entire Deuteronomistic historical work.

[8] Rainer F. Uhlmann, *Segen für die Völker. Einführung ins Alte Testament I: Pentateuch*, 2nd ed. (Norderstedt: Books on Demand GmbH, 2011), 237.

> sured possession. It was not because you were more numerous than any other people that the LORD set his heart on you and chose you, for you were the fewest of all peoples. It was because the LORD loved you and kept the oath that he swore to your ancestors that the LORD has brought you out with a mighty hand and redeemed you from the house of slavery, from the hand of Pharaoh king of Egypt. (Deut 7:6-8)

In another place the book of Deuteronomy can go even farther, saying that Israel lacks "uprightness of heart" (Deut 9:5) and emphasizing its stubbornness (Deut 10:16). But that means that God's love for Israel and, even earlier, for the ancestors Abraham, Isaac, and Jacob is irreducible. It does not rest on Israel's outstanding heritage or some extraordinary moral qualification it has "brought with it." God's love for this one people, like every genuine love, has a focus that surpasses all motivations other than no-longer-explicable free affection and devotion. Ezekiel 16 expresses this even more radically than Deuteronomy 7. There we read how God found Israel: abandoned in the open, a newborn babe that no one wanted.

> Your origin and your birth were in the land of the Canaanites; your father was an Amorite and your mother a Hittite. As for your birth, on the day you were born your navel cord was not cut, nor were you washed with water to cleanse you, nor rubbed with salt, nor wrapped in cloths. No eye pitied you to do any of these things for you out of compassion for you, but you were thrown out in the open field, for you were abhorred on the day you were born. I passed by you and saw you flailing about in your blood. As you lay in your blood, I said to you, "Live! and grow up like a plant of the field." (Ezek 16:3-6)

This passage begins a long narrative of the history of the people of God. What was Israel, then? It was an unloved, abandoned child of miserable parentage, from a pagan mother and father. It was bloody and left to die. God saw it lying on the ground and was seized with pity, rescued it and gave it everything it needed, cared for it, and protected it.

That is how the Bible can depict Israel's beginnings, and Israel itself can do the same. The girl will grow up, become beautiful and desirable and then, as a mature woman, continue the history of her parents with countless "suitors." Israel becomes a whore, offering herself on every street corner and every cultic height. And still, God will continue loving this woman and forgiving her everything (Ezek 16:3-63).

The "Why" and "What For" of Israel's Election

Just as the "where from" of God's love for Israel can ultimately not be accounted for and Sacred Scripture here preserves an inviolable *arcanum*, it also speaks very frequently of the "what for," that is, the purpose of Israel's election.

Within the whole sweep of the biblical narrative this goal is mentioned already in Genesis 12:1-3. Having spoken in its first chapters of humanity as a whole, all the nations (Gen 10), their criminal history and especially the steady growth of ferocious violence, the narrative from Genesis 11 onward focuses on Abraham and his family. Abraham is called by God from among the nations. He is to leave his land, his extended family, and his father's house (Gen 12:1), and he will become the progenitor of a great nation (Gen 12:2). God will bless him, and through him all the nations of the earth will receive blessing: "I will bless you. . . . I will bless those who bless you, and the one who curses you I will curse, and in you all the families of the earth shall be blessed" (Gen 12:3).

This promise to Abraham is fundamental for the whole history of the election of God's people. Genesis 12:3 is already about the "what for" of Israel, since Abraham is its progenitor. He represents the people God chooses as God's own. The salvation or damnation of all peoples (here expressed as "blessing" or "curse") is dependent on their attitude toward Abraham, and thus toward the people of God. Whoever curses Abraham, and thus God's people—that is, whoever regards Israel as an evil—will see evil fall upon themselves, but those who regard Abraham and the people Israel as a blessing and ask for blessing in the name of Abraham will indeed be blessed. Concretely: for them there will be well-being, righteousness, and peace.

As I have already said, Genesis 12:3 is a foundational promise. It is frequently quoted throughout the Bible (e.g., Gen 18:18; 22:18; 26:4; 28:14; Sir 44:21; Jer 4:2; Zech 8:13; Acts 3:25; Gal 3:8), and it says with the utmost clarity why there is a chosen people: God has elected Israel for the sake of the nations. The focus is not first and foremost on Israel; for God, this is about the world. Israel is God's instrument for the salvation of the world—and that in no way contradicts the fact that God's love for Israel is not motivated by any consideration.

The theme of "election for the sake of the nations" that begins with Abraham in Genesis 12 is broadly developed in the book of Isaiah, especially in the figure of the Servant of God, who is Israel itself—not some prophetic or royal figure unknown to us, whose real name must remain a secret. This servant of God who is the subject, again and again, in Isaiah 40–55 is nothing other than a figure of Israel or, more precisely, a figure of the Israel deported to Babylon, suffering there, and doubting God.[9] In Isaiah 40–55 we read repeatedly that God will make this servant a "light for the nations":

> I am the LORD; I have called you to create salvation;[10]
> I have taken you by the hand.
> I have created you
> and destined you to be my covenantal people,[11]
> a light to the nations,
> to open the eyes that are blind,
> and [to free] from the dungeon
> those who sit in darkness. (Isa 42:6-7; from the author's translation)

Who is the subject here? Is the text ultimately about the emperor Cyrus, who is spoken of elsewhere in the book of Isaiah and of whom it can be said that God has chosen him to bring Israel out of its imprisonment in Babylon?[12] That is improbable, if only because the expression "light for the nations" is applied quite unmistakably to Servant Israel in Isaiah 49:6 (cf. Isa 49:3). There God says:

> It is too light a thing that you should be my servant
> to [again] raise up the tribes of Jacob[13]

[9] For a detailed argument let me refer to Gerhard Lohfink and Ludwig Weimer, *Maria – nicht ohne Israel. Eine neue Sicht der Lehre von der Unbefleckten Empfängnis*, 2nd ed. (Freiburg: Herder, 2012), 223–29.

[10] Literally "in [salvation-creative] righteousness."

[11] Not "the covenant for my people" or "as an obligation for the people," as in many translations. The translation I propose is altogether possible on the basis of the Hebrew syntax. The usual translations are governed by the idea that the Servant of God is an individual. [The AV has "I the LORD have called thee in righteousness," using the second-person singular pronoun (thee); similarly at 49:6, "It is a light thing that thou shouldest be my servant." Modern translations such as NRSV simply use "you," which can be understood as singular or plural.—Trans.]

[12] Thus, e.g., Karl Elliger, *Deuterojesaja I. Jesaja 40,1–45,7*, book 11.1 (Neukirchen-Vluyn: Neukirchener Verlag, 1978), 222–40.

[13] For this unusual translation, which, however, is unproblematic on the basis of the syntax of the Hebrew infinitive, cf. at length Norbert Lohfink, "'Israel' in Jes 49,3," in *Wort, Lied und Gottesspruch. Festschrift Joseph Ziegler*, ed. Josef Schreiner, FB 2 (Würzburg: Echter Verlag; Stuttgart: Katholisches Bibelwerk, 1972), 217–29.

and to restore the survivors of Israel;
I will give you as a light to the nations,
that my salvation may reach to the end of the earth. (Isa 49:6)

Thus it is clear that God not only frees Israel from exile, not only raises up Israel and leads it back to its land; Israel now has the duty to liberate the nations. But how is that supposed to happen? It does so inasmuch as Israel becomes a "witness" to the liberating deed of its God (Isa 43:10, 13; 44:8). In that the nations see what God has done for Israel it will become an enduring witness to who its God is: a liberator. That Israel is to become a "light to the nations" thus means that it is to bring liberation and enlightenment to the nations simply by the fact of its rescued existence—or, in another image, to open the blind eyes of the nations and bring them out of their darkness (Isa 42:7; cf. 51:4).

I use the word "enlightenment" deliberately here because the European Enlightenment loved the metaphor of light. English "enlightenment" is German "Aufklärung," French "lumières," Italian "illuminismo." So when Israel is named as "light for the nations" in the book of Isaiah it becomes, in our contemporary terminology, the place of enlightenment that affects the whole world: enlightenment about the true situation of the nations, enlightenment about the true God, enlightenment about how God leads out from the self-created immaturity and darkening of the human spirit.

That may sound too euphoric for some, and we may well ask how this enlightenment of the nations is supposed to happen in actuality. The book of Isaiah offers adequate clarity here, too, because it speaks from the very beginning (Isa 2:1-5) about the "light" that illumines the path of society. There the prophet sees, in a vision, the eschatological pilgrimage of the nations to Zion.[14] Why are they going to Zion, according to Isaiah 2:1-5? It is because they have had enough of endless wars and can no longer endure the rank misery those create. They want the God of Israel to teach them how to beat their swords into plowshares: that is, how to overcome constant rivalries and create peace (2:4). In other words: the nations have recognized

[14] For what follows cf. Michael P. Maier, *Völkerwallfahrt im Jesajabuch*, BZAW 474 (Berlin: de Gruyter, 2016), 95–143.

that their own life-construct is false because it leads only to rivalries and wars. They are looking for a better model of society.

The text presumes—and unfortunately this is usually overlooked—that the immense vision of the future can succeed only because the nations listen to God's instruction (Isa 2:3) and above all because Israel is among them and is already living, or at least striving for, the better order of society. Therefore it is said at the end of the vision, where the prophet turns directly to the Israel that is listening:

> O house of Jacob,
> come, let us walk
> in the light of the LORD! (Isa 2:5 // Mic 4:5)

That means: war is still active in current society. The nations still believe they can solve their problems by the use of force. But it should be different in Israel. Israel should begin, in the power of its God, to live peace within itself, and it should do so now, without delay. In just that way and no other can the world overcome its warring. The people of God must, within itself, in its own heart, begin the lived alternative.

That is a hopeless, impossible task God assigns to this people, and we now have an even better idea of why biblical Israel repeatedly rejected God's plan. Being "a light to the nations" is a ponderous burden and seems impossible to bear. We would fall into a profound misunderstanding, however, if we were to think of the thus-described existence of Israel for the nations as primarily an act of moral strength or ethical achievement. As Isaiah 2:5 shows with utter clarity, it is not Israel's own light that will shine forth but the "light of the LORD" in which the people of God pursues its own alternative path. It only needs to enter into that light, and it already possesses it in the Torah.

A Supplementary Reflection

We have thus arrived at a point where it is time to reflect more directly on all that lies behind such an election. We have seen that God is not thinking, in the first place, about Israel. This is about the salvation of the world. But how can a transformation of world society into worldwide blessing succeed? Many people have tried to change the world. Every revolution seeks to liberate the masses, release people from their misery, radically change conditions. Every genuine revolution has desired a new consciousness, a new society, a new humanity.

Revolutionaries face a problem, however, that creates immense difficulties for them: they don't have time. Individual lifetimes are limited, and the masses are lethargic. If the revolutionaries want to see the new society they are trying to create in their own lifetimes they have to alter the old society from the ground up and do so in a relatively short space of time. They can only do it by force.[15]

Why by force? Quite simply: in the first place for the sake of speed. They want to see the first flowers and fruits of the revolution in their own lifetimes. But the real reason lies much deeper: most revolutionaries do not believe in a free transformation of all relationships. As far as the final form of society is concerned, of course they want it to be free. But in almost all cases they are convinced that violence is necessary in the transitional period because the old society protects itself and its structures are frozen.

In fact, current scholarly definitions of revolution contain at least three elements: (1) it must involve the masses and not just small groups; (2) the overturning of society must take place rapidly, if not even abruptly; and finally (3) that overturning must be accomplished with open and direct violence. We can consider a classic revolutionary text: the last section of the *Communist Manifesto* (1848) reads:

> The Communists disdain to conceal their views and aims. They openly declare that their ends can be attained only by the forcible overthrow of all existing social conditions. Let the ruling classes tremble at a Communistic revolution. The proletarians have nothing to lose but their chains. They have a world to win. Workers of the world, unite!

At the center of this vigorous final paragraph of the *Manifesto* violence is explicitly proclaimed to be the necessary principle of world revolution. There is absolutely no other choice when time is short and the whole world is to be changed at one stroke. In the process, however, human freedom falls by the wayside. Countless people are overpowered and trampled in the dust. There are plenty of bloodcurdling

[15] That is also shown by, among many others, Michael Walzer in his *Exodus and Revolution* (New York: Basic Books, 1995); cf., e.g., p. 17.

illustrations in the French Revolution and the Russian Revolution under Lenin.

God's principle is different. To put it somewhat brashly: God is a better strategist. Like all revolutionaries, the God of the Bible wants a total overturning, a radical transformation of world society, because on that point the revolutionaries are right: this is about the whole world, and the alteration must be radical—simply because the world's misery cries to heaven and because it begins deep within humanity itself. But how can anyone change the world and its society at the root without robbing it of freedom?

It can only happen in that God starts "small," at a single point in the world. There has to be a place—visible, comprehensible, verifiable—where the redemption of the world can begin: that is, where the world becomes what God knows it should be. Then, starting from that place, the new thing can spread throughout the world—but not by persuasion, not by indoctrination, and most certainly not by violence.

People must have the opportunity to appreciate in complete freedom what is new in the world, to examine and test it. When they are convinced, they can let themselves be drawn into the history of reconciliation and peace that God brings into being. That is the only way in which individual freedom can be maintained. What drives people to the new thing must not be compulsion, most certainly not moral pressure, which can be worse than any external force, but only the fascination of a changed world.

God also has to start small, beginning with a little nation, in contrast to the revolutionaries of this world who rely on violence. To be more precise, God cannot even begin with a little nation. God must begin with an individual, because only the individual is the point where God can rely on conversion in freedom. That is exactly what the Bible relates: how God begins with Abraham and his family. The individual must therefore stand at the beginning, but little by little the story has to expand toward a new society, for redemption, salvation, nonviolence, and peace always have, besides—and in fact, primarily—a social dimension. Certainly the people that God wants to make for God's self always contains the indispensability of the individual at its core. God's people can never be a pure collective, a simple mass; it always has to remain "Abraham," that is, a people in which every individual is continually called to her or his task by God. In short: *Because God desires the salvation of the whole world community, that salvation must be prepared and made visible, so to speak, in the experimental sphere of a little people.*

That is God's strategy. Now perhaps we can better understand why there must be election—indeed, why there must be an elect people: *so that the world may freely believe. So that freedom of faith is guaranteed for all. So that no individual or whole group may ever be forced to believe. Election and freedom are profoundly connected.*

Refining the Concept of Mission

What we have here demonstrated by means of central biblical texts has consequences for what the Christian churches call "mission," because everything Isaiah 40–55 has shown us alters the still-widespread concept of Christian mission. In fact, it turns it on its head.

Mission has very often been understood by Christians—especially in the nineteenth century—as the sending of missionaries or messengers to pagan lands to preach the gospel, as individuals or in groups. No question: that preaching was almost always associated with "works": the building of kindergartens, schools, hospitals, and many other charitable institutions. But on the whole the main purpose was to preach and to transplant the gospel, thus far rooted in European culture, in a completely different environment. An infinite amount of good resulted from this missionary method. We have no idea how the world would look today but for the great missionary movement of the nineteenth century (and previous centuries as well).

And yet this missionary "offense" does not really match what we have seen in Isaiah. It does not fit the theme of the pilgrimage of nations as described in Isaiah 2:1-5 and elsewhere in the book (cf., e.g., Isa 11:10; 14:1-2; 18:7; 45:14, 22-25; 49:14-26; 55:1-5; 56:1-9; 60:1-22; 66:15-24). There it is not missionaries who go to the nations but the nations that come to Zion. There the nations are not preached to; they see the works of God in Israel. There it is not Israel that seeks to bring people from among the nations to commitment; instead, people from other nations change their lives and travel to Jerusalem because they recognize that in that place there is instruction to be had from God and that justice and peace are the rule among the people of God (Isa 11:1-12).

Is this true only of the book of Isaiah? No! There are other texts in the Old Testament that have the structure of the pilgrimage of the nations. Compare, for example, 1 Kings 8:41-43; Tobit 13:13; 14:6;

Psalms 87; 96:7-13; 102:23; Jeremiah 3:17; Micah 4:1-5; Zephaniah 3:9-10; Zechariah 2:14-15; 8:20-23; 14:16. A great many more texts in the Old Testament, while they do not speak of the pilgrimage of the nations, presuppose that thought structure. When, for example, the beginning of Psalm 105 reads, "O give thanks to the LORD; call on his name; make known his deeds among the peoples," that certainly does not mean that the assembled festal community should send missionaries to the peoples. Instead, what it says is that Israel itself should recall the miracle God has done for it (v. 5) and remember the faithfulness God has shown toward it (vv. 8-9). When that happens, when the people of God is, at the center of its existence, a living memory and recollection of God's mighty deeds, then the nations, too, will join in praising God. We really should consider the fact that, during the time of biblical Israel, no one ever had the idea of sending messengers, certainly not missionaries, to pagan peoples.[16]

Likewise, there was no mission in that sense in the period of early Judaism.[17] Jews dwelt in many cities of the ancient world, and they had synagogues and communities in a lot of places. There were proselytes from among the Gentiles who joined a community and became Jews. There were the so-called God-fearers who participated in worship at the synagogue but had not yet taken the step to become proselytes. In the time before and after Christ there were even many Jewish writings that scholars call "mission literature." These were narratives, novels, and expositions advocating for Judaism. But their appeal was made by describing Jewish life or the reasonableness of Jewish belief.

If I am correct, there was never a Jewish mission strategy like that of the Christian mission—for example, in the nineteenth century.

[16] Cf. Joachim Jeremias, *Jesus' Promise to the Nations*, trans. S. H. Hooke (London: SCM, 1958): "During its early history Israel was not a missionary people" (p. 11).

[17] Differently Jeremias, *Jesus' Promise*, 11–19. The evidence Jeremias offers points, with a single exception, only to the abundance of so-called mission literature as well as the demand that Jewish communities should be "light for the nations." But texts of that kind do not presuppose the sending of missionaries; rather, they fall within the schema of the pilgrimage of nations. Obviously there were many proselytes in Jewish communities, and clearly they were surrounded by a circle of "God-fearers." But that does not assume the sending out of missionaries. The only clear exception is Matt 23:15, but that text could reflect early Christian polemics. For the whole question see also the reserved stance of Ulrich Luz, *Matthew 21–28*, Hermeneia (Minneapolis: Fortress, 2005), 117–18n45.

Certainly there seem to have been intensive efforts under the Hasmonean rulers to re-Judaize Galilee, which had become dominated by Gentiles. But those attempts do not really fall under the concept of mission we are talking about here. On the whole, Judaism until today has remained faithful to the basic model of the pilgrimage of nations. That is: God's social order must be lived in visible communities. Only in that way can God's purpose in the world be made demonstrable.

If that is right, then at this point the question necessarily arises: What was the situation in Jesus' mission, in the post-Easter communities, and in the early church? Did it hold to the Old Testament basic model of the pilgrimage of nations, or did the young church develop a concept of mission that was fundamentally different from Old Testament and Jewish models? I can only point to an answer here.

Jesus followed the basic structure of the Old Testament pilgrimage of the nations to the letter. He proclaimed the now-inbreaking reign of God in Israel, speaking deliberately and exclusively to Jews. His few encounters with Gentiles are marginal phenomena that happened by accident (Matt 8:5-13; Mark 7:24-30). In fact, Jesus concentrated his mission in the core territory of Judaism and avoided Hellenistic cities lying within the borders of ancient Israel.

Jesus called the community of disciples he gathered around him, as a center for the growth of the now-to-be-assembled eschatological Israel, a "city built on a hill" and "light of the world" (Matt 5:14). The light of his community of disciples should "shine before others" so that they might glorify God (Matt 5:16). Here Jesus is clearly alluding to the idea of the pilgrimage of nations, and he also assumes it largely as a matter of course when he says, for example, that many will come from east and west to recline at table with Abraham, Isaac, and Jacob in the reign of God (Matt 8:11).

The post-Easter community of disciples, originally concentrated in Jerusalem and Judea, acts in the same way: as the first speeches in the Acts of the Apostles show, they turn first to Israel alone, just as the biblical prophets had done. The election of Matthias restores the group of apostles to twelve (Acts 1:15-26), because for Jesus the Twelve already functioned as eschatological witnesses and judges over the twelve tribes of Israel (Luke 22:28-30).

Originally there was no thought of an early Christian mission to the Gentiles. The first incorporations of Gentiles into the church did not result from a planned mission strategy; indeed, they were completely unplanned (Acts 10). When it then appeared that more and more Gentiles were asking to be admitted to the church and thus to eschatological Israel it was evidently interpreted in terms of the pilgrimage of nations. At any rate, in the Acts account of the so-called Apostolic Council, James, the brother of the Lord, argues as follows:

> My brothers, listen to me. Simeon has related how God first looked favorably on the gentiles, to take from among them a people for his name. This agrees with the words of the prophets, as it is written, "After this I will return, and I will rebuild the dwelling of David, which has fallen; from its ruins I will rebuild it, and I will set it up, so that [!] all other peoples may seek the Lord—even all the gentiles over whom my name has been called. Thus says the Lord, who has been making these things known from long ago." Therefore I have reached the decision that we should not trouble those gentiles who are turning to God. (Acts 15:13-19)

James, in his argument, cites Amos 9:11-12 LXX with Isaiah 45:21. The crucial point is that first "the dwelling of David, which has fallen" (that is, Israel) must be restored. This has occurred in the time after Easter described in Acts 1–5, or at least it has begun. Now that it has happened, the Gentiles may come in. James thus uses the pilgrimage of the nations, promised in Scripture, as the basis for his argument. The important point is, as we have seen, that first Israel itself must become a shining city before the nations can start out on the way to it.

The interpretation that Jesus' brother James gave to the mission to the Gentiles, according to Acts, remained fully present to the church in the first century and also in the early centuries of Christianity that followed. The Gentile mission was always seen as a fulfillment of the Old Testament promise of a pilgrimage of the nations to Zion. The church was now Zion. That is quite evident in Paul's writing in Romans 9–11, but not only for Paul. At the beginning of this chapter I had referred to 1 Peter 2:9-10:

> But you are a chosen race, a royal priesthood, a holy nation, God's own people, in order that you may proclaim the mighty acts[18] of him

[18] NRSV. (NRSVue, "excellence"; NABRE, "praises." Cf. Isa 43:21, תהלתי יספרו; LXX τὰς ἀρετάς μου διηγεῖσθαι.)

> who called you out of darkness into his marvelous light. Once you were not a people, but now you are God's people; once you had not received mercy, but now you have received mercy.

This text is saying that as Gentiles the recipients of the letter had been far from God's people Israel. Now, however, they have been implanted in eschatological Israel. The ideas that they have been called into "light" and now proclaim God's "mighty acts" come directly from the motif of the pilgrimage of nations as developed in the book of Isaiah.

The major theologians of the ancient church also interpreted the Gentile mission against that background. The loveliest formulation comes from the great Origen, who interprets the nations that, in accordance with Isaiah 2:3, are coming to "the mountain of the Lord" as the Gentile Christians, and the "mountain of the Lord," which for Isaiah was Mount Zion, as the church:

> Each one of us [Gentile Christians], then, has come in the last days, when our Jesus has appeared visibly among us, to the bright mountain of the Lord, the Word that is above every word, and to the house of God, which is the community of the living God, the pillar and ground of the truth. And we see how it is built upon the tops of the mountains, i.e., the predictions of all the prophets, which are its foundations. . . . And [we], the many nations go forth, admonishing one another to turn to the divine worship that in the last days has shone forth through Jesus Christ: Come, let us go up to the mountain of the Lord, to the house of the God of Jacob; and He will teach us of His ways, and we will walk in them. For the law came forth from the dwellers in Zion, and settled among us as a spiritual law.[19]

Justin, Irenaeus, and Tertullian read Isaiah 2:1-5 similarly. Thus the early church continued to interpret its mission to the Gentiles in light of the prophetic message of the pilgrimage of nations. That horizon of interpretation was very gradually lost by the church as, when considering mission, people concentrated more and more on Jesus' words at the end of Matthew's Gospel:

[19] *Contra Celsum* 5.33; available at https://www.newadvent.org/fathers/0416.htm.

> Go therefore and make disciples of all nations, baptizing them in the name of the Father and of the Son and of the Holy Spirit and teaching them [all] that I have commanded you [to keep]. And remember, I am with you always, to the end of the age. (Matt 28:19-20)

Regrettably, in the history of Christian mission this powerful text was often interpreted very one-sidedly: people saw only the commands to "go" and to "baptize," overlooking "make disciples." But that is the very element that is crucial in Matthew 28:19-20: it means the gathering of communities of disciples. Of course, the references to baptism and to keeping what Jesus commanded also point to that meaning. The "teaching" of Jesus here refers to the Sermon on the Mount and, together with it, the major collections of teachings in the Gospel of Matthew, directed primarily to Jesus' disciples. All this shows that Matthew 28:19 is not about a "rapid" mission with "fast" baptizing and an emergency ration of information from the catechism; rather, it is about a mission that, while it is familiar with missionaries, has as its goal the building up of communities of disciples who live on the basis of the Sermon on the Mount. The many others from among the nations can then run to those communities. Here again, the motif of the pilgrimage of nations is clearly in the background.

It is no different with Paul. While he is quite rightly called the apostle to the Gentiles (cf. 1 Tim 2:7) and the great missionary, if we look closely we see that he consistently follows the Jewish model: he depends on a network of communities stretching through the lands around the Mediterranean. Paul works untiringly and with his whole existence so that these communities may come to life and give living witness to the gospel of Jesus Christ. But then the communities themselves are supposed to attract people and win them over to Christ. They are to "shine like stars in the world" (Phil 2:15). Here we arrive again at a motif from the pilgrimage of the nations. The goal of the apostle to the Gentiles is not a blanket ministry but rather the building up of living communities that can become witnesses to the gospel.

That this basic biblical principle so often fell by the wayside in the course of church history represents a profound loss, because ultimately the fundamental principle of "pilgrimage of the nations" does not imply an "offensive" mission (propaganda, strategies for spreading the faith), but fascination—the fascination of those who see in concrete communities that here there is peace, reconciliation, nonviolence, justice, community. When people see that, it can awaken in them a longing to question their own life-constructs, leave them behind, and find a home in the new Christian way of life developed on the basis of Israel. In this way their adoption of faith can be utterly free.

Please do not misunderstand me! I am not saying that all Christian strategies for mission involved force. Such an assertion would be bitterly unjust—especially toward the countless missionaries in the recent history of mission. But alas, force was applied in the past. Think only of the medieval "mission with the sword" in the East or of the favored strategy of converting leaders, whereupon a whole tribe could be baptized. There were many forms of compulsion in the history of the church's mission. They would never have existed had the church always kept its biblical "model of mission" in mind: that the community of Israel must change itself in order to win over people in freedom.

The Lamb That Was Slain

Now I have said "must change itself"—and precisely at this point one last correction needs to be made. According to Isaiah 52:13–53:12 the Servant of God is not at all someone who needs to be changed, who must become more holy, more moral, more faithful to the law, more believing. Instead, the Servant is led by God into profound suffering, into a condition in which there is nothing more the Servant can do. In this so-called Fourth Servant Song everything previously said about Israel, the Servant of God, achieves an ultimate intensification.

This is so because the nations have gathered together against this Servant of God. The Servant is seized by them and led to judgment (Isa 53:8), is mistreated (Isa 53:7), and yet, like a lamb, does not open his mouth (Isa 53:7), surrenders his life to death (Isa 53:12), and is executed (Isa 53:8), being consigned to a grave among the wicked (Isa 53:9).

If we decode those statements we find that this is about Israel, led away to Babylon. The Servant chosen by God and intimate with God lives in the misery of exile because of his sins. He has become prey to the nations, has no form any longer, is despised by all, and lives in the sphere of death, as if in the grave. And yet, even this beaten and scattered Israel is God's instrument, is "light for the nations."

Indeed, the greater part of this magnificent speech about the Servant of God is a confession made by the kings and the nations (Isa 53:1-11). They suddenly recognize what is really going on with this beaten and deformed creature:

> We accounted him stricken,
> struck down by God, and afflicted.
> But he was wounded for our transgressions,
> crushed for our iniquities. (Isa 53:4-5)

What is here depicted is an unfathomable paradox. It is precisely through beaten and bowed Israel that God's plan will succeed (Isa 53:10). For the Servant astonishes the many nations (Isa 52:15); kings must fall silent before him (Isa 52:15), God's glory is shown through him (Isa 49:3), and through him God's salvation reaches the whole world (Isa 49:6).

The paradox consists precisely in the fact that the Servant of God uses no violence, no instruments of power, no strategies, no offensives, no arts of persuasion. In the end he convinces through his silent suffering, his disfigurement and deformation. It is only by this means that his message gains its full force.

In the ancient world, where serious disease and deformation of the human figure were regarded as divine punishment, this was a scarcely comprehensible revolution in thought. Israel suffers for the "many," that is, for the nations—and in just that way, God's plan succeeds.

Jews have frequently and increasingly interpreted the Servant in Isaiah 40–55 collectively in reference to Israel. Christian reading, from the outset, fastened on Jesus (cf. Acts 8:26-40). The interpretation in terms of Jesus was also quite correct, for in himself Jesus gathered together all the lines of Israel's descent and everything that the people of God should be. At the moment of his death he embodied, all alone in his representative suffering, the Israel that was chosen by God to be salvation for the nations and that, in the sense of Isaiah 40–55, is a better sacrifice than that of "those who conquer by violence."[20]

[20] So formulated in "Gerechter Friede" ("Just Peace"), document 66 of the German Bishops' Conference (Bonn: Sekretariat der Deutschen Bischofskonferenz, 2000), 24.

The thoughts in this chapter began with the concept of election, which has become incomprehensible to so many people. Isn't the statement that Israel was chosen by God from among all the nations simply contrary to all reason? But we have seen that the Bible speaks in very subtle terms about the "what for" of Israel's election. What is decisive is that God's concern is not with Israel but with the world—a world that can enjoy human dignity, justice, peace, and openness to God. We also saw that moving a world living in aggression and violence toward that goal must not and cannot be accomplished through violence. It must happen in freedom; otherwise nothing can change. Therefore God has to begin small, in a particular place, a single part of the world, with a little nation. That nation's way of life must show clearly what justice and peace mean.

Biblical Israel never supposed they could change the nations of the world with missionary strategies, nor did they ever make wars in order to spread their faith. They pictured the transformation of the world in the model of the pilgrimage of nations: the peoples, filled with longing and fascination, come to where justice and peace are lived. Therefore Israel itself must begin to be the alternative.

That could put the people of God under a dreadful pressure to succeed. It could degrade what Israel is meant to be into a society of moral achievement, with all the horrible consequences such attempts always bring with them. The book of Isaiah, however, develops the model of the pilgrimage of nations in a totally different direction: what the nations come to see is not "moral armament" and most certainly not a perfect society of achievement, but an oppressed and defeated nation that becomes a victim.

The model of the pilgrimage of nations, as shown to us first in Isaiah 2:1-5, is already based on pure freedom. If the nations come to Zion it is only because they want to. They come because they are fascinated. They come because they see that a different kind of society is possible. Still, Isaiah 52:13–53:12 radicalizes that freedom: whoever renounces all violence, preferring to be struck down and destroyed rather than to strike back, choosing to become a victim instead of a triumphant victor—that one opens to others a still more profound freedom.

What happens in this space of deliberate nonviolence and the acceptance of suffering is the absolute opposite of all compulsions, all wars of religion, all murder in the name of God (and probably also all previously planned campaigns to spread the faith).

I am by no means renouncing what I have said in the course of these reflections about Isaiah 2:1-5. It is certainly correct. The tides of refugees now flooding Europe and other continents, and steadily increasing, are functioning according to the structural model of Isaiah 2. They show how attractive a society can be when it exhibits justice, guaranteed rights, solidarity, and peace. But Isaiah 53 shows us that ultimately that is not enough, because even a society of guaranteed rights and equality before the law is always endangered. It, too, requires the silent victim who surrenders self on behalf of others: representative suffering, because otherwise it will lose contact with the roots out of which it springs. Those roots, that ground: these are established forever in the death of Jesus. Without his surrender of his life and the freedom he thus instituted, enduring solidarity and democracy cannot last, in Europe or anywhere else.

5

Social Project and Knowledge of God

The exodus narrative (Exodus 1–15) is one of the best-known texts in the Old Testament. When we read it as a unit, however, we soon notice that as a whole it is not nearly as familiar to us as it first seemed, because our attention focuses mainly on individual events: the scene at the burning bush, the Egyptian plagues, the institution of the Passover feast, and then especially the transit through the Sea of Reeds.

Those are indeed high points in the great, connected exodus narrative. Most of us learned them as children, and then later the liturgy opened them to us even further. Still, texts that become significant parts of our awareness conceal a danger: they are all too easily isolated and become separated from their context. And that is dangerous precisely because then it often happens that, as a result, theological connections running throughout the text that were important to the original authors fall out of sight.

Here modern knowledge of the Bible is a great help. It sharpens our perception, within narratives, for the major continuous lines in the text. While older exegesis pursued a distinction of sources at length and often excessively, and found great satisfaction in reconstructing more and more complicated previous layers of the biblical text, recent exegetes have increasingly dealt with the so-called "final text" also, seeing it as a theological whole, even as an "aesthetic subject."[1] This newer exegesis, in succession to structuralism, tries

[1] For the concept of the "aesthetic subject" cf. Helmut Utzschneider, *Gottes langer Atem: die Exoduserzählung (Ex 1–14) in ästhetischer Sicht* (Stuttgart: Katholisches Bibelwerk, 1996). See also Helmut Utzschneider and Wolfgang Oswald, *Exodus 1–15*, trans. Philip Sumpter, IECOT (Stuttgart: Kohlhammer, 2015), 17–20.

to get a sharper picture of the final text, and in doing so it discovers themes that necessarily escaped those who were only interested in distinguishing sources.[2]

The study of the Exodus history is ideal for illustrating all that—and yet, this great narrative can show us something else as well: namely, the profound connection, even interdependence, between social project and knowledge of God.

Society and Its Symbolic World of Meaning

There is a fixed relationship between the real form of society in which people live and their recognition of God. In terms of theory that was most clearly established by the sociologists Peter L. Berger and Thomas Luckmann in their book *The Social Construction of Reality*.[3] Simply put, this important book—together with many others—says that every society establishes a "symbolic world of meaning" for itself, and that symbolic world is the source of interpretation for the life of the society as a whole. It defines every experience within the society, all its marginal situations, its troubles, but also its successes and ecstasies. A symbolic world of meaning must "encompass all reality"—containing it, ordering it, explaining it, and thus protecting it against the chaos of individual lives and social "terror." For, as Berger and Luckmann rightly say:

> All social reality is precarious. All societies are constructions in the face of chaos. The constant possibility of anomic terror is actualized whenever the legitimations that obscure the precariousness are threatened or collapse.[4]

Consequently, there is no society that does not live within a symbolic world of meaning that it has itself produced. This world of meaning creates its identity.

[2] A lively example of the application to the final text is the lecture by Norbert Lohfink, "Mose wird zum Befreier—wie er sich dabei selbst verändert. Biblisches zur Spiritualität der Gerechtigkeit und der Befreiung," at https://www.sankt-georgen.de/fileadmin/user_upload/personen/Lohfink/lohfink22.pdf.

[3] Peter L. Berger and Thomas Luckmann, *The Social Construction of Reality: A Treatise in the Sociology of Knowledge* (New York: Anchor Books, 1967).

[4] Berger and Luckmann, *The Social Construction of Reality*, 103.

To make this a little more concrete: for European societies in the nineteenth century the ideas of home, native land, and the honor of one's own nation were essential components of their world of meaning. That is no longer true to the same extent for the peoples of Western Europe in the twenty-first century. Globalization and ecological problems now play a completely new role that shapes consciousness in that milieu. To exaggerate a little: the purity of the air has replaced the purity of the nation.

Obviously that is not a complete description of the meaning-creating symbolic world of today's Western Europeans, which extends deep into the collective unconscious. Also, previous worlds of meaning such as the "purity of the nation" can return in part. I only want to make somewhat clear what is meant by a symbolic world of meaning. It is certain that religion plays a decisive role in all meaningful symbolic worlds, and with religion so do the gods, or God. Consequently there is a fixed web of relationships between the social system of each society and its image of God.

But let us return to the ancient Near East, or to antiquity as a whole, because that will make the whole thing much clearer. A society with a king as its monarchic head also had a "highest" god at the head of the whole pantheon of gods. The heaven of the gods and the structures of society corresponded. The existence of the highest god legitimated the existence of the king, making him untouchable and sacrosanct.

Likewise, a society based on offensive violence against its neighboring peoples and constant wars of conquest quite naturally anchored those structures of violence in their gods as well. They had a special god of war, as was the case in Greece and Rome: Ares or Mars. Unending wars of conquest were so central to the Roman state that the month in which the campaign season began—namely, March—was dedicated to the war-god Mars.

Above all, when we consider the ancient Near East it is clear that society and the world of the gods corresponded to one another. An inhumanly structured society must necessarily be reflected in the inferiority of its gods—and, on the other hand, knowledge of the true God presupposes a rightly constructed society. A constant interdependence was required.

It should be clear by now what must follow: Israel had to go out from the slave state of Egypt because only in that way could it achieve knowledge of the true God. This God, in fact, desires people who are not enslaved but free. The exodus narrative is very subtle in how it reveals the connection between knowledge of God and social structure. I cannot, of course, investigate the whole of the exodus story; I can only shed light on certain details. I have been greatly aided by Helmut Utzschneider's book, *Gottes langer Atem*, to which I will refer directly. But now, at last, to come to the point!

Israel's Situation in Egypt

The first thing that strikes us in Exodus 1–15 is that the narrative uses an unusual amount of space for the description of the situation of the people in Egypt. Compare, for example, Exodus 1:11-14:

> [The Egyptians] set taskmasters over them to oppress them with forced labor. They built supply cities, Pithom and Rameses, for Pharaoh. But the more they were oppressed, the more they multiplied and spread, so that the Egyptians came to dread the Israelites. The Egyptians subjected the Israelites to hard servitude and made their lives bitter with hard servitude in mortar and bricks and in every kind of field labor. They were ruthless in all the tasks that they imposed on them.

Note the keywords "forced labor" and "hard servitude." I will come back to those. Otherwise the text needs no commentary. Twentieth-century labor camps fully illustrate what forced labor means. When Moses, at God's command, goes to Pharaoh and begs him that he be allowed to go three days' journey into the wilderness with the people in order to offer sacrifice, the work regulations are immediately intensified:

> That same day Pharaoh commanded the taskmasters of the people, as well as their supervisors, "You shall no longer give the people straw to make bricks, as before; let them go and gather straw for themselves. But you shall require of them the same quantity of bricks as they have made previously." (Exod 5:6-8)

This text is already familiar with all the inhumanities of the Gulag: forced labor, deliberate raising of quotas, and finally the capo-system, which recruits the necessary overseers—here called "taskmasters"—from among the oppressed themselves.

Even before the imposition of these harsher measures we have read that the Hebrew midwives have been ordered to kill all boy babies born to the Israelites (Exod 1:15-16). When the midwives contrive to evade the command, the order is intensified: the Egyptians are to throw all boys born to the Israelites into the Nile (Exod 1:22). That command is meant not only to prepare for the story of Moses' rescue. It has another function as well: it is to make clear that the Israelites in Egypt are doomed, that they live in a destructive society, a land of death.

There can be no coexistence with such a society. In the long run one cannot evade it by stealth, as the midwives sought to do (Exod 1:17-21). Nor can one meet it with counter-violence such as Moses attempts when, one day, he slays an Egyptian (Exod 2:11-14). It is impossible even to live in such a society by creating a space for freedom within it, as the repeated request to celebrate a sacrificial feast in the desert indicates (Exod 3:18; 8:21-24, etc.). All those possibilities are presented in the text, evaluated, and then rejected.[5]

The Only Solution: Exodus

The right reaction to a social system of this kind is completely different. It is the solution God uses: the exodus. God leads Israel out of the state of Egypt, built on enslavement, and presents it, at Sinai, with a better system: the social order of the Torah. Thus the exodus from Egypt is not only flight from a closed system that destroys people. Much more important is the goal toward which the exodus is directed: a life of freedom in the land God once promised to Abraham and his progeny. In this way the new existence into which God means to lead Israel is an "alternative world."

The society out of which Israel was taken and the new society that is to flower in the land given by God stand in sharp contrast to one another, a contrast that is especially clear in the creed given in Deuteronomy 26:5-10. It is to be spoken in the temple at Jerusalem as thanksgiving for the harvest, probably at the Festival of Booths:

> A wandering Aramean was my ancestor; he went down into Egypt and lived there as an alien, few in number, and there he became a great

[5] Utzschneider, *Gottes langer Atem*, 92, 97–98; cf. also the essay by Norbert Lohfink, "Mose wird zum Befreier," *passim*.

> nation, mighty and populous. When the Egyptians treated us harshly and afflicted us, by imposing hard labor on us, we cried to the Lord, the God of our ancestors; the Lord heard our voice and saw our affliction, our toil, and our oppression. The Lord brought us out of Egypt with a mighty hand and an outstretched arm, with a terrifying display of power, and with signs and wonders; and he brought us into this place and gave us this land, a land flowing with milk and honey. So now I bring the first of the fruit of the ground that you, O Lord, have given me.

This creed of Israel shows with full clarity that God has heard the cry of Israel in Egypt. But liberation from enslavement would not have been enough. The broad arc of the history of rescue has to lead to a new land, where there will be an abundant harvest. The land yields its fruit. It gives blessing. Israel can gather the yield of its own labor in freedom. The credo in Deuteronomy 26 ends with the motif of the harvest in Israel's own land and so becomes definitively a praise of the liberation God has given.

But what kind of liberation is this? Is it only freedom from the Egyptians' cudgels? Is it only relief from the pressure of constantly increasing work rules? In other words: is liberation in the exodus narrative solely about the social and political dimensions of Israel's existence? Certainly that social dimension of liberation plays an important part in the exodus texts; not a letter may be subtracted from them. But there is more meaning here.

Liberation into Knowledge of God

The appropriate form of a society is connected to the correct form of its worship of God. A free society can, in the long run, exist only where the true God is worshiped. This insight escapes all those who exalt the achievements of the European Enlightenment while repressing the fact that they have something to do with the God-image in the Jewish-Christian history of enlightenment. Should that image of God collapse, so will the Western history of freedom.

The reverse is also the case: the true God can, in the long run, be worshiped only where a society is rightly constructed. Many Christians have suppressed that insight: they believe they can accommodate socially to their neopagan environment, be completely absorbed in society, and still hold fast to their God. That is a mistake that will one day exact a bitter revenge. Christians will only be able to hold fast to the God of Abraham, Isaac, and Jacob, the God of Jesus Christ, if they live socially in contrast to the neopagan society. Berger and Luckmann are quite correct when they write that "counter-definitions of reality require counter-societies."[6]

So, again: an enduringly free and just society can come about only where the true God is worshiped, and in turn the true God can, over time, be known and worshiped only where the society is rightly constructed. Social order and knowledge of God are inextricably interdependent. Israel knew that from long experience.

That is why the theme of the self-revelation of the true God is woven, quite deliberately, throughout the story of liberation in the exodus narrative. That self-disclosure begins right away, in Exodus 3, with the familiar scene in which Moses stands before the burning bush, out of which God is self-revealed as "the God of Abraham, Isaac, and Jacob." God has beheld the people's misery and wills to deliver them from the power of the Egyptians (Exod 3:6-8).

Moses, in the course of the dialogue that begins here, is sent by God to speak to Pharaoh, but Moses resists. Before he can approach the royal court he has to first convince the Israelites themselves of his mission. Moses knows who are the enemies of the exodus: not only Pharaoh, but Israel itself. What is he to say to them when they ask him what this God who is sending him is called? Hereupon Moses receives a most unusual answer from God; interpreters are struggling with it to this day. The whole passage reads:

> But Moses said to God, "If I come to the Israelites and say to them, 'The God of your ancestors has sent me to you,' and they ask me, 'What is his name?' what shall I say to them?" God said to Moses, "I will be what I will be!" And God said further, "Thus you shall say to the Israelites, 'I Will Be' has sent me to you." God also said to Moses, "Thus you shall say to the Israelites, 'YHWH, the God of your ancestors, the God of Abraham, the God of Isaac, and the God of Jacob, has sent me to you. That is my Name forever and my title from generation to generation." (Exod 3:13-15, from the author's translation[7])

[6] Berger and Luckmann, *The Social Construction of Reality*, 184.

[7] Standard English translations since the AV have "I am who I am," from the LXX *egō eimi ho ōn*, but the Hebrew אֶהְיֶה אֲשֶׁר אֶהְיֶה is indeterminate.

God thus solemnly proclaims the divine name here, the name with which people may call on God: YHWH. But did God answer Moses' question about the name of the deity with whom he has spoken? If we look more closely we see that in no way did God answer the question; the divine name YHWH has already been defined as "I will be what I will be!" That puzzling sentence can only mean: "I will not give you a name. I do not allow anyone (at least at this moment) to talk with me about such a thing. You do not need a divine name to know who I am. All you need is this: look at what is about to happen. What is now going to happen to you and the Egyptians will show you who I am. Who I truly am will reveal itself. History will show it, not a name. Therefore: I will be what I will be—that is, through my actions."

We have to paraphrase God's answer in some such words.[8] The result, however, is a crucial statement about the nature of God. This God is not only outside human command but is different from the gods of the nations. This God does not have a name, as the gods all have individual names, to distinguish them from one another and so that they can be reached by prayer. The God of Israel cannot be grasped by means of that kind of name. This God is revealed in saving intervention; God's innermost essence appears in the leading of God's people out of oppression and into freedom, out of the land of exploitation into a "good and spacious land, a land flowing with milk and honey" (Exod 3:8).

Thus the exodus narratives begin with a trumpet sound. They are not only about Israel's rescue from enslavement but simultaneously about God's self-revelation. God is revealed in action. What God will do in powerful, untiring, compassionate acts for Israel—that is God's name. From that point of view, moreover, it makes the greatest theological sense that Jews, and the church with them, have refused from ancient times to speak the word YHWH. But that is only a side note!

Everything that will be told in the subsequent chapters of Exodus, set against the background of this refusal by God to specify a divine name, is a revelation of God's true nature. From an intertextual point of view the theme of Exodus 3:14 is resumed in 34:6-7, where the name of God revealed to Moses in the burning bush is further explained in

[8] Cf. Utzschneider, *Gottes langer Atem*, 59.

solemnly stylized language.[9] There is much in favor of the idea that here, too, initially YHWH is self-described in paradoxical fashion.

> The LORD passed before him [Moses], and proclaimed: "[YHWH is YHWH], a God merciful and gracious, slow to anger, and abounding in steadfast love and faithfulness, keeping steadfast love for the thousandth generation, forgiving iniquity and transgression and sin, yet by no means clearing the guilty, but visiting the iniquity of the parents upon the children and the children's children, to the third and the fourth generation."

What is said here is not a declaration of timeless truth about God. After all, it has been preceded by Israel's breach of the covenant by making the Golden Calf (Exod 32:1-6) and God's declared resolve to have done with Israel (Exod 32:7-10). But then God regrets the evil threatened against Israel, retracts the divine anger, and does not carry out the destruction. God is shown to be a faithful God for Israel. Thus here again we understand that who YHWH really is can be seen in YHWH's merciful actions.

Pharaoh's Resistance

God's self-revelation in the exodus event has another side, too. Through it God reveals the divine Self to Moses and the Israelites. They recognize God through what God does. On the other hand, God also wills to reveal that divine Self to Pharaoh and the Egyptians. They, too, will see God's deeds. They can repent and change their ways. They can let the Israelites go. They can even bless them and praise the God of Israel.

But that is just what does *not* happen. The Egyptians, and primarily Pharaoh, will reject God's self-revelation. That rejection is set before the eyes of readers within the fabric of the exodus narratives in a thoroughly thought-out fashion. The starting point for the whole story of rejection is the depiction of the Pharaoh's complete lack of interest in YHWH. When Moses and Aaron first stand before him and

[9] For Exod 34:6-7 cf. Ruth Scoralick, *Gottes Güte und Gottes Zorn. Die Gottesprädikationen in Ex 34,6f und ihre intertextuellen Beziehungen zum Zwölfprophetenbuch*, HBS 33 (Freiburg: Herder, 2002); for our subject see esp. pp. 1, 42, 103, 105.

ask him to let the Israelites go out into the wilderness to celebrate a feast, the answer they receive is:

> Who is [YHWH], that I should listen to him and let Israel go? I do not know [YHWH], and I will not let Israel go. (Exod 5:2)

In the course of the narrative God will take up this arrogant "I do not know YHWH" and use it against Pharaoh. The god-king of Egypt will come to know who YHWH is. The phrase "he shall know" runs like a refrain through the whole story of the signs God works against Pharaoh and the Egyptians. "You" in the following passages always refers to Pharaoh:

> The Egyptians shall know that I am [YHWH]. (Exod 7:5)
> By this you shall know that I am [YHWH]. (Exod 7:17)
> So that you may know that there is no one like [YHWH] our God. (Exod 8:10 [MT 8:6])
> . . . that you may know that I [YHWH] am in this land. (Exod 8:22 [MT 8:18])
> . . . so that you may know that there is no one like me in all the earth. (Exod 9:14)
> . . . so that you may know that the earth is [YHWH's]. (Exod 9:29)
> . . . and the Egyptians shall know that I am [YHWH]. (Exod 14:4, 18)

The gradual expansion of the formula is worth noting. We have already seen what it means: Israel's God is the one who does not have a name, as the gods of the nations do. This God's name is to be recognized by humans through God's mighty deeds. As such—so the expansion of the formula shows—God is sovereign not only in God's people Israel but also in Egypt. God is Lord within the land of Egypt (Exod 8:22). But more than that: YHWH is sovereign not only in Egypt but throughout the whole earth (Exod 9:14, 29).

How does Pharaoh react to this increasingly urgent self-revelation of God? How does he respond to the dreadful signs God is working, which show that God is master over Egypt and therefore over Pharaoh? We find a whole sheaf of reactions. First Pharaoh tries to compete. He sets the signs worked by his own state and court magicians over against those of YHWH (Exod 7:11, 22; 8:7 [MT 8:3]). When the priest-magicians ultimately fail, Pharaoh tries to compromise. First he says that the feast the Israelites want to celebrate in the wilderness should simply be held in the land of Egypt (Exod 8:25 [MT 8:21]). When Moses refuses, the next suggestion is that they should celebrate in the wilderness, but not far away (Exod 8:29 [MT 8:24]). The third variant on the compromise is that only men should participate in the festival, not women and children (Exod 10:8-11). In other words, the women and children are to remain as hostages. The final offer is that all the people may participate, but they must leave their flocks in Egypt as security (Exod 10:24).

From time to time the Pharaoh even asks Moses and Aaron to pray for him (Exod 8:28 [MT 8:24]), and when hail destroys everything growing in the fields he confesses himself guilty before the God of Israel (9:27-28). Then, when the locusts ravage the land, his confession of sin becomes even more desperate:

> I have sinned against [YHWH] your God, and against you. Do forgive my sin this once, and pray to [YHWH] your God that at the least he remove this deadly thing from me. (Exod 10:16-17)

Still, every time the danger is past and the plague abated, Pharaoh's heart is hardened. There is a constant shifting between confession and renewed hardening, between surrender and another refusal. Pharaoh repeatedly falls back into his stubbornness, even when his officials advise him, finally, to let the Israelites go and celebrate their sacrificial festival (Exod 10:7).

The readers are almost exhausted. Why these monotonous repetitions? Why Pharaoh's overpowering hardness of heart? At first glance the text gives an obvious answer: Pharaoh is so unbending because God has directly hardened him and repeatedly made his heart stubborn (Exod 4:21; 7:3-4; 9:12; 10:20). Likewise, the reason why God does so is clearly stated: God hardens Pharaoh's heart in order, through him, to demonstrate God's glory for all to see (Exod 14:4, 17).

But if we look closely we see that the text is more subtle: it is not God who hardens Pharaoh's heart; Pharaoh does it to himself. That is, he makes it hard, stiffens it, makes it impenetrable. For example, when he has begged that the plague of flies be removed:

> And [YHWH] did as Moses asked: he removed the swarms of flies from Pharaoh, from his officials, and from his people; not one remained. But Pharaoh hardened his heart this time also, and would not let the people go. (Exod 8:31-32 [MT 8:27-28]; cf. 8:15 [MT 8:11])

If we try to reconcile the two sets of formulae, "self-hardening" versus "hardening by God," we have to say that Pharaoh himself rejects God's actions. He refuses to understand because he does not want to let Israel depart. But God even uses that refusal to bring this history to its goal and show the divine glory. Therefore the narrative speaks not only of Pharaoh's self-hardening but also of his being hardened by God.

Consequently, the text itself justifies us in laying aside our modern difficulties with a "hardening by God" and giving all our attention to the phenomenon that here is a human being who, with an unbelievable hard-heartedness and mulish stubbornness, refuses to see and hear, recognizing only his own will. Certainly it is scarcely possible to conceive why the "narrated" Pharaoh cannot understand, after all the horrors that have befallen Egypt, and even the death of the Egyptian firstborn, and why he still pursues the Israelites.

Is the story exaggerated? Is it trying to inflate God's deeds of power? Is it simply working with a climax that is continually delayed in order to raise the tension? No, something else must be going on here. This story speaks about a phenomenon that is characteristic of human rejection of God. The narratives about the hardening of Pharaoh are shaped as a pure example of how darkening and unfreedom come about in the world. They happen because human beings unceasingly defend themselves against God. They refuse to see. They refuse even to learn anything better. They insist on pursuing their own self-glorification. And even when they are made aware they again repress what they have seen.

After the eighth plague Pharaoh at last admits his own guilt and thus confesses the God of Israel as his Lord (Exod 10:16). But after that confession he hardens himself anew and becomes even less approachable than before. After the ninth plague he says to Moses:

> Get away from me! Take care that you do not see my face again, for on the day you see my face you shall die! (Exod 10:28)

It may be that nowhere in the Old Testament is there such an intense depiction of what theological tradition calls "original sin." Human refusal to accede to what God wills is demonstrated here in the figure of Pharaoh. The long series of Pharaoh's hardenings serves, in fact, as a parade example of the history of sin and of entanglement in guilt. Human beings can see, they can understand, and yet they refuse and they harden themselves—contrary to their own experience—within their own ideas and desires.

Thus the narrative of the ten plagues acts out, in the person of "Pharaoh," how it looks when God's self-opening encounters the self-withholding by a human being that resembles original sin. Naturally, that original-sin-like self-withholding is intimately connected, in turn, with the structural mentality within which Pharaoh lives: after all, he is the god-king and lord who is revered by the whole land. How can he acknowledge another master? In doing so he would surrender not only himself but the whole "world of meaning" within which he and all his people exist.

The Enabling of Worship

Still, the narrative has much more to say. As we have already seen, Moses repeatedly asks Pharaoh to allow Israel to go out into the wilderness to offer sacrifice. Superficially this festival appears to be only a tactical pretense, meant to lead Pharaoh by the nose. What it is really about is something different: flight.

Indeed, the sacrificial feast is actually a smokescreen, and yet it expresses a reality that goes far beyond any pretense, because the fact that Israel wants to celebrate a feast in the wilderness is not only about its preparations for escape. The reality is much more profound: Israel cannot celebrate any festival for its God in Egypt because, in the long run, no feast can be celebrated within a falsely constructed society. Worshiping God and serving as slaves are contradictory realities.[10] The true feast (and therefore true worship of God) demands a true society. Therefore Israel must go into the wilderness in order to "serve" God there (Exod 7:16, 26). As long as it is serving Pharaoh it cannot serve God.

From this point of view it is simply fatal that later, at the Sea of Reeds, in the moment when Pharaoh approaches with his chariots, the people break into fearful cries and beg to return to Egyptian slavery:

> As Pharaoh drew near, the Israelites looked back, and there were the Egyptians advancing on them. In great fear the Israelites cried out to the Lord. They said to Moses, "Was it because there were no graves in

[10] The German assonance of "Gottesdienst" (worship/service of God) and "Frondienst" (slavish service) is hard to reproduce in English.—Trans.

> Egypt that you have taken us away to die in the wilderness? What have you done to us, bringing us out of Egypt? Is this not the very thing we told you in Egypt, 'Let us alone so that we can serve the Egyptians'? For it would have been better for us to serve the Egyptians than to die in the wilderness." (Exod 14:10-12)

Here, then, the key word "serve," which we already encountered at the beginning of the story, appears again. "Serving God in the wilderness" and "serving the Egyptians" are thus placed in contrast to one another. They establish an unbridgeable contradiction. Either festival or enslavement! Either worship of God or slavish service! The two are incompatible. Hence the overpowering insistence on a sacrificial feast that has to take place outside the boundaries of Egypt is more than a pretense meant to throw sand in Pharaoh's eyes. The Israelites need that feast before their God if they are to live. The feast is not possible in Egypt; it only becomes so when Israel is free. Then it can begin at once.

That, then, is what happens. The Sea of Reeds has scarcely been crossed, and Pharaoh and his chariots drowned there, when the people Israel begins its first feast as a people. Then Moses lifts up a song that reads, at its center, "Who is like you, O LORD, among the gods? Who is like you, majestic in holiness, awesome in splendor, doing wonders?" (Exod 15:11). With that song the rescue of Israel from Egypt has reached its goal. Enslavement is at an end. Worship, with true veneration of God that is to fill the whole land, has begun. And that worship is tied to a clear knowledge of how God is different: "Who is like you, O LORD, among the gods? Who is like you, majestic in holiness?"

This worship will then continue at Sinai (Exod 3:12), and there it will be established forever. The tent of meeting ("tabernacle") will be part of that established order; its construction is described in Exodus 25–40 in full detail, and in that context, in Exodus 35–36, the subject of "enslavement" and "worship of God" will be taken up again. That is how important it is to these narrators.

The Tabernacle and Free Will

What is so special about the tent-sanctuary? For one thing, it is portable. It can be broken down and rebuilt. It is to accompany Israel during its wandering through the wilderness. Still, despite its portability, it symbolizes *the* sanctuary, God's final resting among God's people, the perfection of the whole creation.

It is said of this tent-sanctuary that it is built for "ministering" or "offering" (Exod 35:19; 36:3). Thus the key idea of "service" appears anew, but here everything is different. The Israelites no longer serve as slaves; they are free. This is evident in the willingness with which they offer the best that they have for the construction of the sanctuary. Their willingness, in fact, becomes the guiding thread of the depiction in Exodus 35–36:

> Take from among you an offering to the LORD; let whoever is of a generous heart bring the LORD's offering: gold, silver, and bronze; blue, purple, and crimson yarns. (Exod 35:5-6)
>
> Then all the congregation of the Israelites withdrew from the presence of Moses. And they came, everyone whose heart was stirred, and everyone whose spirit was willing, and brought the LORD's offering to be used for the tent of meeting and for all its service and for the sacred vestments. So they came, both men and women; all who were of a willing heart brought brooches and earrings and signet rings and pendants, all sorts of gold objects, everyone bringing an offering of gold to the LORD. (Exod 35:20-22)
>
> All the Israelite men and women whose hearts made them willing to bring anything for the work that the LORD had commanded by Moses to be done brought it as a freewill offering to the LORD. (Exod 35:29)

The guiding thread of the quoted statements is obvious:

> everyone whose heart was stirred
> everyone whose spirit was willing
> all who were of a willing heart
> freewill offering

At this point the book of Exodus, through the guiding theme of willingness and spontaneity, renews its emphasis on the contrast with enslavement in Egypt. Now the Israelites, both women and men, are no longer toiling as forced labor for Pharaoh, the supposed god-king; they serve the true God. And that service can be done only in freedom. One's heart must drive one to it. The people are no longer building just anything—tombs, for example. Instead they are building a sanctuary for God in which God's glory may descend and which will reflect the perfection of the world (cf. Exod 39:32, 43 with Gen

2:1-3). Then God will be fully present in Israel and it can at last come to "know" God:

> I will dwell among the Israelites, and I will be their God. And they shall know that I am the LORD their God, who brought them out of the land of Egypt that I might dwell among them; I am the LORD their God. (Exod 29:45-46)

Those two statements are still in the future tense. They will become present tense at the end of the book of Exodus, where God's taking-up-residence among the people of God really happens:

> Then the cloud covered the tent of meeting, and the glory of the LORD filled the tabernacle. Moses was not able to enter the tent of meeting because the cloud settled upon it, and the glory of the LORD filled the tabernacle. (Exod 40:34-35)

Thus here again, as with the song of victory at the Sea of Reeds, it is clear that the exodus from Egypt not only leads from enslavement to freedom and from a falsely constructed state to a new society. It also leads into freedom to recognize the true God, to serve that God, and so to be entirely with this LORD. Human beings are made free from false gods, most of them the personal, self-constructed gods of self-assurance and self-glorification.

God as Liberator

When persons become free from false gods, whether they are called Pharaoh or bear some other name, it becomes possible for them to recognize the true God and open themselves to that God in freedom. The Israelites show us how difficult that is: even after all the signs and wonders they have seen they prefer to be re-enslaved by Pharaoh rather than risk the new freedom with God: "What have you done to us, bringing us out of Egypt? Is this not the very thing we told you in Egypt, 'Let us alone so that we can serve the Egyptians'?" (Exod 14:11-12). At this point, too, the narrative is free from any illusions. It by no means says that it is very difficult to achieve the new freedom. It says, rather, that it is impossible for human beings. The exodus narratives continually point out that neither Moses nor the Israelites can manage to remove themselves from Egypt. They tell us over and over that God alone accomplishes the exodus. It was not Moses, who resisted from the outset (Exod 3:11–4:17). It was certainly not the people, who were always skeptical, ultimately succumbing to panic and begging to be returned to enslavement. It was God alone. The whole exodus was a miracle of pure grace; it was possible only because God was very patient and repeatedly took the initiative.

It was not Israel that fought against the Egyptians; God fought for Israel. That is stated in exemplary fashion in Moses' speech at Exodus 14:13-14. The Israelites have arrived at the Sea of Reeds but have not yet crossed it. They are just gathering themselves for the crossing—finding themselves in a highly precarious situation—when the Egyptians' mounted troops and chariots appear on the horizon. Then Moses says to the people:

> Do not be afraid, stand firm, and see the deliverance that the Lord will accomplish for you today; for the Egyptians whom you see today you shall never see again. The Lord will fight for you, and you have only to keep still. (Exod 14:13-14)

Thus liberation from a false society to that of the people of God is pure grace. A part of that liberation began at that time, in the exodus, and it happened again and again in the course of Israel's story. After all, the exodus narratives are the collected account of Israel's experiences through many centuries.

We may say in conclusion that according to Exodus 1–15 knowledge of God and social structure are intimately connected. So long as the people of God remain in Egypt they cannot be free. If they stay in Egypt there is no path to the true God's self-revelation, and so the people cannot serve God. Still less can Pharaoh recognize the true God. The brief flashes of recognition he experiences are immediately swallowed by deep darkness. After all, Pharaoh is completely entangled in the structures and models of a falsely constructed society.

Knowledge of God and Social Structure in Hosea

Obviously the connection between knowledge of God and ordering of society could be illustrated with the aid of many other biblical texts—including, for example, some from the book of Hosea. In that book especially the connection between social chaos and failure to know God is striking. It is the case with Hosea and other prophets that Israel itself falls back into the situation of a society distant from

God. Injustice and exploitation have spread; political corruption and power politics have replaced care for the community. Therefore in Hosea 11:5 Israel is even threatened that it must return to Egypt, which here serves as a symbol for Assyria. A crucial text for the connection between knowledge of God and models of society is Hosea 4:1-3, which forms a kind of overture to Hosea 4–11:

> Hear the word of the LORD, O people of Israel;
>   for the LORD has an indictment against the inhabitants of the land.
> There is no faithfulness or loyalty,
>   and no knowledge of God in the land.
> Swearing, lying, and murder,
>   and stealing and adultery break out;
>   bloodshed follows bloodshed.
> Therefore the land mourns,
>   and all who live in it languish;
> together with the wild animals
>   and the birds of the air,
>   even the fish of the sea are perishing.

The concept of "knowledge of God" occurs very frequently in the book of Hosea (cf. 4:6; 5:4; 6:3, 6; 8:2; 11:3). For Hosea "knowledge of God" is knowing the one whom Israel has to thank for its existence and the gifts of the land. The quoted text shows that the consequence of contempt for God's social order is that knowledge of God vanishes from the land—and the reverse is likewise true: when Israel forgets the one to whom it owes its existence, its society breaks asunder.

Thus an intensive study of the book of Hosea would have been important to our theme, but I have restricted myself to the exodus narrative because, as regards the connection between knowledge of God and social order, it is precisely that major text that is least familiar.

The Triune God and the Corresponding Society

Before concluding we need to take a brief look at the New Testament. Exodus 1–15 speaks of the liberation of the people of God from false social structures and false gods. With Jesus and the Pentecost descent of the Spirit of Jesus that long history of liberation reached its goal, definitively and unsurpassably. That liberation is celebrated in the Easter Night and the whole great Easter festival of fifty days, concluding with Pentecost.

But during those fifty days and on that Pentecost it is not only their liberation from enslavement that Christians celebrate; it is, at the same time, the gift of God's ultimate self-revelation. For the most beautiful and precious fruit of the ever-deepening knowledge of God within Israel was ultimately the insight that God is not alone and lonely, not a life contained within itself, but rather that God is triune: society, *communio*, shared life, an ongoing conversation.

After everything we have seen it ought to be clear that such an insight and understanding of God's triune nature was not accidental; it was possible only where the people of God themselves lived as *communio*—where believers trusted one another implicitly, were one in spirit, accepted one another mutually in *agapē*, and shared their lives with one another. The insight that God is a triune community presupposes the *communio* of the gathered assembly as a new society.

The reverse is also true: obviously the *communio* thus practiced presupposes the gracious action and self-communication of the triune God. To put it another way, in terms of a "theology from below": only at the moment when, within the evolution of social structures, that form of *communio* was achieved in the original community in Jerusalem, where a social group was held together no longer by power structures but by unanimity, trust, and a shared life—only there could God be recognized as triune.

Therefore the feast of Pentecost as the birthday of the eschatological people of God was the hour in which God was ultimately recognized, for in the wake of the Pentecost feast it could be said that

> All who believed were together and had all things in common; they would sell their possessions and goods and distribute the proceeds to all, as any had need. Day by day, as they spent much time together in the temple, they broke bread at home and ate their food with glad and generous hearts. (Acts 2:44-46)

When the author of Acts writes that way he is not depicting a utopia or a romantic idealization of the original community; he is describing what constituted the innermost essence of the church. Nevertheless it needs to be said: we must turn back, again and again, to that form of the church through an unceasing reformation.

6

Trinitarian Faith and Imperial Monotheism

The confession of the triune God is one of the innermost aspects of Christian faith. That is the very reason why it is so difficult to explain to non-Christians what this confession means and how it came about. It is just too foreign to them. A Japanese visitor to a baroque church in Bavaria, viewing a fresco representing the Trinity, said:

> God the father: that I can understand. That God has a son I can also understand. But I really can't conceive why there should be a holy bird, too.

Probably this was meant to be a polite rejection of Christianity—but certainly it was a fundamental misunderstanding of what confession of the triune God is meant to express.

Excursus: Analogous Concepts

Why is it a fundamental misunderstanding? For one thing, God does not "have" a son, as the Japanese viewer supposed, nor is this about a "son" like the sons human beings have. Most Christians, as well as non-Christians, fail to understand that we are always speaking of God in images and parables.

To put it in technical terms: all statements about God are *analogous*. In this case "analogous" means that we can only ever speak about God in concepts with which the dissimilarity between the original idea and God is always greater than the similarity. In the present case this means that "son" does not *univocally* refer to a son like those that human parents have. "Son" here means, in an analogous sense, the inconceivable communion between God and Jesus—but obviously the word "communion" in that statement also has to be understood analogously: that is, not as communion involving all the distance and reservations human beings experience in their relationships. And obviously the "dove" the Japanese visitor was contemplating is a pure image that has to be relativized by other images.

But above all—and many theologians are unaware of this—even the "three" in expressions about the Trinity and the "one" used in speaking about belief in one God are, in theological terms, analogous concepts and thus cannot be simply equated with the "one" and "three" in our numerical series. The "three" must be understood as dissimilar—that is, analogous—to the same degree as all other statements about God.

To that extent the jeering with which Mephistopheles ridicules the dogma of the Trinity in Goethe's *Faust* as a kind of skewed mathematics completely misses the reality of Christian faith:

> Ancient the art and modern too, my friend.
> 'Tis still the fashion as it used to be,
> Error instead of truth abroad to send
> By means of three and one, and one and three.
> 'Tis ever taught and babbled in the schools.
> Who'd take the trouble to dispute with fools?
> When words men hear, in sooth, they usually believe.
> That there must needs therein be something to conceive.
> (*Faust*, part 1, "The Witches' Kitchen")[1]

Not the Brainchild of Theologians

But far more serious than the ridicule or lack of understanding on the part of non-Christians is the fact that faith in the triune God has become foreign even to many Christians. They ask themselves uneasily, sometimes even worriedly, whether it is not enough to join

[1] Text at https://www.gutenberg.org/cache/epub/3023/pg3023.html.

Israel in believing in the *one* God.—Is it really necessary to understand and pray to this one God as also triune? Trinity—isn't that just pure theory, artificial speculation by theologians, a mere figment of their imaginations?

No, it is not! Belief in the Father, Son, and Holy Spirit is not a construction by theologians; it came about because of real experience—experience that took place, in fact, within Israel.

First there is the experience of the Old Testament people of God with the one who brought them out of Egypt, traveled with them through the wilderness, led them, rescued them, forgave their sins, is close to them. This is a saving God, one who comes to the aid of the people God has chosen. Israel already called this God by one of the loveliest names God can have: "Father."

This fundamental experience of closeness that Israel always enjoyed with its God then acquired a new dimension in Jesus. In him God was finally and definitively present within God's people. Jesus' disciples could not describe it in any other way. They had to say: Jesus is God's ultimate word. In him God is completely communicated. In him God has said everything, once and forever. In him God finds full self-expression, and in him God has also fully and finally acted. In short: who sees Jesus, sees the Father (John 14:9). And because he is altogether the image, the reflection of the Father, they had to say: He is the "Son" (Matt 11:25-27). That does *not* mean that he is a "second" God but rather that he is the definitive presence of the Father in the world. Therefore, within the people of God, prayer can no longer ignore Jesus. All prayer to the God of Israel now takes place "with Jesus" and "in his name" (John 14:13-14).

On the day of Pentecost, then, all that was deepened by a third fundamental experience: Jesus—from a superficial point of view—is no longer here. His disciples can no longer see him. No one can still hear him. And yet he is not separated from his disciples; he is in their midst (Matt 28:20). He is with them when they gather. He is even nearer to them than he had ever been before. He is with them through his Spirit. That is the fundamental experience of Easter and Pentecost, and the basic experience of the church as a whole: Jesus is present in the Holy Spirit, and with Jesus the Father is likewise present.

If the church, then, no longer speaks of God without distinction, but instead of "Father," "Son," and "Spirit," that is not an amendment of its belief, and it is most certainly not an ideology in opposition to

Israel's belief in one God. That would have been historically impossible, because the experiences thus described took place within Israel, that is, fully within the strictest possible monotheism.

Those who formulated the faith in the triune God were, in fact, not Christians drawn from among the Gentiles but Jewish Christians firmly rooted in Israel's faith. And the theologians who in subsequent centuries penetrated more and more deeply into the mystery of the triune God in order to protect it against misunderstandings were not thinkers in the tradition of Greek philosophy. They were not concerned with Hellenistic speculations about gods but thought in terms of the New Testament.

Thus belief in the Father, the Son, and the Spirit rests on spiritual experience of God's self-opening. The one God has become present in the world in such a way that all God's previous becoming-present has reached its goal and perfection. Therefore the Son and the Spirit are not two new gods but the opening of the one God to the world in which God is entirely present—in the face of the Son and the power of the Spirit. None of that has anything at all to do with polytheism; what it is really about is the ungraspable and overflowing love of God for the world.

But even when all that has been said, much remains unanswered. For example, there is the question of what faith in a triune God has to do with our daily lives. Does it change anything about the reality of my life whether, as a faithful Jew, I believe in the *one* God or, as a Christian, in the *one* God in three persons? Certainly I insist that Jesus was more than a rabbi and more than a prophet. I also maintain that God has spoken God's self entirely and definitively in this human being. But does that make any difference in my real life, here in the world?

The answer can only be: Yes, it makes a fundamental difference in many ways, for in that case I insist that Jesus' Sermon on the Mount is the definitive interpretation of the Torah, with all that follows from that (Matt 5:21-48). I affirm that, with Jesus and the coming of the Holy Spirit at Pentecost, there has begun within Israel what the prophets longed for (Acts 2:14-21). Then I know that the church is the place of the *eschatological* worship of God (Phil 2:5-11).

Thus belief in the triune God changes lives—but not only those of individuals and of the people of God. It changes the life of society as a whole. Whether there is faith in the triune God or not has enormous consequences. I want to illustrate that now with a concrete example, namely, what historians today call "imperial monotheism."[2] But to do that I must broaden the picture.

The Roman Principate and Its Background

When the young church was spreading slowly in all directions it did so on the ground of the Roman Empire, the *Imperium Romanum*. Prior to that time Rome had suffered a century of civil warfare; it was only Augustus who succeeded in putting an end to those wars. He created a new political system, the principate, aiming at monarchical rule, though primarily in terms of a veiled one-man governance. That completely came to light only during the reigns of Augustus's successors. Augustus himself still knew how to hold matters in a clever balance; the Senate continued to exist, together with many institutions of the ancient Roman republic, but *de facto* the Roman emperor ruled, gradually with more openness, as the sole monarch.

This profound alteration of the Roman constitution by Augustus and the later emperors was not merely the usurpation of power, and it arose not only from the need to hold the empire together. It also corresponded to the new religious ideas of the Roman upper class: educated persons had already long ceased to believe simply in the ancient gods of popular religion. Ovid, in his *Art of Love*, urged young women to make false promises and swear lying oaths. Jupiter could only laugh at such things; after all, he himself had sworn falsely. Then comes the famous verse:

> *Expedit esse deos,*
> *et, ut expedit esse putemus.*
>
> *Gods are useful:*
> *As they're useful, let's think they're there.*[3]

[2] The category of "imperial monotheism" was introduced to historical scholarship by Garth Fowden in his book *Empire to Commonwealth: Consequences of Monotheism in Late Antiquity* (Princeton: Princeton University Press, 1993). For what follows I have also consulted the lengthy *Habilitationsarbeit* by Almut Höfert, *Kaisertum und Kalifat. Der imperiale Monotheismus im Früh- und Hochmittelalter*, Globalgeschichte 21 (Frankfurt: Campus, 2015), as well as Wolfram Drews, Antje Flüchter, et al., *Monarchische Herrschaftsformen der Vormoderne in transkultureller Perspektive*, Europa im Mittelalter 26 (Berlin: de Gruyter, 2015).

[3] Ovid, *Ars Amatoria* 1.16.7. Translation by A. S. Kline, ©2001, available at https://www.poetryintranslation.com/PITBR/Latin/ArtofLoveBkI.php.

Greek philosophy had led to an altered view of the world that would fully develop later in Neoplatonism.[4] The elites believed in a highest principle that was, so to speak, the pinnacle of the cosmos, the first cause of all order in the world. This supreme divine power, this godly *monarchia*, ruled and ordered the whole world and was the ultimate basis for the unity of all things. It pervaded the whole cosmos and held it together. In this system the ancient gods were certainly not meaningless, but they sank to the level of secondary cosmic powers—subordinated to the unique, all-ruling world-principle.

This idea of an ultimate and highest cosmic *monarchia* was now the precise model for the new structure of the Roman *imperium*. It was the task of the Roman legions to subordinate all the peoples of the earth, and at the pinnacle of the gigantic empire thus created stood the Roman emperor as sole ruler. We only need to read the official titles of Octavianus Augustus: *Imperator. Caesar. Divi filius.*[5] *Augustus. Pater patriae. Pontifex maximus*. The titles applied to him in the cities of the East went much, much further. There not only was the *genius* of Octavian worshiped as divine; Octavian himself was regarded as God.[6]

The ancient gods had been engaged in dreadful conflict among themselves. The horrible civil wars, so it was believed, mirrored their strife. Now, however, the Roman emperors, as images of the one world principle, secured eternal peace, the *Pax Romana*. The divine order of the universe and the reality of the Roman constitution had become completely synonymous and produced a cosmic harmony. That is what was propagated; that is what people believed. They confidently quoted the famous verse from Homer (*Iliad* 2.204): "Lordship for many is no good thing. Let there be one ruler, one king."[7]

[4] For what follows see Erik Peterson, "Der Monotheismus als politisches Problem," in *Theologische Traktate*. Ausgewählte Schriften 1 (Würzburg: Echter, 1994), 23–81. (Originally in his *Der Monotheismus als politisches Problem: ein Beitrag zur Geschichte der politischen Theologie im Imperium Romanum* [Leipzig: Hegner, 1935]). In this now-famous treatment Peterson investigates political theology from Aristotle to Eusebius with respect to God's *monarchia*.

[5] *Divi filius* means "member of the family of the [*Divus*] *Caesar*, declared by the Senate in the year 42 to be God."

[6] Cf. Karl Christ, *Geschichte der römischen Kaiserzeit von Augustus bis zu Konstantin* (Munich: Beck, 1988), 165.

[7] Homer, *The Iliad*, trans. Richard Lattimore (Chicago: Phoenix Books, 1951), 2, 204.

Hence the emperor was worshiped as the image of divine order—indeed, incense was offered to his *genius*—but thereby the Roman state was worshiped as a divine creation and hence as sacrosanct, that is, a holy and cast-iron force for order.

A New Experience of the World

Now, into this cosmic order, this world picture arising out of Greek philosophy and ultimately supported by belief in a single highest Being, the Christians suddenly erupt. It is true that they comply with the civil order: they pay their taxes and even pray for the emperor and his officials, that they may rule justly. But essentially they represent a counter-world in the center of the *Imperium Romanum*, something that quickly came to be seen as areligious, godless, and incendiary. They are accused of "insurrection" (*stasis*)—rebellion against the civil and thus the cosmic order. They refuse to worship the emperor, and thus the state, as divine. Instead, in their assemblies they call on Christ as their *kyrios*, their lord. It is not the emperor who is "son of God," even though he is called that in the eastern regions. The true lord, the true son, is Jesus and only Jesus.

Consequently, the Christians did not take part in the imperial festivals, the great civil holidays with their public processions and free banquets. They kept their distance from many of the customs of pagan society. They did not attend the circuses to ogle the bloody gladiatorial contests or to honor the emperor with their acclamations. They did not abort or expose unwanted children; instead, they took care that none among them should suffer want. What they sought for themselves was not wealth, power, and an easy life but *agapē*, the love between sisters and brothers that unites all and requires ongoing reconciliation. In this *agapē* they united their lives so that communities arose within the cities, societies that conceived themselves differently from the Roman state.

Now for the crucial question: what was the ground, the ultimate reason, the condition for the possibility of this new social project? It was not simply belief in the one unique God, because in those days even pagan society believed in a single, ultimate divine Principle that gave life and ordered all things; at least the elites did so.

The reason for Christian distancing from the imperial cult and the pagan ways of life was something Christians had in common with

Jews: the biblical theology of the de-divinization of the world and of the state. Those who held to what the biblical books said had to reject the cult of the emperor. Those who wanted to belong to the holy people of God could no longer take part in many pagan ways of living without cutting themselves off from their own roots.

Moreover, this Jewish-Christian distancing from the Roman state and its ruler-cult was rendered still more profound by Christians' belief in the triune God who is genuine community within God's self: the ultimate and unutterable community of the Father with the Son, the Son with the Father, the communion of Holy Spirit with the Father and the Son; a single God and yet a "we," a triune life that is in itself pure *agapē*, pure love.

Genuine love is not self-enclosed, is never merely self-love. It always extends itself to another. So God's self is essentially nothing but devoted *agapē*—for the Son, for the Holy Spirit. And yet this overflowing love in God desires to spread itself much farther. It creates worlds and communities within our world: the church, Christian communities that live in and out of God's *agapē*.

Obviously such a world design, such a view of God, world, and society, had to clash profoundly with the world-construct of the *Imperium Romanum*, since Christians were a new society within the ancient world, a different kind of *politeuma* (Phil 3:20), arising out of a completely different idea of God. Here the state ideology of *one god, one emperor, one empire, one religion* no longer applied. The equivalent was now *one God who is community within God—thus not necessarily a single ruler—therefore also not necessarily a single empire governing the whole world—and therefore, also, no state religion that demands absolute allegiance.*

I think it must be clear by now that belief in the triune God has consequences that extend deep into the social conception of reality. The *Imperium Romanum* was, in fact, not an accidental entity that could have been altogether different; it was profoundly connected with the image of god and world proposed by Neo-Pythagoreanism and developing into middle Platonism and then Neoplatonism.[8] The *monarchia* of the emperor corresponded to the *monarchia* of the one, divine world principle. In contrast, the Christian view of the

[8] The Stoa also contributed, in its own way, to the creation of the imperial monotheism of the Roman imperial period.

world and the real form of Christian communities were profoundly connected with belief in the triune God. Belief in the Trinity had to oppose absolute state monarchy—in the long run, at least.

Now, ideas of history that connect real history with philosophical proposals, as sketched here, always have their profound difficulties. Isn't this just a construct? Doesn't it connect things that cannot be related to one another because they operate on totally different levels? This objection must be taken seriously. Therefore in what follows I will undertake a kind of test of what I have just said: a test that begins at a very different point in history, namely, in our own time.

The Unity of Religion and State in Islam

There are societies in the world today, indeed very powerful and apparently ever-mightier societies, based altogether on monotheism, the belief in one God; they condemn Christian belief in the triune God as primitive idolatry and pagan polytheism. I am referring to Islam. At the center of the Islamic confession of faith is the Qur'anic *Sura* 112, which reads:

> In the name of Allah, Most Gracious, Most Merciful.
> Say: He is Allah, the One and Only;
> Allah, the Eternal, Absolute [ruler];[9]
> He begets not, nor is He begotten;
> And there is none like unto Him.[10]

The Orientalist and poet Friedrich Rückert (1788–1866) sought to reflect the linguistic brilliance of the Qur'an in German. He translated *Sura* 112 as:

> In the Name of God, the all-merciful Merciful One;
> Say: God is One, eternally Pure,
> Has not begotten nor been begotten by any,
> And there is none like Him.[11]

[9] The translation here is uncertain. Also possible are "who rules unchangeably in himself" or "the Unchangeable."

[10] English translations of the Qu'ran, unless otherwise indicated, from Abdullah Yusuf Ali, *The Qu'ran: Translation* (Elmhurst, NY: Tahrike Tarsile Qu'ran, Inc., 1995).

[11] Trans. LMM.

The "has not begotten nor been begotten by any" of course recalls what is said of Christ in the Nicene-Constantinopolitan Creed: "begotten, not made, of one being with the Father." Originally "has not begotten" in *Sura* 112 was probably aimed at Arabic forms of polytheism, but today it is understood by Muslims as a solemn and categorical condemnation of Christian trinitarian theology: God has not begotten a son; God has no partner; there is no participation in God's divine sovereignty and dignity. God is undivided majesty. In the Qur'an itself Christ's divine sonship is rejected in the sharpest terms, especially in *Sura* 5.73:

> They do blaspheme who say: God is one of three in a Trinity: for there is no god except one God (Allah). If they do not desist from their word (of blasphemy), verily a grievous penalty will befall the blasphemers among them.

This divine monocracy, which is stated in the Qur'an again and again and is likewise the center of Islamic faith, from a social point of view quite often matches the monarchy of the ruler. An especially marked form is found today in Saudi Arabia, whose kingship is an absolute monarchy. The king is head of state, head of government, custodian of the sacred cities, supreme head of security, supreme commander of the armed forces, and chief of the ministerial council. He is *legibus solutus*, that is, he is not subject to the laws he himself creates.

This form of Islam, called Wahabism, is the state religion of Saudi Arabia. No Muslim citizen there has the right to become a Christian. Doing so is a defection from Islam, which is punishable by death. Christians living in Saudi Arabia are not allowed to hold worship services, receive any sacraments, or build any churches. Fundamental elements of democracy such as division of powers or freedom of opinion are not permitted or are rigidly limited.

It is quite obvious that this form of the state is deeply connected, historically, with Islamic monotheism. The national flag of Saudi Arabia bears a giant sword over which is written the *shahada*, the central confession of Islamic faith:

> There is no god but God,
> And Mohammed is God's prophet.

If we compare the polity of Saudi Arabia to the basic law of the *Imperium Romanum* we can see the commonalities right away: *one god as ultimate and highest principle of the world, one ruler, one religion that is the religion of the state.* What is absent is the "world empire," which played such a dominant role in the Romans' ideology of the state, but it is not far from Muslim thought. Islamic faith is intended to dominate the whole world. Of course, so is Christian faith. But when state and religion are completely synonymous, the missionary spread of Islam would necessarily and inevitably yield a worldwide empire.

Of course, Saudi Arabia is an extreme example of the model of the society we are describing here. Probably the only entity that is more extreme is the Islamic State (commonly referred to as ISIS or the IS), which is explicitly intended to renew the classic caliphate and aims at world rule. In its sphere *sharia* law is rigorously enforced in both public and private life. All those who deviate from its own ideology, even if they are Muslims, are regarded as "unbelievers" and are executed. For the IS the principle of a pure culture is *one God–one ruler–one world empire–one faith.*

In other, territorial Islamic states—for example, Pakistan, Bangladesh, or Yemen—this is much more complicated. That is, the Islamic model state exists in various shadings. Especially in states with Islamic majorities things are constantly shifting. There are democratizations toward more human rights[12] and there are also radicalizations in a more strongly fundamentalist direction. In any case, however, there are lands in which Islam is the state religion so that religion and state are fully synonymous, as was once the case in the *Imperium Romanum.*[13]

Is there a continuity between Rome, Riyadh, and Sana'a, between the Roman imperial state and Islamic states, between Augustus and today's Islamic potentates, whether they now call themselves kings, caliphs, or presidents?

Imperial Monotheism

Now for a brief look backward! We have seen that the Roman imperial system did not arise by accident or happenstance. It was preceded by the horrors of the civil wars. In the background, and still

[12] The best example is probably Jordan.—Trans.

[13] This is true at least of the *Imperium Romanum* beginning with Theodosius, and prior to that the cult of the emperor was obligatory official religion. The fact that there was room for private cults alongside that of the emperor is another subject. Jews had been granted a special status by Caesar.

present, however, was also a shift in ancient religious history: at least among the educated people polytheism was losing its plausibility to a greater and greater degree. They could understand the battles between the gods that they had read about in Homer and Hesiod, under the instruction of their tutors, only in a symbolic sense: as allegorical depictions of the battles that rage within every individual and also in society itself. For Neoplatonism and its precursors the true godhead could only be transcendent and perfect, and above all it was an absolute unity. It was *The One*.

Here, then, the image of god and the structure of society were fully identical. The *one* Roman Empire matched the *one* god. The governance of the *one* god was altogether like the unitary rule of the Roman emperor. There could no longer be plurality in this construction of reality because there was no such thing in the deity, who was *the absolute One*.

Consequently, the Roman state could not tolerate Christian faith either. With its belief in Christ as the true *Kyrios* and true God it not only called into question the Roman emperor and the whole ideology of the state he embodied but also challenged the educated class's Neoplatonic image of God.

This is what I am getting at: This state ideology did not end on the day when the emperor Constantine (ca. 280–337 CE) turned to the Christian faith. It continued on.

First of all, it continued in the Christian imperial system. After Constantine it was increasingly important to the Roman emperors that—in support of imperial unity—there should no longer be a plurality of religious cults in the lands under Roman jurisdiction.[14] Instead, the Christian faith became the official religion, and the church became an imperial institution.

This development, as I have said, began under Constantine, who granted privileges to the church. It reached its high point under Emperor Theodosius I (347–395 CE). Emperor Justinian I (ca. 482–565 CE) completed the development of the imperial church. Under Theodosius, Christianity became the state religion, to all intents and purposes. His constitution *De fide catholica* leveled penalties on pagan

[14] An obvious exception is the brief period under Emperor Julian ("the Apostate") (360–363).

cults and on Judaism; temples were closed;[15] above all, Theodosius declared the Nicene Creed to be the official confession of faith. Any bishop who did not accede to Nicaea could now be regarded as a heretic and be banished. Obviously all that accorded with the guiding principle just described: *one God–one emperor–one world empire–one faith.*

There were two telltale features in this whole development: first, that in the early stages it repeatedly drove the Christian emperors to the Arians' side, since they often thought that they could ensure the unity of the empire on the basis of Arianism.[16] That is easy to understand when we consider that the theology of Arianism was very similar to the monarchical God-image of Neoplatonism: in Arianism, after all, theology and state ideology were an incomparably better match than in a Christology founded on the New Testament.

Likewise revealing, however, was the fact that the Jews came increasingly under pressure. It is true that there were other reasons for the increasing persecutions of Jews. One of the most important was the false and dangerous position of many Christian theologians who asserted that Israel had lost its election and the church had taken its place as the "new" people of God. The rapidly spreading persecutions of Jews were, however, caused primarily by the state ideology, which depended on a unitary faith.

The transformation into an "imperial church" was a disastrous development: it was not only damaging to the church; it was dangerous as well. Moreover, the fact that the church became an "imperial" institution in which the emperor was in charge of church and cult, in which it was he who summoned councils and claimed to be, in himself, the symbol of orthodoxy, was by no means something unavoidable. Bishops and theologians could have recalled the resistance to the Roman state ideology in the first three centuries. They could have remembered the skepticism with which the Old Testament spoke of kingship. They could have thought of Jesus' critical statements. He by no means questioned the necessity of the state, but he did not embrace it (cf. Luke 22:25-26). Above all: the theologians and bishops could have recalled that at one time they had asked for

[15] But evidently, at first, not synagogues: see above, chap. 1, "Is the Church Required to Undergo Enlightenment?," p. 17, n. 34. [Theodosius]

[16] Cf. Peterson, "Monotheismus," 57.

tolerance toward themselves—and consequently had called for pluralism on the part of the state when it came to matters of faith.

But evidently joy at the end of the time of persecution was greater than critical recollection of that kind, and apparently the advantages of the new situation were tempting: bishops could now travel to councils by means of the imperial post system and the emperor imposed his full authority to bring about church unity in times of conflict over matters of faith. But above all: there must have been an incredible fascination in the model of *one God–one emperor–one world empire–one faith*.

In this matter Bishop Eusebius of Caesarea (ca. 260–340 CE) played an inglorious role. In his *Life of Constantine* and especially in an official festival oration on the emperor's thirty-year regnal anniversary he proposed a political theology that would prove catastrophic in subsequent years. For Eusebius the Roman Empire since Constantine was an image of the heavenly realm. As in the heavenly sphere there was only the one reigning God, so in its earthly image there was only one emperor, and it was his duty to carry out God's plan of salvation, liberate humans from the power of polytheism, and bring them to acknowledge the true God. The emperor is God's vicar on earth and is Lord Protector of the church. State and church, while they are not identical, are coterminous.

We cannot say that this imperial ideology was accepted by the whole church and all its bishops, but its effects are evident, especially in the East and in the later Orthodox Church. What Eusebius celebrated was really what a number of today's historians call "imperial monotheism," that is, the principle of *one God, one emperor, one faith, one world empire*.[17] It shaped European history for many centuries: the politics of Charlemagne, the policies and social system of the medieval emperors. It marked the Byzantine church-state in particular; it was more sharply defined there than in the West.[18] Also, by way of Byzantium this construction of reality expanded into and through Islam. In the same year (622) when Muhammad made his *hijra* from Mecca to Medina, the Byzantine Empire embraced a bold imperial monotheism, namely:

[17] Höfert, *Kaisertum*, 84, 145–50.

[18] The emperor Justinian, unlike those before him, no longer derived his rule from the Senate and the masses but only from God. Neither did he allow himself to be crowned in the Hippodrome with the acclamation of the people; the coronation took place in the imperial palace. He abolished the office of consul.

> A world empire under one God with the emperor as the image of God who shows believers the way to right belief, persecutes pagans, Jews, and heretics, and celebrates himself as "*victor omnium gentium*" (conqueror of all nations) because he claims to place the whole *œcumene* under God's rule. That was the starting-point for the Umayyad caliphs, who took up residence in Damascus in 661 and established the Muslim world empire, incorporating the Christian elites.[19]

That is the basis in particular for a history and analysis of the caliphate. I cannot attempt that, of course. But there is much historical evidence in favor of the idea that the strict *unity among monotheism, imperial rule, and faith* that marked the caliphate can be traced to the Byzantine ideology of the state and thus, ultimately, to Roman imperialism.[20]

Certainly we must add that Jews and Christians were tolerated as "peoples of the book," even though their freedom was severely limited. And obviously Islam excludes any similarity between the monarch and God; however, the idea that the ruler is God's representative was certainly adopted.[21] The intolerance in Islamic *sharia* as illustrated at present in Saudi Arabia, for example, arises historically from imperial monotheism and the rigorous autocracy of the late *Imperium Romanum*.

That the unified idea of *one God, one ruler*, which also postulated a single empire, was never actually realized except in imperfect form is irrelevant. After the death of Theodosius I in the year 395 the *Imperium Romanum* divided permanently into the Western and Eastern Roman Empires.[22] The Western Roman *Imperium* ended in 476 when the emperor Romulus Augustulus was deposed by a German force and it was only restored, under new auspices, by Charlemagne.[23] The Umayyad caliphate (661–750) was followed by the differently oriented caliphate of the Abbasids in Baghdad (750–1258) and then

[19] Höfert, *Kaisertum*, 237.

[20] In addition, influences from the Sasanian (New Persian) Empire (224–642) must have played a role.

[21] Cf. Höfert, *Kaisertum*, 301.

[22] In addition, from the time of Diocletian (ca. 240–312) it was common for a number of rulers to exercise imperial authority within the Roman Empire. That still did not change the notion of the unity of the imperial concept.

[23] The elevation of Charlemagne introduced a duality into the original constellation of imperial monotheism (*one God, one emperor, one world empire, one faith*). There were now two universal monarchies: the Latin and the Byzantine. Thus Höfert, *Kaisertum*, 397.

by other Islamic systems of rule. Islamic unity dissolved permanently, in the ninth century, into Sunni and Shi'a. But none of these antagonisms and separations changed the fact that the guiding idea of the unity of *God–ruler–empire–faith* ran through it all like a scarlet thread, maintaining itself throughout, and indeed with a highly impressive obtrusiveness.

We can see this continuity very clearly in the series of titles with which Charlemagne introduced his decrees and charters. An official document produced by his chancellery in May 801 in Bologna begins as follows:

> In the Name of the Father, the Son, and the Holy Spirit. Charles, *serenissimus Augustus*, crowned by God, great peace-bringing Roman emperor, who rules the empire, and by the mercy of God king of the Franks and the Lombards.[24]

The Western Way

The Western church and Western society have traveled a difficult path over centuries to free themselves from this dangerous ideology of unity; nor is it the case that there was no church resistance in the East to the emperors' ecclesiastical politics.[25] But in the West the resistance was tougher and lasted longer. Whereas in the East the link between church and *imperium* became ever more a matter of course as time went on and later established itself in Russia as well, in the church of the West there was increasing demand for ecclesiastical autonomy. That conflict reached its climax between 1076 and 1122 in the Investiture Controversy.

Resistance to imperial church politics began very early, in the fourth century. It appeared especially in the opposition of many bishops to the emperor Constantius II (317–361), who favored the Arians and, in his role as head of the church, meddled in many decisions, demanding that the church be subjected to the *imperium*. The great bishop Athanasius of Alexandria (298–373) was prominent in

[24] Engelbert Mühlbacher, *Die Urkunden der Karolinger*, MGH DD Kar 1 (Hannover: Hahn, 1906), 197.

[25] The resistance in the East also is rightly emphasized by Höfert, *Kaisertum*, 197–237. John Chrysostom played an especially important role there.

defending against such a claim. As a result he was condemned by a council ordered by the emperor and was forced to go underground. Athanasius was banned by various emperors at least five times. Certainly he was not the only bishop in the West who stood against the emperor; others did the same.

Let me at this point refer to an instructive book by Hugo Rahner that first appeared in 1943, not accidentally in the period of National Socialism. It was called *Abendländische Kirchenfreiheit: Dokumente über Kirche und Staat im frühen Christentum* (Freedom of the Church in the West: Documents on Church and State in Early Christianity). A new edition was published in 1961, now titled *Kirche und Staat im frühen Christentum*.[26] Hugo Rahner presents thirty-five crucial documents from the first to the ninth centuries, with commentary. They shed light on the church's struggle for freedom from the Roman state, which repeatedly sought to oversee the church, to regulate it, and to force it into the imperial system.

To take just one example: the elderly bishop Hosius of Córdoba (ca. 256–358) sent a letter to Constantius against his meddling in church affairs:

> Intrude not yourself into Ecclesiastical matters. . . . God has put into your hands the kingdom [*basileia*]; to us [God] has entrusted the affairs of the Church; and as anyone who would steal the empire [*archē*] from you would resist the ordinance of God, so likewise [be afraid] on your part lest by taking upon yourself the government of the Church, you become guilty of a great offense. It is written, "Render unto Caesar the things that are Caesar's, and unto God the things that are God's!" Neither therefore is it permitted unto us to exercise an earthly rule [*archein*], nor have you, Sir, any authority to burn incense [*thymian*].[27]

Why, among all the "affairs of the Church" in which the emperor should not meddle, did Hosius choose the burning of incense in particular? Could he not have given a more serious example? The explanation is simple: the bishop is alluding to 2 Chronicles 26:16-21, where priests forbid King Uzziah to offer incense with his own hand

[26] Hugo Rahner, *Church and State in Early Christianity*, trans. Leo Donald Davis (San Francisco: Ignatius Press, 1992; repr. 2005).

[27] Athanasius, *History of the Arians* 6.44 [alt.] at https://www.newadvent.org/fathers/28156.htm.

in the Jerusalem temple; he must confine himself to his role as king. Priestly functions in the temple are taboo for him. That is, however, only incidental! More important is that the bishop's expressions rest on a kind of "theory of two powers." The emperor is to govern earthly things and the bishops the heavenly matters. The church repeatedly brought this two-powers theory to the fore, but *de facto* the overlaps between empire and church—in the Middle Ages between *regnum* and *sacerdotium*—remained.

The struggle to free the church from secular authority would continue for many centuries. The battle would be long, but it was real. It was the early stage of the later separation between church and state in the West. That salutary separation was thus not forced by the European Enlightenment. It arose just as much out of the church's profound awareness of its nature and mission.

The decisive force that drove this Western history of freedom forward was Jewish-Christian belief in a personal God who acts in history and repeatedly relativizes all human governance, breaking its spell, demythologizing it, and indeed de-divinizing it.

Nevertheless, I am convinced that Jewish-Christian monotheism alone would not have been enough to make possible the free societies of the West. Much more was needed, even though that is completely unknown to most of our contemporaries. Required was belief in the triune God: the God who is indeed unique, the ultimate Unity, and yet is God in three persons, that is, community and, if we do not misunderstand the word, plurality. God is one, says Hilary of Poitiers, but God is not alone.[28] To put it in strictly theological terms: God is One in the difference of Father, Son, and Holy Spirit.

If this thesis seems too elevated, too theological, too extravagant and lacking in sociological foundation, the following may help: In about the year 325 the monastic Pachomius founded a first *coenobium* in an abandoned village in Upper Egypt. It would be followed by many more: monks who previously had lived solitary lives in the wilderness, praying and weaving baskets in order to earn their living, now dwelt together in monastic communities, praying and working together. Thus at the very moment when the church was gradually starting to become an imperial church, a church of the

[28] Hilary of Poitiers, *De trinitate* 6.19; 7.8. Cf. Robert L. Wilken, *The Spirit of Early Christian Thought: Seeking the Face of God* (New Haven: Yale University Press, 2008), 92.

masses in which no one needed any longer to make a decision about her or his belief but simply was a Christian without any opportunity to choose[29]—at precisely that moment a movement began within the church that rested on free decision, that strove for a free communion according to the gospel, and that was the exact opposite of imperial monotheism.

There began in Upper Egypt a movement that, from the fourth century to today, would be the salt in the church, a movement that would repeatedly stimulate, reform, and bring the church back to the gospel. In most monastic orders the abbot or superior was elected by a local or general chapter: that is, there was a fundamentally democratic structure.[30] And the original model for monastic communities was not a monarchical God but the communion of the Father with the Son and the Holy Spirit.

[29] The emperor Justinian (482–565) then later introduced compulsory baptism of children; apostasy from Christianity was considered a crime (*Codex Iustinianus* 1.11.10).

[30] Let me give as an example the Rule of Benedict 64. For the rules of other orders cf. Hans Urs von Balthasar, ed., *Die großen Ordensregeln* (Einsiedeln: Benziger, 1961), 103, 251, 318, 399.

7

Did the First Christians Understand Jesus?

There are texts that are so intriguing that they are repeatedly cited. One such is the saying of the French biblical scholar Alfred Loisy from over a century ago: "Jesus foretold the kingdom, and it was the Church that came."[1] I will not pursue the question of how Loisy himself understood his statement.[2] What interests me, rather, is how it is interpreted by those who love to quote it. They usually read it as bitterly ironic.

On the one hand there is the reign of God as Jesus is supposed to have proclaimed it: the great, all-encompassing, unimaginable transformation of the world under the rule of God—and then, after Easter, the church, an entity with all the limitations associated with a socially structured entity. So: a yawning gulf between Jesus' proclamation and the post-Easter reality! Here the glory of God's reign—there the bitter meagerness of the church as it really exists.

Let me say right away what I think of such a contrast between the reign of God and the church: Nothing, absolutely nothing! For it opens a gulf between what Jesus wanted and the church's reality that does justice neither to Jesus nor to the church. Why?

In the first place because Jesus also described the tiny, almost invisible beginnings of the reign of God. I am reminded of the meta-

[1] Alfred Loisy, *The Gospel and the Church*, trans. Christopher Home (London: Isbister, 1903), 166.

[2] On this see, at length, Gerhard Heinz, *Das Problem der Kirchenentstehung in der deutschen protestantischen Theologie des 20. Jahrhunderts*, TTS 4 (Mainz: Grünewald, 1974), 122–39.

phors: mustard seed, yeast, endangered seed, and seed that grows in secret.[3]

Second, because the reign of God that Jesus preached is not a reality apart from society. People have repeatedly tried to make it be that: pushing it into the far future of absolute transcendence or the depths of the human soul. But, in fact, for Jesus the reign of God means concrete social reality. God's *basileia* has its starting point in a real people. The transformation of the world by the reign of God has to begin in Israel.[4]

It is true that the reign of God and the people of God are not the same thing, but they have a solid and fixed correlation. In the second petition of the Our Father, Jesus orders prayer for the coming of God's reign; but immediately before, in the first petition, he directs prayer for the gathering and sanctification of God's people. That, in fact, is the meaning of the petition "hallowed be Thy Name."[5] The background for this is the theology of the book of Ezekiel.[6]

Jesus proclaims the reign of God, but he does more than that: he begins the real transformation of the world, which is what the reign of God means, in the midst of Israel. The proclamation of the reign of God is linked to the gathering of Israel.[7] And because the church is nothing other than the Israel that hears Jesus, follows him, and is sanctified by him, the reign of God and the church are related as closely as they can be. That Jesus proclaimed the reign and then, after Easter, the church came to be—that is not a tragic collapse, not a bitter irony of history, not a perversion of the will of Jesus: it was consonant with the social dimension of Jesus' proclamation of the reign of God.

Against that background, in what follows I want to pursue the question of whether the early church understood and lived what Jesus

[3] Mustard seed: Mark 4:30-32; yeast: Matt 13:33; endangered seed: Mark 4:1-9; seed growing secretly: Mark 4:26-29.

[4] This is demonstrated quite charmingly by an entire book: Scot McKnight, *Kingdom Conspiracy: Returning to the Radical Mission of the Local Church* (Grand Rapids: Brazos, 2014).

[5] Cf. Gerhard Lohfink, *The Our Father: A New Reading*, trans. Linda M. Maloney (Collegeville, MN: Liturgical Press, 2021), 31–42.

[6] Cf. esp. Ezek 20:22, 41, 44; 36:22-28.

[7] For the Jesuanic correlation between proclamation of the reign of God and gathering of the people of God see, in detail, Gerhard Lohfink, *Jesus of Nazareth: What He Wanted, Who He Was*, trans. Linda M. Maloney (Collegeville, MN: Liturgical Press, 2015), 59–71.

wanted. Such a broad theme really requires a great deal more time. Hence I will attempt by means of three examples to address what can be investigated in terms of many phenomena: (1) nonviolence, (2) love of neighbor, and (3) imminent expectation. I will give reasons in each case for why I have chosen these particular examples.

Nonviolence of Jesus and in the Early Church

Why this particular example, "nonviolence"? The reason is obvious. In recent decades Islam has spread throughout the world, and it has acquired a new self-awareness. There is absolutely nothing to be said against that! But regrettably, within the Islamic nations there are an increasing number of terrorist-islam*istic* movements that not only practice "holy war" but explicitly make violence a part of their *ethos*, and they appeal to the Qur'an for support.[8] These movements call murder a form of service to God.

That kind of misanthropic, inhuman violence causes many enlightened women and men to experience an increase in the aversion to religion they already entertain. Christianity (and Judaism) are included within the scope of that dislike. We increasingly hear people say even that all monotheistic religions have a natural inclination to violence. Here again Judaism, Christianity, and Islam are named in the same breath.

To the contrary, it cannot be said often enough or clearly enough that Old Testament Israel already spoke against violence in its key religious texts. Jesus' radical nonviolence was rooted in the Old Testament, particularly in the texts about the Suffering Servant that are found in Isaiah 40–55. The "servant" reference is to Israel, deported to Babylon. Israel, God's beloved servant, does not cry or shout (Isa 42:2). From God alone does this chosen one hope for justification in face of the injustice suffered (Isa 49:4). The Servant gives his back to those who beat him (Isa 50:6) and, like a lamb, does not open her mouth when led to slaughter (Isa 53:7). The so-called Servant Songs in Isaiah speak of the beaten, exiled, enslaved Israel that relies on

[8] See the brief and highly precise sketch of this whole question in Christian W. Troll, "Koran, Gewalt, Theologie," *CiG* 43 (2014): 485–86.

God alone and, precisely through its absolute rejection of violence, becomes salvation for the nations.[9]

The truth is, however, that it was precisely the book of Isaiah that abolished the previous state of things in Israel, whereby alien gods were thought to exist although only YHWH was worshiped, and replaced it with pure monotheism. This means that in the precise time and place where monotheism triumphed in Israel it also received the most unequivocal texts supporting radical nonviolence. Conclusion: those seeking to link monotheism with violence may try to find support in the Qur'an but should keep hands off the Bible, lest they reveal their crass ignorance.

On the other hand, we must naturally admit that religion appears in raping and murdering Islam*ism* in such a repulsive form that the anger of many people against religion as such is understandable. It is all the more necessary in the current state of things that we confront Jesus' *ethos*: his absolute nonviolence, his demand that one should lose one's honor by allowing oneself to be hit in the face rather than strike back (Matt 5:38-42). Jesus was convinced that it was only in that way that, ultimately, the eruptions of violence in society could be curbed.

I think I need not rehearse the whole list of Jesus' commands to nonviolence in the Sermon on the Mount.[10] Let me simply make four points:

1. The Sermon on the Mount is addressed to Jesus' disciples and, beyond them, to the whole people of Israel. Jesus' commands to nonviolence are not a program for the civil state. The state must not give to everyone who asks; it may not turn the other cheek; it cannot follow the precept "do not resist an evildoer" (Matt 5:39). The Sermon on the Mount is intended for a people of God that lives Jesus' practice of the reign of God as a people within the nations and so becomes a sign of peace for them all.

[9] For more detail see Gerhard Lohfink and Ludwig Weimer, *Maria – nicht ohne Israel. Eine neue Sicht der Lehre von der Unbefleckten Empfängnis*, 2nd ed. (Freiburg: Herder, 2012), 223–29.

[10] In detail: Gerhard Lohfink, *Wem gilt die Bergpredigt? Beiträge zu einer christlichen Ethik* (Freiburg: Herder, 1988), 42–45.

2. In his injunctions to nonviolence Jesus speaks in prophetic-focused language, as in many other places. That, however, does not change the fact that he aims at real attitudes that are to be carried out in action and illuminate the analogies that serve as models. Jesus really does forbid his disciples to use violence, and he is convinced that anyone who accepts his word can live without counter-violence and vengeance.

3. The nonviolence Jesus demands is not some passive, powerless acceptance of the opponent's violence. The concrete examples given in the Sermon on the Mount all have some provocative feature intended to change the one exercising violence by making her or him feel touched by it and brought to think it over. The very act of turning the other cheek (Matt 5:39) is meant to startle, even frighten the attacker. And if someone who is taken to court and required to surrender his or her undergarment then tosses in the outer garment along with it (Matt 5:40), the result is a shameful situation: the poor and unprivileged person stands there naked. This is not submissive, doglike acceptance; it is *nonviolent resistance*.[11]

4. Jesus' demands for nonviolence are not found only in the Sermon on the Mount. They are also part of the mission instructions in Mark 6, Matthew 10, and Luke 9 and 10.[12] Jesus forbids his disciples to wear sandals when they travel through Israel to proclaim the reign of God everywhere (Luke 10:4); neither are they to carry a staff (Luke 9:3) or have money in their purses (Luke 10:4). They are not even to take bread with them (Mark 6:8).

   This is not at all intended to imitate some kind of denial of material needs such as itinerant Cynic philosophers demonstrated at that time. Rather, the disciples' lack of equipment is to be seen as a sign that distinguishes them from the anti-Roman resistance's readiness to fight. Someone who has no staff cannot

[11] Further on this third point: Walter Wink, *The Powers That Be: Theology for a New Millennium* (New York: Doubleday, 1998).

[12] For a more precise tradition-historical analysis let me point to Christoph Heil, "Die Missionsinstruktion in Q 10,2-16. Transformationen der Jesusüberlieferung im Spruchevangelium Q," in *Das Spruchevangelium Q und der historische Jesus*, SBAB 58 (Stuttgart: Katholisches Bibelwerk, 2014), 119–46.

> defend herself; someone who has no shoes on his feet cannot even flee, given the stony ground of Palestine. Someone without money is without means, is helpless, and is completely dependent on sympathizers within the Jesus movement. For Jesus this immediately obvious difference between his disciples and the "warriors for God" in his time was fundamentally necessary. The Jesus movement must not be confused with the strategies of the Zealots.

Did the young church then understand and live this radical nonviolence that, for Jesus, was a signal of the approaching reign of God? That is the first question to be addressed here.

Answering this question, however, presents two problems. First: it would be wonderful if we knew a great deal more about the real lives of Christians in the first three centuries, but the sources are not especially bubbling over with information. We are forced to draw conclusions from the sermons of the early church fathers or the writings of the so-called Apologists who defended Christian faith against pagan attacks.

Besides that, of course, there is the question whether a faith community should be judged solely by what it lives *de facto*. Jews and Christians always knew that they fell far short of what they ought to do. They were aware that serious faults were committed even in their own midst: murder, quarreling, adultery, rivalries, religious disputes, crimes of every sort. Both Jews and Christians knew that they were continually working against God in ever-new ways, grumbling about God's promises, and that they therefore had to repent constantly.

So in what follows I by no means want to praise a romantic and glorified picture of a faultless and heroic early time of the church. Even then there was dreadful misery within the church itself, pathetic cowardice and profound guilt. But because today almost everyone is interested only in the criminal history of Christianity we have to speak all the more urgently about the other side as well: the fidelity of the early church to the Gospel. Also, we dare not look only at what Christians were; we must also consider what they wanted to be.

This is immediately obvious when we consider a first text: 1 Corinthians 6:1-8. It shows that members of the Christian community in Corinth were bringing lawsuits against one another and thus going before pagan judges. Paul is outraged at that; he sees it as a perversion of the Gospel. The community members should settle their quarrels between themselves. Paul presents a series of arguments in favor of that position, but then he delves even deeper, referring to Jesus' Sermon on the Mount. He writes to the community at Corinth (1 Cor 6:7): Why are you defending yourselves at all? Why not better suffer injustice? Why not let yourselves be robbed?

Thus 1 Corinthians 6 makes it clear that the pagan way of life is still deeply rooted in the Corinthian community: strife, rivalries, legal quarrels! Paul therefore tells them this must not be. Such a way of life has nothing to do with the reign of God (6:10). You have been sanctified through Christ (6:11)!

Thus as regards the questions we are now considering it is not merely a matter of successful accomplishment but also of the consciousness that shapes reality. Was the young church familiar with the Sermon on the Mount? Was there a lively awareness that Jesus called for nonviolence?

When we pose the question at this level we discover a truly amazing phenomenon. The second chapter of the book of Isaiah had described how, one day, the pagan peoples would come to Mount Zion.[13] They would come, out of the crisis of their existence and their bafflement at how to escape it, out of the horrors of their unending wars. They would come in order to learn from Israel—above all to learn how to put an end to the world-ravaging wars—for from Zion went forth the clarifying and all-illuminating word of God. That is the precise context of the famous passage: "they shall beat their swords into plowshares and their spears into pruning hooks; nation shall not lift up sword against nation; neither shall they learn war any more" (Isa 2:4).

The theologians of the young church applied that prophetic word to the Gentile nations.[14] They said: Mount Zion is the church, and from it comes the word of Jesus. We, the Gentile Christians, have set ourselves on the way to the true God. When we were baptized we learned to lay down our weapons. We have beaten our swords and spears into instruments of peace. We no longer prepare for war. Isaiah 2 is already fulfilled; what it prophesied has become reality. We have no further need of violence.

[13] Cf. Michael P. Maier, *Völkerwallfahrt im Jesajabuch*, BZAW 474 (Berlin: de Gruyter, 2016), 95–143.

[14] For a fuller discussion of what follows see Lohfink, *Wem Gilt die Bergpredigt?* 161–92.

We find this interpretation of Isaiah 2 in all the great theologians of the young church: Justin, Irenaeus, Tertullian, Origen, Athanasius. But did their interpretations truly represent reality? Or was it "only" theology? That in itself would have been a great deal. Still, it would have been lovely if the theologians had not only said all that but if the Christian communities had also lived it. And at this point the so-called Apologists enter the picture.[15]

The Apologists, who themselves had often been pagan philosophers before becoming Christians, defended the Christians' way of life. Because they simply refused to participate in many pagan customs and practices they were called "haters of humanity"[16] and accused of every possible kind of atrocities. The Apologists contradicted these accusations by describing the real lives of Christians. All their writings are imbued with a powerful and unshakable trust that Christian praxis itself would be persuasive. They repeatedly told their pagan readers: we have not only the true philosophy but right practice as well, and the two are profoundly connected. Thus, for example, Athenagoras of Athens wrote in his *Presbeia*, around the year 177:

> Among us you will find uneducated persons, and artisans, and old women, who, if they are unable in words to prove the benefit of their teaching, yet by their deeds exhibit the benefit arising from their persuasion of its truth, they do not rehearse speeches but exhibit good works; when struck, they do not strike again; when robbed, they do not go to law; they give to those that ask of them, and love their neighbors as themselves.[17]

Here, then, we find a direct citation of the Sermon on the Mount. The case is the same with many early Christian defenses of Christianity. I need not cite more texts; it seems to me that one thing is clear: a writing in defense of Christian faith had to be able to appeal to real forms of Christian life; otherwise it would have been clatter and smoke.

Nevertheless, an important question remains in this context: What was the early church's attitude toward war? Did its bishops forbid

[15] On this, with many source references, cf. Gerhard Lohfink, *Jesus and Community: The Social Dimension of Christian Faith*, trans. John P. Galvin (Philadelphia: Fortress Press, 1982), part 4, "The Ancient Church in the Discipleship of Jesus." [This edition is out of print; a new translation of the revised edition published by KBW will be available from Fortress Press in 2026.]

[16] E.g., Tacitus, *Annals* 15.44.2-5.

[17] Athenagoras of Athens, *Presbeia* (A Plea for the Christians) 11, translation at https://www.newadvent.org/fathers/0205.htm.

believers' service in the Roman armies? That would be a test that could clarify a good deal, but the state of research is complicated.[18] Many of those baptized were soldiers, and many more soldiers were accepting baptism. That is easily shown from the historical record.[19] Moreover, there was no such thing as a general rule of Christian pacifism in the early church,[20] nor should we expect such a thing since, as we have already seen, the Sermon on the Mount is not a rule for public life. It governed the lives of Jesus' disciples among themselves. That, then, is one side that must be stressed: there were many soldiers who were Christians.

On the other hand, there were indeed theologians of the ancient church who denied that Christians could engage in military service.[21] The most important was Origen. Celsus, who was hostile to Christians, had written a work against them in which he accused them of not participating in support of the state and of setting themselves apart from Roman society. For example, they did not stand by the emperor in his campaign against the barbarians who were already overrunning the frontiers of the empire.

Origen responded this way in the year 248 in his work *Contra Celsum*:[22] You do not require your priests to be soldiers either, but in fact we Christians are all priests in the sense that we sanctify the society in which we live. We pray for the emperor; we ask for just

[18] For a selection of important literature on this topic see Adolf von Harnack, *Militia Christi: The Christian Religion and the Military in the First Three Centuries*, trans. David McInnes Gracie (Philadelphia: Fortress, 1981); Hans von Campenhausen, "Der Kriegsdienst der Christen in der Kirche des Altertums," *Universitas* 12 (1957): 1147–56; Heinrich Karpp, "Die Stellung der Alten Kirche zu Kriegsdienst und Krieg," *EvTh* 17 (1957): 496–515; but especially Hans Christof Brennecke, "'An fidelis ad militiam converti possit?' [Tertullian, *De idolatria* 19.1]. Frühchristliches Bekenntnis und Militärdienst im Widerspruch?," in *Die Weltlichkeit des Glaubens in der Alten Kirche, FS Ulrich Wickert*, ed. Dietmar Wyrwa, BZNW 85 (Berlin: de Gruyter, 1997), 45–100.

[19] Cf. Tertullian, *De corona* 1 (*solus fortis inter tot fratres commilitones*), 42–43; *Apologeticum* 5.6; 37.4; 42.3; Eusebius, *Church History* 6.41.22-23; 7.11.20; 7.15-16; 8.1.7.

[20] von Campenhausen, "Kriegsdienst," 1148: "Not a single church father doubted that, in the world as it is, wars must be conducted, and accordingly they found no reason to condemn military service in particular."—Trans. LMM.

[21] Besides Origen, see also Tertullian, *De corona* and *De idolatria* 19; and cf. Lactantius, *Institutiones divinae* 6.20.15-17. The discussion about whether a Christian could be a soldier thus began only in the third century.

[22] Cf. Origen, *Contra Celsum* 8.68, 73, 75.

government and that only just wars be pursued. That is more important than for us to engage in wars ourselves.

Here, then, we have an altogether clear position on the question of whether a Christian can be a soldier, and above all a solid awareness of the church's own and most important duty to society. It is to preserve pagan society from destroying itself in wars conducted out of greed and lust for conquest. Here we are very close to the Sermon on the Mount and to what, in Jesus' mind, the people of God ought to be: yeast for society—precisely by means of their nonviolence.

Moreover, it is by no means the case that we have only the voices of theologians to guide us regarding military service. The whole question is also treated in legal terms in at least *one* church order,[23] the *Traditio Apostolica* attributed to Hippolytus (ca. 170–235), though we are not certain when and where it was applied. There[24] we read:

> A soldier[25] who finds himself in a certain authority, let him not kill; and also if he is ordered, let him not offer sacrifice, swear [the military oath], and not put wreaths on the head. One who executes with the sword, or a ruler of a city or one who wears the purple, let him cease or otherwise be rejected. A catechumen or one of the faithful, if he desires to be enlisted [in the army], let him be rejected because he did a wrong to the Lord.

Let me emphasize that this church order was by no means circulated throughout the church; however, it does show that Jesus' nonviolence had not completely disappeared from Christian consciousness—with respect to military service as well. The *Traditio Apostolica*, while it

[23] In contrast, however, the Canons of Elvira completely ignore the question of military service by Christians, despite the fact that they deal extensively with questions of Christian life within pagan society. See Brennecke, "Frühchristliches Bekenntnis," 93.

[24] Paul F. Bradshaw, *Apostolic Tradition: A New Commentary* (Collegeville, MN: Liturgical Press Academic, 2023), B.16, 105–6 (pp. 53–54). For the Latin original see Bernard Botte, *La Tradition Apostolique de Saint Hippolyte. Essai de Reconstitution*, Liturgiewissenschaftliche Quellen und Forschungen 39, 3rd ed. (Münster: Aschendorff, 1966), 36.

[25] In the *Imperium Romanum*, civil and military service were not separate. *Militia* can mean both. *Miles* normally means "soldier," but it can also designate an imperial officer who bears arms.

acknowledges the existence of Christian soldiers, says that anyone who has become a catechumen may no longer serve in the military.

Jesus' Love of Neighbor and That of the Early Church

As a second example I have chosen the theme of love of neighbor because this topic in particular is burdened with severe misunderstanding at present. We are constantly told: "You can only love the other if you first love yourself." It is not only psychologists and psychiatrists who say it; it is the principal theme of "edifying" religious literature in the twenty-first century.

Certainly it is not altogether wrong. Self-acceptance is important and can even be profoundly Christian. The statement is false only if it aims at unswerving, pleasurable self-discovery. Above all, it is wrong when the assertion is made that "as yourself" in the love commandment is the basis of self-love and self-acceptance, because in the Bible self-acceptance is in no way the basis for love of neighbor. The Bible says nothing about self-acceptance; it speaks of repentance. Nor does it talk of reconciliation with oneself, only of reconciliation with God and neighbor.

In the Bible "you shall love your neighbor as yourself" does not refer in any way to the individual "I" in the modern sense. "I" here is one's family. We can see that very clearly in the calling of Abraham, when God says to him: "I will make of you a great nation, and I will bless you and make your name great, so that you will be a blessing" (Gen 12:2). What does "you" mean here? Abraham, of course, but not only he, since his wife Sarai, his nephew Lot, and many women and men in service to them, people they had acquired as possessions in Haran, went with him (Gen 12:4-5). That is: Abraham traveled toward Canaan with his whole extended family, his flocks, and his tents.

Against this background, which is a matter of course for the Old Testament, the commandment of love of neighbor in Leviticus 19:18, 34, means the help and solidarity everyone in Israel owes to her or his relations and especially the immediate family—that is to be extended to all Israel. The boundaries of the immediate family are to be breached in favor of all sisters and brothers in the people of God, and for strangers as well—even those who are regarded as enemies to one's own family and relations. That is what Leviticus 19 means to say, and it is a universe away from the individual self-love that is preached at us from every direction today.

Leviticus 19 even explodes the inner solidarity due to the "I"—that is, the family and clan, extending it to all Israel. Even foreigners among the people of God now have a claim on the same solidarity that belongs to those genetically connected. According to Leviticus 19, strangers in the land are to be sisters and brothers to the long-settled inhabitants. That was anything but a matter of course. It ran contrary to all then-current values and rules.

Jesus now takes up precisely this revolutionary step in Israel's exilic theology; in fact, he radicalizes it. In the Pentateuch the commandments to love God and to love the neighbor stand independently alongside one another—the first in Deuteronomy 6, the second in Leviticus 19. Jesus joins the two commandments.[26] Not only that, he makes the command to love the neighbor equal in importance to the one about love of God (Matt 22:37-40). For him, the two are inseparable; both are at the center of Torah.

For Jesus, in fact, that does not remain merely a beautiful theory; it becomes the center of all he does. When Jesus began his work the people of God was profoundly divided and split apart into Samaritans, Sadducees, Pharisees, Zealots, and Essenes. Each of those groups and religious parties was hostile to the others and claimed to be the "true Israel," the only one corresponding to the will of God. If we look closely we can see that Jesus was confronted with precisely the same scandal we face today: the division of the people of God.

What does he do in this situation? The aim of all his work, of all his praxis of the reign of God, was to gather together this shattered Israel in light of the nearness of the reign of God, to unite and renew it. And his command to love neighbors and enemies belongs precisely in that context. It is not about some kind of love for those most distant, embracing all humanity, so to speak, and making them neighbors "in spirit." No, it is very concretely about eliminating hostilities within

[26] There were no texts in ancient Judaism that juxtaposed love of God and love of neighbor, linked them together, and set them at the center of Torah as Jesus did. The closest parallels are texts in the Testaments of the Twelve Patriarchs, although it is still disputed whether what we have here is a Jewish-Christian document or a basic Jewish document with Christian interpolations. For the question of the juxtaposition of love of God and love of neighbor in ancient Judaism see the broad-ranging study by Andreas Nissen, *Gott und der Nächste im antiken Judentum. Untersuchungen zum Doppelgebot der Liebe*, WUNT 15 (Tübingen: Mohr, 1974), esp. 230–44. Nissen emphasizes that "in fact, a linking of Deut 6:5 with Lev 19:18 is nowhere attested in ancient Jewish literature, at least before the Middle Ages" (241n642).—Trans. LMM.

the people of God and even dealing with all the foreigners living among them in brotherly and sisterly fashion. To put it another way: it is about treating foreigners in such a way that they are received into the protected space of mutual respect and solidarity. That is precisely what biblical *agapē* means.

Did the young church understand and live this radical love of neighbor that, for Jesus, was a sign of the onrushing reign of God? At this point it would make sense to engage deeply with the letters of Paul, because they show not only how central intra-community *agapē* was for him but also that, for him as well, *agapē* consisted, already in the Old Testament, not of pleasant feelings but of mutual acceptance and respect, help and solidarity. For Paul that solidarity extends even beyond the Christian communities. In that context, certainly, he does not speak of *agapē* but of "doing good."[27] Ultimately Paul's letters show that the most profound basis for Christian *agapē* is Jesus giving himself on the cross.

But I will not pursue the subject of Paul further; instead let me turn immediately to the young church in the second and third centuries. Did it live mutual *agapē*, the center of Jesus' reign-of-God practice? I could offer many instances from the writings of the great early church theologians as well as those of the Apologists. For now I will choose three Christian texts.

The first is an important passage from Justin's *Apology*, written around the years 150 to 155. The text is so noteworthy because here, in the sixty-seventh chapter, we find the oldest account of the Christian celebration of the Eucharist. Justin first describes the Liturgy of the Word, then speaks of the homily, and afterward of petitions, the preparation of the gifts, the Eucharistic Prayer with the community's "Amen," and the distribution of communion. Finally, at the end of his description, he says something more about the collection:

> And they who are well to do, and willing, give what each thinks fit; and what is collected is deposited with the president, who succors the orphans and widows and those who, through sickness or any other cause, are in want, and those who are in bonds and the strangers sojourning among us.[28]

[27] Cf. 1 Thess 5:15; Gal 6:9-10; also 1 Pet 2:17.

[28] Justin, *Apol.* 1.67. Text at https://www.newadvent.org/fathers/0126.htm.

Thus the Sunday collection was at the service of all those in the community who were in need of help, especially widows, orphans, the old, the sick, the unemployed, prisoners and fellow-Christians who were banned, Christians passing through on journeys, and all those in the congregation with special needs. Care was also taken to see that the poor should receive decent burial.

This produced a network of social solidarity that was unique in antiquity, resting on mutual aid and voluntary donations that were collected at the Eucharist. When early Christians spoke of *agapē*, love of neighbor, they meant precisely this mutual help. *Agapē*, however, extended beyond the local congregation. Thus Bishop Dionysios of Corinth wrote, around the year 170, to the community in Rome:

> From the beginning it has been your practice to do good to all the brethren in various ways, and to send contributions to many churches in every city. Thus relieving the want of the needy, and making provision for the brethren in the mines by the gifts which you have sent from the beginning, you Romans keep up the hereditary customs of the Romans, which your blessed bishop Soter has not only maintained, but also added to, furnishing an abundance of supplies to the saints, and encouraging the brethren from abroad with blessed words, as a loving father his children. This has been your custom from the beginning, to do good to all the brethren in various ways, and to send resources to many churches which are in every city. Through the resources which you have sent from the beginning, you Romans, following a custom of the Romans, have refreshed the poverty of the needy, and granted subsidies to the brethren who are in the mines.[29] Your blessed Bishop Soter has not only preserved, but added to this custom.[30]

Hence love of neighbor did not remain an empty word either within individual communities or in the church as a whole. *Agapē* proved to be a tangible tool for resolving economic and social need within the church. Certainly this was not simply about money matters. When plague was raging in the city of Alexandria in about the year 260 the local bishop Dionysios wrote in a letter:

[29] This refers to Christians who had been deported to toil in the mines: for example, the iron mines of Sardinia. On this see Adalbert G. Hamman, *Die ersten Christen* (Stuttgart: Reclam, 1985), 155–56.

[30] Eusebius, *Church History* 4.23.10. Translation at https://www.newadvent.org/fathers/250104.htm.

> At all events most of the brethren through their love and brotherly affection for us spared not themselves nor abandoned one another, but without regard to their own peril visited those who fell sick, diligently looking after and ministering to them and cheerfully shared their fate with them. . . . At all events, the very pick of our brethren lost their lives in this way, both priests and deacons and some highly praised ones from among the laity . . . taking up the bodies of the saints on their arms and breasts, closing their eyes and shutting their mouths, bearing them on their shoulders and laying them out for burial, clinging to them, embracing them, washing them, decking them out, they not long after had the same services rendered to them; for many of the survivors followed in their train.
>
> But the Gentiles behaved quite differently: those who were beginning to fall sick they thrust away, and their dearest they fled from, or cast them half dead into the roads: unburied bodies they treated as vile refuse.[31]

When reading such texts, today's Christians are inclined to say: "We must not generalize. This reveals the black-and-white character of legend. There are always Christians who fail, and there is always model behavior among non-Christians." Obviously that is true. Nevertheless, we dare not simply accuse the quoted text from Bishop Dionysios of falsifying the facts. Even if we were to do so we would have to admit that, in any case, that is how Christians saw themselves and wanted themselves to be.

To this point I have referred to Christian sources, and so I want to cite at least *one* pagan writer—not the only one who could be mentioned. In about the year 362 the emperor Julian,[32] a fervent enemy of Christianity, wrote to Arsakios, the pagan high priest of Galatia:

> Why do we not observe that it is their benevolence [*philanthrōpia*] to strangers, their care for the graves of the dead and the pretended holiness of their lives that have done most to increase atheism [i.e., Christianity]? . . . The impious Galileans support not only their own poor but ours as well; [everyone sees] that our people lack aid from us.[33]

[31] Dionysios, bishop of Corinth, fragments from a letter to the Roman church. Adapted from https://www.earlychristianwritings.com/text/dionysius.html. "Gentiles" refers to pagans: those neither Christian nor Jewish.

[32] "The Apostate"—Trans.

[33] Julian, *Epistola* 22: To Arsacius, high-priest of Galatia. Available at https://en.wikisource.org/wiki/Letters_of_Julian/Letter_22.

He also wrote, in a similarly programmatic letter to Theodoros, high priest for the province of Asia:

> Since, as I think, the poor are ignored and neglected by our priests, the impious Galileans, seeing this, have adopted this practice of benevolence [*philanthrōpia*].[34]

This, of course, is a distortion of Christian *agapē*. The Christians did not pretend to it in order to entice pagans but because Torah and Jesus demand *agapē* as a response to the love of God.

This letter from the emperor Julian also shows that apparently what the Apologists wrote about Christians' internal solidarity was true. The Christian social system functioned so well that even non-Christians could be supported by it. This solidarity must have made a deep impression on outsiders; it is one of the reasons why Christianity spread so rapidly.

Incidentally, Julian attempted to imitate the community support system in order to deprive Christians of that weapon. His aim was to establish a kind of Hellenic "church" that would imitate the Christians in caring for the poor and holding worship services that included preaching.

After reigning for two years, Emperor Julian was killed in a battle with the Persians. His effort would certainly have failed. The strength and inimitability of the church's system of support lay precisely in the fact that it was not centralized and decreed from above but was rooted in individual communities and was constantly reborn there out of inner conviction and free consent. Its ultimate source was sisterly and brotherly love, and its proper place was the eucharistic celebration of the community assembled on the Lord's Day.

Imminent Expectation: Jesus and the Early Church

I deliberately chose this example because hardly anyone can deal with the idea of imminent expectation at present—bishops and priests not excepted. The subject of "imminent expectation" is a dead letter. That is why it is so necessary to speak of it.

Jesus preached the reign of God, the sovereignty of God. But that in itself would have been nothing new. Many people in Israel believed

[34] Julian, *Epistola* 48, 305 C.

in the reign of God, and there were even Jewish groups in Jesus' time who hoped that it would soon reveal itself, that it would appear in the near future and would conquer. Those included the Zealots and the community whose writings were discovered at Qumran.

What was unique with Jesus was that he preached that the reign of God is not coming in the near future; it is coming now. It is already present, said Jesus, in the mighty deeds he is doing by the power of God,[35] and it is now, step by step and unstoppably, transforming the people of God, and through them the whole world.

One could speak dialectically about a concealed/revealed presence of God's reign, as it is realized in broader and broader contexts. Only to that degree can the reign still "come," and its "coming" must be prayed for. It is not yet present in its fullness and completeness. But it is near. It is so near that Jesus' hearers have to repent *now*. There is no more time left in which repentance can be delayed. Now, today, Jesus' listeners must decide to receive God's reign in faith and begin to act in its power. Moreover, they must not decide simply for God's sake but also because of Israel's critical situation and the world's immeasurable suffering.

I wonder whether there was any other way Jesus, surrounded as he was by such a climate of eschatological thinking—in which he himself was also deeply rooted—could have expressed in words the urgent "now" that called for decision in terms other than those of imminent temporal expectation. Are we ourselves, with our mental horizon of continuing, unending time in which there is no longer any such thing as a *kairos*, but only *events*, really closer to the truth of our existence and of human history than Jesus was with his pointed eschatological emphasis? I seriously doubt it.

Obviously we have to translate Jesus' eschatological language. When we do so we can see that it was not Jesus who was mistaken: we ourselves are continually deceiving ourselves—not only about the fragility and exposure of our lives, but also about the nearness of God.

Now once more the question: Did the early church also follow Jesus in this? Did it remain faithful to him here also? We dare not pose that question in superficial fashion. That is, we must not ask: Did the church of the beginnings and in its earliest centuries adopt

[35] Cf. esp. Luke 11:20; 17:21.

and retain the model of imminent temporal expectation? Instead, we must ask: Did the earliest church understand the core meaning of the model of temporal imminent expectation and live it? Did it grasp the presence of the reign of God? Did it understand that the decisive thing is happening already, that liberation and salvation are present now? And did it comprehend the onrushing nearness of God's reign, which allows no more time for delaying our repentance?

The answer can only be: yes, it did grasp the presence and nearness of the reign of God. It even made use of the concept of temporal imminent expectation for some decades. In the middle of the first century Paul could still write: "you know what time it is, how it is already the moment for you to wake from sleep. For salvation is nearer to us now than when we became believers; the night is far gone; the day is near" (Rom 13:11-12).

Thus for a time the church held to the model of temporal imminent expectation, but while using the concept it also reconstructed it. It spoke less and less of the reign of God or rule of God and more and more infrequently of temporal imminent expectation. Those ideas were replaced by something else that corresponded exactly to what they meant within the horizon of Jewish thought. That is the Spirit theology of the early church, the assertion of the presence of the Spirit. The Holy Spirit is the beginning of the end time.[36] The Holy Spirit is the down payment on fulfillment. In the Holy Spirit the world is being newly created toward its perfection.[37] In the Holy Spirit the Risen One is continually present and fills the church with the power of his resurrection.[38] The Spirit theology of the early church is thus the equivalent and precise continuation of Jesus' proclamation of the reign of God. When we pray, "Send forth your Spirit and all shall be re-created, and you will renew the face of the earth," we enter into Jesus' preaching of the reign of God.

Still, something more must be added. As Jesus' proclamation of the reign of God was accompanied by sign-actions—his deeds of power were signs of its inbreaking—so also the church's reception of the Spirit continues in visible, tangible signs: I am speaking, of course, of the sacraments. They are eschatological sign-actions.

[36] Cf. Acts 2:14-21.

[37] Cf. Matt 12:28; Rom 8:18-30; 2 Cor 1:22; 5:5; Heb 6:4-5.

[38] Cf. Rom 8:9-11.

That is obvious in the Eucharist, which was marked in the earliest church by the cry: "Come, Lord Jesus,"[39] continued today in the response: "We proclaim your Death, O Lord, and profess your Resurrection, until you come again." Similarly with baptism: it is an eschatological sign; it seals in light of the end—and yet precisely this sacrament obligates us to a new life in the world. Whoever has died with Christ in baptism is reborn into the new society of the church. The sacrament of reconciliation is likewise eschatological. Those who confess their guilt in the presence of the church submit themselves to God's final judgment. The church's words in response anticipate the judge's ultimate pronouncement—forgiveness and reconciliation.

The sacraments contain eschatological dynamite, and they are the place where the church has adopted Jesus' present eschatology and continues to make it a reality even today—or, unfortunately, very often does not do so because the inner connection between the sacraments and the coming of the reign of God is altogether foreign to many Christians.

Should I proceed to cite a series of texts on early Christian experience of the Spirit and sacramental theology in the first three centuries? That would altogether explode the limits of this essay, so I will conclude with a single text by the great theologian and bishop Cyprian from his *Ad Donatum*. That writing is drenched in the impressions of the baptism that Cyprian had received shortly before (probably in the year 245). It had transformed him.

In a "confession" that anticipates those of Augustine, Cyprian refers to the insecurities of his previous life—the shadows, the false directions, the moral errors, the hardenings, the deeply rooted sins, the doubts. Cyprian says he considered it impossible to put off the old self.

> But after . . . by the help of the water of new birth, the stain of former years had been washed away, and a light from above, serene and pure, had been infused into my reconciled heart—after . . . , by the agency of the Spirit breathed from heaven, a second birth had restored me to a new man—then, in a wondrous manner, doubtful things at once began to assure themselves to me, hidden things to be revealed, dark things to be enlightened, what before had seemed difficult began to

[39] Cf. 1 Cor 16:22; Rev 22:20; *Didachē* 10.6.

> suggest a means of accomplishment, what had been thought impossible, to be capable of being achieved; so that I was enabled to acknowledge that what previously, being born of the flesh, had been living in the practice of sins, was of the earth earthly, but had now begun to be of God, and was animated by the Spirit of holiness.[40]

Cyprian thus describes his baptism by using words from Scripture, but his own all-encompassing experience sustains and saturates the text. The experience of countless Christians must have been quite similar: otherwise how could we explain the courage of the many who accepted persecution and martyrdom at the hands of the imperial authorities? Cyprian also died a martyr: he was beheaded in the Valentinian persecution, near Carthage on September 14, 258.

Perhaps you have noticed that Cyprian uses the words "light" and "enlightened" in describing his baptism. He was not alone in that. Baptism was already understood in the New Testament as "enlightenment" (Eph 5:14; Heb 6:4; 10:32). The ancient church's theologians then adopted that way of speaking. For them "enlightenment" (*phōtismos, illuminatio*) became a common designation for baptism.

The European Enlightenment later laid claim to that concept to describe its fundamental concern: that human beings should depart from the darkness of hollow tradition and enter the light of independent-minded reason. Christians are in a position to combine both: baptism is the exodus from the darkness of pagan unreason and entry into the church as the space of enlightened tradition—the genuine enlightenment as regards violence and nonviolence, the possibility of solidary community, and the unfathomable nature of "today" that Jesus unlocked in his proclamation of the reign of God.

[40] Cyprian, *Ad Donatum* 4; available at https://www.newadvent.org/fathers/050601.htm.

8

Murder in the Name of God?

"Religion and violence" is surely one of the most urgent topics in recent years. In the print media, on the radio, on television, on the internet—we now constantly encounter this theme. The reason is clear. For years now we have been faced with an Islamist fundamentalism that has not the least hesitation in destroying ancient cultural monuments and relics, flattening churches with bulldozers, abducting people, raping women, brutally murdering those who think differently, and even displaying their executions on the internet. Those who do it claim to be acting "in the name of God." And this is not solely the province of Islamists—this religious fanaticism that believes it is permissible to murder and destroy "in the name of God."

The Accusation

Many people's aversion to that kind of religion is so great as to produce a generalized suspicion: that is what religion is like; that is how it has always been. That is the way all religions are, even Hinduism and, of course, Christianity. And since no one can find any encouragement for the use of violence in the New Testament, at least, people shake their fingers at the Old Testament.

In the Old Testament murder was also committed in the name of God; there, too, we find "holy war" and God demands that the Israelites exterminate whole peoples. Still more: there God personally exercises violence: for example, God drowns an entire Egyptian army in the Sea of Reeds. So the Old Testament and the Qur'an are named in the same breath, paralleled with one another, and disqualified as texts of violence.

Let me give a typical example, representative of many others: the social scientist Wolfgang Freund recently reviewed a new work by Jürgen Todenhöfer in the *Süddeutsche Zeitung*. The review was titled "Chaos im Orient." Freund remarked critically:

> In a skillful pedagogy aimed at the readers, Todenhöfer lists at the end of the book a number of verses from the Qur'an that are intended to establish that true Islam is anything but an instruction for the world-wide liquidation of all non-Muslims or "false" Muslims. The only problem is that there are just as many passages in the Qur'an that clearly preach violence and war, whether "holy" or not, very much as the Bible and even the New Testament do.[1]

Evidently Wolfgang Freund has not a clue about proper interpretation of the Old Testament, and I would really like to hear from him where he finds the New Testament preaching and exhorting to violence.[2] Calling the Bible, including the New Testament, violent in this sense is itself a violent act, the use of verbal violence. But hasty and dilettantish shifts from the Qur'an to the Bible like this one are quite characteristic of the present time. They are irresponsible, and they reveal the ignorance of their authors.

Still, it is no use to complain. In the face of such charges we must not put our heads in the sand; we have to resist them. We have to look directly at the texts and learn how to make distinctions. I will begin with the phrase "holy war." Does it appear in the Old Testament?

Holy War in the Old Testament?

To put it as clearly as I possibly can: if the phrase "holy war" is to be found in the Old Testament at all, it is in only one verse, Joel 3:9. But in that verse it is precisely the nations hostile to God who are

[1] Wolfgang Freund, "Chaos im Orient" [Chaos in the Orient], *Süddeutsche Zeitung* 124 (June 2, 2015): 13.

[2] Matthew 10:34 ("Do not think that I have come to bring peace to the earth; I have not come to bring peace but a sword") is cited to prove that Jesus exhorted his followers to prepare for violence, but that is childish. As the context shows, this is a metaphor for divisions within families. Some follow Jesus; others do not.

called to wage "holy war" against the people of God, something that will result in a final judgment on the nations.[3]

The idea of "the Wars of the Lord [YHWH]" or "YHWH's battles" appears at three places in the Old Testament,[4] and words to the effect that YHWH fights for Israel or makes war on Israel's behalf are fairly frequent.[5] The meaning is that it is God who acts; human beings need take no part.

Also, the idea of "holy war" is so vague and nebulous that it is hard to work with. In the ancient Near East, in Greece, and even in the Roman Empire it was more or less a given that all official wars were conducted at divine command. Before beginning a war it was necessary to inquire of the gods, and the help of the gods was implored through prayers and sacrifices; afterward, a portion of the spoils of the war or even the whole of them were dedicated to the gods as thanks for the victory.

There was even a sense to such rituals: people wanted to be assured that the war was just. It was thought that unjust wars would embitter the gods and make enemies of them. So all wars in the ancient Near East as well as in Greek and Roman antiquity were conducted "in the name of God" or "in the name of the gods." In this, what Israel did was largely the same as the practice of all nations at that time. Fighting "in the name of God" (2 Chr 14:10) was thus not something unique to Israel.

It is true that the narratives of the Old Testament include the war by which Israel conquered its future territory. I will speak of that at length presently. But that war of conquest was not about the spread of the faith. Israel conducts no war in the Old Testament in order to introduce belief in YHWH to other peoples. In that sense the Old Testament—in contrast to Islam—knows no wars of religion.

The Extermination of Peoples

The case with another group of texts is much more problematic. The Old Testament contains God's command to Israel to conquer the

[3] On Joel 3:9 ("Consecrate yourselves for war") [Heb 3:9: "Sanctify war"], see Hans Walter Wolff, *Dodekapropheton 2. Joel und Amos*, BKAT 14, 2 (Neukirchen-Vluyn: Neukirchener Verlag, 1969), 95–96.

[4] Cf. Num 21:14; 1 Sam 18:17; 25:28; see also 1 Sam 17:47.

[5] Cf. Exod 14:14, 25; Deut 1:30; 3:22; 20:4; Josh 10:14, 42; 23:3, 10; 2 Chr 20:29; 32:8; Zech 14:3.

promised land and to root out all the peoples who dwell there. Let me illustrate this by quoting Deuteronomy 7:1-3:

> When the LORD your God brings you into the land that you are about to enter and occupy and he clears away many nations before you—the Hittites, the Girgashites, the Amorites, the Canaanites, the Perizzites, the Hivites, and the Jebusites, seven nations more numerous and mightier than you—and when the LORD your God gives them over to you and you defeat them, then you must utterly destroy them. Make no covenant with them and show them no mercy. Do not intermarry with them.

The book of Joshua depicts the events accordingly. I will quote the beginning of the summary that confirms the carrying out of this divine command: namely, Joshua 11:15-20:

> As the LORD had commanded his servant Moses, so Moses commanded Joshua, and so Joshua did; he left nothing undone of all that the LORD had commanded Moses.
>
> So Joshua took all that land: the hill country and all the Negeb and all the land of Goshen and the lowland and the Arabah and the hill country of Israel and its lowland, from Mount Halak, which rises toward Seir, as far as Baal-gad in the valley of Lebanon below Mount Hermon. . . . There was not a town that made peace with the Israelites except the Hivites, the inhabitants of Gibeon; all were taken in battle. For it was the LORD's doing to harden their hearts so that they would come against Israel in battle, in order that they might be utterly destroyed and might receive no mercy but be exterminated, just as the LORD had commanded Moses.

The first question we must pose in light of these "extermination texts" is this: are we dealing here with historical accounts, a kind of "documentation," a historical reconstruction of Israel's beginnings? The answer is: no, not at all.[6] As archaeology has long since shown, the groups of peoples from which Israel later arose only infiltrated these lands over a long period of time, or else they left the Canaanite cities and joined with slowly developing Israel. These groups at first lived

[6] Cf. Norbert Lohfink, "Landeroberung und Heimkehr. Hermeneutisches zum heutigen Umgang mit dem Josuabuch," in *Biblische Hermeneutik*, ed. Ingo Baldermann, et al., JBT 12 (Neukirchen-Vluyn: Neukirchener Verlag, 1998), 3–24, at 9–15.

solely in the hills, places with poor soil, locations where there had been no settlements previously. The immigrants were much too weak to be able to attack the fortified Canaanite cities in the fruitful lowlands.[7] Therefore: historically there was no extermination of other peoples in the initial period of Israel's existence.

That does not, however, explain much. Ultimately, our concern is with the image of God in the Old Testament. How could the Hebrew Bible permit texts in which God orders the literal destruction of whole city-states along with all their inhabitants? For that it is necessary to know that the texts in question were formulated at a time when Israel itself was in danger of falling and being made extinct.

In the eighth century BCE the Assyrians began, with a brutality previously unknown in the ancient Near East, to destroy whole peoples or resettle them and thus rob them of their identity. In 722 they conquered Samaria, and from that point onward the Northern Kingdom of Israel ceased to exist. The whole northern part of Israel became an Assyrian province. Parts of the population were deported and a new pagan upper class from the East was settled in the conquered land.

Judah, in the Southern Kingdom, became a vassal state of Assyria in that same century, thus also falling under foreign domination. After the collapse of Assyria, Judah was conquered by the Neo-Babylonian Empire. Jerusalem and the cities of Judah were destroyed. The whole Southern Kingdom became Babylonian territory, and the Babylonians had no interest in rebuilding. For several generations there was scarcely a population worth mentioning in all of Judah.[8] Nor was there a new governmental organization installed by the Babylonians. Many Israelites emigrated or died of plagues.

At the moment when it became clear that Assyria was coming to an end, but when the new constellation in the Land Between the Rivers, with Babylon at its head, was not yet really visible, there must have been a plan or at least an attempt, under King Josiah of Judah (641–609

[7] The findings of archaeology are confirmed by notices in the book of Judges. Cf. Judg 1:18-19, 27-28, 29, 30, 31-32, 33; 2:21-23; 3:1-6.

[8] This is confirmed by recent excavations: no Greek imported wares appear during a period of several decades. The previous assumption that, in contrast to Assyrian practice, the Babylonians only deported the elite members of the population, the scribes, and the artisans to the East has been rendered questionable by these findings.

BCE) to restore the older Israel. It seems that the first part of the book of Joshua may have been written at that time, as a kind of propaganda for the royal agenda and based on memories of ancient sagas.

Thus the book of Joshua was created, at the earliest, half a millennium after the settlement of the Promised Land. The commands for extermination in this book (and in Deut 7:1-3) are an effort to secure the further existence of the people Israel. They are meant to tell the endangered and despondent people in the Southern Kingdom: This land belongs to you. God gave it to you as a gift. You will not be destroyed. God is on your side, if only you trust radically!

We could see the words of God to Joshua at the very beginning of the book as consolation in the face of Israel's desperate situation at the end of the royal era: "I hereby command you: Be strong and courageous; do not be frightened or dismayed, for the LORD your God is with you wherever you go" (Josh 1:9).

The commands to exterminate, placed in a fictive situation already centuries in the past, were thus not such, but were words of encouragement intended to secure the identity of the remnant of Israel in the face of brutal threats from foreign nations.[9] A narrative like that of the destruction of the city of Ai (Josh 8:1-29) was created as a "counter-history" to fortify people against the fear and horror created by the spreading propaganda of Israel's enemies. Assyria in particular worked not only with physical violence but with its verbal counterpart as well. It developed a genuine propaganda of terror in order to demoralize other nations.

Thus Israel responded to the fear-arousing propaganda of its more powerful opponents with counter-propaganda that was, at the same time, meant to console its own people. The Old Testament—just like the New—is indeed the word of God in human words, and as human words it plays on the whole keyboard of human language.

To put it another way: the Old Testament commands to extirpate people are not commands but appeals. They are not intended to offer descriptions of past events or to demonstrate historically that God had in former times issued a command to exterminate. Instead, they mean to console those who hear them: "Don't be afraid. God once

[9] For what follows, cf. Norbert Lohfink, "Die Schichten des Pentateuch und der Krieg," in *Gewalt und Gewaltlosigkeit im Alten Testament*, ed. Norbert Lohfink, QD 96 (Freiburg: Herder, 1983), 51–110, at 74–75.

gave you the land, and God will give it to you again!" Thus we have to look carefully to see what kind of text we have in front of us in each case. The same is true, incidentally, of the New Testament. When Jesus says that "it is easier for a camel to go through the eye of a needle than for someone who is rich to enter the [reign] of God" (Matt 19:24) he does not mean to affirm that no rich person will ever get in. Instead, he is appealing to the rich: Use your wealth rightly! Use it to help the poor. Otherwise you cannot have a part in the reign of God! But it is said in a sharp, positively provocative tone: otherwise the rich people will not even listen. In the same way, the texts that order extermination are not orders; they are appeals to the depressed and suffering people in Judah.

Moreover: the commands to exterminate peoples in the book of Joshua are already relativized within the Old Testament itself: the book of Deuteronomy distinguishes sharply between the destruction of cities during the conquest of the Promised Land and all later wars (Deut 20:10-20).

It is necessary, then, first of all to read the texts of the Old Testament rightly. Let me emphasize again that the Bible is the word of God in human words. God speaks and acts through people, and people try, tentatively and with the language tools of their own time, to put the will and the word of God into their own words.

A great deal more could be said about texts regarding violence in the Old Testament.[10] Of course they exist, but they must be read rightly. The exodus narrative, for example, must also be rightly read, since in it God personally destroys Pharaoh's whole army. One can only understand that narrative if one has first read the account of Pharaoh's permanent and hard-headed refusal to allow enslaved and defiled Israel to depart. The sequence of his refusals is meant to illustrate, narratively, how human beings (and especially the powerful) can become frozen in brutal violence and hard-heartedness, whereby they bring disaster on themselves and their own people. We have to

[10] See esp. "Gerechter Friede" ("Just Peace"), document 66 of the German Bishops' Conference (Bonn: Sekretariat der Deutschen Bischofskonferenz, 2000); Norbert Lohfink and Rudolf Pesch, *Weltgestaltung und Gewaltlosigkeit. Ethische Aspekte des Alten und Neuen Testaments in ihrer Einheit und ihrem Gegensatz*, Schriften der Katholischen Akademie in Bayern 87 (Düsseldorf: Patmos, 1978); Norbert Lohfink, "Gewalt und Monotheismus. Beispiel Altes Testament," *ThPQ* 153 (2005): 149–62.

understand God's destruction of Pharaoh in some such terms today. But at the same time we must not fail to recognize that God, by obliterating Pharaoh and his army, personally restores the law that has been broken and destroyed. God cares for those without rights and takes personal responsibility for right itself.

This brings us to another very important point that needs noticing: where the Old Testament speaks of violence originating with God, perhaps even connected with words such as "vengeance" and "retribution," the background is a different set of ideas from those connected with "vengeance" and "retribution" in our Western culture.[11] When one of us takes revenge, the act is contrary to the lawful order of things. The avenger oversteps the bounds of social control and legitimation, surrendering to his or her own rage, striking back, getting even, settling a score. In contrast, when the Old Testament speaks of God's vengeance we have to assume that it means something quite different: God puts things right, restores the lawful order within the people of God. God heals the injustice done to God's own and helps them to recover their rights. Consider, for example, Isaiah 35:3-6:

> Strengthen the weak hands
> and make firm the feeble knees.
> Say to those who are of a fearful heart,
> "Be strong, do not fear!
> Here is your God.
> He will come with vengeance,
> with terrible recompense.
> He will come and save you."
> Then the eyes of the blind shall shall see,
> and the ears of the deaf shall be opened;
> then the lame shall leap like a deer,
> and the tongue of the speechless sing for joy.*

Here the concepts of "revenge" and "reprisal" clearly move in a different field of ideas than they do with us. They are components of legal language. Wrong that is suffered "will be offset by punishment

[11] For what follows cf. Rüdiger Lux, "Moses Schwanengesang. Gott und die Gewalt im Alten Testament," *Freiburger Rundbrief* 17 (2010): 102–11.

* NRSV alt.

and so eliminated."[12] Right will be restored. But this "restoration of the right can be put into words by using metaphors of violence."[13]

Old Testament Critique of Violence

In addition, we have to be clear about this—and it is now nearly the most important of all: Even in the Old Testament itself we find an increasingly powerful critique of violence. It appears especially in late, postexilic texts in which Israel looks back at its own history—a history that was filled to the brim with violence from without and even from within the people of God itself.

At the very beginning of the Bible, within the so-called primordial history, violence is condemned in the sharpest terms, in the story of Cain and Abel. It is important in this connection to ask: what exactly does "primordial history" mean? It is not the same as "early history" or "protohistory," the things that happened in the very first beginnings. Primordial history, rather, focuses on what always is, what always happens, in every phase of real history. We must read the story of Cain and Abel in that context. Cain kills his brother Abel, even though he has been expressly warned not to perform that violent act. God says to Cain:

> Why are you angry, and why has your countenance fallen? If you do well, will you not be accepted? And if you do not do well, sin is lurking at the door; its desire is for you, but you must master it. (Gen 4:6-7)

That is precisely the unmasking of rivalry and violence—exposure of the fearful violence that runs throughout history to this day. A few chapters later God looks at creation and sees that the world has not become what God wills it should be: it is filled with violence. Genesis 6:11-12 says explicitly:

[12] Hans Wildberger, *Jesaja* 3, BK 10.3 (Neukirchen-Vluyn: Neukirchener Verlag, 1982), 1344.

[13] Thus Ludger Schwienhorst-Schönberger, "Recht und Gewalt im Alten Testament," in *Macht–Gewalt–Krieg im Alten Testament. Gesellschaftliche Problematik und das Problem ihrer Repräsentation*, ed. Irmtraud Fischer, QD 254 (Freiburg: Herder, 2013), 318–51, at 349.

> Now the earth was corrupt in God's sight, and the earth was filled with violence. And God saw that the earth was corrupt, for all flesh had corrupted its ways upon the earth.

That statement applies, in turn, to the whole of human history. God does not approve of violence in the world. Force applied against our fellow human beings stems from sin. God willed and wills a different world, one free from violence. God desires a world society in which limits are placed on violence, in which it is shut down. God wants a world in which people can live in peace with one another.

Swords into Plowshares

But how can such world peace be created? The Old Testament, in another passage, gives an astonishing answer: not by the existence, within the world, of a people that is more powerful than every other society—a people that subdues every outbreak of violence with still greater force and thus can play the role of a world police.

The temptation to think that way is very great, because there are advantages to having a world police. They are even necessary—as much as police and judiciaries within individual nations. And yet the Old Testament, in its definitive prophetic texts within which Israel's centuries of experiences and hopes are concentrated, does not expect the end of violence to come through counter-violence.

That is evident, for example, in Isaiah 2:2-5. Here world peace is *not* established by a nation that has more modern weapons and is better organized or that fights with more abandon than all others. Instead, it comes through the people of God that listens to the guidance of its God, lives as a just society, and relies on nonviolence. This is how Israel can become the city on a hill to which all nations look—to which, indeed, all nations come in order to learn from it how a right society could be constructed.[14]

It is still a vision. According to Isaiah 2, that state of the world has not yet been achieved. But the people of God must begin *now* to live this vision of a new, alternative society. Then the longed-for

[14] On Isa 2:1-5 see the interpretation by Norbert Lohfink, *Die messianische Alternative. Adventsreden* (Freiburg: Herder, 1981), 12–26, but especially Michael P. Maier, *Völkerwallfahrt im Jesajabuch*, BZAW 474 (Berlin: de Gruyter, 2016), 95–143.

community will also come—for the whole world. The unbelievably bold text, which is paralleled in Micah 4:1-5, reads as follows:

> The word that Isaiah son of Amoz saw concerning Judah and Jerusalem.
>
> In days to come
> the mountain of the LORD's house
> shall be established as the highest of the mountains
> and shall be raised above the hills;
> all the nations shall stream to it.
> Many peoples shall come and say,
> "Come, let us go up to the mountain of the LORD,
> to the house of the God of Jacob,
> that he may teach us his ways
> and that we may walk in his paths."
> For out of Zion shall go forth instruction
> and the word of the LORD from Jerusalem.
> He shall judge between the nations
> and shall arbitrate for many peoples;
> they shall beat their swords into plowshares
> and their spears into pruning hooks;
> nation shall not lift up sword against nation;
> neither shall they learn war any more.
> O house of Jacob,
> come, let us walk
> in the light of the LORD! (Isa 2:1-5)

This, a central prophetic text in the Old Testament, thus asserts that world peace will be achieved only through nonviolence, but—note—through the nonviolence of the people of God that realizes within itself God's instruction and thus God's nonviolence. Hence the cry at the end of the vision: "O house of Jacob, come, let us walk in the light of the LORD!"

The Nonviolent Servant of God

But the Old Testament goes much further. It knows from its own history that the one who renounces violence must often suffer violence, being ruthlessly destroyed by those who rely on power alone. Hence Deutero-Isaiah, writing in light of the experience of Israel, oppressed and trodden down by the nations, writes the songs of God's servant, using that title to represent Israel, exiled to Babylon.

The nations have gathered together against this "servant of God," the people of God. They strike down God's servant; indeed, they try to destroy him, but he remains true to his God and takes refuge in God alone. The servant does not strike back against the violence that is focused on her, nor does she retreat. And, precisely in that way, the Servant amazes the world of the nations. In Isaiah 53 we suddenly hear a confession of the kings and the mighty who have raged against God's servant. The nations and their rulers acknowledge what this rejected one was and what God wanted with it. They have to confess: "we accounted him stricken, struck down by God, and afflicted. But he was wounded for our transgressions, crushed for our iniquities" (Isa 53:4-5).

This theology of the Servant of God arrives at a point that can never be surpassed. It is an utterly devastating revolution in thought, and it already appears in the Old Testament. "It is the insight that it is better to be a victim than a violent victor."[15] It is the insight that true peace in the world can come only from the victims and never from the victors.

It is true that, at the present time, interpreters do not agree whether the Servant in Isaiah is simply representative of the Israel exiled to Babylon or is perhaps an individual who reflects Israel's history. It is true that there are serious reasons to think that, in the book of Isaiah, the Servant represents deported Israel and nothing else.[16] I am absolutely convinced of it. But at this point I can leave the whole question open.

The Messiah on the Donkey

There are, after all, texts in the Old Testament that could resolve the question of "individual" or "collective" in favor of a single person. For example, in Zechariah 9:9-10, a very late Old Testament text, the Messiah (an individual figure) brings peace to Israel and the world.

Probably this idea also rests on one of Israel's most profound experiences: certainly it is better to be a victim than a violent victor, but a whole nation cannot sustain being a pure victim. To put it better: the people of God can maintain that stance only if an individual

[15] This statement is found in "Gerechter Friede," 24, which describes the Old Testament contexts succinctly and with utter clarity.

[16] See Gerhard Lohfink and Ludwig Weimer, *Maria – nicht ohne Israel. Eine neue Sicht der Lehre von der Unbefleckten Empfängnis*, 2nd ed. (Freiburg: Herder, 2012), 223–30.

precedes it on the path to absolute nonviolence. That is precisely what Zechariah 9:9-10 is about:

> Rejoice greatly, O daughter Zion!
> Shout aloud, O daughter Jerusalem!
> See, your king comes to you;
> triumphant and victorious is he,
> humble and riding on a donkey,
> on a colt, the foal of a donkey.
> [I][17] will cut off the chariot from Ephraim
> and the war horse from Jerusalem;
> and the battle bow shall be cut off,
> and he [i.e., the messianic king] shall command peace to the nations;
> his dominion shall be from sea to sea
> and from the River to the ends of the earth.

The Messiah, who causes all Jerusalem to break forth in a joyful shout, comes on a donkey, the poor person's mount. Obviously no one can make war while riding on a donkey. Thus the messianic ruler comes as a nonviolent person, someone both peaceable and peace-bringing. This one will do away with the chariots of Ephraim and the war horses of Jerusalem. Note: it is not the weapons of Israel's enemies that will be destroyed; God's people will disarm themselves when this ruler comes. Thus this late text again emphasizes what the book of Isaiah has already said, but it interprets Isaiah's collective texts in terms of a single figure, the Messiah who is to come.

As we have already seen, the text of Zechariah 9 is late. When it was formulated, Alexander the Great, with his Macedonian military technique, had already conquered a world empire that stretched from Egypt to India. The Messiah on the donkey is, in all probability, a consciously constructed counterimage to the world conqueror Alexander on his warhorse. This Jewish messianic ruler has no power—or, better, this one's powers are mildness and humility. But precisely those powers are greater than that of Alexander.

Thus we find concentrated in Zechariah a long line of Old Testament tradition. We could describe it as follows: God does not desire a world full of violence. God's means of healing is a nation that lives

[17] Author's translation; thus also the AV.—Trans.

nonviolence. But that inevitably means that this nation will become a victim. And because a whole nation cannot sustain such a thing there must be one who precedes it on the path of nonviolence so that the many people of God can follow in that one's footsteps. It is an incredibly radical theology, unique in the world. That is how revolutionary the thought of the Old Testament is.

Unnerving Dissonances?

Now let us look back again at the Old Testament as a whole. Its books contain texts of shocking violence. I could have presented many more of them: texts that never appear in the liturgy, that are profoundly repugnant to us, such as the revenge of Jacob's sons on the men of Shechem (Gen 34) or the Levites' merciless killing of the three thousand men who worshiped the golden calf (Exod 32:26-29), or the destruction of the Levite Korah and all his followers (Num 16). These last are literally swallowed up by the ground.

Still, we need not be shocked by such texts because they show that Israel only came to know God through a long process. Initially, Israel participated in the nations' systems of violence and, accordingly, its God was taken to be a violent deity. Slowly, through many stages, but sometimes with revolutionary force, Israel's image of its God changed, and with it the nation's view of social violence. Or should we say that Israel's view of violence changed, and with it the nation's image of its God? Probably both formulations would be correct.

What is crucial, at any rate, is that already within the Old Testament itself there was a development that overturned everything: from violence to nonviolence. Thus the Old Testament is not an ugly collection of texts that celebrate and expose violence, nor is it an infuriating concert in which the harmonies of nonviolence contend with the cacophonies of violence in annoying dissonances.

Rather, the Old Testament itself reveals a clear tendency to nonviolence—and to that extent it can by no means be compared to the Qur'an. We have seen that the development of world society toward violence is condemned at the very beginning of the Old Testament, in the book of Genesis. We have also seen that in the book of Zechariah, one of the latest prophetic books of the Old Testament, the image of a nonviolent messianic ruler appears as the product of a long history of reflection and enlightenment in Israel.

One more note at this point: everyone knows the famous saying, "An eye for an eye, a tooth for a tooth," which is continually cited as proof of a supposedly consistent mentality of vengeance and violence in the Old Testament. It is the magic formula with which both intellectuals and nonintellectuals swiftly and concisely dismiss the whole Old Testament. Literally and completely, this legal decree says: "eye for eye, tooth for tooth, hand for hand, foot for foot, burn for burn, wound for wound, stripe for stripe" (Exod 21:24-25).

The saying does not, however, necessarily prove what it is supposed to prove. In ancient Near Eastern law it certainly refers to literal revenge for violence—in order to prevent it. The Codex Hammurabi reads: "If a man destroy the eye of another man, they shall destroy his eye. . . . If a man knock out a tooth of a man of his own rank, they shall knock out his tooth."[18] The oldest evidence inside the Bible, namely, Exodus 21:24-25, stands in a context that prescribes "compensations": see Exodus 21:18-19, 22, 30, 32. If we consider the context to be decisive, then the decree means here that someone who has struck out another's eye must pay compensation to the value of an eye. Someone who has knocked out another's tooth must pay compensation to the value of a tooth. And so on. Thus, in the earliest place where it appears in the Bible, the saying "an eye for an eye"—given its context[19]—simply does not refer to limitless violence in the sense of "what you do to me, I will do to you!" but basically represents a humanization of the law.[20]

Incidentally: the principle of *talion* in Codex Hammurabi is itself an extremely late arrival. Older Mesopotamian law collections contain no trace of literal recompense. They already have a clear system of compensations. Hammurabi reintroduces an archaic, older, and harder justice, not for everyone but for a newly arisen leadership group. Such things do happen in history.

[18] *The Code of Hammurabi, King of Babylon*, trans. Robert Francis Harper (Chicago: University of Chicago Press, 1904), nos. 196, 200. Available at https://en.wikisource.org/wiki/The_Code_of_Hammurabi_(Harper_translation). Cf. E. S. Gerstenberger, *Leviticus: A Commentary*, trans. Douglas W. Stott, OTL (Louisville: Westminster John Knox, 1996), 366–68.

[19] Cf. Frank Crüsemann, *The Torah: Theology and Social History of Old Testament Law*, trans. Allan W. Mahnke (Minneapolis: Fortress Press, 1996), 148–49.

[20] The situation in Lev 24:17-21 and Deut 19:21 is different. There it appears that the legal principle is again being used in its original sense, that is, according to the principle of *talion*.

Fulfillment in Jesus

But still I have not said everything. I have proceeded thus far as if the Old Testament could be considered in isolation, cleanly separated from the New—as though Old and New Testaments were two different books. They are not. From a Christian point of view they are inseparably connected with one another; they are a single book. Christians call that one book "the Bible."

For Christians the New Testament is not the Bible proper, whereas the Old Testament would be only a "prehistory." No, the New Testament is the final redactional layer, and at the same time it is the closing chapter of the one great book that is the Bible. And that means, to continue the same image, that all the previous chapters of this great book are to be read and understood in light of its last chapter. That is a principle that is simply taken for granted in the case, for example, of juristic documents: a law book must be interpreted in terms of the lawgiver's final redaction.

Now I am saying the same thing about Jesus. In him the long process of enlightenment that began in Israel with Abraham has reached its end. The many steps Israel walked have brought it to its goal. In Jesus, Israel has come to know God completely. To say it the other way around: God is fully self-expressed in him. Therefore everything that was said previously must be understood in light of Jesus.

But that does not mean a complete rupture, a totally new beginning, the retraction of what preceded. We have already seen that the Old Testament itself contains the insight that nonviolence is better than violence, that it is better to be a victim than a violent victor. Jesus took up the best texts and lines of tradition in the Old Testament with incredible instinct and an unheard-of assurance. He lived entirely on the basis of the Old Testament and perfected it in every way.

Jesus adopted the Servant Songs from Isaiah, and as he entered Jerusalem for his death, for Passover, he literally made a reality of the figure of the king of peace who rides on a donkey. Also, in the Sermon on the Plain, he calls for nonviolence in the most drastic way:

> I say to you who are listening: Love your enemies; do good to those who hate you; bless those who curse you; pray for those who mistreat you. If anyone strikes you on the cheek, offer the other also, and from anyone who takes away your coat do not withhold even your shirt. Give to everyone who asks of you, and if anyone takes away what is yours, do not ask for it back again. (Luke 6:27-30)

Jesus radically distanced himself from the Zealots, the warriors for God in his own time. His disciples must not even use a staff when they travel.

Thus Jesus perfected everything. He brought what was already present in the Old Testament into full light. He clarified the Old Testament—not only in his words, but in his own person. He preferred to let himself be killed rather than to use violence. In the end he was hanged on a cross. It is scarcely possible to imagine a greater contrast to Muhammad.

But if everything is fulfilled in Jesus, if everything is made clear in him, if in him everything in the Old Testament that is not completely obvious achieves its utmost clarity—why isn't the church simply satisfied with the New Testament? That question floats around in many Christian heads today, even those of theology professors.[21] Why doesn't the church exclude the Old Testament from the canon?

In the first place, it is simply because we cannot set ourselves above Jesus. If Jesus lived entirely from the Old Testament we also must live from it—or, to put it another way, Jesus himself traveled Israel's long path in his own person and brought it to its fullness. Jesus would not have been possible without Israel's sacred scriptures.

Should it be different for us? Must not we also, in our lives, accompany him on that whole path: believing as Abraham did, being led out of Egypt as Israel was, being tested in the wilderness, slowly coming to know, step by step, what violence really is and what it causes? Must we not listen to the critical words of the prophets and, like the book of Isaiah, take leave of every kind of violence and rely only on peace and reconciliation?

Christianity is not founded on a teaching that fell from heaven or was dictated from above. It lives—and this, precisely, is the rationality of Christianity—out of a long and difficult process of recognition that had to be traveled by a whole people. It lives out of the long path that Israel journeyed through history. There can be no such thing as Christianity unless the church again and again, ever anew, travels the road taken by the Old Testament people of God. Only then can it arrive where Jesus is.

[21] Cf., e.g., Notger Slenczka, "Die Kirche und das Alte Testament," in *Das Alte Testament in der Theologie*, ed. Elisabeth Gräb-Schmidt and Reiner Preul, Marburger Jahrbuch Theologie 25 (Leipzig: Evangelische Verlagsanstalt, 2013), 83–119; rightly to the contrary Ludger Schwienhorst-Schönberger, "Die Rückkehr Markions," *IKaZ* 44 (2015): 286–302.

9

Did Easter Change History?

Did Easter change anything in the course of the world? Or did everything stay the same as it had always been? Still the same misery? More and more wars, deportations, expulsions? More and more rape, poverty, sickness, misery? Still the human being as wolf? Ultimately the whole question culminates in this: Did Christians' faith in the resurrection change the world?

Some thirty years ago I preached on this question at Easter, and I said everything that I had thought about, up to that time, about this question. Did Easter, Jesus' resurrection, the Easter faith of countless Christians change the course of the world in any way? Here I will present that sermon once again, and then I will argue with it—not in the sense that I question it, but I want to shed more light on its theological background and take a closer look at problems that were not discussed in the sermon.

The outward impulse for the sermon at that time was a newspaper article related to the coming feast of Easter, written by Nikolaus Lobkowicz, then rector of the Catholic University of Eichstätt. I still recall how his Easter article irritated me at that time. Essentially, the whole sermon was nothing but an argument against it. Here, then, to start with, is the complete text of my sermon just as I then preached it.

An Easter Sermon

I am holding in my hand the lead article from a newspaper on the subject of Easter! It appeared yesterday. The article is titled "What Has Improved because of Easter?" The title, at least, I find to be very good. What has gotten better because of Easter? We may well ask.

The answer that the author then gives, however, is not so good. It is, in fact, extremely weak. It says, namely, that almost nothing has changed because of Easter. On the other hand, everything has changed because of Easter. The reasoning is as follows:

In the real world, in the course of history, almost nothing ever changes. It is true there has been a Christian culture for centuries, but in the two thousand years of Christianity humans have not gotten better. They are, now as then, the most cruel of all living things. And yet everything has changed because, thanks to Jesus' resurrection, our lives have acquired a meaning beyond death. Since Jesus has risen, there is eternal life for us, and that has made everything different.

At first that does not seem so bad. After all, the author is a believing Christian. After all, we can be happy when the media do not ridicule the great feasts of Christian faith or—as is increasingly normal—simply ignore them.

Still, this lead article is irritating because it is based on a profound skepticism—about whether faith can in any way change history. Hence, ultimately, the article is faithless. It may even be more dangerous than a lead article that disdains Christianity, because this author shifts everything into a world beyond. *There* the world will be transformed. *Here*, however, in this history, (almost) nothing changes. Only hope in the world beyond is firmly grounded in Jesus' resurrection, and to that extent everything in the world is, in fact, changed.

But that is precisely *not* the meaning the New Testament gives to Jesus' resurrection. Just read through all its Easter narratives!—in all four Gospels! You will not find a single Easter text that is meant to shift our attention to a world beyond. Moreover, can you find a single passage in the New Testament in which the Risen One says to his disciples: "Rejoice, because I have opened heaven for you. As I myself have risen, so you, too, will rise"? I am not aware of any such text within the Easter stories. I even know of a counter-text. In Acts 1, after Jesus' ascension, the two angels say to the disciples: "Why do you stand looking up toward heaven?" (Acts 1:11). This reproof from the angels points Jesus' disciples to their mission. They are to be Jesus' "witnesses in Jerusalem, in all Judea and Samaria, and to the ends of the earth" (Acts 1:8).

The case is just the same in the other Easter narratives as well. They all culminate in the sending of the disciples by the Risen One. The disciples are sent out to proclaim the Gospel and to gather communities that live on the basis of the Easter forgiveness and so become a living witness to the power of God, already in this world.

But precisely that—God's power in this world—is something many Christians no longer believe in nowadays. At most they believe only in God's past deeds, not in any such works today: hence their profound resignation as regards the church and its mission to change the world.

Whence that resignation? There are many reasons for it. One of them is certainly the deep-seated inferiority complex of a lot of Christians in Europe. Since the time of the European Enlightenment it has been unceasingly hammered into Christians that, alas, Christianity has not changed anything on earth for the better. There is nothing to be seen, not a trace in all the world, of a redemption of humanity. Karl Marx formulated this permanent accusation addressed to the church with smug irony: "The social principles of Christianity have now had eighteen hundred years to be developed, and need no further development."[1] No change, not the least, has been effected by the church, says Karl Marx. Now *we* must take charge. And we will.

"Nothing has changed in the world because of Christianity. Nothing. Nothing at all!" Those words are only a few of the many lies that are constantly preached at us—to the point that, gradually, our brains have become cloudy and we are no longer in a position to see the simplest things. Christianity has not changed anything in the world for the better? Is that really true?

All the Christian martyrs, from the first century till today, who preferred to die rather than betray the truth of their faith—can it be that they, with their resistance against the omnipotence of the state, effected no change in the world?

All the saints, from those altogether unknown among us to Francis of Assisi or Mother Teresa: their joy in doing the will of God is not supposed to have changed anything?

All the mothers who sat, night by night, at their children's bedsides, recited evening prayers with them, and looked back at the day just past with the eyes of faith: they are not supposed to have changed the world in any way?

[1] "The Communism of the Paper *Rheinischer Beobachter*," *Deutsche-Brüsseler Zeitung* 73 (September 12, 1847), Extract (Moscow: Foreign Languages Publishing, 1957; repr. Mineola, NY: Dover Publications, 2008), 82–87, at 83.

All the married couples who did not give in to society's trends, did not divorce, but remained faithful to each other and repeatedly forgave each other: they changed nothing in the world?

All the convents and monasteries that have spread across our land like stars in the heavens, since the early Middle Ages—with their schools, their dispensaries, their workshops, their *scriptoria,* their skills in building and agriculture—none of that changed anything in the world?

Martin Luther King Jr., who stood up as a Christian, nonviolently, for the abolition of racial separation in the United States, who made the civil rights movement a mass phenomenon and was rewarded with assassination: he changed nothing in the world?

We have no idea how the world would look today if not for the world-changing work of countless Christians.

Every one of us has, at some time or other, used a scale that has to be balanced by hand, by pushing weights back and forth. There is a point at which the balance is achieved. If the weight is just a little off, the beam of the scale tips.

It may be that our society, with its greed, rage for destruction, and death wish, is constantly on the point of tipping—and above all it is believers, with their courage, patience, and unceasing actions against chaos, who keep it in balance.

If Jesus had not risen from the dead, and if his resurrection had not initiated a quiet but unceasing revolution—among many non-Christians as well—the world would look different today. In our oldest and most beautiful Easter song, "Christ Is Arisen," we sing: "Had he not risen, the world would have perished." I am convinced that there is more truth in that statement than we can ever imagine. Had Jesus not risen from the dead, and were he not present in the life witness of countless Christians in society, the world would look very different today: indeed, it might long since have been destroyed.

So let's not believe the stupid statement that Christianity has not changed the world. When someone approaches me with such a moronic assertion, I simply ask: "How do you know that? How do you know what the world would look like if there had never been Abraham, Moses, Israel's prophets, and above all the loveliest fruit of Israel, Jesus Christ? How do you know what the world would look like if Jesus' Sermon on the Mount and Christians' Easter faith did not exist?"

But it is better if we, for once, ask the opposite question: if we do not talk about the world in general but about ourselves. Changing the world—that starts with us; after all, it starts with me. I myself decide whether Easter has changed the world or not—I do it with my own life.

If I accommodate to society, to its self-made gods, its fashions, its trends, its relativism, its unbelief—if my comfort, my private well-being, my personal successes are the most important things in life, then I contribute to a situation in which Easter no longer happens and no one understands it.

Consequently I will say, in contrast with Nikolaus Lobkowicz's article, that as soon as I believe that the power of the risen Jesus can change the world and constantly does change it; as soon as I stop asking, "What improves my reputation?" but instead, "What adds to respect for God?"; as soon as I seek not just my own little pleasures but join in helping the new thing God wants to create in the world through the church to happen, I contribute to making Easter happen today—because then I provide an opportunity for God to make the power of the resurrection visible even today, here in this world.

Then I can no longer ask, "Has Easter changed anything?" I have to ask, "Am I ready to let myself be changed by the Gospel?" Then, in fact, Easter changes the world. In that sense I wish you all a blessed Easter, with all the joy the resurrection of Jesus brings us.

Constant Progress?

That was my Easter sermon thirty years ago. I still think it is correct. I might preach it again today, just as it is. Still, in the meantime a lot of questions have arisen for me, and I would like to talk about them now, because one thing is clearer to me than it was then: the question about whether Christian faith changes the world is one of the most difficult problems in theology. In what follows I can introduce only a few points of view, and in doing so I will probably ask more questions than I can give answers for.

First let me propose a theological concept that plays an important role in this context: "perfectibility." That term is intended to express the idea that humanity is capable of constant improvement. It is true that humanity can also fail. It can fall back into barbarism. But in principle it is possible for humanity to move forward and steadily develop itself toward perfection, so that in the end reason conquers completely.

We may think: yes, that is how the great spirits of the eighteenth century thought. "Perfectibility" is a concept from the European Enlightenment, which was about human progress, the upbuilding of humanity and morality. It was the European Enlightenment that, in the eighteenth century, constantly applied the concept of perfectibility. It was of extraordinary importance.

But what is crucial is what happened to that idea in the nineteenth century. The pure possibility of human perfection became the philosophical assertion that humanity would, in fact, constantly grow more perfect—not only in terms of science and technology but also culturally and morally. Civilization, culture, and humanity would move upward in a steady curve until the true freedom of humanity and the happiness of all were achieved.

It is popular, in that context, to point to the elimination of slavery, the emancipation of women, the enormous improvement in living conditions, the speedier communications, the building-up of human rights. The growing industrialization and the ever-improving state of popular education were supposed to lead to an ever-more-profound humanization of society.

That faith in progress was often combined with a positively naïve optimism about it. Thus, for example, Ludwig Feuerbach praised the modern insurance systems, the recently invented railroads and steam engines, the newly created collections of paintings and museums of natural history, and above all the academies for war and business. Such institutions were supposed to signify the gigantic progress of humanity, and that immense progress was said to prove that Christianity had played itself out. All that can be found in Feuerbach's bestseller, *The Essence of Christianity*.[2]

This nineteenth-century optimism about progress, based on the eighteenth-century Enlightenment and subsequently combined with biological models of evolution, was destroyed in gruesome fashion in the twentieth century. Then the Enlightenment revealed its ugly dialectical face: two world wars in which French and Germans and many other nations engaged in mutual slaughter; a diabolically

[2] Ludwig Feuerbach, *The Essence of Christianity*, trans. Marian Evans (London: John Chapman, 1854), preface to the 2nd ed., v–xvii.

fraudulent propaganda against the current enemy; the industrial-style murder of six million Jewish children, women, and men; the brutal destruction of whole cities, with countless dead victims; the dropping of two atomic bombs on Hiroshima and Nagasaki; the deporting of whole peoples—all that and much more called the dream of constant human moral progress radically into question.

Still, that dream appears to be rooted quite deeply in human consciousness, for when the Soviet Union fell in 1991 and 1992 the American author Francis Fukuyama, in his book *The End of History*, asserted that now Western democracy and, with it, free orders of society had finally and forever asserted themselves in the world, eliminating and putting an end to all the tensions and conflicts of world history in the Hegelian sense.[3] As the course of history has shown, and as Putin or the Islamic State are showing us once again, that thesis was likewise marked by unbounded naïveté.

Looking at scientific and technical development in world civilization does not reduce our skepticism. In these first decades of the twenty-first century we are experiencing fast-paced technical developments that no non-expert can any longer comprehend. The digitalization and, with it, the networking of society is increasing with breathtaking speed. There is rising anxiety that we humans are not equal to keeping control of technology, since it appears that not only dictatorships but democracies, to the same degree, are exploiting every technological opportunity to create a world that conforms to their wishes, both economically and in terms of power relationships. I am thinking of the NSA, the major foreign intelligence service of the United States, and its cooperation with the internet giants. Here, and for a long time now, a permanent perversion of the rule of law is taking place.

Anyone who has followed, even casually, what Edward Snowden has revealed will ask herself or himself, increasingly, whether the image of history in the book of Revelation is not much closer to reality than all the utopias of progress—since, that is, the powers of obfuscating propaganda and demonic accumulations of force are not growing weaker in our world but constantly strengthening, forcing Christians to an ultimate faith decision.

[3] Francis Fukuyama, *The End of History and the Last Man* (New York: Perennial, 1992).

But here we can leave that question open and return to the idea of human perfectibility, the great dream of the Enlightenment! I spoke about how the "enlighteners" of the eighteenth century still considered it possible that humanity could also retreat into barbarism, but by the nineteenth century the idea of constant and unstoppable human progress had conquered.

If we look more closely at this development of the idea of progress we discover a phenomenon that is of great interest in our context: toward the end of the eighteenth century a part of Protestant theology adopted the idea of perfectibility and interpreted the history of Christianity as an unstoppable progressive movement: Christianity would increasingly dominate the world, demonstrate its superiority more and more clearly, suppress all other religions, and achieve a purer and purer form.

This *Christian* optimism about progress and the future has also since been defeated. Islam has entered an era of astonishing success, and in Europe the numbers of those who profess Christianity are falling rapidly. At present there are more Muslim students than Catholics in the primary, high, and technical schools in Vienna.

In Germany today we live together with Muslims, Hindus, Buddhists, Baha'i, and even members of the voodoo cult. But above all we are more and more surrounded by people of no "confession," who call themselves atheists, agnostics, or simply "nones." In the year 1970 the percentage of the population registered as "of no religion" was 3.9; by 1987 the percentage was 11.4. After the reunion with the DDR the number rose to 22.4 percent, and in 2013 there were 36.6 percent who were nonreligious. The trend is obvious.

A Revolutionary Theology

As a New Testament scholar I naturally ask myself in this context what the Bible itself has to say about this whole problem. In the view of the Bible, did faith in the God of Abraham and of the God of Jesus Christ change the world? Will Christian faith ultimately succeed more and more, in spite of all setbacks? And in the end will it lead, after all, to an unstoppable humanization of the world?

I had not yet asked myself those questions thirty years ago when I preached that Easter sermon. Does the Bible offer an answer—a clear and unmistakable one? Let me attempt to approach the problem in several ways.

First I will look at the Old Testament, and in particular at the motif of the so-called pilgrimage of the nations. It played an important role for the prophets and above all in the book of Isaiah.

According, for example, to Isaiah 2, at the end of days God will cause Mount Zion to attract representatives of all the nations to itself, because a fascination will go forth from that mountain—that is, from Jerusalem, from Israel—that will overwhelm all peoples. What the nations will see in Zion is an order of society that is shaped by nonviolence and reconciliation, by justice and peace. The fascination of that society will cause the nations to change their own guiding principles and learn from the people of God. It is precisely in this context that we find the famous words: "They shall beat their swords into plowshares and their swords into pruning hooks; nation shall not lift up sword against nation; neither shall they learn war any more" (Isa 2:4).

Note: all that is not taking place in an afterlife but here, in this history. And the people of God are urged, at the end of this vision, to live the fulfillment of the promise *now*, already, by walking "in the light of the LORD."

So: a shining end to history? Unstoppable progress toward a nonviolent and finally peaceful world society? It is not that simple, for the book of Isaiah again takes up, primarily in chapters 40–55, the theme initiated in its second chapter. There we read again and again about a "Servant of God." Who is that?

In Isaiah the Servant is none other than Israel, suffering and deported to Babylon. But that means the "Servant of God" in Isaiah is a symbolic figure: it is a collective.

In itself that is not a problem. We, too, are familiar with such symbolic figures. Think of the "German Michel" or the figure of *Germania* above Rüdesheim.[4] In the sense intended by their creators they represent the whole nation. Or consider the figure of "Bavaria" on the border of the Oktoberfest meadow in Munich: she symbolizes all Bavaria. Please excuse these banal comparisons. I only use them in order to show that the figure of an individual can represent a whole people. It is no different with the Servant of God, who represents the countless Jews who had been deported to the Land Between the Rivers.

But now to get to the point: what is said of this Servant of God in the book of Isaiah is truly amazing: God rescues the Servant from

[4] In the American context we could say "Uncle Sam" and the Statue of Liberty.—Trans.

suffering and mortal danger. Still more: God makes use of the Servant to advance the divine plan for the world:

> The divine spirit is laid upon the Servant (Isa 42:1).
>
> The Servant witnesses to God's deeds (43:10).
>
> God makes the Servant a light for the nations (42:6).

But how does that happen? How can the Servant Israel reach the nations? How is it that the beaten and despised one will become a means of salvation for the peoples? It will not be through great and noble deeds the Servant will accomplish personally. No, it will be very different: "like a lamb that is led to the slaughter and like a sheep that before its shearers is silent, so he did not open his mouth" (Isa 53:7).

This statement in Isaiah 53:7 is of the greatest importance for our question, because it says that Israel will achieve the transformation of the world not through brilliant successes, not by noble deeds, not by its heroic efforts, but through its suffering and failure. It will be led like a lamb to the slaughter. This statement is repeated in various forms:

> The Servant refuses to use any violence (50:6).
>
> The Servant is mistreated (53:7).
>
> The Servant is killed (53:8).

That precisely this beaten and despised Servant will be healing for the nations is thus an absolute paradox, one that is described in this way:

> This one's life is given as an offering for sin (53:10).
>
> The Servant bears the sicknesses [of the nations] (53:4) and is wounded for their transgressions (53:5).
>
> God lays the iniquity of the nations upon this person (53:6), and it is by this Servant's wounds that they are healed (53:5).
>
> The Servant makes the "many" (that is: the many nations) righteous (53:11).

Only because the Servant of God bows under God's will—silent as a lamb—is this dreadful suffering not for nothing:

God's Servant does not end in shame (50:7) but will find success and be exalted (52:13).

The Servant's reward will be descendants and a long life (53:10), and it is through the Servant that the LORD's plan will succeed (53:10).

If we survey all these statements about the Servant we can see that they not only constitute a solid fabric of meaning: more than that, they reveal a drama. Israel, the servant chosen by God and wedded to God, is living in the misery of exile because of its sins. Israel has become the nations' plunder and no longer has any shape; it is despised by all. Israel is living in the sphere of death, as if in the grave.

But this very beaten and downtrodden Israel is God's instrument. God makes it a "light for the nations." Through Israel, the Servant, God brings salvation to the ends of the earth. But this happens, as we have said, not by the exercise of power and violence; it happens through Israel's mute suffering.

Let me now apply all that to my initial question: does the people of God—or, better, does God, through God's people, change the course of the world, of history? The answer is an unqualified "yes." For

The Servant's wounds bring about the healing of the nations (53:5).

The LORD's plan will succeed through the Servant (53:10), and the Servant of God justifies the "many"—that is, the many nations (53:11).

Thus change does happen in the world—right down to its roots. But this alteration of the world does not take place as a result of external success, of world-shaking achievements. It comes through the passion of the Servant of God, the hideous fate this Servant must accept.

A Squalid Death

It will be no different—and here I take another step—for Jesus. The whole destiny of Israel is concentrated in his person. Jesus gathers within himself everything that constitutes the faithful Israel that trusts in its God alone.

Jesus proclaims the reign of God, and not only proclaims it but makes it present. He tells the poor that their miserable situation will soon change. He tells the weeping that they will soon laugh. He heals the sick. He frees those who are tortured by the demons of society from their obsessions. He gathers people around himself to form the new family that from now on will seek only the will of God.

All that does not, for the present, mean a world beyond this one; it is about the history in which we live. Jesus wants a silent revolution, and by gathering and transforming Israel he desires—through and beyond Israel—the transformation of the world. Jesus assumes the pilgrimage of nations proclaimed by the prophets as a matter of course. That, in fact, is why he focuses on Israel and does not go to Alexandria, Athens, or Rome. He knows that only when the people of God repent and do justice to their election can the world be changed.

Did Jesus achieve what he wanted? Was his public appearance, his preaching of the reign of God, a story of success? No. After an astonishing beginning, Jesus died a shameful, squalid death on the cross. He must have become aware, very soon, that it would come to that. It was not for nothing that he told the parable of the scattered seed and its enemies as an image of the coming of the reign of God: some of the seed would be pecked by the birds, some would dry up, some would be choked by thorns. Certainly the portion of the seed the parable speaks of at the end yields an abundant harvest. But the parable shows that Jesus has no illusions: he knows how much resistance and hostility the reign of God must expect to encounter. In the end, Jesus is executed.

It is impossible to separate this, Jesus' end, from his message about the coming of God's reign. We dare not think of his preaching of the rule of God and his cross as two completely different things that have nothing to do with one another.

Jesus' death on the cross again modifies his proclamation of the reign of God. It does not erase the good news of the beginning; it does demonstrate the authenticity of Jesus' preaching. His death now definitively reveals the character of the reign of God: its hiddenness and its lowliness. What does that mean? It means that the reign of God will not come without persecution and without sacrifice. Indeed, it cannot come without daily dying. There is no other way.

What was hidden in Jesus' preaching from the beginning becomes completely clear in his death: the reign of God demands a change of sovereigns that human beings must accomplish. It calls for letting-happen and self-surrender. The reign of God will not come without pure receptivity, which is always also suffering. Jesus was by no means far from the reign of God in his passion. Indeed, the reign of God comes precisely in the "hour" in which Jesus himself can do nothing more; he must simply hand himself over and surrender to the reality of God. That is precisely the basis of the Gospel of John. The "hour" of most profound "humiliation" is the hour of his "glorification," that is, the hour in which the glory of God embraces the whole of Jesus' "work."

So, through his death, Jesus' promise of the reign of God acquires, once again, a final clarification and focus: from that point on, the concept of "reign of God" can no longer be used unless one speaks at the same time of Jesus' surrender, even to death. For Jesus' followers that means they cannot live within the reign of God without obedience to what it brings with it—and within a resistant society and a reluctant church that cannot happen without suffering, without sacrifice, without passion stories.

Ultimately, Jesus' death uncovers all the self-glorification of the human being and with it every kind of superficial and presumptuous idea of the reign of God. God's reign can only happen where people reach their limits, when they no longer know where they are surrendering, where they are making room only for God so that God can act. Only there, in the space of continual dying and rising, does the reign of God begin.

But that brings us directly back to Isaiah 52–53. The church has rightly seen Jesus as the one in whom everything the book of Isaiah said is concentrated and fulfilled.

A History of Triumph?

All that produces a decisive change of direction for our question about whether the faith of Israel and the church really changes the world. It is not yet a clear answer, but it is a shift. I would state it this way:

Isaiah, the prophets, the whole Old Testament: they are all about changing the world. Creation should look as God imagined it. World society should become what God planned for it: a community free from violence, living in peace and reconciliation.

The same is true for Jesus. He lives entirely on the basis of his Bible, the Old Testament, and it is therefore obvious to him that it is all about changing the world into one of freedom, reconciliation, and righteousness. That is precisely the meaning of the reign of God he preaches.

That changing of the world about which Jesus and the prophets before him spoke is, however, not a superficial history of success. It is a road with infinite resistances, a path in the face of naked hostility, a way in darkness and apparent failure. There can be no other way for Jesus' disciples than the one Jesus and the Servant of God, Israel, have already traveled.

Given all this, we should be skeptical about any and all depictions of Christianity that attempt a triumphal account. There are certainly narratives in existence that portray the church's path as a victory parade. The lives of the first Christians, those of the saints, those of Christian communities, or the work of great pastors were frequently painted in triumphalistic hues. Today, of course, that is less and less common. Nowadays the tellers of stories are fonder of Christianity's criminal history. What is altogether lacking, and what no one accepts any longer, not even professors of church history, is a salvation history of Christianity like what Luke ventured for the church's first years. Why has that become so hard?

It is probably because no one dares any longer to speak of the works of God in our day. While it is true that God's deeds continue in history, that they not only happened in biblical times, we scarcely dare to speak of them now. That is certainly connected to the fact that no individual can afford to offer such an interpretation of history. There is a need for experienced theologians who can say, against the background of faithful communities, and even in company with them: "The Lord has done this." When Paul and Barnabas returned to Antioch from their first missionary journey

> they called the church together and related all that God had done with them and how God had opened a door of faith for the gentiles. (Acts 14:27)

Who among us could dare to offer such an interpretation of history today? The objection would immediately be raised: that kind of language is evangelical; it smells of fundamentalism; that kind of biblicist attitude is definitively not allowed any longer.

God's Incognito

Certainly there is also a more profound reason why interpreting history in terms of faith is so difficult for us. In what is probably the most magnificent book he wrote, namely, his *Introduction to Christianity*, Joseph Ratzinger spoke of "Christian structures." He lists six such Christian structures that are to be found everywhere.[5] He calls one of them "The Law of Disguise." There he says that God is not only the Wholly Other. God is also the absolutely hidden, the unrecognizable. Whenever God appears it is in such lowliness that God is easily overlooked, almost impossible to recognize. God is revealed only by appearing to disappear in lowliness:

> First there is the Earth, a mere nothing in the cosmos, which was to be the point of divine activity in the cosmos. Then comes Israel, a cipher among the powers, which was to be the point of [God's] appearance in the world. Then comes Nazareth, again a cipher within Israel, which was to be the point of [God's] definitive arrival. Then at the end there is the Cross, on which a man was to hang, a man whose life had been a failure; yet this was to be the point at which one can actually touch God. Finally there is the Church, the questionable shape of our history, which claims to be the abiding site of [God's] revelation.[6]

Thus, according to Ratzinger, God's law of disguise also applies to the church. God is also in the church—and thereby also in what the church changes in the world—invisible, hidden, unrecognizable, and self-revealed, here too in lowliness.

Now let me attempt to apply those statements to our question. It can then be seen that even when decisive changes happen in the world through Jesus' resurrection, through the church, through Christians, that agency remains disguised, hidden under the veil of lowliness, obscured from nonbelievers and not recognizable by them.

To put it still more clearly: as in my Easter sermon thirty years ago, I am still profoundly convinced that Easter and the Easter faith of Christians have changed the world and history at depth and continue

[5] Joseph Ratzinger, *Introduction to Christianity*, trans. J. R. Foster (San Francisco: Ignatius Press, 2004).

[6] Ratzinger, *Introduction to Christianity*, 256, alt.

to change them. But those radical changes, if they are genuine and not staged, remain disguised. They can be suppressed, misunderstood, denied, and reinterpreted, or they may remain completely hidden from nonbelievers.

To take one example: The French Revolution proclaimed freedom, equality, and fraternity/sorority. Let us set aside for the moment the fact that from the beginning it trod those magnificent demands under foot. Even so: those three magnificent words were shouted aloud in the world. But even today they are identified as achievements of the Enlightenment, of European emancipation, of the modern history of freedom. It is denied that they have anything to do with Christianity and instead they are attributed to the modern freedom movements. But in reality those three things have their deepest roots in the Bible and the people of God.

Israel's exodus from Egypt was a road to freedom, an emancipation from an enslaving, freedom-destroying state. It is precisely in that sense that even today Jews and Christians remember and celebrate the exodus as their "foundational event." The apparently secular modern history of freedom was altogether based on and sustained by the memory of Israel's exodus. That is abundantly clear from the history of the English Revolution under Cromwell and of the American Revolution—liberation from the power of England. In both revolutions, politicians explicitly referred to the biblical exodus.

Likewise, the concept of equality is biblical. Ultimately it rests on the knowledge that human beings are created in the "image" of God (Gen 1:27). Even though the ancient Stoa spoke of the equality of all human beings, it was still something entirely different when, in the earliest Christian communities, women and men, slaves and free, Jews and Greeks sat together, with equal rights, at the table of the Eucharist.

What about the concept of brotherhood/sisterhood? It comes from the biblical book of Deuteronomy, the basis from which the language of Jewish and Christian community stems.

But all that is absent from the minds of most intellectuals in our time. It has been and is simply suppressed. It just cannot be true that the most profound roots of the Western history of freedom are to be found in the Bible.

Probably it has to be that way. God remains hidden, and so do God's deeds. So also the radical changes that happened in the world because of Good Friday and Easter remain secret. They only open themselves to the astonished eyes of faith.

Paul, who dared in Romans 11 to speak of the fact that one day the Gentile church will bring Israel to belief because, at some time, Israel will see that the church lives messianically—that therefore the Messiah must already have come—Paul, who dared that unbelievable interpretation and theology of history, concludes it with statements that show the limits of such daring:

> O the depth of the riches and wisdom and knowledge of God! How unsearchable are his judgments and how inscrutable his ways! "For who has known the mind of the Lord? Or who has been his counselor?" "Or who has given a gift to him, to receive a gift in return?" For from him and through him and to him are all things. To him be glory forever. Amen. (Rom 11:33-36)

Only those who believe, who give all honor to God, can recognize God's ways in history, can grasp how profoundly Easter has changed the world. But even believers—as Paul says, deeply shocked by the audacity of his chapters on Israel—even they find God's ways in history unfathomable.

So, did Easter change anything? Most certainly. It transformed the world to its depths, and since then it continually transforms history. It does so whenever Christians believe in Jesus' resurrection and, through their lives, become witnesses to Easter. Theoretical speculations about Christian alteration of history make no sense. Only one thing is powerful: an Easter existence. We ourselves decide whether Easter has changed the world or not—and we decide by means of our own lives.

10

Easter and the Enlightenment

Every year again, the feast of Easter comes and sets the media in confusion. Their cluelessness is even greater than at Christmas: then at least family and the sweetness of a child come into play. The possibilities are much fewer at Easter. There are all too many treatments of the Easter promenade from Goethe's *Faust*, and the Easter egg, its origins and history, has already been exhausted as a subject. What should we do?

Warmed-over Rationalism

Gerd Lüdemann, professor of theology in Göttingen, has rushed to the aid of the media. He wrote a book on Jesus' resurrection in time for the feast, denying that there was such a thing.[1] The tomb was not empty; it was full. The stories of the women at the tomb—late legends! The appearances of the Risen One—nothing but terrified reactions, projections of the unconscious, or, in the case of the five hundred sisters and brothers who, according to Paul, had seen the risen Jesus (1 Cor 15:6), a collective hallucination driven by "animal instincts and emotions"! And Paul on the road to Damascus? Well, he was stricken by a hysterical blindness that was evoked by his journey. Besides, he had a Christ-complex.

[1] Gerd Lüdemann, *Die Auferstehung Jesu. Historie, Erfahrung, Theologie* (Göttingen: Vandenhoeck & Ruprecht, 1994). English: *The Resurrection of Jesus: History, Experience, Theology*, trans. John Bowden (Minneapolis: Fortress Press, 1994). See also his *Die Auferweckung Jesu von den Toten. Ursprung und Geschichte einer Selbsttäuschung* (Springe: Zu Klampen, 2001), and *The Resurrection of Christ: A Historical Enquiry* (Amherst, NY: Prometheus, 2004).

Certainly Lüdemann does not want to assert that the Easter accounts in the Gospels are of no value. Their historical core is to be found in impressions and feelings that should be taken seriously. He refers to these feelings as "intimations of a Beyond" or sudden grasping of what "life" is. And what the two disciples in Luke 24:13-35 experienced was something like "the experience of eternity."

Lüdemann's theses, including those about the historical Jesus,[2] are old-hat. They derive from the early period of the Enlightenment when people were only prepared to accept as historically plausible what, in principle, could be repeated at any time and could therefore, in principle, be possible for anyone to see and hear. Hence Lüdemann's reductionism. Anyone may ultimately shudder at the mystery of life, and intimations of eternity are everywhere.

The methods used by Lüdemann in his attempt to interpret the resurrection texts in terms of detached religious experiences have nothing to do with historical honesty and theological integrity. Still, he succeeded in one respect: the Easter feast in the year in question acquired a whiff of greater genuineness than at other times. Suddenly it was about more than harmless feature articles. It was necessary to take a stand.

Klaus Berger, then professor of New Testament theology in Heidelberg, did that with the utmost clarity. He published a review of Lüdemann's book in the *Frankfurter Allgemeine Zeitung*,[3] and a little later, in the Easter edition, presented a more basic essay titled "Die andere Wahrnehmung."[4] Berger's Easter essay clarifies an aspect of distinguishing what is Christian. Hence it is worthwhile to read him at more length, but at the same time to carry his thinking further.

[2] Gerd Lüdemann, *The Great Deception: And What Jesus Really Said and Did* (Amherst, NY: Prometheus, 1999).

[3] Klaus Berger, "43 Witwen und 19 Witwer widerlegen die Bibel. Wie der Göttinger Neutestamentler Gerd Lüdemann mit der Auferstehung Jesu fertig wird" [43 Widows and 19 Widowers refute the Bible. How the Göttingen New Testament scholar Gerd Lüdemann deals with Jesus' resurrection], *FAZ* 30 (March 1994).

[4] Klaus Berger, "Die andere Wahrnehmung. War das Grab leer? Weshalb Rationalisten und Fundamentalisten an der Osterbotschaft scheitern" [The Different Perception: Was the Tomb Empty? Why Rationalists and Fundamentalists Run Aground on the Easter Message], *FAZ* 77 (April 2, 1994).

Preliminary Decisions

Klaus Berger rightly points out that prior decisions play a role in a great many statements about Jesus' resurrection. If it is taken as a given that our natural-historical image of the world excludes any form of physical resurrection, it only remains to explain away the substance of the Easter message. In fact, since the advent of critical, liberal interpretation of the Bible that has happened again and again. The modes, of course, have shifted.[5]

For older Enlightenment scholars it was obvious that Jesus was a simple rabbi whose divinization had begun with the invention of the Easter events. His tomb was empty only because his disciples had removed the body or had mistakenly confused his grave with one that had not yet been used. Or else it was that Jesus had only appeared to die and, after reawakening, had swiftly and silently departed, going far away, possibly to India.

Since David Friedrich Strauß,[6] however, those who disputed Jesus' resurrection no longer felt satisfied with rationalistic hypotheses of apparent death, theft, and confusion. There was not much discussion any more about visions and the tomb; instead, Easter was simply declared to be a myth—told not on the basis of real events but arising solely and uniquely out of the disciples' belief. And what, for Strauß, was a myth? In the words of Marius Reiser: simply anything "that breaks out of the frame of ordinary experience and natural laws, everything supernatural, and every religious exaltation of a historical person."[7]

Of course it still always depended on determining the "message" of these mythic texts. Here again, modes shifted over time. Some said that the Easter faith is the recognition that God is on the side of all those who are weak, suffering, and deprived of rights. Others said more simply that Easter is the insight that we are altogether accepted by God.

[5] For what follows see the solid presentation by Marius Reiser, *Kritische Geschichte der Jesusforschung. Von Kelsos und Origenes bis heute*, SBS 235 (Stuttgart: Katholisches Bibelwerk, 2015).

[6] David Friedrich Strauß, *Das Leben Jesu, kritisch bearbeitet*, 2 vols. (Tübingen: Osiander, 1835, 1836). There are many editions of this work in English. See, e.g., *The Life of Jesus Critically Examined*, trans. George Eliot, 3 vols. (London: Continuum, 2005; original publication 1892).

[7] Reiser, *Kritische Geschichte*, 44.

When the Easter accounts have been reduced that far, the degree to which false presuppositions have entered the picture must be obvious. How could it come to this: that the Easter event is reduced to a simple insight about God? Why is a genuine action by God on the dead Jesus thought impossible? Isn't this an effect of the prior decision that, really, a human being is a spirit, a self? Is it true that only the human spirit is worthy of God, and ultimately God cannot have anything to do with matter? But on the basis of such presuppositions Christianity is divorced from history and church and becomes a religion of the individual and of one's inner subjectivity.

From such arrogance toward creation it is then only a small step to absolutizing human knowledge and equating the individual spirit with the Holy Spirit. Then Easter faith is, logically, nothing more than a new, autonomous understanding of what is human. To this Klaus Berger rightly says:

> The "Word of God" always reaches its goal first of all in corporeality; God wants to be recognized here, on this field, and see his commandment followed concretely and physically. Hence the way we talk about resurrection always has something to do with our particular understanding of body. Whoever reduces the resurrection to one's pure internal self-concept separates Christianity from the concrete and physical following of the commandments and the equally concrete community of the church.[8]

At first glance that all seems to be leading us away from the question of Jesus' resurrection, and yet it is precisely here that the preliminary decisions about faith in Jesus' real, physical resurrection are made. It is no accident that Berger speaks in this connection about the "physical following of the commandments." He has thus arrived at the place where the Old Testament, Judaism, and obviously the New Testament all make essential distinctions.

Physical Redemption

Let me go deeper, in light of the Old and New Testaments, into what Klaus Berger only hints at: for the Old Testament and Judaism,

[8] Berger, "Die andere Wahrnehmung."—Trans.

redemption is a comprehensive event. Redemption encompasses everything: soul, body, environment, history, all of life. That understanding of redemption is concentrated in the Torah. It is instruction for Israel, a gracious gift. It is given so that all of life may be turned toward God and thus liberated. Nothing is excluded; everything is included within its power to design and shape—from credit for poor Israelites (Deut 15:7-11) to protection for the enemy's trees in wartime (Deut 20:19-20) and the prohibition against surrendering escaped slaves (Deut 23:15-16) to the requirement that parapets be placed on roof terraces (Deut 22:8).

Anyone who supposes that the young church abandoned this concrete and vivid understanding of redemption by spiritualizing it has fallen into a serious and consequential error. The first Christians were Jews, just as Jesus was. They knew that Jesus had laid hands on the sick; he had freed those who were possessed; he had traveled to Jerusalem for the Passover feast and ridden into the city on a donkey; he had told a blind person to wash his eyes in the pool of Siloam; he had reclined at table with his disciples, washed their feet, and shared bread with them. The whole person was always included: not just her spirituality, but her body as well.

It is only in bodiliness that God attains any goal. Only those who take this Jewish-Christian axiom seriously and live within its light can approach the resurrection texts with the right pre-understanding. One then has a different understanding of reality—of the whole, undivided reality of the world, which God means to redeem.

What Does "Really" Mean?

Only when that is clear can we take another step and ask what "reality" is, after all. Klaus Berger makes that question central to his essay: "Can the worldview of modern physics guarantee that it is the only approach to what one may truly understand as reality?" I would add: the natural sciences can only deal with things that are measurable and—to quote a famous saying of Galileo—they can attempt to make measurable what is thus far immeasurable. This methodological self-limitation was and is altogether successful, but it touches only a fragment of reality. Other spheres of human life, in fact the most important, resist the objectifying methods of natural science and of all the exact sciences. When discussing this complex question I always have to recall an anecdote about Albert Einstein:

> Einstein was addressing a select group on the subject of his theory of relativity when a member of the audience stood up and jeered: "My sound human understanding rejects everything that cannot be seen." Einstein replied calmly: "Then please come up here and place your sound human understanding on the table!"

In fact: human understanding, human dignity, responsibility, freedom, love, longing, beauty—the greatest human matters—cannot ultimately be measured and sized, even though there are measurable elements in all of them. From this point of view the assertion that today's worldview does not admit of the idea of a physical resurrection is simply a violation of boundaries that has nothing to do with scientific method. Nothing forces us to restrict reality in such a way that Jesus cannot really have risen from the dead.

Obviously Jesus' resurrection is not a historical event in space and time, as his death and burial were historical happenings. Jesus' resurrection surpasses our earthly space and time, but it is not less real because of that. It is related to history because in it Jesus' own history arrives at its fulfillment, but it is itself not an earthly event. It is related to matter because in it matter is transformed and redeemed, but it is not the restoration of a body to earthly life.

A Different Perception

In his essay Klaus Berger uses the concept of "a different perception," which gives his work its title. He says:

> The Easter events in the Bible—like other biblical experiences of visions and miracles, transfigurations and heavenly journeys—derive from a different culture of perception. It is a matter of different approaches to what really is. . . . Anyone who thinks that our way of perceiving, as well as the scope of all that may be regarded as real, is generally applicable, that scientific standards of proof are the criteria for each and every reality, is living in the sphere of a grievous and presumptuous cultural imperialism.[9]

That is correct, for a start. Genuine reality cannot be limited to what is subject to scientific methods of numbering and measuring. It is

[9] Berger, "Die andere Wahrnehmung."—Trans.

equally impossible to define from the outset what human perception is capable of. The Easter accounts in the Gospels speak very realistically about seeing and hearing, even of the disciples' touching and sensing the Risen One. Every interpreter must take that seriously and must not declare it from the outset to be unacceptable: as myth, as community legend, as primitive invention, or as symbolic speech. What Gerd Lüdemann altogether lacks is respect for the text, for what is strange and resistant in it. To immediately co-opt a text by trimming it to the point at which it fits within one's own tiny worldview is indeed a fetid example of cultural imperialism.

At the same time, I have questions for Klaus Berger, too. It is certainly true that other cultures exhibit very different ways of perceiving than our own. But that must not prevent us from applying the critical probes of reason and theological insight to those ways of perception that are foreign to us. I cannot just say that visions and heavenly journeys are purely a different method of perception, one that is lacking in our cultural circles and that I simply must respect. Obviously I have to respect them, but may I not scrutinize them—and do so with the appropriate respect and recognizing the depth dimension they possess?[10]

To put it concretely: I may thus take seriously the fact that in appearances, visions, auditory phenomena, mystical phenomena, and the whole range of things that are called "transcendental" or "extrasensory" there are things in play that are, to some degree, accessible to psychology. Must I then exclude the possibility that there are natural structures that are operative in the Easter experiences—more precisely, in the visions of the Easter witnesses?

God, in acting on human persons, does not make them passive objects of that action; in such cases God acts with and through them. That is: God does not eliminate the structures, laws, designs, and potentialities of the world; rather, God acts precisely *with* their help and in cooperation with them. Hence a genuine vision is both: entirely the product of the human, and altogether the work of God.

A genuine vision is, first of all, a human product. It is the bringing-into-play of one's history, one's past, one's experiences, one's knowledge, one's hopes, one's imaginings—and all of it, of course, in an unconscious process that the person in question cannot control and

[10] I have treated this subject at length in my book, *Jesus of Nazareth: What He Wanted, Who He Was*, trans. Linda M. Maloney (Collegeville, MN: Liturgical Press, 2015), 288–307.

in which period style and culturally conditioned forms of ideas play an important role.

The time is long since ripe for us to again honor visions as a genuine human possibility. If we were to do that we could, in fact, also take them seriously as a way by which God could be self-revealed to human beings within the structure of what is human, and nowhere else. For as every vision is wholly and completely a human work, so it can at the same time be wholly and entirely the work of God, who then makes use of the productive imaginative power of the human to communicate God's self in the midst of history.[11]

The principle of the theology of grace, undisputed today, that God's action does not suppress those of human beings but instead sets them free must be applied to the inner structure of the Easter visions. This means that the disciples' Easter experiences can, theologically speaking, be regarded really and truly as appearances of the Risen One in which God has revealed the Son, powerful and in his whole glory (Gal 1:16)—and yet, psychologically, as visions in which the imaginative power of the disciples constituted the visual perception of the Risen One. The two are by no means mutually exclusive. It is only when one understands the Easter appearances in the way just described that one takes them seriously, both theologically and anthropologically. This aspect, which is ultimately connected to a rational doctrine of grace, is something I find lacking in Klaus Berger's writing.

Another thing I miss: the idea that we encounter a different culture of perception in the Bible and in other places where it is formulated is indeed quite correct. But Berger should at least have mentioned that this different perception is still possible today or, better, that it can happen today wherever Christians live their faith in the biblical sense. Now I want to expand on that somewhat.

The Basis of All Easter Experience

Even today, everyone can share in the Easter experience of the first witnesses and can stand within the same field of awareness in which Jesus' disciples then stood. That is the basis, the ground of all Easter

[11] What I speak of here is not to be understood as isolated communication, singular intervention by God. God communicates to the world uninterruptedly and everywhere but is not perceived everywhere and by all.

experience. This commonality, this communal basis that profoundly unites us with Jesus' disciples and the Easter witnesses of that time is what I would call baptismal grace or the baptismal experience.

After all, the Easter narratives in the Gospels are not everyday texts. They are based on real experiences of the Risen One by the first Easter witnesses, people who had previously left everything to follow Jesus and ventured on a new way of life. The Easter narratives were handed down in the circle of the disciples who had left everything behind and dared, with Jesus, the new thing of the reign of God. They were then handed on further through believing communities. Therefore they are all directly or indirectly connected to the earliest Christian baptismal experience.[12] The fact that by the second century CE Easter had already become the liturgical *locus* of baptism was only a natural consequence and is reflected even today in the Christian celebration of the Easter Vigil.

In general we are too little aware of what a profound watershed baptism constituted in the lives of the early Christians. Baptism was not only an impressive ritual to which one submitted. It was not only an "induction" into the mysteries of Christianity. It was entry into the new way of life called "community," which was fundamentally different from the life forms of the pagan world. Baptism therefore always meant exodus. It was a change of rulers. It was a turning away from the gods and demons of pagan society and entry into the church as the space of Christ's rule.

It was all quite concrete: the candidate for baptism had to offer a guarantee representing the seriousness of her or his repentance. Candidates had to participate in a relatively long process of baptismal instruction that carefully introduced them to Jewish-Christian ways of discernment and the life form of faith. The ancient church assumed with the utmost confidence that the Christian life of the baptismal candidates did not originate with themselves but had to be learned. It also took into account that evil is powerful and every foot of the reign of God had to be fought for.

[12] Of course, that does not mean that all Jesus' disciples were baptized, before or after Easter. It signifies that they were already located within the same field of experience that would later be characteristic of primitive Christian baptism. That field included repentance, discipleship, and exodus from the past.

Therefore the instruction of catechumens and baptism itself were accompanied by sign-actions that expressed Christians' struggle: exorcisms, anointings, solemn renunciations of Satan and his pomps. Certainly Christians also discovered—and this was the fundamental experience of baptism—that in the church, in the sphere of Christ's rule, they received a new life.

Baptism as New Creation

The inbreaking of the radically new thing into an old, antiquated world is a basic idea in eschatology. When Christian instruction says that in baptism the old human being is stripped off and a new one is put on (cf. Col 3:9-10), that shows the degree to which baptism was experienced as an eschatological event, an unearned and undeserved "new creation." Paul had written of baptism: "[I]f anyone is in Christ, there is a new creation: everything old has passed away; look, new things have come into being!" (2 Cor 5:17). Consequently, nothing in the life of the newly baptized could remain as it once was. A good many kinds of pagan activity were no longer possible for Christians. Attending gladiatorial contests and blood sports was frowned upon; taking part in pagan processions and displays was forbidden, as was participation in public meals and banquets—for example, on imperial holidays. We could extend this list of Christian refusals to cooperate much, much farther.

But what was more important was that the newly baptized were incorporated into a community in which people joined their lives together, bore one another's burdens, and took responsibility for one another. What the early church called *agapē*, being no longer for oneself but for God and the sisters and brothers in the communities, was thus a radical change, a new life in contrast to pagan existence.

Being Brought from Death to Life

This radical change is most profoundly reflected in Paul's baptismal theology. Quite certainly it was not lived everywhere in the early church, but at least it formulated the difference between the new life and mere religion, and it made clear to all Christians what was offered them. Paul says bluntly that Christians have died in baptism—they have died because, through baptism, they are incorporated in

God's saving action in and for Christ. Those who are baptized die with Christ and are buried with him. They die to the old world that is ruled by the power of sin. And as Christ was raised, so also the baptized already live a new life with Christ. Although, as before, they are "mortal bodies," they have already "been brought from death to life" (Rom 6:12-13). The new existence given to them is life in the Christian community.

For Paul those are not empty assertions. Just as the confession of faith that was entrusted to the baptizands in early Christian baptismal rites spoke of Christ's dying and rising, so Paul's vision of the lives of believers is very concrete. They live within the space of Christ's rule: concretely in the space of the church, where they have the opportunity to live free of the power of sin and to be, henceforward, free for God and God's cause.

From that point of view Klaus Berger is altogether correct when he speaks in his essay of a "different perception." No historian, no sociologist, no psychologist can have that perception unless, in faith, they surrender their existence to the new thing that has come with Christ. The experience of baptism, of "being in Christ" that I have tried to picture, is another, a fully different kind of experience, one closed to common knowledge. Therefore exegetes may not apply irrelevant categories or the average experiences in our society to the resurrection texts. They must, instead, bring these texts closer to the level of experience for which they were written: namely, the experiential level of faith, the ground of believing experience of community, the basis of an existence lived in and through baptism.

To repeat: the Easter narratives stem from witnesses who followed Jesus and invested their whole lives in him and his message. Their narratives were heard and handed on in a church in which conversion, baptism, and exit from the former life were the fundamental realities—but that means a life in which there was the experience of dying with Christ and of "new creation" and "new life."

That experience—dying to the old world and its powers and entering already into a new life—is something from which the church has never parted. Those who do not live in that experiential space, who have never experienced what exodus means, have never sensed what it means to surrender one's own desires and plans, have never sensed the joy of repentance and conversion in their own bodies—they are incompetent to interpret the Easter texts correctly. They simply cannot understand them. They will suppress them or even hate them.

Those who want to talk about Jesus' resurrection cannot do it only from a desk. The question whether Jesus has really risen from the dead and has appeared to his own is something that can be decided only with one's life.

11

How Paul Talks to His Communities

How we would have loved to be present when the community in Philippi gathered in the home of Lydia, the dealer in purple,[1] when the Torah and the prophets were read aloud, when Paul explained the Scriptures, interpreting them in light of Jesus Christ, when he then discussed concrete problems in the Philippi congregation, with lively participation by the whole assembly, and when he admonished the community to be "of the same mind, having the same love, being in full accord and of one mind" (Phil 2:2). How exciting would it have been to be there and to hear Paul speak in his own voice!

Alas, the necessary time-travel into the past is not yet technically possible,[2] and unfortunately no recordings of Paul's voice have been preserved. Or maybe there have been? In some other form? Basically, the authentic letters of Paul—Romans, 1 and 2 Corinthians, Galatians, 1 Thessalonians, those to the Philippians and Philemon—are extremely vivid examples of how Paul talked to his communities. Why is that?

Paul's letters are something special. They are clearly different from the letters written by other people in antiquity—and not only because

[1] There is much in favor of the idea that the house of Lydia was the gathering place of the community in Philippi: cf. Acts 16:15, 40. Moreover, *syzygos* in Phil 4:3 could refer to Lydia. This is argued, with good support, by Peter Eckstein, *Gemeinde, Brief und Heilsbotschaft. Ein phänomenologischer Vergleich zwischen Paulus und Epikur*, HBS 42 (Freiburg: Herder, 2004), 190–91.

[2] Here, of course, I am thinking of H. G. Wells's utopian novel, *The Time Machine* (1895). Wells's machine, however, transfers people into the future, not the past. Other authors have then pursued time-travel into the past, in utopian or dystopian tales.

Paul's letters are much longer.[3] Most ancient letters were as short as the little one to Philemon, that is, only what a single sheet of papyrus could hold.[4]

But why were Paul's letters longer? Simply because they are snippets of life! In his letters Paul mostly writes as passionately as if he were in the presence of the community he is addressing—and it appears that Paul often talked at great length! Once, in Troas, he spoke until midnight, so that a young man named Eutychus, who was sitting on the windowsill, went to sleep and fell out (cf. Acts 20:7-12). Paul's letters still reflect those long speeches. He has the community before his eyes; he talks with them; he hears their objections, sees their questioning expressions, and allows himself to get so caught up in what he is saying that his sentence constructions often go off the rails.

One example of such passionate speech is Galatians 2:1-10. New Testament scholar Marius Reiser has analyzed that piece of text very closely and shows what a wealth of parentheses, afterthoughts, shifts in construction, and incongruities it contains.[5] Unfortunately, we can only study all that in the Greek text. Our translations mainly try for a smooth reading, which is a shame since we are robbed of the feeling that what we have before us is a piece of highly vivid and emotional speech. Marius Reiser says, quite correctly: "Paul writes in such a fresh and natural way that in many places it is possible to hear him speak, even to sense when he draws breath. There is scarcely anything comparable in ancient literature."[6]

Paul can positively gather around him the people he has in view. When a member of the community in Corinth acts against both Roman and Jewish law[7] and all moral sensibility by living in concubinage with his stepmother (his father has evidently died), Paul

[3] Certainly there are exceptions. These always occur when letters are basically not private but take the form of tracts, as is the case with the letters of Epicurus. Cf. Eckstein, *Gemeinde*.

[4] Within the New Testament the letter to Philemon offers a good idea of how short an ancient letter normally was, as do 2 and 3 John; another example is the letter to the community in Antioch in Acts 15:23-29.

[5] Marius Reiser, "Paulus als Stilist," *Svensk Exegetisk Årbeitsbok* 66 (2001): 151–65, at 158–61.

[6] Marius Reiser in a lecture entitled "Das Neue Testament als Buch der Christenheit."

[7] Cf. Lev 18:8; 20:11; Deut 23:1; 27:20.

orders that the man be expelled from the community. But it is not his sole decision. He knows that the exclusion must be done in concert with the members. And when that does not happen—and Paul is far away in Ephesus—he at least gathers the whole Corinthian community "in spirit":

> It is actually reported that there is sexual immorality among you and the sort of sexual immorality that is not found even among gentiles, for a man is living with his father's wife. And you are arrogant! Should you not rather have mourned, so that he who has done this would have been removed from among you? For I, though absent in body, am present in spirit, and as if present I have already pronounced judgment in the name of the Lord Jesus on the man who has done such a thing. When you are assembled and my spirit is present with the power of our Lord Jesus, you are to hand this man over to Satan for the destruction of the flesh, so that the spirit may be saved in the day of the Lord. (1 Cor 5:1-5)

"Handing [someone] over to Satan" means—in that he must live outside the Christian community—surrendering him to the powers of evil,[8] so that he may come to his senses and repent.[9]

This text is an extreme example of the intensity with which Paul is connected to his communities. As he is dictating the letter to the Corinthians he is *in* the congregation, is gathered with them, speaks to them, and suffers profoundly at the condition of the community that has simply accepted the outrage without doing anything about it.

So we do not need either a time machine that will take us back into the past or sound recordings. We have only to read Paul's letters

[8] Wolfgang Schrage is correct when he writes: "Someone who is excluded from the community falls back into the hands of the destroying powers." *Der erste Brief an die Korinther*, KEK VII 1 (Zürich: Benziger; Neukirchen-Vluyn: Neukirchener Verlag, 1991), 375—Trans.

[9] Certainly the meaning of "handing over to Satan" is disputed. There are also authors who regard exclusion from the community as a curse that will cause the man to die. If that is the fact, however, it is not clear how "his spirit" can be saved. Should we, in that case, regard his death as a penitential and reparative punishment? One representative of the curse theory is Hans Conzelmann, *Der erste Brief an die Korinther*, KEK, 11th ed. (Göttingen: Vandenhoeck & Ruprecht, 1969), 115–17. (Cf. idem, *1 Corinthians: A Commentary on the First Epistle to the Corinthians*, trans. James W. Leitch, Hermeneia [Philadelphia: Fortress Press, 1975], 94.)

sympathetically—and then we are already in the midst of the communities of Paul's time.

Still, Paul's letters reveal something else that distinguishes them from most ancient letters. They are not only longer: they also show us a person who has opened his heart so widely that we can see into it. Thus in the second letter to the community in Corinth we read: "I wrote you out of much distress and anguish of heart and with many tears, not to cause you grief but to let you know the abundant love that I have for you" (2 Cor 2:4). A little later he says:

> We have spoken frankly to you Corinthians; our heart is wide open to you. There is no restriction in our affections but only in yours. In return—I speak as to [my] children—open wide your hearts also. (2 Cor 6:11-13)

At the very beginning of this agitated and often even imploring letter[10] Paul had said: "We do not want you to be ignorant, brothers and sisters, of the affliction we experienced in Asia, for we were so utterly, unbearably crushed that we despaired of life itself" (2 Cor 1:8). That kind of language is highly unusual in antiquity, at any rate in letters, in which one did not so readily allow a glimpse into one's heart. Letter writers held to forms and formulas, remained disciplined and restrained, valued calm and composure.[11] We only have to compare the highly detached style of 2 and 3 John with Paul's letters, especially the two written to Corinth as well as Galatians and Philippians. Paul reveals all his emotions to his communities; he opens his heart.

Let me offer just one tiny detail to illustrate this.[12] In the four volumes of "Discourses" by the philosopher Epictetus (ca. 50–138) the word "heart" appears only once. In Paul's letter to the Romans it occurs fifteen times. You may chuckle at such a statistical comparison. Such numbers are really squishy. But if you page through the fifteen passages in Romans you will quickly stumble over 9:1-3, where Paul

[10] It is possible that 2 Corinthians is a composite of a number of shorter letters by Paul to the community in Corinth, but that is disputed. I need not go into that question here.

[11] A characteristic example is the letter Plutarch wrote to his wife in order to console her on the death of their daughter. This famous letter contains beautiful philosophical reflections, but almost nothing of a personal nature.

[12] I am grateful to Prof. Dr. Marius Reiser for the reference to Epictetus.

mourns the fact that only a small number of the Jewish people, to whom he himself belongs, believe in Christ. He writes:

> I am speaking the truth in Christ—I am not lying; my conscience confirms it by the Holy Spirit—I have great sorrow and unceasing anguish in my heart. For I could wish that I myself were accused and cut off from Christ for the sake of my own brothers and sisters, my own flesh and blood. (Rom 9:1-3)

When we read words such as those we sense Paul's passion. I do not hesitate to use a cliché: he wrote his letters "with his heart's blood." It is truly rewarding to read these letters intently while keeping in mind one question: How does he really talk to his communities? Then Paul will quite naturally show himself to us as a pastor, and it will be clear that Paul not only opened his heart and fought passionately over the truth of the gospel; he also relied on the rationality of his congregations and did not hesitate to argue at length, to give reasons, to explain and clarify.

The Whole Range of Human Language

Human language is capable of an unbelievable number of things. It can inform, report, narrate, and describe. It can clarify, expound, discuss, instruct, and justify. It can lament, accuse, rebuke, encourage, correct, implore. It can command and forbid, mandate and order. It can warn, comfort, console, praise, thank, confess, eulogize—and a great deal more.

We find all those forms of speech in Paul's letters. He plays on the whole keyboard of language, and in the process the form and intention can shift rapidly. Take, for example, the eloquent and moving conclusion to 1 Thessalonians, where Paul writes:

> We appeal to you, brothers and sisters, to respect those who labor among you and have charge of you in the Lord and admonish you; esteem them very highly in love because of their work. Be at peace among yourselves. And we urge you, brothers and sisters, to admonish the idlers, encourage the fainthearted, help the weak, be patient with all of them. See that none of you repays evil for evil, but always seek to do good to one another and to all. Rejoice always, pray without ceasing, give thanks in all circumstances, for this is the will of God in

Christ Jesus for you. Do not quench the Spirit. Do not despise prophecies, but test everything; hold fast to what is good; abstain from every form of evil.

May the God of peace himself sanctify you entirely, and may your spirit and soul and body be kept sound and blameless at the coming of our Lord Jesus Christ. The one who calls you is faithful, and he will do this.

Brothers and sisters, pray for us.

Greet all the brothers and sisters with a holy kiss. I solemnly command you by the Lord that this letter be read to all the brothers and sisters.

The grace of our Lord Jesus Christ be with you. (1 Thess 5:12-28)

This ending of the letter, which takes on a more and more liturgical character as it proceeds,[13] contains the greatest variety of rhetorical forms, almost interwoven and without transition: plea, admonition, promise, consolation, invocation, and a final blessing.

The letter to the Romans offers an especially beautiful example of how Paul could shift between rhetorical forms—indeed, how they could suddenly reverse themselves. In chapters 9–11 Paul reflected at length on Israel. Why had a great number of the people of God not come to believe in Christ? The apostle seeks an answer, and its boldness is still not acknowledged or appreciated by many Christians today:

That most of Israel did not come to believe, says Paul, led to salvation's reaching the Gentiles. That salvation happened because of Israel's error (Rom 11:11). So God had to be behind this hardening of Israel. Was it God's plan? Did God interfere in history? Did God personally harden Israel and make it obdurate in order that salvation might reach the Gentiles (11:7-10)?

Paul thinks still further: If salvation reaches the Gentiles everywhere, throughout the world, that very thing could lead Israel to become jealous (11:11, 14). To put it in our own terms: if Israel sees vital Gentile-Christian communities it may understand that Messiah has already come—because Israel will find messianic communities throughout the world. That, in turn, must bring not-yet-believing Israel to accept the Messiah—and so Israel will reach "full inclusion" (11:12), that is, its full number in faith. But if all Israel comes to believe,

[13] The kiss of peace that is recommended at the end of some of Paul's letters (cf. 1 Cor 16:20; 2 Cor 13:12) was part of the liturgy.

that will have consequences for the whole world. Paul is evidently thinking at this point of the great pilgrimage to Zion that was promised by the prophets.[14] So he can write: "For if their [Israel's] rejection is the reconciliation of the world [i.e., the Gentile world], what will their acceptance be but life from the dead?" (11:15). But that means that then Israel will live up to the role originally planned for it, and it will be reconciliation and salvation for the whole world. So all Israel will be saved (11:26), and through Israel "life will emerge from death" for the whole world. Paul summarizes this altogether audacious view of salvation history: "For God has imprisoned all in disobedience [in order to] be merciful to all" (11:32).

Was that only airy speculation? Or was it taking seriously the promises received through the prophets and, at the same time, a Spirit-filled theology of history that very accurately predicted the breathtaking mission to the Gentiles that was then taking place? In Paul's view it was most certainly a legitimate theology of history. But in formulating it—and this is my focus here—he himself was terrified at the possibility of arrogating to himself the right to peek at God's cards. Suddenly his language veers. He draws back, corrects, relativizes everything he has said and subjects it to the caveat of the inscrutability of God's ways:

> O the depth of the riches and wisdom and knowledge of God! How unsearchable are his judgments and how inscrutable his ways! "For who has known the mind of the Lord? Or who has been his counselor?" "Or who has given a gift to him, to receive a gift in return?" For from him and through him and to him are all things. To him be the glory forever. Amen. (11:33-36)

Now, in spite of the letter form, we are again in the midst of a community gathering. The proclamatory, knowledge-seeking prophetic language struggling for certainty has become pure praise, and the (fictively present) congregation responds with "Amen."

We can observe similar corrections at many points in the Pauline letters. To take just one more example: at the beginning of the letter

[14] For the motif of the pilgrimage of nations in Romans 9–11, cf. chap. 12, "Was Paul Anti-Jewish?," in this volume.

to the Romans Paul tries to indicate to the community in Rome, still strangers to him, why he wants to visit them. In that context he writes:

> Without ceasing I remember you always in my prayers, asking that by God's will I may somehow at last succeed in coming to you. For I long to see you so that I may share with you some spiritual gift so that you may be strengthened. (Rom 1:9-11)

"Share with you some spiritual gift"—Paul had scarcely dictated those words to his scribe, Tertius,[15] when he sensed that his formulation was not appropriate and might even be impolite. That is not how community should be thought of, with one person conveying spiritual gifts and all the others being mere recipients. Consequently, Paul continues, correcting himself: "or rather so that we may be mutually encouraged by each other's faith, both yours and mine" (Rom 1:12).

Hence mutual exchange of spiritual gifts: Paul strengthens the community in Rome and the community in Rome strengthens Paul. Both at the end of the chapters on Israel and here, at the beginning of Romans, we can see how Paul's language radically shifts. But it can also happen that his language is multilevel from the start: for example, in the brief and very valuable letter to Philemon.[16]

Philemon's enslaved man Onesimus had run away from him and evidently had found in Paul, who was then in prison,[17] a person to whom he could pour out his heart. At the same time he was a great help to Paul. In those times people who were imprisoned were sustained by their relatives and friends; the city-state's only interest was in keeping them from running away. Paul must have had long talks with Onesimus and then had baptized him. He sends him back to Colossae with a letter to Philemon and his household, asking them to forgive Onesimus and receive him back, now as a brother in Christ. Although Onesimus was a great help to Paul in his imprisoned state and Paul would have greatly preferred to have him stay, he sends him back and asks the household only to receive this enslaved man,

[15] Cf. Rom 16:22: "I Tertius, the writer of this letter, greet you in the Lord." Given the technical difficulties of writing on raw papyrus it was uncommon in antiquity for letters to be written by the actual sender. Cf. 1 Cor 16:21.

[16] For the letter to Philemon see esp. Peter Stuhlmacher, *Der Brief an Philemon*, 2nd ed., EKKNT 18 (Zürich: Benziger; Neukirchen-Vluyn: Neukirchener Verlag, 1981).

[17] Probably in Ephesus.

who had probably been "useless" (v. 11), "as you would welcome me" (v. 17)—"no longer as a slave but more than a slave, a beloved brother" (v. 16).

What is decisive in our context is that Paul could order Philemon and his household to do this by virtue of his authority as an apostle, and yet he deliberately does not do so. It is true that he writes this, as he does all of his letters, as an apostle called by Christ and in the full authority of his office—and yet the whole letter is an affectionate and brotherly plea:

> Though I am more than bold enough in Christ to command you to do the right thing, yet I would rather appeal to you on the basis of love—and I, Paul, do this as an old man and now also as a prisoner of Christ Jesus. I am appealing to you for my child, Onesimus, whose father I have become during my imprisonment. (vv. 8-10)

Paul is even prepared to compensate Philemon for any wrong Onesimus has done to him. This is a letter that glows with Paul's full authority and yet is nothing but pure, humble petition. Paul has command of all the possibilities of human language, but he does not play on them. Instead, they emerge from the depths of absolute authenticity.

Richness of Imagery

Paul commands all the nuances of human language—should I bother to demonstrate that he could also speak with extreme irony[18] and even sarcastically?[19] The "fool's speech" in 2 Corinthians 11:16–12:13, in which he defends himself against his opponents, is deadly serious and at the same time supple irony. But I want to look at another aspect of his language: its wealth of imagery.

In Paul's letters we encounter a full range of similes and metaphors. The ancients loved pictorial language, but Israel surpassed them in that. To see this, one only has to read the psalms. Paul's life was shaped

[18] For Pauline irony cf., e.g., 2 Cor 11:19 ("For you gladly put up with fools, being wise yourselves!"); 12:13 ("How have you been worse off than the other churches, except that I myself did not burden you? Forgive me this wrong!").

[19] Sarcasm: e.g., when Paul calls his opponents "super-apostles" (2 Cor 11:5; 12:11) or "false apostles" (2 Cor 11:13) and recommends that they castrate themselves (Gal 5:12; cf. Phil 3:2).

by both: the Greek wealth of imagery and Israel's vivid language. Like the Roman Menenius Agrippa, Paul speaks of the body and its members as an organism in which all the parts are dependent on each other,[20] but he also writes language like that of the prophet Jeremiah about pulling down, building up, and planting.[21]

Paul has been accused of being awkward in his use of imagery. Often enough his images crashed: people point especially to the famous one of the olive tree in Romans 11. There Paul speaks of the noble olive tree of Israel into which God has grafted the Gentiles like the branches of a wild olive (11:17). It is said that the metaphor is really false because, as is well known, agricultural practice is precisely the reverse: shoots of carefully cultivated trees are grafted into strong wild stock.

I, however, do not find this objection the least bit persuasive. Obviously cultivated stock is grafted into wild, and not the reverse. Paul knew that, too. In Romans 11:24 he deliberately describes what is now happening in the history of Israel and the Gentiles as *para physin*, "against nature." In doing so he points to a fundamental principle of salvation history.

When God acts there is a constant disruption of the so-called "normal," natural, foreseeable, and predictable. The whole of salvation history is one of "impossibilities." To take one example: when God chooses someone, the choice mostly falls not on those who are naturally apt. The prophet Samuel thinks God has chosen one of Jesse's tall, imposing sons to be Saul's successor: Eliab, Abinadab, or Shammah. But God, oddly enough, has chosen the youngest, whom no one thinks of: David, who is far away in the fields, herding the sheep (1 Sam 16:1-13).

It had already been the same with Esau and Jacob. God chose not the firstborn but the second: Jacob, not Esau. God chooses whom God will, often against human notions of what is proper. God exalts not the strong and powerful but the lowly. God ministers not to the sated but to the hungry (Luke 1:51-53). Paul has that law of salvation history

[20] The fable of the bodily organs quarrelling with the stomach, which Menenius Agrippa supposedly told the plebeians in 494 BCE after their secession and withdrawal to the Aventine, is found in Livy, *History of Rome* 2.32, in Dionysius of Halicarnassos, *Roman Antiquities* 6.86, and numerous other authors.

[21] Cf. Jer 1:10; Gal 2:18; 1 Cor 3:6.

in mind; in our context he even emphasizes it directly (Rom 9:6-13). Thus no one should accuse Paul of using a false metaphor in his olive-tree comparison. From a biological point of view it is certainly wrong, but Paul is not thinking here in terms of pure biology; his thought has to do with salvation history, and he has the whole Bible on his side.

So let us not carp at Paul's metaphorical language but rejoice in it. We can be glad that we are "God's coworkers," "God's field," "God's building," even "God's temple" (1 Cor 3:9, 17). Consider what it means that in baptism we are "buried with Christ" in order to live with him (Rom 6:1-11), and let us stand astonished that Paul, like a best man at a wedding, leads us "to Christ" (2 Cor 11:2). Let us take in, at depth, that "the whole creation has been groaning together as it suffers together the pains of labor" (Rom 8:22), that it "waits with eager longing for the revealing of the children of God" (Rom 8:19), that we already have "the first fruits of the Spirit" (Rom 8:23), the Holy Spirit who prays in us "with groanings too deep for words" (Rom 8:26), who "searches everything, even the depths of God" (1 Cor 2:10).

These are urgent images Paul uses: believers as runners in a stadium (1 Cor 9:24-25), whom Christ equips with the "breastplate of faith and love and for a helmet the hope of salvation" (1 Thess 5:8), who are still constantly "doing military service" (1 Cor 9:7) and yet are already being led by Christ "in triumphal procession" (2 Cor 2:14).

Still, the most powerful images are those in which Paul has to defend himself and—against his will—speak about his apostolic existence:

> We are afflicted in every way but not crushed, perplexed but not driven to despair, persecuted but not forsaken, struck down but not destroyed, always carrying around in the body the death of Jesus, so that the life of Jesus may also be made visible in our bodies. For we who are living are always being handed over to death for Jesus' sake, so that the life of Jesus may also be made visible in our mortal flesh. (2 Cor 4:8-11)

Paul does not hesitate to point to the order of apostles and to name himself as a "miscarriage" ("one untimely born") at the end of the list (1 Cor 15:8). But for Christ's sake he has abandoned everything and regards it as "rubbish" (Phil 3:8) in order to gain Christ. Indeed,

Paul does not speak of "things of value" as our correct society inculcates in us, but of *skybalon*—rubbish, refuse, dirt, garbage. And he tells us that it is possible to build a life with "gold, silver, precious stones" but also with "wood, hay, straw." We have to choose. In the end it will be evident, as if "with fire," what we have used to build the houses of our lives (1 Cor 3:12-13).

Memorability

Paul, however, does not intensify what he says simply with images and similes. He can also write with brevity, compactness, and pointedness. He can say that God "justifies the ungodly" (Rom 4:5), and he can remind us that we were all "enemies" of God (Rom 5:10). He often brings the subject so sharply and acutely to the point that his phrases almost have the character of aphorisms or suggest themselves as maxims. Once heard, they are unforgettable. Here I will simply list some of these memorable and trenchant sentences:

> *Many live as enemies of the cross of Christ. . . . Their end is destruction, their god is the belly.* (Phil 3:18-19)
>
> *Work on your own salvation with fear and trembling.* (Phil 2:12)
>
> *The letter kills, but the Spirit gives life.* (2 Cor 3:6)
>
> *Bear one another's burdens, and in this way you will fulfill the law of Christ.* (Gal 6:2)
>
> *Do we then overthrow the law through this faith? By no means! On the contrary, we uphold the law.* (Rom 3:31)
>
> *Love does no wrong to a neighbor.* (Rom 13:10)
>
> *Love is the fulfilling of the law.* (Rom 13:10)
>
> *God's love has been poured into our hearts through the Holy Spirit that has been given to us.* (Rom 5:5)
>
> *Where the Spirit of the Lord is, there is freedom.* (2 Cor 3:17)
>
> *If anyone is in Christ, there is a new creation.* (2 Cor 5:17)
>
> *Knowledge puffs up, but love builds up.* (1 Cor 8:1)
>
> *We know that all things work together for good for those who love God.* (Rom 8:28)

> [*I forget*] *what lies behind and* [*strain*] *forward to what lies ahead*. (Phil 3:13)
>
> *Even though our outer nature is wasting away, our inner nature is being renewed day by day*. (2 Cor 4:16)
>
> [*We do not*] *lord it over your faith; rather, we are workers with you for your joy*. (2 Cor 1:24)
>
> *World or life or death or the present or the future—all are yours, and you are Christ's, and Christ is God's*. (1 Cor 3:22-23)

Such statements, which could easily be multiplied, show that Paul not only spoke in difficult arguments that are not immediately accessible. He could find extremely brief formulations that shed light on the subject, often in the middle of speech constructions in which he was struggling to find an appropriate expression. Listeners at the time would have thanked him for it, and so do we.

Clarity

If we try to feel our way into Paul's language we immediately notice how exact he is. He does not talk around things or make them vague. He does not depend on pious commonplaces that are never completely false but do not touch the center of faith, remaining instead in the realm of the merely "religious" and producing boredom. Paul's language is combative; it pushes thought forward and drives it more and more pointedly to the issue at hand.

This rhetorical style appears most clearly when Paul is dealing with the topic of "law and redemption." Here he is inexorable: no surrender and no compromise. Salvation—Paul speaks almost always about the salvific "righteousness of God"—does not come from the law, but from Christ alone. That is why the faith that relies on Christ is what is crucial, and not a righteousness of the law. As Paul presents the principal theme of his letter to the community at Rome:

> But now, apart from the law, the [saving] righteousness of God has been disclosed and is attested by the Law and the Prophets, the righteousness of God through the faith of Jesus Christ for all who believe. For there is no distinction, since all [Gentiles as well as Jews] have sinned and fall short of the glory of God; they are now justified by his grace as a gift, through the redemption that is in Christ Jesus. (Rom 3:21-24)

Paul defends this basic thesis relentlessly against all softening and false compromise. His rigidity in the question of law is especially evident in Galatians. Jewish-Christian agitators[22] had entered the community in Galatia, which Paul had founded, and they demanded that the Galatian men let themselves be circumcised and that the entire community should follow the whole Old Testament law because obedience to the law is necessary for salvation.[23]

Paul defends against this uncompromising theology of the invaders with the utmost determination because he knows that it denies that redemption comes through Christ alone and thus it destroys the gospel:

> I am astonished that you are so quickly deserting the one who called you in the grace of Christ and are turning to a different gospel—not that there is another gospel, but there are some who are confusing you and want to pervert the gospel of Christ. But even if we or an angel from heaven should proclaim to you a gospel contrary to what we proclaimed to you, let that one be accursed! As we have said before, so now I repeat, if anyone proclaims to you a gospel contrary to what you received, let that one be accursed! (Gal 1:6-9)

The question of the law, then, is ultimately about Christ. If simply following Torah brought salvation, then Christ would be superfluous: he would have lived for nothing, proclaimed the gospel for nothing, and died for no reason.[24] Hence Paul's severity and decisiveness on this point.

Of course, that brings him into difficulties. Because he rejected any kind of law-righteousness in the sharpest terms (Rom 3:20; Gal 2:16) he could be suspected of declaring the law, and thus also obedience to the commandments, to be superfluous. It would have been all too easy to accuse him of saying "Everything is permitted, because everything

[22] What is certain is that it was Jewish Christians who insisted in principle on circumcision and Torah observance. It is improbable, however, that the intruders were acting on direct orders from Jerusalem. There is a good overview of the question of Paul's opponents in Galatia in Heinrich Hübner, art. "Galaterbrief," *TRE* 12:5–14.

[23] Cf. Gal 4:8-10, 16-20; 5:1-12; 6:11-16.

[24] Cf. Gal 2:21: "If righteousness comes through the law, then Christ died for nothing."

is grace, and we are saved even if we sin." In Romans Paul works step by step through this possible objection to his preaching.[25]

He thus had to fight on two fronts: against law-righteousness and at the same time against lawlessness. That two-front war sometimes occasions confusion on our part when we deal with his argumentation in Romans and Galatians, but it was necessary, and it preserved the church from immense errors.

Paul was so deeply involved in this battle over the truth of the gospel that one aspect of his theology is not really clear: the law from Sinai does not demand works-righteousness.[26] Here, as elsewhere, human beings are not saved by individual acts of "keeping the law" but by the saving works of God that precede the law from Sinai.[27] Keeping Torah is grateful obedience for the fact that God has already acted. Still more: God has not only acted graciously in the past; the gift of Torah is itself pure grace.[28]

In that sense "redemption by grace" is already a basic structure of Old Testament law. That is not always clear in Paul's writing when he is struggling against law-righteousness. Some allowances can be made here, because he may be thinking more about the concrete practice of his contemporaries than about basic principles of Old Testament theology of the law. Actual behavior contained a real and elementary danger—not only for Jews but equally for Christians—

[25] Cf. Rom 3:8; 6:1, 15. The phrase "everything is permitted to me" in 1 Cor 6:12; 10:23 can scarcely be attributed to opponents who accused Paul of adopting that position. It could come from the Corinthians themselves, as a misunderstanding of Paul's teaching about freedom in Christ.

[26] It is true that Paul accuses Israel of works-righteousness: see esp. Rom 9:32; 10:3, 5; cf. Rom 3:20; Gal 2:16. It is not impossible that such was true of the Judaism of his time, but it is in no way true of the Old Testament.

[27] Before the Torah was given to the people at Sinai they had been rescued from Egypt, and the Ten Commandments have a prologue: "I am YHWH your God, who brought you out of the land of Egypt, out of the house of slavery" (Exod 20:2). Thus the saving action of God precedes all commandments and obedience to them.

[28] For the whole question cf. Norbert Lohfink, "Gesetz und Gnade," in *Das Siegeslied am Schilfmeer. Christliche Auseinandersetzungen mit dem Alten Testament* (Frankfurt: Knecht, 1965), 151–73; = "Law and Grace," in *The Christian Meaning of the Old Testament*, trans. R. A. Wilson (Milwaukee: Bruce, 1968), 103–20. See also E. P. Sanders, *Paul and Palestinian Judaism: A Comparison of Patterns of Religion*, 40th anniv. ed. (Minneapolis: Fortress, 2017); Volker Stolle, *Luther und Paulus. Die exegetischen und hermeneutischen Grundlagen der lutherischen Rechtfertigungslehre im Paulinismus Luthers*, ABG 10 (Leipzig: Evangelische Verlagsanstalt, 2002), 16, 43, 197–98, 447–48 (!).

that in practice they might be relying on their own works, abilities, and wisdom as well as their own command of the world.

Paul understood at depth that this reliance on one's own knowledge, action, and rituals is a fundamental danger to human beings, including and especially religious people. Their reliance on a law wrongly understood had led to Jesus' crucifixion. To that extent Paul's battle against law-righteousness revealed a profound danger to human beings and their self-created religion.

Thus we must make the sharpest possible distinction: the Torah of the Hebrew Bible is not built on righteousness according to the law, nor is Judaism. But both Jews and Christians can fall victim to law-righteousness and works-righteousness—and then they destroy their faith in God's saving acts. Paul is struggling to ensure that his communities hold fast to Torah in the right way and at the same time believe in Christ as the world's redeemer and savior. Hence his phrasings that seem almost antithetical. On the one hand:

> If righteousness comes through the law, then Christ died for nothing. (Gal 2:21)

On the other hand:

> Do we then overthrow the law through this faith? By no means! On the contrary, we uphold the law. (Rom 3:31)

For Paul the resolution to this apparent contradiction lies in the fact that Torah has found its fulfillment in Christ: concretely, in the love commandment as Jesus proclaimed it and as it found its fulfillment in his living it even unto death. "Love is the fulfilling of the law" (Rom 13:10).

Obviously there are other points on which Paul is clear and unyielding: for example, regarding his call and sending by the Risen One. Paul allows no one to detract from his apostolic office and authority. His personal experience of the Christ, risen and justified by God, is indeed the most profound basis for his claim against the law as the way of salvation. The prescript of the letter to the Galatians reads:

> Paul, an apostle—sent neither by human commission nor from human authorities but through Jesus Christ and God the Father, who raised him from the dead—and all the brothers and sisters with me, To the

> churches of Galatia: Grace to you and peace from God our Father and the Lord Jesus Christ, who gave himself for our sins to set us free from the present evil age, according to the will of our God and Father, to whom be the glory forever and ever. Amen. (Gal 1:1-5)

Similarly, Paul stresses his calling and his apostolic office in numerous introductions to his letters. As we have said: in this matter also, Paul is absolutely clear. His calling and his apostolic office are, for him, inviolable.

There are many other matters in which Paul reveals no ambiguity or lack of clarity. To name only a single point: in all his letters Paul speaks of judgment, but he does not go on about it at length. That God will judge the world and, obviously, Christians also through Christ is simply obvious to him. He presupposes it and hence he never has to do more than refer to it in passing, for example in 2 Corinthians 5:10: "For all of us must appear before the judgment seat of Christ, so that each may receive due recompense for actions done in the body, whether good or evil."

In light of the fact that many theologians today, and even those who hold office in the church, only speak of God's mercy, kindness, beneficence, and tenderness, this clarity is vitally important for the church, for there may be no detracting from the dialectic of mercy and justice, grace and judgment, redemption and yet the eschatological clarification of all injustice. It is good that we have Paul, his gospel, and his clarity!

Moreover, this would all be one-sided if I did not add at this point: despite all his firmness and clarity, Paul can also be very expansive and open. He was constantly dealing with "missionaries" who exploited his communities in his absence and made use of the gospel for their own benefit—or confused his congregations by trying to correct his gospel. Paul can be profoundly horrified at such preachers, but he can also say:

> Some proclaim Christ from envy and rivalry but others from goodwill. These proclaim Christ out of love; . . . others proclaim Christ out of selfish ambition, not sincerely. . . . What does it matter? Just this, that Christ is proclaimed in every way, whether out of false motives or true, and in that I rejoice. (Phil 1:15-18)

Arguing

In the course of exploring the clarity of Paul's language we have arrived at a principal theme of his theology: the question of law and grace. Here Paul argues, and he does so broadly and intensely—but not only here. It is characteristic of Paul's way of speaking and writing that he explains, expands on, clarifies, gives reasons, argues. Long sections of his letters are passionate and at the same time patient works of argumentation, no matter whether they are about the salvific righteousness of God (Rom 1–11), his own apostolic office (2 Cor 5–6; 10–12), charisms in the community (1 Cor 12–14), the character of the resurrection body (1 Cor 15), or the question of meat offered to idols.

Paul writes at great length about that last question in 1 Corinthians, especially in 8:1-13. What he says there is continued in 10:14–11:1. For the moment let us linger on these two texts and see more precisely *how* Paul argues there. But first we have to be clear about why the subject of "meat offered to idols" was such a hot topic in Corinth. It was connected with the fact that in antiquity almost all of both public and private life was influenced by religion. Concretely, "influenced by religion" meant that sacrifices to the gods, whether offerings of drink or of food, played an immense role.[29]

When a public festival was celebrated in the *polis*, that is, the city-state, as a matter of course it involved the slaughter of sacrificial animals. Certain parts of the animal were burned and so presented to the gods; other parts were eaten in public banquets as part of the feast. When a high official entered office there were sacrifices to the gods, and meals featuring the meat of the sacrifices. When a birthday, a wedding, a funeral, or a memorial for the dead was in order there were sacrifices to the gods, and meals at which the sacrificial meats were served. When the members of an association met and enjoyed a common meal it was preceded by a sacrifice to the god who was responsible for the guild, and there was sacrificial meat on the table. Many such associations were cultic in nature: they were founded only for that purpose, so that their members could celebrate a festive

[29] For the ancient background on the eating of sacrificial meats cf. esp. Wolfgang Schrage, *Der erste Brief an die Korinther* 2. *1 Kor 6,12–11,16*. EKKNT 7/2 (Zürich: Benziger; Neukirchen-Vluyn: Neukirchener Verlag, 1995), 216–17.

banquet in honor of a particular god once or several times a year—of course with a sacrifice and the associated sacrificial meats.

Invitations to dinner often involved meals in the spacious interiors of temples. Some such halls could properly be called temple restaurants. What was on the menu there? Sacrificed meats, of course! But even if someone just went to the *macellum*, the market, and bought meat at the butchers' stalls, the meat received was in most cases from sacrifices—either offerings in the temple that were sold to the merchants by the priests, or killed by the butcher. In the latter case at least a forelock of the slaughtered young animal, calf, or pig had been presented to the gods in a sacrificial fire.

The poor in particular, who normally had only vegetables or baked goods on their tables, at least got meat on their plates at public meals or when invited to family feasts. Then, if they were Christians, they had to expect they would be offered meat that had been sacrificed to idols.

That was the situation in Corinth, and in principle it was the same throughout the Roman Empire. In light of this the Jews in the Diaspora had established a radical separation: they ate meat only from a Jewish butcher or if they had slaughtered it themselves, guaranteeing that they would not have to eat meat sacrificed to idols. Or else, to be absolutely certain, they ate no meat at all. They simply did not accept invitations to pagan feasts. Many Christians chose a similar course. The agreement reported in Acts 15:28-29 (in connection with the so-called Apostolic Council) made it a rule for Gentile Christians that they must not eat any meat sacrificed to idols. That was meant to make a common life possible for Jewish and Gentile Christians.

But in Corinth (and probably not only there[30]) some Christians—stimulated by the Pauline gospel—had developed their own opinions about this matter. They said: Christ has made us free (1 Cor 8:9). Hence we have achieved a more profound *gnōsis*, that is, a deeper "knowledge."[31] We know that the pagan gods do not exist; they

[30] There must have been similar problems in Rome: cf. Rom 14:1–15:6 and the excursus "Die 'Starken' und 'Schwachen' in Rom," in Ulrich Wilckens, *Der Brief an die Römer. Röm 12–16*, EKKNT 6/3 (Zürich: Benziger; Neukirchen-Vluyn: Neukirchener Verlag, 1982), 109–15.

[31] It is striking how often the keyword *gnōsis*, "knowledge" [or: "insight"], or the corresponding verb appears in this context; cf. 1 Cor 8:1, 2, 7, 10, 11. The "strong" must have been proud of their "knowledge" or "insight." Paul does not reject the concept, but he reinterprets it.

simply are not real. Therefore the cultic practices dedicated to the gods are also empty and completely meaningless. So we may eat meat offered to idols in the pagan cults. We are completely free in this matter. On the basis of Romans 15:1, New Testament scholars generally call this group in Corinth "the strong." It must have been a title they claimed for themselves: "We, the strong."

But they were only one part of the Corinthian community. Other Christians, whom Paul calls the "weak" (1 Cor 8:9-11), refused to eat meat from pagan sacrifices. Some of them may have feared that the meat itself was demonically "infected" and thus dangerous (1 Cor 8:7).

Still, there must have been a more important motive: the desire to avoid any kind of participation in pagan cultic acts. People would have said: if we eat meat that is connected to a cultic action it is like participating in the pagan cult itself. Probably those Christians ate no meat at all, out of caution, and drank no wine (cf. Rom 14:21). Even in the case of wine a small portion might have been poured out as a libation to the gods.

There must have been serious conflict between the two groups. The "weak" were offended by the laxity of the "strong." They condemned the attitude of the "strong" as lawlessness and sin; they "judged" those who ate meat. The "strong," in turn, believed they were in the right. They "despised" the scruples of the "weak" (cf. Rom 14:10). They said "everything is clean" (cf. Rom 14:20) and "all things are permitted" (1 Cor 10:23).

Paul had received an inquiry from Corinth (1 Cor 8:1) about what should be done in face of this conflict that was splitting the community. What did Paul do? How did he deal with this strife-bringing conflict? How did he argue?

To a certain degree Paul affirmed what the "strong" said, because the pagan gods do not exist. There is only the one, true God who created the world and everything in it (1 Cor 8:4-6). Hence all created things belong to God, including food. Therefore when one eats after giving thanks, the eating is done under God's blessing (1 Cor 10:30; cf. Rom 14:6). No one need fear that it is under the influence of demons. To that extent the "strong" do, in fact, have "knowledge."

But, says Paul, there are two sides to "knowledge." Often it makes people conceited—that is, arrogant—so that they despise others and traumatize their consciences. True knowledge, in contrast, builds up (1 Cor 8:1). It is borne by love and therefore cannot bear to see the "weak" shamed, confused, or injured. Everything that wounds a brother or a sister in the community is wrong. Paul writes: "Therefore, if food is a cause of [offense to my sister or brother], I prefer never again to eat meat, so that I may not offend one of them" (1 Cor 8:13, author's translation). Refusal to ruthlessly impose one's own ideas: that is true knowledge. On that basis, in chapters 8 and 10 Paul develops some concrete rules of behavior.

It is absolutely forbidden for Christians to take a direct role in pagan cultic actions, that is, sacrificial rituals and all the practices associated with them. In that connection Paul even refers to demons. Whoever takes part in pagan cultic practices, he says, enters into the company of demons: "You cannot drink the cup of the Lord and the cup of demons. You cannot partake of the table of the Lord and the table of demons" (1 Cor 10:21). In such a case the Corinthians would share in the demonic—or, as we would say now, they would participate in the evil that the pagan "gods" represented and the evil for whose purpose those "gods" were used—and that can and must not be. They are not cultic companions of the pagan gods; rather, they are cultic partners with Christ:

> The cup of blessing that we bless, is it not a sharing in the blood of Christ? The bread that we break, is it not a sharing in the body of Christ? Because there is one bread, we who are many are one body, for we all partake of the one bread. (1 Cor 10:16-17)

Direct participation in pagan worship is thus completely forbidden. But it is another matter if a Christian shops in the market for meat. Then she does not need to ask whether it was somehow connected to cultic actions (1 Cor 10:25). The same is true if one is invited to a meal; one may eat what is offered without making prior inquiries (1 Cor 10:27). Still, this Christian freedom becomes questionable if someone says explicitly, "This has been offered in sacrifice" (1 Cor 10:28), or if eating it would offend someone who has problems of conscience in this regard. Then every action must be determined by *agapē*.

So how does Paul proceed in this whole question? He allows the Corinthians the greatest possible freedom, far beyond what the agreement in Acts 15:28-29 had permitted, and he gives reasons for that freedom: everything comes from God, and what is of God can be eaten with thanksgiving. Still, that knowledge has to be subordinated to another insight: namely, that mutual love in the community is the highest good and must never be wounded in any way. It is about building up the community, not imposing knowledge (1 Cor 8:1).

So Paul argues, and he does so in successive steps. He argues on the basis of faith in the one, true God and of *agapē*, setting clear boundaries. Direct participation in pagan sacrifices is always out of the question, as is any damage done to *agapē*. Between these there is a broad space for freedom. Paul even enters casuistically into different situations within that sphere of freedom: shopping at the butcher's (1 Cor 10:25), being a guest at a meal (1 Cor 10:27), perhaps even in the temple bistro (1 Cor 8:10).

We could give many more examples of Paul's careful, prudent, balanced argumentation, but I have chosen these to show that Paul does not simply issue decrees. He wants to win over the community and all the groups within it to the right point of view. Therefore he makes a great effort. His letters are long. His speeches in the communities must have been much longer still.

What Paul is pursuing is enlightenment in the real sense. He wants the Corinthians to use their heads but also to view their sisters and brothers in the community with love. And in everything he desires that the community be built up, because it is the place where God's rationality must be made visible.

Creating Community

How did Paul talk to his communities? I have thus far spoken about the many forms of discourse he used, the wealth of imagery in his language, the clarity of his speech, and the fact that he did not simply give orders but argued his points. Much more could be said—for with Paul one never reaches an end—but here I want to emphasize just one point: the communicative character of his language. Paul continually worked to establish community. The sisterly and brotherly togetherness in his congregations, which were supposed to be one body in Christ: that was his whole desire, and it is evident in everything, down to the linguistic form of his letters. Their very beginnings show it.

Letters have always had a certain shape. Modern ones, too, follow conventions that are constantly reaffirmed. But this was especially true of ancient letters.[32] They began, in the so-called prescript, with

[32] There is a good overview of the ancient letter form in Marius Reiser, *Sprache und literarische Formen des Neuen Testaments*, UTB 2197 (Paderborn: Schöningh, 2001), 116–25.

the name of the sender, followed by that of the addressee and then a greeting. One example, representative of many other letter-beginnings along the same lines: *Cicero Atticum salutem*,[33] "Cicero greets Atticus." In ancient letters that was the whole beginning, and thereafter the writer came directly to the point. There might be, at most, a short transition: in Latin letters, for example, there was the abbreviation SVBEEV, which said:

> SI VALES BENE EST, EGO VALEO.
> If you are well, it is good; I am well.

According to ancient conventions the letter to Philemon really should have begun: "Paul greets Philemon," and so should all the Pauline letters. But the letter to Philemon starts differently:

> Paul, a prisoner of Christ Jesus, and Timothy our brother, to our beloved coworker Philemon, to our sister Apphia, to our fellow soldier Archippus, and to the church in your house: Grace to you and peace from God our Father and the Lord Jesus Christ. (Phlm 1-3)

You will have noticed immediately that as far as the basic structure is concerned that is precisely the ancient letter formula: sender, addressee, greeting. And yet, what has Paul made of the short letter formula of his contemporaries!

Paul introduces himself as sender not simply by name; he calls himself "a prisoner of Christ Jesus." That is: he is in the service of Jesus Christ, and it is on Jesus Christ's account that he is in prison. Moreover, in this letter's beginning Paul names not only himself but Timothy, one of his most important coworkers. Paul does not name him because he was co-sender of the letter; no, it is because Paul is not presenting himself as an individual and isolated figure who preaches the gospel; he thus indicates that he is in profound communion with his coworkers.

Still more: Paul does not simply name Philemon as the addressee but says "to our beloved coworker Philemon, to our sister Apphia, to our fellow soldier Archippus, and to the church in your house."

[33] "*Dicit*" is understood: literally "Cicero awards health [or: wellbeing] to Atticus." But the sentence is as formulaic as our "Good day," which, of course, is not about someone's state on the present day, but is simply a greeting.

Apphia was probably Philemon's wife. Christian couples played a significant part in the early Christian mission, and women had a crucial role in the ancient household. Philemon's wife would certainly have had something to say about the treatment of the escaped slave Onesimus. But Paul addresses not only the couple; he adds another coworker named Archippus and then the whole congregation that gathered in Philemon's (and Apphia's?) house.

Here, then, the narrow framework of a private letter has been expanded quite a lot. The case of the escaped Onesimus concerns the whole congregation. He is not only to be rooted once more in the family of Philemon; he is to become a fellow Christian and a brother in faith to the whole community.

One final observation: the extremely brief greeting in the ancient prescript has been significantly expanded by Paul: it has become a solemn blessing formula with liturgical character. Paul knew that his letter would be read aloud in the community assembly.

There is not a single example in pre-Christian antiquity of a letter with a beginning that is so rich in its wording, so weighty, and so solemn. Moreover, it is obvious why Paul opens the letter to Philemon, and all his letters, at such length: he wants to establish communion between himself and the addressees. "Himself," moreover, is not him alone but also his coworkers. And his addressee—this is not a single person; it is the whole community.

Moreover, we should not focus only on these formal structures in the prescripts of Paul's letters. We also have to appreciate the sincerity and respect with which he greets his addressees. Philemon, after all, is not just Philemon; he is Paul's "beloved coworker." And when Paul writes to the community in Corinth, where there are strife, rivalries, divisions, and other sources of potential ruin, he speaks of the Christians there as "sanctified" and "called" (1 Cor 1:2). Moreover, Paul not only "greets" but blesses, announcing "grace and peace from God our Father and the Lord Jesus Christ."

In his letters, immediately after the prescript, Paul always thanks God for the community to which he is writing, and he assures them that he prays for them without ceasing.[34] Again, there is no such extended and solemn thanksgiving to be found in any pre-Christian

[34] The only exception is Galatians, which lacks a thanksgiving. Paul is disgusted and saddened by the deviation of the Galatian community from the gospel he preached to them.

letter, and it once more shows the communicative nature of Paul's writing. He seeks communion with his congregations even in the external form of his letters. In the one to the community at Philippi the thanksgiving reads:

> I thank my God for every remembrance of you, always in every one of my prayers for all of you, praying with joy for your partnership in the gospel from the first day until now. I am confident of this, that the one who began a good work in you will continue to complete it until the day of Jesus Christ. It is right for me to think this way about all of you, because I hold you in my heart. (Phil 1:3-7)

Once again: I am concerned to show that the very stylistic genre of Paul's letters reveals the communicative nature of his speech, even prior to any content. The same thing is evident in another linguistic phenomenon that is typical of Paul: the frequent use of reciprocal pronouns. Again and again in Paul's letters we find the Greek word *allēlōn*, "one another." Some examples:

> *Love one another with mutual affection.* (Rom 12:10)
>
> *Live in harmony with one another.* (Rom 12:16)
>
> *Welcome one another.* (Rom 15:7)
>
> *You yourselves are . . . able to instruct one another.* (Rom 15:14)
>
> *When you come together to eat, wait for one another.* (1 Cor 11:33)
>
> *Have the same care for one another.* (1 Cor 12:25)
>
> *Through love become enslaved to one another.* (Gal 5:13)
>
> *Bear one another's burdens.* (Gal 6:2)
>
> *Encourage one another.* (1 Thess 5:11)
>
> *Always seek to do good to one another.* (1 Thess 5:15)

This is only a small selection from among many.[35] With his frequent use of the little word *allēlōn* Paul shows us what the gospel intends: not in the first place the spiritual upbuilding of one's own self but the

[35] For more on Paul's use of the reciprocal pronoun and a collection of all occurrences see Gerhard Lohfink, *Jesus and Community: The Social Dimension of Christian*

building up of the community as the place where communion with Christ in the world can acquire a visible shape. Christians live "with one another" and "for one another"—and precisely in this way they are making a reality of the world-changing power of the gospel.

Paul's language is communicative. There is another linguistic phenomenon in his letters that reveals his efforts at shaping *communio* with his congregations: again and again, in all his letters, we find places where Paul says he will come soon, or that he cannot come at the moment, or in which he simply reports his situation to his addressees. Characteristic, for example, is the following section from the letter to the Philippians. It is not read in the liturgy and consequently is scarcely familiar to many churchgoers, and yet it says so much about Paul and his pastoral sense:

> I hope in the Lord Jesus to send Timothy to you soon, so that I, too, may be consoled by news of you. I have no one so like myself who will be genuinely concerned for your welfare. All of them are seeking their own interests, not those of Jesus Christ. But Timothy's worth you know, how like a son with a father he has served with me in the work of the gospel. I hope therefore to send him as soon as I see how things go with me, and I trust in the Lord that I will also come soon.
>
> Still, I think it necessary to send to you Epaphroditus—my brother and coworker and fellow soldier, your messenger and minister to my need, for he has been longing for all of you and has been distressed because you heard that he was ill. He was indeed so ill that he nearly died. But God had mercy on him, and not only on him but on me also, so that I would not have one sorrow after another. I am the more eager to send him, therefore, in order that you may rejoice at seeing him again and that I may be less anxious. Welcome him, then, in the Lord with all joy, and honor such people, because he came close to death for the work of Christ, risking his life. (Phil 2:19-30)

I have deliberately placed this rather long text here because it not only offers a single example of Paul's dedication and his constant *communio* with his congregations. It also shows how communication among communities took place in the early years of Christianity: by means of letters that were read aloud in the congregational assemblies

---

Faith, trans. John P. Galvin (Philadelphia: Fortress Press, 1982), at n. 107; cf. also Eckstein, *Gemeinde*, 192–93.

and through messengers who were sent (in this case Timothy and Epaphroditus). The result was an amazingly broad net of mutual connections.

Another phenomenon should be mentioned in the same context. It is remarkable how many names appear in Paul's letters. Almost all of them are those of Paul's coworkers or of persons who were important for his missionary work. I once collected a list of such names from the authentic letters of Paul, simply in the order in which they appear in the New Testament corpus:

> Phoebe, Prisca, Aquila, Epaenetus, Mary, Andronicus, Junia, Ampliatus, Urbanus, Stachys, Apelles, Aristobulus, Herodion, Narcissus, Tryphaena, Tryphosa, Persis, Rufus, Asyncritus, Phlegon, Hermes, Patrobas, Hermas, Philologus, Julia, Nereus, Olympas, Timothy, Lucius, Jason, Sosipater, Tertius, Gaius, Erastus, Quartus, Sosthenes, Chloe, Apollos, Crispus, Stephanas, Fortunatus, Achaicus, Silvanus, Titus, Epaphroditus, Evodia, Syntyche, Philemon, Apphia, Archippus, Epaphras, Mark, Aristarchus, Demas, Luke.

Such a number of names in only seven letters is absolutely unique in antiquity. The list suggests how the Christian faith spread in the early years of the church: from person to person, face to face. The list also shows how Paul conducted his pastoral work: he sought to have as many coworkers as possible, to preach the gospel and create communities together with them. They were women and men, married couples and the unmarried, companions who accompanied Paul on his journeys and fellow workers who were resident in the individual communities. Paul was not a lone wolf; many others worked with and around him, and he spoke of them with great respect and love.

How did Paul talk to his communities? We have seen that he could discuss and argue, praise and admonish, warn and comfort, give orders and make requests. He could speak with the greatest decisiveness and hope for agreement like a lover. He could join with others in joy and sorrow.

There is *one* form of address I have not mentioned, and I will do so now to conclude this whole discussion. Paul could speak with unshakeable hope and infinite confidence and convey both to his hearers. In one of his loveliest texts he tells the community in Rome, after he has offered a whole series of arguments about the burden of sin, the calamity of human guilt, and the saving righteousness of God's justice:

> If God is for us, who is against us? He who did not withhold his own Son but gave him up for all of us, how will he not with him also give us everything else? Who will bring any charge against God's elect? It is God who justifies. Who is to condemn? It is Christ who died, or rather, who was raised, who is also at the right hand of God, who also intercedes for us. Who will separate us from the love of Christ? Will affliction or distress or persecution or famine or nakedness or peril or sword? . . . I am convinced that neither death, nor life, nor angels, nor rulers, nor things present, nor things to come, nor powers, nor height, nor depth, nor anything else in all creation will be able to separate us from the love of God that is in Christ Jesus our Lord. (Rom 8:31-39)

12

Was Paul Anti-Jewish?

Anti-Judaism has left its disgusting tracks throughout the history of the church. If we picture what people baptized into Jesus Christ have done to their Jewish sisters and brothers over centuries, or how they have looked away when, instead, solidarity was called for, we can only be shocked to our depths.

It is right, therefore, that Christians pray again and again, in worship, for forgiveness of their sins. They beg God to pardon them for having distanced themselves so greatly from Jesus and the New Testament. In that light it would certainly be fatal if the New Testament itself displayed anti-Judaism, if reality were obscured and hatred sown in the place where true enlightenment has its home. There is nothing worse than the pollution of the very source, and there could be nothing more diabolical than for truth to be perverted at its origin.

It is from this point of view that I will examine Paul's letters here.[1] My purpose is not to cleanse them as needed but to get to the basic truth. Is there anti-Judaism in Paul's letters? I have deliberately chosen these letters in particular because nowhere else in the New Testament is the question of the relationship between Israel and the church posed so radically and at such length as in Romans 9–11. What follows will therefore focus particularly on that passage. All other New Testament texts need to be understood in light of these three chapters—that is,

[1] The following essay is based on a paper delivered at an international symposium at the Vatican in Rome (October 30–November 1, 1997). The papers given there by exegetes and historians were published in *Radici dell'antigiudaismo in ambiente cristiano. Colloquio intra-ecclesiale* (Libreria Editrice Vaticana: Citta del Vaticano, 2000). I have reread and expanded the lecture published there (pp. 163–96) for this book.

if we are prepared to read the New Testament not as a somewhat accidental collection of individual writings but as a single text.

So, is there anti-Judaism in Paul's letters? It does not seem particularly likely in the work of Paul, the Jew. After all, he emphasizes that he is a Hebrew born of Hebrews, that he was circumcised on the eighth day, that he belongs to the people Israel (Phil 3:5) and is a descendant of Abraham (2 Cor 11:22). If there is such a thing as anti-Judaism in Paul's letters, then 1 Thessalonians 2:14-16 is the most likely passage.

Anti-Judaism in 1 Thessalonians 2:14-16?

Here Paul compares the situation of the young community in Thessalonica with the case of that in Judea. As the Christians there were persecuted by the Jews, so now the Christians in Thessalonica were being put under social pressure, or even persecuted,[2] by their neighbors in the sections of the city where they lived.[3]

> For you, brothers and sisters, became imitators of the churches of God in Christ Jesus that are in Judea, for you suffered the same things from your own compatriots as they did from the Jews who killed both the Lord Jesus and the prophets and drove us out;[4] they displease God and oppose everyone by hindering us from speaking to the gentiles so that they may be saved. Thus they have constantly been filling up the measure of their sins, but wrath has overtaken them at last. (1 Thess 2:14-16)

[2] The acerbic nature of the language in 1 Thess 2:15-16 is best explained if we trust the account in Acts 17:5-13 and suppose that Paul's missionary work among the God-fearers in Thessalonica had aroused the local Jews against him. What the Christians in Thessalonica were then experiencing at the hands of their pagan neighbors, since Paul had been driven out, may also have been brought about by the arousal of the local Jews, who stirred up the pagans against the Christian community. That is the only way in which the comparison in 2:14 fully makes sense. Cf. Traugott Holtz, *Der erste Brief an die Thessalonicher*, EKKNT 13 (Zürich: Benziger; Neukirchen-Vluyn: Neukirchener Verlag, 1986), 110–11.

[3] The *phylai* assumed in 1 Thess 2:14 had long since ceased to be groups of people related by ancestry but were districts within the *polis*, subdivided into neighborhoods. Cf. Christian Maurer, *TDNT* 9:245–50.

[4] In the LXX it is only in 1 Kgs 30:10 that *ekdiōkein* certainly means "persecute." Otherwise it is always read as "cast out," "hunt out," "drive out," "root out." Cf. Deut 6:19; 1 Chr 8:13; 12:16; Pss 36:28; 100:5; Joel 2:20 (!); Jer 27:44; 29:19; Dan 4:22, 29, 30; 5:21 (!). The parallel in Luke 11:49 (in some of the mss.) by no means permits the flat translation "persecute."

This text has to be suspected of anti-Judaism because at first glance it seems to adopt both of the main accusations leveled in antiquity at Jews: their contempt for the gods and their supposed hatred of humanity. It was a fixed *topos* that Jews are hostile to all other people,[5] and the idea that they would displease God recalls Tacitus's formulation, "they are hated by the gods."[6] This last is merely a sharpening of the charge that Jews are godless (*atheoi*).[7]

This accusation that Jews are hostile to all humanity is absolutely unique within the Corpus Paulinum. That has caused a large number of exegetes to declare that 1 Thessalonians 2:14-16 is not by Paul and was inserted by another hand.[8] There are, however, no solid reasons for that assumption. It is not only that the two verses in question fit smoothly within their context.[9] A closer inspection also shows that the two anti-Jewish sayings by Paul are treated differently; in fact, their sense is altered.

First of all, there is that expression "displease God," which has very little, in fact absolutely nothing, to do with the pagan accusation of godlessness. In Paul's writing "to please" always describes something one does, an active way of behaving.[10] In verse 15 Paul is say-

[5] Cf. Tacitus, *Historiae* 5.5: "they are obstinately loyal to each other, and always ready to show compassion, whereas they feel nothing but hatred and enmity for the rest of the world [*apud ipsos fides obstinata, misericordia in promptu, sed adversus omnes alios hostile odium*]"; also Juvenal, *Satirae* 14.103–4; Diodorus Siculus, *Bibliotheca historica* 40.3 §4; Josephus, *Contra Apionem* 1.34; 2.8, 10, 14.

[6] Tacitus, *Historiae* 5.3.

[7] Cf., e.g., Pliny, *Naturalis historia* 13.4.46: "a race remarkable for their contempt for the divine powers [*gens contumelia numinum insignis*]"; Tacitus, *Historiae* 5.5, "despise the gods" (*contemnere deos*); Josephus, *Contra Apionem* 2.14.

[8] There is a good review of the discussion in Joseph Coppens, "Miscellanies bibliques. LXXX. Une diatribe antijuive dans 1 Thess., II,13-16," *ETL* 51 (1975): 90–95. Cf. also Ingo Broer, "'Antisemitismus' und Judenpolemik im Neuen Testament," in *Religion und Verantwortung als Elemente gesellschaftlicher Ordnung*, ed. Bodo B. Gemper, Beiheft zu den Siegener Studien (Siegen: Vorländer, 1982), 734–72, at 741–46. Current discussion of a later redaction is most commonly associated with the supposition that 1 Thessalonians was subsequently assembled out of two shorter letters between Paul and the Thessalonian community. One starting point for this hypothesis is the renewed thanksgiving in 2:13. Cf., e.g., Franz Laub, *1. und 2. Thessalonicherbrief*, NEB 13 (Würzburg: Echter, 1985), 21–22.

[9] *Kai hymeis* in 2:13 must not be overemphasized. Cf. Ernst von Dobschütz, *Die Thessalonicherbriefe* (Göttingen: Vandenhoeck & Ruprecht, 1974 [repr. of the 1909 ed.]), 103.

[10] So esp. Werner Foerster, art. ἀρέσκω, κτλ., *TDNT* 1, 455. Cf. esp. Rom 15:1-3; 1 Cor 10:33; 1 Thess 4:1.

ing: The Jews are not living as is pleasing to God, that is, they are not doing God's will. That, however, is altogether biblical in its sense and is unmistakably bound up with Paul's concrete experience: his fellow Jews persecute him and try by every means possible to obstruct[11] his mission among the Gentiles (more precisely: among the "God-fearers"). In doing so they are opposing the salvation of the Gentiles and so are working against God's plan for history. The pagan accusation of godlessness, in contrast, referred to the fact that the Jews did not participate in the official cult or take a role in state festivals. It thus had nothing at all to do with a current historical situation.

The accusation of hostility to humanity also has a different sense in Paul's writing than it had on the lips of Gentiles. The pagan accusation refers to *amixia*, Jewish separation. Greeks and Romans of course noticed that on certain points the Jews maintained distance from them; the reason they gave for that was the "uncleanness" of pagans. Paul, on the other hand, here again refers to his personal experience in the course of his missionary work. Jews tried to prevent salvation from reaching the Gentiles. In that (and in no other way!) they showed themselves hostile to other humans.[12]

Thus on the surface Paul may make use of Gentile accusations against Jews, but for him they have a different meaning. They no longer characterize the "nature" of Jews as the Gentiles then saw it but the concrete historical rejection by the synagogues that set themselves against God. Paul does not speak here as the Gentiles do, but as a Jew who interprets the refusal of his fellow believers in terms of basic experiences with Sacred Scripture.

Ultimately, the extent to which Paul thinks in historical-situational terms in our text is shown by the fact that he places his own experience

[11] Cf. the corresponding texts of Acts in 9:29; 13:45, 50; 14:2, 19; 17:5, 13; 18:12; 22:22-23; 23:12-15. Certainly the wrath of the synagogues is understandable. Paul's mission was most successful precisely among those Gentiles who were already living in relationship to the synagogues as "God-fearers." Cf. Marius Reiser, "Hat Paulus Heiden bekehrt?," *BZ* 39 (1995): 76–91.

[12] This connection is also clearly indicated syntactically in the text: *kōluontōn*, added asyndetically after the threefold *kai*, epexegetically continues the preceding *kai pasin anthrōpois enantiōn*. Thus correctly von Dobschütz, *Thessalonicherbriefe*, 111. It is possible that, given its generalized form, the accusation of hatred for humanity even refers to a similarly generalized accusation from the side of the Jews like that found in Acts 17:6—Paul and his coworkers are trying to "turn the world upside down." If that accusation had actually been raised by the politarchs in Thessalonica it shows that 1 Thess 2:15 was uttered in light of a concrete situation and was tied to it.

of mission within a broader historical framework: the history of Israel's disobedience, wherein even the prophets were killed (1 Thess 2:15) and in which guilt was heaped upon guilt (1 Thess 2:16). By his use of this "deuteronomistic" frame of argumentation[13] Paul definitively signals that he is not speaking on the level of a pagan anti-Judaism. He says only what could be and had been said in Israel against their own people from the time of Amos and Hosea: Israel rejects its God.[14] It persecutes and kills the prophets.[15] With its lack of faith it obstructs God's plan and thereby causes God's wrath to be enflamed against it.[16]

Verse 16c scarcely seems to say that this wrathful divine judgment is final and will last for all eternity. *Eis telos* can, indeed, mean "forever" or "eternally."[17] But it can also simply mean "completely," "altogether," "to the utmost extent."[18] Here the second meaning is more likely. God's wrathful judgment has already broken over Israel, and to the fullest extent. It is thoroughly biblical to think that such wrathful judgment can also, once again, change to mercy—not only when Israel repents, but in some circumstances even without repentance—through the pure love of God that excludes any possibility that God will surrender this people and extend divine wrath over them to the full.[19] Paul will also write in Romans 9:22 of the wrath

[13] For the "deuteronomistic" *schema* cf. Odil Hannes Steck, *Israel und das gewaltsame Geschick der Propheten*, WMANT 23 (Neukirchen-Vluyn: Neukirchener Verlag, 1967). Otto Michel ("Fragen zu 1 Thessalonicher 2,14-16: Antijüdische Polemik bei Paulus," in Willehad Paul Eckert, Nathan P. Levinson, and Martin Stöhr, *Antijudaismus im Neuen Testament? Exegetische und systematische Beiträge*, ACJD 2 [Munich: Beck, 1967], 50–59, at 52–58) considers that 1 Thess 2:14-16 may be a reworking of pre-shaped Christian tradition. That is possible in principle, but the text shows no real indications of it. It appears, rather, to be working with fixed motifs such as "notorious murdering of the prophets." Ultimately the demonstration of an already-formed tradition would be irrelevant for us, at any rate. We are concerned with the interpretation of the final text.

[14] Exod 15:24; 16:2, 8 (!); 17:3, 7; Num 11:1-6; 14; 17:6-7; 20:2-13; 21:5; Deut 1:26-46; Neh 9:6-37; Pss 78; 106; Jer 2:4-13; 3:19-25; Ezek 16; 20; 23; Hos 2:4-17; 4:1-3; 8–10; Amos 2:4–3:2, and frequently.

[15] 1 Kgs 19:10, 14; 2 Chr 24:20-22; Neh 9:26; Jer 2:30; 11:18-23; 26:8, 20-24.

[16] Cf. Exod 32:10; Deut 9:19; 29:26-27; Judg 2:13-14; 2 Kgs 17:18; 2 Chr 36:14-16 (!); Ps 78:59; Isa 5:25; Jer 7:20; 23:20; Ezek 21:36-37, and frequently.

[17] Cf., e.g., Pss 9:19; 76:9 LXX; 102:9 LXX; 1 Chr 28:9; Dan 3:34.

[18] Cf. Deut 31:24; 2 Chr 12:12; Jdt 14:13; PsSol 1:1; 2:5.

[19] See especially the whole composition in Hosea 4–11, with the turn in 11:8-9. On this cf. Norbert Lohfink, "'Ich komme nicht in Zornesglut' (Hos 11:9). Skizze einer

of God and the "objects of wrath," and yet only a short time later the text speaks instead of God's having "imprisoned all in disobedience so that [God] may be merciful to all" (Rom 11:32).[20]

Conclusion: as close as Paul comes in 1 Thessalonians 2:14-16 to the cliché of ancient anti-Judaism, on closer inspection we see that his argument is biblical. We must even say that he argues within Judaism. Nevertheless, we must admit that this text from the oldest surviving letter of Paul can easily be read differently. Ancient society already contained an enormous potential for hatred of Jews. To speak, within such a social context, of Jewish "hatred of humanity" was not only to open oneself to misunderstanding:[21] it was highly dangerous. A few years later Paul took his reflections on Israel in an unmistakably different direction, in chapters 9–11 of the letter to the Romans.

Romans 9–11 within the Whole Letter to the Romans

Romans 9–11 must also be examined in regard to possible anti-Judaism, or at least to see whether these three chapters could be understood as anti-Jewish. What about, for example, the statement about grafting, which plays such an extraordinarily large role in the argumentation of Romans 9–11? Does it betray anti-Jewish tendencies?

As in the case of 1 Thessalonians 2:14-16, so also with regard to Romans 9–11 it seems right to examine not only isolated motifs and themes but also their respective locations in the historical context and, beyond that, to inquire into the basic statement of the three chapters. What is Paul's overall concern?

That in turn is closely involved with another question: what is the place of Romans 9–11 in the whole context of the letter to the Romans? It is clear that chapters 1–11 constitute the more "basic" part of the letter and that there is a clear break at chapter 12, where the *paraklēsis* (encouragement) begins. But what is the function of chapters 9–11

---

synchronen Leseanweisung für das Hoseabuch," in *Ce Dieu qui vient. Mélanges offert à Bernard Renaud*, ed. Raymond Kuntzmann, LD 159 (Paris: Cerf, 1995), 163–90.

[20] If it were true that Paul, contrary to the position I have argued for, spoke of a *definitive* judgment of Israel in 1 Thess 2:16d, he later changed his mind in Rom 9–11. In that case this change of mind would be controlling as far as the final statement of the Corpus Paulinum on the question of Israel is concerned.

[21] The reception history of 1 Thess 2:14-16 has yet to be written.

within the first part of Romans? Are they a kind of excursus, or only an appendix? In neither case would their function be impacted.

Biblical scholarship today is in broad agreement that chapters 9–11 are organically tied to what has been said previously in Romans, "because everything the apostle presented in the first eight chapters of the letter to the Romans inevitably demands a theological clarification of the problem of Israel."[22]

In order to see this connection we must briefly review the situation in which the letter to the Romans originated. Paul is planning to travel to Jerusalem to deliver the collection that has long since been gathered in his communities in Macedonia and Achaia (Rom 15:26-28). After that he intends to journey to Spain because he wants to carry his missionary work, begun in the East, to its completion in the most distant West (Rom 15:28). For that he needs the aid of the Roman community (Rom 15:24), and he has to suppose that the accusations emanating from Jews and Jewish Christians, which are a terribly heavy obstacle to his missionary work, have already reached Rome. Therefore his letter describes the gospel he proclaims everywhere,[23] and at the same time he addresses the attacks of his opponents.

Consequently, the letter to the Romans becomes not only a presentation of Paul's gospel but at the same time a "dialogue with a (fictional) Jewish interlocutor."[24] This fictive opposite represents Paul's Judaizing Jewish-Christian opponents who follow him everywhere and cause turmoil in the communities of the Pauline mission because they demand that the newly converted Gentiles accept male circumcision and keep the whole Torah. They consider Paul a pseudo-apostle and a dangerous apostate. They accuse him of invalidating Torah and denying Israel's election. Paul confronts both accusations at length: in Romans 6–8 he addresses the charge of lawlessness, and in Romans 9–11 he meets the accusation that he teaches the rejection of Israel and thus identifies with anti-Judaism.

[22] Otfried Hofius, "Das Evangelium und Israel. Erwägungen zu Römer 9–11," *ZThK* 83 (1986): 299. Cf. also Ulrich Wilckens, *Der Brief an die Römer (Röm 1–5)*, EKKNT 6/1 (Zürich: Benziger; Neukirchen-Vluyn: Neukirchener Verlag, 1978), 19 and *passim*.

[23] Cf. Rom 1:1, 9, 16-17; 2:16; 15:19.

[24] Rudolf Pesch, *Römerbrief*, NEB (Würzburg: Echter, 1983), 11. Cf. also Wilckens, *Brief an die Römer (Röm 1–5)*, 46.

Paul's concern, however, is not merely an apologetic against outsiders. He wants to give a personal assessment of the consequences of his theology as they affect Israel. For if not only the Gentile world but all Israel are subject to the wrath of God (Rom 1:18–3:20), and if salvation for Jews as well as Gentiles comes only through faith in Jesus Christ (Rom 3:21–8:39), but the majority of Israel does not believe the gospel of Jesus Christ (Rom 10:16-21), then the hard and urgent question is this: why does the gospel that, according to Romans 1:16, is "God's saving power for everyone who believes, for the Jew first and also for the Greek," appear to be powerless for the Jews?[25]

Has Israel then dropped out of the history of salvation? Has its election become obsolete, and has the church taken its place? Thus the question of the salvation of Israel is the test case for what Paul says about salvation and redemption. The unbelief of the people of God raises the question of the validity of God's promises. Does God keep promises once given, or not?

The close linkage of this question to the center of Pauline theology is already evident, purely on the surface, from the fact that it accompanies his exposition in Romans from the very beginning. As early as Romans 3:3-4, Paul writes: "What if some were unfaithful? Will their faithlessness nullify the faithfulness of God? By no means!"

We must not simply identify this question regarding Israel's position in salvation history with that of Jews' postmortem salvation. Obviously when Paul speaks of "redemption" the question of eternal salvation or damnation comes into the picture, together with the fate of individuals. But its most urgent concern is with the ways of God within history, as the closing doxology in Romans 11:33 shows: "O the depth of the riches and wisdom and knowledge of God! How unsearchable are God's judgments and how inscrutable [God's] ways!"

Paul, like the whole of the Old Testament, is concerned with the world. Will God accomplish salvation in it, despite the resistance of human beings, and so prove that the divine promises are genuine? This question of salvation within history, for Paul, refers to the redemption of the world—but it is indissolubly connected to the question of Israel's salvation. If God "who justifies the ungodly" (Rom 4:5) saves the Gentiles by pure grace, must that same God not also

[25] Cf. Hofius, "Evangelium," 299.

save Israel, first chosen as God's own people and intended to be "light for the nations"?[26] Thus in concluding the presentation of his gospel Paul is positively forced to ask about Israel's fate. The basic question in Romans 9–11 is, in short: does the righteousness that God gives freely in Christ also mean salvation for Israel, so that it remains true that God keeps every promise?

Israel's Hardness of Heart and the Awakening of Its Jealousy

The first answer Paul gives to this question is the assertion that "not all those descended from Israel are Israelites" (Rom 9:6). In consequence, Paul distinguishes between the "children of the flesh," that is, the physical-biological descendants of Abraham, and the "children of the promise" (Rom 9:8). In fact, that results in a distinction between an Israel "according to the flesh" (1 Cor 10:18) and the true Israel, that is, the Israel that is the community of salvation. That distinction, which Paul develops on the basis of the election of Isaac and Jacob—that is, based on Torah—makes it possible for him to say that God's word of promise is true for the "children of the promise," that is, the Israel made up of Jews and Gentiles to whom God's promise applies; indeed, it is present now (Rom 9:6-29).

Thus God's election already creates a division within Israel. Paul then pursues this idea in Romans 11:1-10 with the aid of another Old Testament category, namely, the idea of the "remnant of Israel."[27] By this he means the Jewish-Christian church, which belongs entirely to Israel but differs from the rest of the people of God because it believes in Israel's Messiah. Here, at least, a part of Israel has come to faith and thus to salvation or redemption. It is God's choice that there should be a "remnant" of Israel.[28] It is the work of God's electing grace (Rom 11:5-6). Then, however, it is already established that God has not broken the words of divine promise and maintains fidelity to God's people.

[26] Cf. Isa 42:6; 49:6; 60:1-2, taken up by Paul in Rom 2:19.

[27] For the concept of the "remnant" in Rom 9–11, cf. 9:27, 29; 11:5, 7. On the idea of a remnant in the Old Testament cf. now esp. Jutta Hausmann, *Israels Rest. Studien zum Selbstverständnis der nachexilischen Gemeinde*, BWANT 124 (Stuttgart: Kohlhammer, 1987).

[28] Hausmann, *Israels Rest*, 207.

But is this demonstration sufficient? Not for Paul: he insists on asking "what about the rest of Israel?"—that is, the Israel that apparently remains stubborn and so does not believe in Jesus Christ as the fulfillment of the promises.

Paul had already introduced the biblical concept of "hardening hearts" in Romans 9:18.[29] That idea has become foreign to people today. It may be that post-Christian contemporaries will still admit that people can "harden" themselves, but that God could harden the hearts of individuals and even entire peoples is something not even believing Christians would say now.

Certainly, even in Romans 9–11 the idea of hardening that is solely of divine origin does not stand alone. Paul can use other concepts as well; these show that hardening by God does not eliminate human freedom. He speaks of "contrary" Israel (Rom 10:21), of its disobedience (Rom 10:3, 21), its unbelief (Rom 10:16; 11:20, 23), even its ungodliness (Rom 11:26), either in formulaic language or by citing Scripture. It is probable that the principal goal of Romans 9:30–10:21 is to demonstrate Israel's guilty rejection of the gospel.[30]

Beyond that we should also note that the idea of hardening is *functional* for Paul. That is: God does not harden people and nations at random but for a particular purpose.[31] This is most clearly expressed in Romans 11:7-11. God has hardened Israel so that the gospel may also be preached to the Gentiles:

> Israel has not achieved what it was pursuing. The elect have achieved it, but the rest were hardened. . . . So I ask, have they stumbled so as to fall [perish]? By no means! But through their misstep[32] salvation has come to the gentiles, so as to make Israel jealous. (Rom 11:7, 11)

[29] After 9:18 the concept of hardening is taken up again in 11:7-10, 25. The Old Testament is familiar not only with hardening by God but also with self-hardening, the hardening of the heart: cf. Ps 95:7-11.

[30] Thus Hans-Martin Lübking, *Paulus und Israel im Römerbrief. Eine Untersuchung zu Röm 9–11*, EHS.T 260 (Frankfurt: Lang, 1986), 79–97.

[31] Pharaoh is hardened in order that the news of God's deeds may spread throughout the world. Cf. Exod 9:16 in Rom 9:17.

[32] We may best translate *paraptōma* here with "misstep" so as not to disrupt the logic of the simile. Israel has only "tripped" (11:11) and been caused to "stumble" in the sense of encountering a "stone that will make people stumble" (9:32). But in Isa 8:14-15, the text Paul has in mind in Rom 9:32-33 and that he partly quotes, *piptein* means a destroying fall. Cf. Hofius, "Evangelium," 298–99, 306–7.

Thus the hardening of Israel is for the purpose of salvation, the rescue of the Gentiles, yet the salvation of the Gentiles is not simply for their own sake. It is, in turn, part of a greater and much broader event, because the salvation that has come to the Gentiles as the result of Israel's hardening works back, beyond and through the Gentiles, on Israel itself. It is to "make Israel jealous" (Rom 10:19; 11:11, 14). That, at any rate, is how most translators render the *parazēloō* in the Greek text. The translation is by no means wrong, because when Paul quotes Deuteronomy 32:21 in Romans 10:19 *parazēloō* certainly has that meaning: "I will use those who are not a nation to make you jealous; with a foolish nation I will provoke you" (Rom 10:19). But it should be noted that already in Deuteronomy 32:21 the jealousy to which Israel is to be led is a reflection of divine jealousy:

> They have aroused me to jealousy toward a not-God,
> awakened my wrath with their idols.
> So I will make them jealous toward what is no people,
> provoke them to wrath with a foolish nation. (Deut 32:21 LXX)

God is jealous for the sake of God's own people and fights for this chosen people. Israel is to adopt this divine jealousy and pursue God's cause with the same zeal. The jealousy God wants to arouse in Israel is thus already in Romans 10:19 (= Deut 32:21) something different from human jealousy. This is about that passion for God that is found elsewhere in Sacred Scripture and refers to the dedication of the whole person to God's cause.[33] For example, Phinehas is jealous (or: zealous) for God in that sense,[34] and so are Elijah[35] and Jehu.[36]

That Paul also understood *parazēloō* in Romans 11:11, 14 in that way is evident already in 10:2, where the apostle emphasizes that Israel has "zeal for God," but it is "not based on knowledge." The idea here, of course, is not some kind of "jealousy" but the commitment of one's whole existence. All that is lacking in Jewish zeal is the insight into how God's righteousness is truly to be acquired (Rom

[33] See, in the New Testament, Rom 10:2 (!) [zeal]; 1 Cor 12:31 [verb: strive]; 14:1, 30 [as in 12:31]; 2 Cor 7:7 [zeal], 11 [zeal]; 9:2 [zeal]; 11:2 [divine jealousy (felt by Paul)].

[34] Cf. Num 25:11 [jealousy (God's)], 13 [zealous (Phinehas)]; 1 Macc 2:24-26 [zeal], 54 [zealous]; Sir 45:23 [zealous].

[35] Cf. 1 Kgs 19:10, 14; 1 Macc 2:58 [zeal]; Sir 48:2 [zeal].

[36] Cf. 2 Kgs 10:16 [zeal for the Lord].

10:3), but the Jews could achieve that insight by looking at the righteousness-through-faith of the Gentiles and thus transform their false zeal into a correct one.

Therefore in Romans 11:14 Paul says that he himself desires, through his apostolic service among the Gentiles, to make "his own flesh"—that is, the Israel that does not yet believe in Christ— zealous for God so that "some" may be saved. Modesty forbids him to say more at this point.[37] Of course he means more than only "some."

> Inasmuch as [or: precisely because] I am an apostle to the gentiles, I celebrate my ministry in order to make my own people jealous and thus save some of them. (Rom 11:13-14)

But Paul can also speak differently about this *parazēloō*. As high as he considers his own office to be (cf. Rom 1:5), he knows that the conversion of the nations to the gospel and thus the incitement of Israel are parts of a more comprehensive event (cf. Rom 11:15). Therefore, already in Romans 11:11 and quite independently of his own office, he writes: "through their stumbling salvation has come to the gentiles, so as to make Israel jealous."

But what, exactly, is that jealousy to consist of? Does it include an eventual coming of Israel to belief? Romans 11:14, at any rate, speaks in favor of that, because there *parazēloō* is immediately followed substantially (not temporally) by "and thus save." Apparently, for Paul, becoming jealous is largely equivalent to coming to faith. That faith can only be aroused when Israel sees God's action, namely, God's merciful acts. Concretely: Israel can see in the Gentile church a "people" (Rom 9:25; 10:19) that lives in a righteousness by faith (Rom 9:30) that Torah's social order shows can be fulfilled in *agapē* (Rom 13:8-10) and so attests to the fact that salvation has already come.[38] The correct definition of *parazēloō* thus proves to be the exegetical key to a right understanding of what, according to Romans 11:25-26, will lead Israel to conversion.

Oddly enough, some interpreters scarcely pay any attention to *parazēloō*, or at least they grant it no theological significance for Israel's

[37] "Some" (*tines*) should therefore not be stressed. It is an expression of modesty, corresponding to the clear parallel in 1 Cor 9:22 where *tines* means "as many as possible."

[38] Cf. Pesch, *Römerbrief*, 22.

path.[39] Others draw a sharp line of separation between a merely temporary *parazēloō* and the act of final salvation of Israel by God alone.[40] In recent decades some have even taken the position that the conversion of still-unbelieving Israel will take place independently of the church, indeed "without reference to the church" before Christ's *parousia*.[41] The text that is said to undergird this thesis is

[39] Cf., e.g., Franz Mussner, " 'Ganz Israel wird gerettet werden' (Röm 11,26)," *Kairos* 18 (1976): 241–55. According to Mussner we can no longer discern what Paul meant by the motif of *parazēlōsai*, and it is "without importance for our subject" (p. 246). Likewise Otfried Hofius and Michael Theobald do not discuss *parazēlōsai* in their helpful and important essays on Romans 9–11. Cf. Hofius, "Evangelium,"; Michael Theobald, "Kirche und Israel nach Röm 9–11," *Kairos* 29 (1987): 1–22.

[40] Thus Berthold Klappert, "Traktat für Israel (Röm 9–11)," in *Jüdische Existenz und die Erneuerung der christlichen Theologie*, ed. Martin Stöhr, ACJD 11 (Munich: Kaiser, 1981), 58–137, at 81–82: "PARAZEELOOSAI characterizes the *sending of the nations as preparation for the way of the Messiah and thus not as an endpoint, but instead as an 'interlude' in God's history with Israel* and tasks the Gentile church—though this has been betrayed throughout the church's history—through its messianic attractiveness in word and deed to cause the synagogal majority of Israel to pay attention, so that ultimately it may recognize in the way and actions of the church the messianic preparation of the way and the messianic splinters." [Trans. LMM]. As correct as much of this is, on the whole it is an attempt at a sharp separation between the time of the *parazēlōsai* and the act of Israel's final salvation by God. Therefore the messianic preparation of the way for Israel by the church can only be an "interlude" in which the "messianic splinters" become evident. Such exegesis is an exemplary case demonstrating how the church's actual experience can influence interpretation: many theologians do not really believe that God acts through the church, and they certainly do not trust the church to allow God to act on it.

[41] Cf. esp. Christoph Plag, *Israels Wege zum Heil. Eine Untersuchung zu Röm 9–11*, Arbeiten zur Theologie 40 (Stuttgart: Calwer, 1969), 37, 68. Franz Mussner, *Tractate on the Jews: The Significance of Judaism for Christian Faith*, trans. Leonard Swidler (Philadelphia: Fortress Press, 1984), 34: Israel will be saved "simply and only through the initiative of a God merciful *to all*, completely independent of the attitude of Israel and the rest of humanity, which will consist concretely in the *parousia* of Jesus. The *parousia* [of] Christ saves all Israel without a preceding 'conversion' of the Jews to the gospel." Klappert, "Traktat," 85–86: "This eschatological hope for the rescue of all Israel by God is for Paul trans-kerygmatic and trans-eschatological, and this means a critique of the church in the true sense of the word. In that Paul expects the salvation of all Israel first of all from the Parousia of the coming *kyrios*-human one and not from the mission to the nations as ordered in the gospel, he recognizes an *immediate application of the coming Parousia of the Kyrios to all Israel without reference to the church.*" [Trans. LMM]. Theobald, "Kirche," 14: "Salvation for all only through Jesus Christ (*solus Christus*), but in the case of Israel therefore also (and perhaps not only in the case of Israel): salvation independent of the church!" [Trans. LMM]. All the named authors emphasize the graciousness of Israel's salvation at the *parousia* and the necessity of Israel's belief in Christ's *parousia*. Hofius, "Evangelium," 319–20, stresses in

Romans 11:25-27, where Paul speaks of the "mystery" of Israel's future and gives a proof for it from Isaiah 59:20-21; 27:9:

> I want you to understand this mystery, brothers and sisters, so that you may not claim to be wiser than you are: a hardening[42] has come upon part of Israel until the full number of the gentiles has come in. And in this way all Israel will be saved, as it is written,
> "Out of Zion will come the Deliverer;
> he will banish ungodliness from Jacob."
> "And this [will be the fulfillment of the] covenant [I affirm],
> [that I will] take away their sins."

The crucial question for this text, which is the goal of everything that has been said in Romans 9–11, is: According to Paul, is the cause of Israel's conversion the vision of the *parousia* of Christ, the "savior" from Zion? Or is Paul thinking primarily of Israel's being-brought-to-zeal-for-God, which has been referred to several times previously? An exegetically satisfying answer requires us to note two things:

1. The thesis that a "special path for Israel" cannot be derived from Paul's own formulations but comes solely from a scriptural citation is highly dubious. The formal difference between the formulation of the "mystery" and the subsequent scriptural quotation must be taken seriously. To put it another way: the formulation of the mystery must be coherent in itself, that is, it must not reveal any gap that needs to be filled by a scriptural citation. The application of Isaiah 59 and 27 is intended as substantiation for the already-described process of Israel's salvation; in itself it does not introduce crucial elements of the process to the minds of the hearers or readers. That is the only way in which a formal scriptural citation like that in Romans 11:26-27 functions.

2. The "mystery" formulated in Romans 11:25-26 does not stand alone in the text like something that has fallen from heaven. Paul has carefully prepared for it in a whole series of arguments. We cannot examine them in detail here; let me simply point to the fact that readers have already heard about the hardening of

---

addition that Israel will not come to salvation through the preaching of the gospel but that in the return of the *Kyrios* it will implicitly encounter the gospel as well.

[42] *Apo merous* may be adnomial to "hardening." Cf. Hofius, "Evangelium," 312. The modern translations need to be somewhat freer here.

> Israel's heart.[43] But they have also heard about the "part of Israel," that is, the division within Israel[44] as well as the "fullness of the Gentiles."[45] They even know of the temporal limits of the hardening,[46] and that all Israel will be brought home.[47] All that is new is the concrete form of the limitation: namely, that Israel's hardening will have an end as soon as the "full number of the gentiles" has been reached.

If we take seriously the fact that Paul has prepared for the formulation of the mystery with the utmost care we will know it is necessary also to seek within what has already been said for the mode in which Israel's hardening will come to an end. Then the only question is about the arousing of Israel's jealousy, already referred to in Romans 10:19; 11:11, 14. The "mystery" can then be described as follows:

> God has imposed a partial hardening on Israel until the time when the fullness of the Gentile nations has entered into the true Israel, that is, the eschatological people of God made up of Jews and Gentiles. Then God will bring an end to the hardening of the still-unbelieving Israel. From Israel's side this absolutely gracious action corresponds to zeal for God, or a turning that takes place in light of the "fullness" of the Gentiles. "In this way" (*kai houtōs*) all Israel will be saved.

"In this way" could really, by itself, settle the whole disputed question because, as Pauline parallels show, *kai houtōs* can only refer to what has been said previously, not to the scriptural citation that follows. Apart from Romans 11:26, *kai houtōs* appears in Paul's writings also in Romans 5:12; 1 Corinthians 7:17, 36; 11:28; 14:21, 25; Galatians 6:2; 1 Thessalonians 4:17. In all these passages, without exception, it points back.[48] Thus "in this way all Israel will be saved" by no means

[43] Of "hardening" already in Rom 9:18; 11:7-10.

[44] Of "parts" already in Rom 9:6-13; 11:1-7.

[45] Of the "fullness" of the Gentiles already in Rom 11:12 (*ploutos ethnōn*).

[46] For the temporal limits of the hardening cf. already Rom 11:12 (the "reduction" to a remnant is followed by the "filling" of the remnant to the full number) and 11:15 ("rejection" is followed by "acceptance" by God). Cf. Hofius, "Evangelium," 308.

[47] For the "bringing home of all Israel" cf. already Rom 11:12, 15, 23-24.

[48] Likewise, simple *houtōs* in Paul is almost always a backward reference. The few cases in which it points to something that is to follow are syntactically quite clear: cf., e.g., Rom 10:6; 1 Cor 9:26. In 1 Cor 15:45 simple *houtōs* introduces a quotation and is thereby likewise a reference backward.

says that Israel's salvation will take place in the form described in the subsequent scriptural citation; rather, it will happen as previously described, thus primarily by the "coming in of the full number of the gentiles." That is what will introduce Israel's salvation.

There are probably two reasons why the theological construct of a "special path for Israel" arose at all, though the reasons lie on two very different levels. On the one hand there is the actual history. Israel has, in fact, followed a separate path to this day, and the church shares in the guilt for that: Jewish Christianity was marginalized and the synagogue banished to the ghetto. Finally, after Auschwitz, it seemed appropriate to some theologians that a special path to salvation, apart from the church, should be assumed as a kind of theological reparation for Israel.

There is, however, another reason. Anyone who engages with the literature on Romans 9–11, which is almost without compass, cannot avoid the impression that some interpreters have been unable to imagine God's actions and those of Israel as compatible. Evidently they believe that the absolute graciousness of God's actions can be maintained only if Israel itself does nothing. For that very reason *parazēloō* is downplayed, and the turning of Israel is situated, in almost magical fashion, outside of history and far distant from the faith community of the church. But that is a false interpretation of the relationship between grace and freedom. The letter to the Romans does not support it. God's action (removal of the hardening) and Israel's response (becoming zealous) are not contradictory in Paul's eyes. They are "unmixed and unseparated," the divine and human sides of one and the same event.[49]

After all that it is no longer difficult to determine the real purpose of the scriptural quotation in Romans 11:26-27. The weight of the combined citation lies not so much on the "Deliverer from Zion" as on the taking away of the hardening (= removal of ungodliness) and God's faithfulness to the covenant. Both were referred to previously, and both are intended to be emphasized by the scriptural reference.

[49] For the possibility of the "interpenetration" of divine and human action cf. Gerhard Lohfink, "Die Not der Exegese mit der Reich-Gottes-Verkündigung Jesu," *ThQ* 168 (1988): 1–15; repr. in idem, *Studien zum Neuen Testament*, SBAB 5 (Stuttgart: Katholisches Bibelwerk, 1989), 383–402; Gerhard Lohfink and Ludwig Weimer, *Die Lust an Gott und seiner Sache oder: Lassen sich Gnade und Freiheit, Glaube und Vernunft, Erlösung und Befreiung vereinbaren?*, 2nd ed. (Freiburg: Herder, 1982).

Like the "Deliverer from Zion," so also the theme of covenant in Romans 11:27 is often falsely interpreted. It is not directly about the "new covenant" of Jeremiah 31:31; rather, it concerns the covenant with the patriarchs (Genesis 17; Exodus 6; Leviticus 26),[50] for immediately afterward we read in Romans 11:28: "As regards the gospel they are enemies for your sake, but as regards election they are beloved for the sake of their ancestors." Because God promised salvation to the ancestors and solemnly affirmed it, God will remain faithful to Israel and maintain the covenant made with the patriarchs. Concretely: God will remove all that is godless from Jacob (= Israel) and take away the sins of the people of God through God's Christ. Here, in the combined quotation, the "Deliverer from Zion" is replaced, without notice of the fact, by the "I" of YHWH:[51] Christ, the "Deliverer from Zion," removes the "ungodliness from Jacob," but it is God who takes away their sins.

Both couplets refer to the same thing: both "ungodliness" and "sins" are Israel's violations of the covenant.[52] The combined quotation is linked by the keywords "Jacob" and "take away their sins." That the shift in the logical subject is simply ignored shows that the emphasis lies not on the "Deliverer from Zion" but on God's fidelity to the covenant. To that extent it is again evident that the scriptural reference is not the first description of the mode of Israel's turning; it only employs scripture to emphasize the mystery already proclaimed.

Obviously Paul could have found more texts on the theme of "God's fidelity to the covenant" and "salvation of all Israel."[53] The fact that he chose a text in which the "Deliverer from Zion" appears could be related to his having spoken previously, in Romans 9:32-33, of the "stum-

[50] It is true that Isa 59:21 does not speak directly about the covenant with the *patriarchs*. The reference is to what is called an "eternal covenant" in Isa 55:3; 61:8. But Gen 17:7 speaks directly of the covenant with Abraham as an "eternal covenant." Cf. Norbert Lohfink, *Der niemals gekündigte Bund. Exegetische Gedanken zum christlich-jüdischen Gespräch* (Freiburg: Herder, 1989), 87–91. [English: *The Covenant Never Revoked: Biblical Reflections on Christian-Jewish Dialogue*, trans. John J. Scullion (New York: Paulist, 1991), 58–74.]

[51] Given the direct shift to the "I" of YHWH, one might even argue that the "Deliverer from Zion" refers not to Christ but to YHWH. Against that, however, are Rom 9:32-33 (motif of Zion) and 1 Thess 1:10 (motif of the savior). In addition, such unevennesses are common in combined quotations.

[52] In the Old Testament the motif of forgiveness of sins is part of the theme of the "new covenant." That strict connection faded, however, in early Judaism.

[53] For God's fidelity to the covenant cf., e.g., Jer 31:31-34; 32:37-41; Ezek 37:26. For the salvation of all Israel see, e.g., Isa 45:17, 25.

bling stone" in Zion. It may be that, as is often the case in rabbinic exegesis, the quotation is simultaneously a pointer to a broader text-complex within which it belongs; the hearer or reader should have the whole context in mind. Isaiah 59:20-21, in fact, is followed immediately by the great chapter on the pilgrimage of the nations to Zion, and just before it we read: "[T]hose [nations] in the west shall fear the name of the LORD, and those [nations] in the east, his [glorious Name]" (Isa 59:19). Although that statement is embedded in a context of sayings about judgment, Paul could certainly have applied it to God's saving action for distant nations that will bring them to call on the Name of the Lord—even before the saving of Jacob.[54]

Consequently, on the basis of Romans 11:25-27 we should also speak of the idea of the pilgrimage of the nations within the three chapters on Israel. It is, however, necessary first to say something basic about the subject of "Israel's special path." We have already distinguished between the divine and human sides of Israel's eschatological returning. On the divine side there is the absolute, gracious removal of the sin of breaking the covenant (Rom 11:27). Also on the divine side is the appearance of Christ's *parousia*, which removes all godlessness from Jacob (Rom 11:26). On the human (but likewise grace-filled) side of the same event lies what happens within history: the growth of the Gentile church to its full number and the jealousy of Israel awakened by that full number.

The two must not be set in opposition, above all because both are open to dramatic historical processes. We must never forget that, for Paul, Christ's *parousia* is not something far distant but is dramatically close at hand; still more, its nearness is setting in motion a history that will overturn everything. Paul sees and experiences that history in an utterly concentrated form, completely simultaneous. For us, however, it has come apart. A few years have turned into altogether endless lengths of time. Methodologically, then, it is inappropriate to mechanically situate events that Paul sees as tightly combined in the *parousia*, that is, in the very immediate future, in our present idea of history and so locate them on "the last day," that is, to imagine them as taking place in some nebulous distance.

That, however, is precisely what the hypothesis of the "special path" does. If it were consistent in its simplistic application of the text it should

[54] Cf. Hofius, "Evangelium," 324.

expect, even today, that the *parousia* would take place within a few years. Of course, none of its advocates do that. But even if they did, the whole hypothesis would still be deficient because it works with the motif of conquest, of overpowering: what God does not succeed in accomplishing within ongoing history will finally be achieved by a violent end to history through the all-conquering appearance of Christ.

I think that is a miserable theology: God must act with sovereign force, at the absolute limit of history, basically "beyond history," to drive unbelieving Israel to Christ in order that it can at last understand, and thus God's plan for history can finally succeed. But the worst thing about that theology is that it relieves the church of the necessity to be a messianic people in order that Israel may at last understand. The church does not need to change in the face of seeking and hoping Israel; it must only see to it that it does not conduct a mission to Israel and, beyond that it must leave everything to God.

Paul thinks altogether differently here. It is true that the "Deliverer from Zion" appears in his text, too, but the deliverer's appearance is preceded by Israel's becoming jealous. With the aid of that motif Paul makes room for the human partner—more precisely, the interaction between the church and Israel. In this way he gives a proper place to history (which, certainly, in his view rightly develops in terms of and toward the *parousia*). The idea of the pilgrimage of nations aids him in this. We need to give some attention to that idea, because without it we cannot understand Romans 9–11.

The Horizon of the Pilgrimage of Nations

According to the complex of imagery and ideas that emerges so often in the Old Testament, eschatological salvation will shine forth before all nations "at the end of days" from Zion, that is, from the center of Israel, and its fascination will draw them to journey to Jerusalem to see salvation there.[55]

[55] Still a good overview of the Old Testament idea of the pilgrimage of nations: Joachim Jeremias, *Jesus' Promise to the Nations*, trans. S. H. Hooke (London: SCM, 1958). More recent individual studies by Old Testament experts, who have the advantage of being able to tap the concerns of canonical exegesis, include Norbert Lohfink and Erich Zenger, *The God of Israel and the Nations: Studies in Isaiah and the Psalms*, trans. Everett R. Kalin (Collegeville, MN: Liturgical Press, 2000), and above all Michael P. Maier, *Völkerwallfahrt im Jesajabuch*, BZAW 474 (Berlin: de Gruyter, 2016).

For Paul the promised pilgrimage of nations is already in progress[56]—though for the moment not in the sense that the fascination that streams forth from Israel draws the nations to Zion. Rather, it is that the hardening of Israel has driven Jesus' messengers to the Gentiles (Rom 11:11; 10:16-19), so that now salvation is visible not in Jerusalem but among the Gentiles, more precisely in the Gentile Christian communities around the Mediterranean. Even so, Paul writes "until the full number of the gentiles has come in" (Rom 11:25), thus interpreting the unbelievable event that now Gentiles everywhere are coming to believe and are becoming heirs of Abraham and so are constituting the already-happening eschatological pilgrimage to the true Israel, that is, the Jewish-Christian church.

According to Paul, however, that very thing will bring Israel to jealous zeal: it will turn again and believe. In this way the progress of the pilgrimage of the nations—so far as its direction is concerned—is being reversed in a positively paradoxical way. It is not that the nations come to believe because of what they see in Israel but that Israel is coming to believe by looking at the nations or, more precisely, at the Gentile church.

What will Israel see in the Gentile Christians? First of all, there is their fullness (*plērōma*), that is, their numbers (Rom 11:25). The reference is not to their numerical completeness but to the number determined by God and known to God alone.[57] It is an overpowering multiplicity that must cause every Jew to think twice. The "full number of the gentiles," however, means still more: it is also the fullness of human salvation that is dawning in the church.[58] Paul speaks of this richness (*ploutos*) of salvation, again echoing a motif of the pilgrimage of nations, because according to Isaiah 60:6, 16 (LXX) the nations will

[56] Early church interpreters thought like Paul on this point: the pilgrimage of nations is already happening. Cf. Gerhard Lohfink, "'Schwerter zu Pflugscharen.' Die Rezeption von Jes 2,1-5 par Mi 4,1-5 in der Alten Kirche und im Neuen Testament," *ThQ* 166 (1986): 184–209.

[57] The most extended investigation of the subject is found in Rainer Stuhlmann, *Das eschatologische Maß im Neuen Testament*, FRLANT 132 (Göttingen: Vandenhoeck & Ruprecht, 1983); see there esp. 173–78.

[58] This is also the tendency of Klappert, "Traktat," when he speaks of the "messianic attractiveness" of the church "in word and deed" (pp. 81–82, 93). Out of fear that this "messianic attractiveness" might be confused with the idea of a *mission to the Jews*, however, he reduces it to an "incident."

bring their treasures to God's people. Israel can thus see in the "fullness of the gentiles" the blessing that is already on its way to them.

But even with that the unfolding of the "mystery"—of which Paul speaks from Romans 10:1 onward, but above all after 11:11, and then summarizes in 11:25—is not at its end. There is not only a "full number of gentiles" but also a "full number/fullness" of Jews. When Israel has, through its repentance and belief in the Messiah, arrived at the full number determined by God (Rom 11:12), so that one may speak of the "salvation of all Israel" (Rom 11:26), it will in turn have a profound effect on the whole world of the nations. Namely:

> [I]f their stumbling means riches for the world and if their loss[59] means riches for gentiles, how much more will their full inclusion mean! (Rom 11:12)

A little later Paul writes a variation on the same idea:

> For if their rejection is the reconciliation of the world, what will their acceptance be but life from the dead? (Rom 11:15)

Again, we can only interpret this further intensification within the model of the pilgrimage of nations—now, certainly, in its original Old Testament sense: the turning of all Israel will begin the ultimate coming of the Gentiles to Zion, to the true Israel, and thus introduce the transformation of the whole world. The model is:

Hardening of Israel

Salvation for the Gentiles

Repentance/Return of all Israel

Salvation for the whole world

[59] Here the Greek text has the rare word *hēttēma*. In Romans 11 it is an antonym to *plērōma* and means the "reduction of this full number" that has come about because of the "downfall" of the unbelieving Jews. Cf. Ulrich Wilckens, *Der Brief an die Römer (Röm 6–11)*, EKKNT 6/2 (Zürich: Benziger; Neukirchen-Vluyn: Neukirchener Verlag, 1980), 243.

It is a breathtaking view of history. Paul cannot see the resistance he experiences on the part of the synagogues as entirely negative. He gives it a positive explanation as the hardening of Israel by God with the direct intent of bringing salvation to the Gentiles. Still, he cannot view the impressive success of his mission among the Gentiles in isolation. In God's mind its purpose is to bring Israel back to its own mission: to be a light to the nations (Rom 2:19). Once that has been achieved, the eschatological pilgrimage of the nations will again be directed in the way proclaimed by the prophets.

Here, then, Paul interprets history in terms of a thrillingly audacious historical theology. As in 1 Thessalonians 2:14-16, but now with an incomparably greater breadth, he interprets what he and his communities are experiencing in the present—but not through ungrounded speculation. He uses models long since prepared for him by Israel's tradition: hardening, holy remnant, promise to the nations, covenant, and above all the pilgrimage of the nations to Zion.

According to Paul even the idea that God advances the history of Israel with its God precisely by calling a people of God's own from among the Gentiles is recorded in Sacred Scripture in advance. Zephaniah[60] writes that the time of God's wrath will come to an end when God makes a new beginning with the nations who dwell at the farthest limits of the world (Zeph 2:11). In a radical revolution, God will cause distant pagans—almost easily—to do what Israel finds so difficult:[61] praising God with clean lips and serving God with one mind:

[60] In interpreting Zephaniah's theology I am primarily following Michael Weigl, *Zefanja und das "Israel der Armen": Eine Untersuchung zur Theologie des Buches Zefanja*, OBS 13 (Klosterneuburg: Österreichisches Katholisches Bibelwerk, 1994). Weigl describes Zephaniah's view thus: "Of all people, the previously unappreciated poor become, in Zephaniah, the sole hope for a continuance of salvation history. Parallel to this revolution in Israel another development, by no means less explosive, will take place: the most distant nations, who previously had existed only as 'islands' in the social imagination, will be transformed into believers by YHWH's initiative; they will come to Jerusalem to offer YHWH the share of tribute that belongs to him. A new salvation for Jerusalem, indeed for all Israel, can only come from this togetherness and mutuality of the historical forces newly constituted by YHWH. The demand with which Zephaniah confronts his hearers/readers is that they recognize that, in light of previous historical reality, every hope for salvation 'from above' [Weigl refers to the upper social classes—GL] and 'from within' is exhausted. YHWH will therefore choose a salvation-historical alternative by causing a new future to grow 'from below' and 'from without'" (p. 256).—Trans. LMM. In Paul's view all that is very near at hand. Cf. also Norbert Lohfink, "Zefanja und das Israel der Armen," *BiKi* 39 (1984): 100–108.

[61] Weigl, *Zefanja*, 132–34.

> At that time I will change the speech of the peoples to a pure speech,
> that all of them may call on the name of the LORD and serve him with one accord. (Zeph 3:9)

Then those who worship YHWH from among all the nations will come from afar to Jerusalem (Zeph 3:10). There they will find the believing "remnant" of Israel, the "humble" and "lowly" who, unlike the rich and satisfied, have remained on YHWH's side. The fact that they still exist in Israel is pure grace. They are the nucleus of the new salvation for the whole people of God and the "guarantors of the continuity of salvation history."[62]

> For I will leave in the midst of you
> a people humble and lowly.
> They shall seek refuge in the name of YHWH—
> the remnant of Israel;
> they shall do no wrong
> and utter no lies,
> nor shall a deceitful tongue
> be found in their mouths. (Zeph 3:12-13)

This whole complex of Old Testament motifs is familiar to Paul, even when he does not quote them all. It is from these that he shapes his image of God's present and future actions.[63] This fabric of motifs has nothing at all to do with airy speculations. It had come to exist in Israel on the basis of real, often painful experience and lived faith in God's promises. In addition, it was grounded in the unforeseeable miracle of the mission to the Gentiles.

The Dramatic Image of the Olive Tree

In Romans 9–11 Paul introduces still another pattern for interpreting his missionary experience, one I have previously set aside: that of the olive tree. Like the model of the pilgrimage of nations, this one was already present in the Old Testament.[64] Thus Jeremiah 11:16

[62] Weigl, *Zefanja*, 216.

[63] Paul could have drawn the "mystery" of Rom 11:25-26 entirely from his scriptures. Cf. the argumentation on this point by Hofius, "Evangelium," 322–24.

[64] See, in addition to Jer 11:16, especially Hos 14:7.

reads: "The LORD once called you, 'A green olive tree, fair with goodly fruit.'" Paul also uses the image of Israel as an olive tree, even though in itself it is somewhat static, to depict the drama of salvation history: the Gentile Christians who are Paul's primary addressees in Romans 11:16-24 have been brought from among the nations into the history of the people of God. Those Jews, in contrast, who have not believed in Jesus as Messiah, have been broken off of their own trunk, or their own roots:

> But if some of the branches were broken off, and you, a wild olive shoot, were grafted among the others to share the rich root of the olive tree, do not boast over the branches. If you do boast, remember: you do not support the root, but the root supports you. (Rom 11:17-18)

But the historical drama goes still further. Previously Paul has regularly written "against nature." After all, no one grafts in "wild" shoots, but only "premium" ones. The roots, in contrast, must be "wild." It shows a complete misunderstanding of Pauline theology when exegetes seek for ancient methods that Paul could justify "biologically"—or when they accuse him of using mistaken imagery. Paul's intention is, in fact, to make it clear that the history God is pursuing in the world is more than mere nature. It is a history of "impossibilities."

In what follows, Paul continues to sharpen the extraordinary and unusual features of the thing: even the branches that have been cut off—still-unbelieving Israel—will not parch on the ground and certainly will not be burned: instead, they will be reimplanted in the old trunk:

> And even those of Israel, if they do not continue in unbelief, will be grafted in, for God has the power to graft them in again. For if you have been cut from what is by nature a wild olive tree and grafted, contrary to nature, into a cultivated olive tree, how much more will these natural branches be grafted back into their own olive tree. (Rom 11:23-24)

As harshly as Romans 11:16-24 deals with the Jews, it is still clear that the scope of the whole is by no means directed against Israel. Instead, Paul uses the image of the olive tree in order to warn the Gentile Christians. The addressee of Romans 11:16-24 is not the synagogue but the church, and within it the Gentile church. Evidently Paul had sensed the danger that the Gentile Christian communities would separate themselves, internally and externally, from their mother earth, Israel, and so would be robbed of their strength.[65] But what is the mother earth, Israel? At this point we cannot avoid attempting a closer definition of the relationship between Israel and the church on the basis of Romans 9–11.

The Relationship of Israel and the Church According to Romans 9–11

Much in Romans 9–11 favors the idea that for Paul the church made up of Jews and Gentiles is the "true Israel." That seems indicated by the statements at the beginning of chapter 9 that are deeply provocative for any Jew:

> [N]ot all those descended from Israel are Israelites, and not all of Abraham's children are his descendants, but "it is through Isaac that descendants shall be named for you" [Gen 21:12 LXX]. This means that it is not the children of the flesh who are the children of God, but the children of the promise are counted as descendants. (Rom 9:6-8)

With this Paul apparently means to say that Gentile Christians, alongside Jewish Christians, are true children of Abraham and genuine heirs of the promise, since a little later he emphasizes that those whom God calls freely, out of mercy and a desire to continue this history with them, come not only from the Jews but also from the Gentiles (Rom 9:24). Immediately thereafter he seeks to show, with help from Hosea, that those who had not belonged to the people are now called "God's people." Those who formerly were "no people" are now called children of the living God (Rom 9:25-26).

It is true that the argumentation with the concepts of "not my people/my people" does not touch what Hosea was writing about,[66] but it makes it all the more obvious that Paul regards the Gentile Christian communities, together with the church drawn from the Jews, as the true Israel. The whole letter to the Romans moves in that

[65] Evidently the author of the letter to the Ephesians sees a similar danger at a later date. Cf. Eph 2:11-22.

[66] By "not my people" Hosea means the Israel rejected by God, not the Gentiles.

direction. Certainly its exposition as a whole points to the conclusion that all have sinned, Jews as well as Gentiles (Rom 3:9, 22-23), that only belief in God's saving act in Jesus Christ brings people to salvation, and that in that respect there is no longer any difference between Jews and Greeks (Rom 3:30).

In light of this basic theme of the letter to the Romans it is all the more striking that Paul does not call the church the "true Israel," either here or anywhere else in his letters—with the partial exception of Galatians 6:16.[67] This finding applies to the other New Testament writings as well. Luke, for example, makes it unmistakably clear by the sequence of his double work that he regards the church as the true, eschatological Israel,[68] but nowhere does he say it directly and literally. There must be reasons for this restraint, and they should be taken seriously by theologians.

If we want to understand this we must consider the basic salvation-historical structure that is taken as a given in broad stretches of the Old Testament: God desires the salvation of the whole world, but for the sake of the nations' freedom this can be achieved only if there is one people in the world in which God's will and plan are visible. God's salvation is to reach all nations by means of this one people. That is precisely the scope of the pilgrimage-of-the-nations model. But even the promise to Abraham in Genesis 12:1-3 says nothing different. Even the saving event in Jesus Christ does not alter this basic structure in the least.

The Gentile church is never the origin, the means, the proper instrument, or whatever one might call it. The Gentiles are and remain shoots grafted into the root, sharing in, sustained by, added to, and drawn into Israel's portion, because to Israel alone belong "the adoption, the glory, the covenants, the giving of the law, the worship, and the promises; to them belong the patriarchs, and from them, according to the flesh, comes the [Messiah]" (Rom 9:4-5). The whole sweep of Romans 9–11 shows us how important for Paul this *pre-* of Israel

[67] Michael Theobald rightly points out ("Kirche," 6), regarding Gal 6:16, that the Christians in Galatia "represent for him 'the Israel of God,' the true Israel; they are God's new creation in which this world's criteria of distinction, circumcision or uncircumcision, Jew or Gentile (Gal 3:28) have lost their validity."

[68] Cf. Gerhard Lohfink, *Die Sammlung Israels. Eine Untersuchung zur lukanischen Ekklesiologie*, SANT 39 (Munich: Kösel, 1975).

is.[69] The course of the history of salvation that Paul paints with all its turns and twists aims precisely at the desired end: that all Israel, even its now-still-unbelieving part and not merely its already believing Jewish-Christian part, will be saved. Why? Because from the beginning Israel has been God's instrument for the healing of the world: because the world can find its way to salvation only through Israel and its history of freedom and enlightenment.

Calling the church simply the "true" or "eschatological" Israel would gloss over all that. It is true that the beginning of the eschatological Israel is present in the church, but it is not yet complete. The church must never forget that, by its very nature, it remains tied to Israel as a whole,[70] but not only in the sense that even today by far the greater part of the synagogue has not yet come to believe in Christ. The church must also never forget that, to the extent that it is largely a "church of the Gentiles," it has a duty toward Israel that is immensely urgent. The nature of that duty can be discerned in the plan of history that Paul proposes in Romans 9–11.

We have seen that the model of the pilgrimage of nations underlies this whole history. But for Paul the sense of the direction of the pilgrimage of nations has been reversed at the moment: it is not the Gentiles who come to Zion, attracted by the brilliance emanating from Israel and its social order, but unbelieving Israel is looking at the Gentile church—shocked, goaded, a little jealous, but also burning with zeal and resolved to repent.

If we are correct in supposing that Paul is playing on the model of the pilgrimage of nations in Romans 9–11, then we are certainly thinking in the same direction if we suppose that Israel comes to faith because it is fascinated by the brilliance of the Gentile church, that is, not only its numbers but also its abundance. We have already spoken of that, too. "Fascination" is part of the very nature of the Old Testament idea of the pilgrimage of nations.[71] The Gentiles are not

[69] Cf. esp. the parable of the olive tree (Rom 11:13-24), but also earlier at Rom 1:16.

[70] Cf. Gerhard Lohfink, "Jesus und die Kirche," in *Handbuch der Fundamentaltheologie*, ed. Walter Kern, Hermann Josef Pottmeyer, and Max Seckler, vol. 3, Traktat "Kirche" (Freiburg: Herder, 1996), 49–96, at 94–95.

[71] This is especially clear in Isa 60:1-3: the light and glory of YHWH that light Jerusalem draw the nations to themselves. Cf. also Isa 2:1-5 *par* Mic 4:1-5.

missionized; they are attracted by what they see. Certainly the brilliance that draws them to the people of God is not its own light but the glory of the Lord that shines over Israel.[72]

If, in accordance with Pauline theology, the Gentile church has slipped into Israel's own role because of Israel's unbelief, it would therefore be the church's duty to show that the Messiah has indeed come, and to do so not only with the lips but by living as a messianic people. In other words: it would be the duty of the Gentile church to live what was bestowed on Israel—inheritance as daughters and sons, glory, covenants, Torah, worship, and the promises—in their original fullness. Only when the synagogue can see in the church itself the fascination of what it has always sought and hoped for can it enter, through the church, into that "zeal for God" of which Paul speaks.

Again: when many interpreters, basing their thinking on Romans 11:26, claim that there is a "special path" for Israel that can only be completed with Christ's *parousia* and that proceeds altogether independently of the church,[73] they fail to see that Paul regards the relationship between synagogue and church as a dramatic history in which the two parts are inseparably ordered and related to one another.[74] The Gentiles come to believe because Israel has not believed; Israel will be jealous because the Gentile church believes; Israel in turn, having come to faith, will be life from death—for the whole world. The Gentile church needs Israel; Israel needs the church; the whole world needs the church and Israel to find each other.

The construction "special path" disqualifies this dramatic being-together and being-for-one-another that Paul has in view. It is a thoroughly disastrous construct that theologians should never have thought of. It is based on resignation about the church and only justifies the development that—contrary to Paul's hopes—actually happened in the history of the church: for what Paul prophesied as Israel's true zeal has not yet come to pass. Instead, what has happened is what he urgently warns the Gentile church must not come to pass: the church has become arrogant and for centuries has haughtily looked

[72] Cf. esp. Isa 2:5; 51:4; 60:1-3.

[73] See n. 41 above.

[74] For the "drama" of the history of Israel and the church cf. Norbert Lohfink, *The Covenant Never Revoked*, 58–74; Lohfink and Zenger, *The God of Israel and the Nations*, 179–85.

down on the synagogue.[75] The church scarcely had its own time of persecution behind it and was finally free when persecution of the Jews began, followed almost immediately by the first burnings of synagogues.

One instance is often cited because of its inglorious aftermath: In Kallinikon on the Euphrates, Christians encouraged by their bishop reduced a Jewish synagogue to ashes. When Emperor Theodosius I, then resident in Milan, angrily ordered that the synagogue be rebuilt at the expense of the perpetrators, Bishop Ambrose of Milan forced him to annul the edict. During the subsequent reign of Theodosius II the burning of synagogues became so frequent that the subject of most of that emperor's edicts was the protection of synagogues and Jewish private houses.[76]

In light of that development and in the face of its Christian persecutors, how was the synagogue to recognize the fullness of messianic reality in the church? Until today it remains true that what Paul saw in prophetic vision has not come to pass. His image of the olive tree and the drama with which he resolved the image has been overlooked or reinterpreted through the centuries.

It is not only the image of the olive tree, however, that has been played down, suppressed, reinterpreted, and even repudiated. The whole text-complex of Romans 9–11 is, still today, one of the most misunderstood sections of the New Testament. The church fathers—and many others in their wake—were like deer in the headlights when they faced Romans 9:14-29 and the problem of freedom versus predestination. In the process they overlooked Paul's real point about God's action in history—for God's people and beyond them for the world. Many interpreters in the ancient church read the statement that all Israel will be saved to apply only to the true Israel of believ-

[75] This is vividly expressed by medieval representations of *Ecclesia* and *Synagoga* over the doors of cathedrals. Late medieval iconography even included a perverse representation of the so-called living cross, in which one arm of the cross thrusts a sword into the breast of the female figure of the synagogue who stands beneath the cross. Cf. W. P. Eckert, "Antisemitismus V," *TRE* 3, 137–43, at 138. Imagery can be found esp. in Herbert Jochum, ed., *Ecclesia und Synagoga. Das Judentum in der christlichen Kunst. Ausstellungskatalog*, Alte Synagoge Essen & Regionalgeschichtliches Museum Saarbrücken, 1993.

[76] Cf. Peter Schäfer, *The History of the Jews in the Greco-Roman World*, trans. David Chowcat (London: Routledge, 2003), 186–88.

ers, that is, Christians. The dramatic interpretation of history that is essential for Paul—namely, that precisely the Israel that still does not believe will come to faith—was thus elegantly avoided.

Anti-Judaism in Romans 9–11?

All that makes it superfluous to ask whether there are beginnings or even initial traces of anti-Judaism in Romans 9–11.[77] The three chapters were, in fact, written by Paul against that accusation, among others of the same sort. What might appear to a biased reader as anti-Judaism is in fact a glowing affirmation of Israel.

Even the idea of hardening, in which one might most probably suspect an attack on the Jews, is not introduced by Paul to exclude Israel from salvation history but to assert its election. Even if it clings to unbelief, God will still turn the disobedience of God's own people into salvation for the world. Israel's hardening has a salvation-historical function.

Then is the provocative distinction between an "Israel according to the flesh" and a true Israel anti-Jewish? Here again it is the case that Paul is working with distinctions that had long had a place in Israel's tradition and history. From Hosea and the book of Deuteronomy to as late as Qumran[78] there was an unending struggle over the "true Israel." That had nothing at all to do with anti-Judaism, not

[77] Gregory Baum does differ, even seeing anti-Judaism at work in Romans 9–11: "All attempts of Christian theologians to derive a more positive conclusion from Paul's teaching in Romans 9–11 (and I have done this as much as others) are grounded in wishful thinking. What Paul and the entire Christian tradition taught is unmistakably negative: the religion of Israel is now superseded, the Torah abrogated, the promises fulfilled in the Christian Church, the Jews struck with blindness, and whatever remains [to Israel] of the election rests as a burden upon them in the present age" ("Introduction" to Rosemary Radford Ruether, *Faith and Fratricide: The Theological Roots of Anti-Semitism* [Eugene, OR: Wipf & Stock, 1997], 6). Baum's summary shows Paul in a distorting mirror: for Paul, God's history with Israel is not superseded in Christ but is fulfilled; the Torah is not abrogated but raised up and concentrated in the love commandment; Israel is not struck blind *forever*; its election sustains the church and is a blessing to the whole world.

[78] For the distinction in the *Hodayot* found in Qumran between the "true Israel" and the Israel that does not correspond to the will of God cf., e.g., 1QH 7.10 ("holy community") on the one hand and 1QH 2.12 ("assembly of the godless") on the other. In contrast to the *Hodayot* and other Qumran writings, Paul uses the idea of a remnant but does not stop with it.

in the least. Otherwise all the prophets and many groups within early Judaism would have to be called "anti-Jewish."

Romans 9–11 is not anti-Jewish; it is a moving affirmation of Israel. The church is conceived entirely in terms of Israel. Gentile Christians are warned against feeling themselves superior to Israel, whose salvation-historical function is emphasized.

Had the Christian communities taken the letter to the Romans seriously, the relationship between church and synagogue would have developed differently. The merciless persecution of Jews, the countless forced baptisms starting in the early Middle Ages, the fearful pogroms, the demonizing of the Jews by Martin Luther in his later years, the silence of German Christians as their Jewish fellow citizens were transported to the death camps—that would scarcely have been possible. The Christians would have known that they themselves had, by the mercy of God, been grafted into the olive tree that is Israel and that the Jews are their sisters and brothers and stand for all time within God's covenant fidelity, "for the gifts and the calling of God are irrevocable" (Rom 11:29).

We saw, in interpreting 1 Thessalonians 2:14-16, that Paul did not speak about the "nature" of the Jews but about their concrete historical rejection of God's way. This accusation by Paul against unbelieving Israel applies today to Christians themselves. They have not observed and embraced their duty toward Israel: to live as a messianic people and so cause Israel to think twice. They have preferred to turn to violence. The image of the olive tree is fading further and further into oblivion.

It was only Vatican II that finally dared to include the Pauline image in an official church teaching document. In the crucial article 4 of the "Declaration on the Relation of the Church to Non-Christian Religions" (*Nostra Aetate*) we read:

> The Church, therefore, cannot forget that she received the revelation of the Old Testament through the people with whom God in His inexpressible mercy concluded the Ancient Covenant. Nor can she forget that she draws sustenance from the root of that well-cultivated olive tree onto which have been grafted the wild shoots, the Gentiles.[79]

[79] *Nostra Aetate* 4, *AAS* 58 (1966): 740–44.

This text marks a rediscovery within the church's faithful "memory" of something that is part of its very nature: its existence coming from Israel, its acceptance into the history of election since Abraham. *Nostra Aetate* opens the way for the church's greatest and most important task in this millennium: to become a messianic people, "to be re-rooted in what is Jewish," in order thereby "to wholly recover that which is Catholic"[80] so that Israel can at last believe in its Messiah.

[80] This follows a publication of the Katholische Integrierte Gemeinde in which it gives an account of its history and mission: Traudl Wallbrecher, ed., *Heute. Pro ecclesia viva: Vom Wieder-Einwurzeln im Jüdischen als einer Bedingung für das Einholen des Katholischen*, 2nd ed. (Bad Tölz: Urfeld Verlag, 1995).

13

How Does the Church Gather?

The evangelist Luke did not just write a Gospel; he continued his work with a second book that was originally connected directly to the Gospel. Why did he do that? Why a second book? Why the so-called Acts of the Apostles?

Luke wanted to show the Christians of his time something: namely, what had crystallized within only a few decades as the enduring structure of the church or, in other words, how the church should live. In the very first chapter of Acts he paints a picture of what "church" is.

Pentecost is at hand. The young community has gathered in Jerusalem in an upper story of a house and is awaiting the Holy Spirit. If "upper story" does not mean much to you, think of it this way: houses throughout the Levant possessed a room above the ground floor with larger windows and better air.

Luke portrays this Jerusalem gathering in vivid language. He writes in Acts 1:12-14:

> Then they returned to Jerusalem from the mount called Olivet, which is near Jerusalem, a Sabbath day's journey away. When they had entered the city, they went to the room upstairs where they were staying: Peter, and John, and James, and Andrew, Philip and Thomas, Bartholomew and Matthew, James son of Alphaeus, and Simon the Zealot, and Judas son of James. All these were constantly devoting themselves to prayer, together with certain women, including Mary the mother of Jesus, as well as his brothers.

All I want to do now is to interpret this little text from Acts in seven steps.[1] I do so because there is something about this text: it contains a whole theology of what community, what church is. If the church did nothing but live this one text it would soon be unrecognizable.

Certainly we should keep the following in mind when interpreting this text: Luke's intention, in writing these two volumes, was not to produce a theological textbook but rather to offer images to the readers and to tell them stories. This text in Acts 1:12-14 is also primarily an image, one that is so vivid that it was repeatedly painted in subsequent centuries (in combination with the Pentecost event) and produced an impressive iconographic tradition.

Luke offers us a picture, but it is not a snapshot of a moment. It does not present a group photo of the assembled community six weeks after Good Friday, but instead a many-layered image that brings together, organizes, and concentrates decades of experience in the early church.

Moreover, the picture that is painted is not a model for imitation. Instead, it is a primal image, comparable to the picture of the exodus that the Old Testament places before us. Primal images have a unique effectiveness. The biblical exodus is not something one can imitate in a superficial fashion, and yet the exodus texts in the Old Testament have moved the people of God to this day, and those texts' life is continually being renewed in them. It happens in a departure from the ordinary and from the familiar ways in which we have settled and felt secure; it consists in daring to live a new life for the sake of the gospel.

The church would quickly come to an end, and so would our communities, if we were not continually experiencing this exodus, this exit from the ordinary—for the sake of the gospel. Israel's exodus from Egypt has always been a powerful image for the church. The same is true of the images of the community gathered in Jerusalem between the ascension and the feast of Pentecost in Jerusalem. But what does this "image" at the beginning of Acts show us?

[1] Let me refer here to the essential interpretation by Hans Hubert Klein, *Sie waren versammelt. Die Anfänge christlicher Versammlungen nach Apg 1–6*, FTS 72 (Münster: Aschendorff, 2015), 75–92.

The Church Is Constant Gathering

First of all, this image shows the church as assembly—more precisely, a constant, ongoing assembly. Obviously Luke does not mean to say that Jesus' followers never separated from one another, but rather that their lives had become an unceasing, constantly renewed coming-together.

There was a very real prehistory to this coming-together of the disciples. They had indeed scattered after Jesus' death. Peter and his fellow fishers from Lake Gennesaret went back north: the first Easter appearances took place in Galilee. In other words: the Galilean fisherfolk had returned home and taken up their old occupation. Others went west—Luke tells of two disciples who were traveling to Emmaus, devastated by Jesus' execution. Still others stayed hidden in the capital city.

It is one of the miracles of the history of Christian origins that these little groups of Jesus-followers, fleeing in terror or anxiously hiding, suddenly came together again—and in the capital city, precisely where they were in the most danger.

The scattering, the separation, the division: all that is normal in our world. Unified gathering around a center—and not by force, not in group frenzy, but freely—is, in contrast, quite unusual and contrary to normal experience. It is one of the Easter miracles. Without the Risen One, without the Easter experience of Jesus' disciples and sympathizers, this miracle could not have happened.

I think it is good to picture in our minds how things went in Jerusalem at that time: for example, what was the dwelling like? After all, these Galileans who had returned to Jerusalem had to find lodging there somewhere. Did they have money to rent rooms? Those were always expensive in the cities. Or did they find a group shelter? Or were there disciples in the capital city who had received them into their homes?

And what about their occupations? After all, Jesus' followers had to earn their living somehow. The fishers from Capernaum could not go fishing in Jerusalem, and did Levi the toll collector find a position there? New employment had to be sought, and that certainly could not happen without the help and the sisterhood and brotherhood of those already resident in the city. The Acts of the Apostles offers us some hints: for example, when Peter was thrown into prison by King

Herod Agrippa I a part of the Jerusalem community gathered in the house of a certain Mary, the mother of one John Mark, where they prayed for Peter (Acts 12:12). As the narrative shows, it must have been a substantial dwelling because it had a gatehouse on the street (Acts 12:13).[2] So there were Christians in Jerusalem who opened their houses to the new arrivals.

We have to keep that whole background in mind if we want to understand the full dramatic effect of the statement that Jesus' disciples regularly gathered together. The mere fact that they could come together presupposes solidarity and unanimity. Interpreting Luke's text in that way certainly is not fantasizing or psychologizing; it means recognizing in the New Testament text what community is: seeking shelter, creating jobs, establishing a gathering place, finding people who are prepared to receive guests into their homes—that, too, is essential to a community—and none of it is a matter of course.

We need only to expand our local horizon and think of the Christians in China, Pakistan, or Syria to make it all very contemporary. Precisely there it will become obvious whether a community is just an anonymous, nonbinding Sunday gathering that exists only for the moment or whether it remains community throughout the week. Jesus' disciples were a "constant community": that is, they not only held prayer meetings or gathered for liturgical evening prayer; they had joined their lives as fishnets are joined.

Paul will then later say that community is a single "body." According to Luke and the whole New Testament, that being-together as a single body is essential to Christian community. The world contains many types of communities, from chess clubs to climbing clubs, from online gaming groups to the Mafia. They all have noble or not-so-noble purposes. What distinguishes the church from them? If we were to ask the New Testament, "What, then, is the critical difference between a Christian community and all the groups, associations, and clubs in the world?" it would reply, "It is that here people join their lives in unanimity, so that their communion becomes an image of the triune God." Community means persons

[2] Ernst Haenchen, *The Acts of the Apostles: A Commentary*, trans. Bernard Noble, Gerald Shinn with Hugh Anderson, rev. R. McLean Wilson (Philadelphia: Westminster Press, 1971), 385.

who, for the most part, are extraordinarily different from one another, and yet are one in Jesus Christ.

Difference in persons, unity in being: that is precisely what the church's creed says of the triune God. Profound differences among those who belong to a Christian community (how varied are the Christians in any one community as regards their origins and history!) and yet unanimity in what they will and what they are called to be, followers of Jesus: precisely that is of the essence of the church and of community.

What else does the image Luke paints for us in the Acts of the Apostles tell us?

The Twelve Are the Center of the Assembly

Let me again pose the question very simply: who are these people, precisely, who are gathered in the upper room, the people of whom the text speaks? Luke's words are clear and precise: first of all, the Twelve have assembled. Their number will be made complete in the immediately following account of the choice of Matthias in Acts 1:15-26. The full number of apostles is important because they are to appear before Israel on Pentecost as the beginning of the eschatological people of the twelve tribes. The Twelve are the center of the assembly, the center of the *ekklēsia*.

Their names are listed—first of all that of Peter—because Jesus' cause, for which they are the official witnesses, can be handed on only from person to person, face to face. Then-Cardinal Ratzinger once said: "God did not build his church on principles, but on people." And these people are just what people always are. Reading the list of names of the Twelve in our text attentively can make us think twice, because the Twelve are a highly unstable mixture. They include former disciples of John the Baptizer such as Andrew, Simon Peter's brother. There is a former toll collector named Matthew and a Zealot named Simon. A toll collector and a Zealot, however, represent the most violently opposed forces in Israel at that time, and here they are together in a single group. Toll collectors joined the Romans in extracting taxes from the people, while the Zealots rejected the Roman occupation force as sharply as possible, seeing it as incompatible with the rule of God.

We have to picture what it was like when such different people sat at the same table. It is like imagining fire and water together. But that is precisely where the miracle of the eschatological people of God really begins. If each person lives strictly for herself or himself and cultivates the self, there can be no visible sign of the reign of God. The fascination of that reign will appear only when people with different origins, different gifts, skins of different colors, women and men, sit together at the same table, join their lives together in order to serve God's cause in unity—and yet each remains herself or himself in unmistakable individuality.

Why are the Twelve so important to Luke that he lists their names again? After all, he had already named them in his Gospel. One reason I have already mentioned: they are to appear before Israel on the day of Pentecost as the beginning of the eschatological people of the twelve tribes. But there is another reason: Luke uses the figure of the Twelve to symbolize the apostolicity of the church. We may simply say that they represent church office. Here Luke already has the official church of his own time in view. Office is essential to the church's existence; without official witness, mission, commissioning, responsibility, and service to the whole body, the church would long ago have ceased to exist. All those are elements of what we call "office."

The concept of office, however, falls short of a full description of what the Twelve mean for Luke. In that symbol Luke also wants to show that the church needs a center, one by which it is united. That is, in fact, a phenomenon of life in general: a stone or a hunk of iron has no center, but *life* is organized in such a way that it cannot exist without one. That is biologically clear in the nuclei of cells, which contain the chromosomes, the genetic information. In social terms we can see it in our ancient cities: at the center was the cathedral, and the marketplace was next to it. The soullessness and inhospitable nature of modern cities is evident precisely in the fact that they no longer have any real center. They are only proliferations.

For Luke, the Twelve are the center of the assembly because they are the enduring memory of what Jesus did and taught. They represent the authenticity, the genuineness of the Jesus-tradition. The Twelve, Luke says explicitly, were present in the time when Jesus went in and out among his own (Acts 1:21-22).

Later, in battling heresy, the church would repeatedly look back to this apostolic center as its "genetic information." At the time when Luke wrote the Acts of the Apostles the church was already engaged in battle with Christian *gnosis*, which had abandoned the Jewish heritage and transformed the faith of the people of God into an esoteric, spiritualized, individualized doctrine of salvation. Luke thus knew precisely why, in picturing the church at the very beginning of Acts, he had to make the Twelve the center of the assembly.

The Twelve, however, while they are the center, are not alone in the space. They most certainly are not seated in a conference room: they are at the center of an assembly. Here we have a positively revolutionary theology of office, for this means that the apostolic office is not superior to the church, or alongside it; its place is in the center of the assembly.

To put it still more clearly: office is entirely built into the life and the togetherness of the rest of the community, for what Luke depicts here is not only a gathering for prayer, assembled for half an hour in the evening for a novena. These are people who share their lives and bear all their burdens together. The officeholders remain what they are, but they live in the midst of the community and have joined their lives with those of the community members.

What does this image Luke paints in Acts 1 show us? It depicts even more, much more, about the inner being of the church.

Community Must Be Readily Visible

Immediately following our text, Luke states that 120 persons were gathered (cf. Acts 1:15). Obviously the number 120 points to the twelve tribes of Israel and the twelve apostles. If the church is really to be church, it has to stand within the history of the People of the Twelve Tribes. It is also apostolic and organized around the Twelve as its center.

At the same time, the number 120 also expresses the real experience that a community must not be too large. It has to be a comprehensible assembly in which each can know the needs and gifts, the cares and joys of the others. How can it be possible in a mega-church to truly join in sustaining the faith of others?

Certainly we are not talking here about a ghetto or separate world but instead about tantalizing vitality. The subsequent decades would show how excitingly vital the little community of disciples in Jerusalem was.

What does the picture Luke paints in Acts 1 show us? Still much more!

The Church Is Not Just Men

Our text, after listing the names of the Twelve, does something extremely important: Luke names another group of persons, namely, the women and Mary the mother of Jesus. Evidently the author is thinking especially of the women who followed Jesus from Galilee onward and supported his work with their means (Luke 8:1-3).[3]

Why does Luke mention the women immediately after the apostles? Evidently to prevent his readers from misunderstanding the picture of the early church he is sketching here as composed only of men. Christian art has only strengthened the image by seating Mary at the center of the Pentecost assembly, with the apostles standing to her left and right. In this way Mary herself is also made an image of the *ekklēsia*, its primal image, the real symbol of faithful listening and receiving.

At this point I want to quote some very important words of Pope Benedict XVI in which he says something essential about the roles of women in the church. At a meeting with the priests of the city of Rome he said:

> The Church [owes] a great debt of gratitude to women. . . . [A]t a charismatic level women do so much, I would dare to say, for the government of the Church, starting with women religious, with the sisters of the great Fathers of the Church such as St. Ambrose, to the great women of the Middle Ages—St. Hildegard, St. Catherine of Siena, then St. Teresa of Avila—and lastly, Mother Teresa.
>
> I would say that this charismatic sector is undoubtedly distinguished [from] the ministerial sector in the strict sense of the term, but it is a true and deep participation in the government of the Church. How could we imagine the government of the Church without this contribution, which sometimes becomes very visible, such as when St. Hildegard criticized the Bishops or when St. Bridget offered recommendations and St. Catherine of Siena obtained the return of the Popes to Rome? It has always been a crucial factor without which the Church cannot survive.[4]

[3] For a recent assessment of the roles of women in Acts see Linda M. Maloney with Ivoni Richter Reimer, *Acts of the Apostles*, Wisdom Commentary 45 (Collegeville, MN: Liturgical Press, 2022). Linda Maloney was Gerhard Lohfink's doctoral student and wrote her dissertation on community in Acts. (See ch. 14 n. 1 below).—Trans.

[4] Benedict XVI, "Meeting with the Members of the Roman Clergy," March 2, 2006, at https://www.vatican.va/content/benedict-xvi/en/speeches/2006/march/documents/hf_ben-xvi_spe_20060302_roman-clergy.html.

Thus Benedict XVI. With these words he wanted to say that the church is not altogether made up of men, and it dare not be. Luke already expressed that by giving Mary and the other women a central place in his image of the church.

But still more: what else does the picture Luke paints in Acts 1 tell us?

The Church Is New Family

After Mary and the other women, Luke mentions still a third group of persons: the "brothers of Jesus," that is, his relatives. They, too, are now present—even though, not long before this, Jesus had been forced to distance himself from them (Luke 8:19-21). All the Gospels show how Jesus encountered twofold resistance when he made his public appearance in Galilee. On the one side were the theologians of his day; on the other side was the opposition of his own family.

Clan, family, blood—then, as now, they had extraordinary power. Jesus' family came to Capernaum in order to force Jesus to return home, where they could put him under house arrest. At that point Jesus had to formally separate from his family: "Here are my mother and my brothers! Whoever does the will of God is my brother and sister and mother" (Mark 3:34-35).

It is important to understand what this radical Jesus saying means by "the will of God." It is not simply a matter of the Ten Commandments or the instructions of Torah, as important as they are. "The will of God," here as in the third petition of the Our Father, means God's "plan," the history God has now put into action in the midst of Israel.

"Jesus' brothers" must initially have refused that concrete historical will of God. We do not know what drove his family to oppose Jesus, but we might imagine it. For one of themselves, someone from their own family, to travel through Galilee, gathering disciples and asserting, "God's new world is beginning now, with those who follow me, in table-fellowship with me!"—they must have thought that was sheer insanity. They may have said to Jesus: "Other people are responsible for the renewal of Israel: the scribes, the priests, the council. You can see to it that worship in our village synagogue is improved. Stay home and keep Torah!"

However things played themselves out, Jesus met massive resistance from his relations. It is important that he did not simply separate from his natural family; he created "new family." He said:

whoever does the will of God—that is, who travels the Way with me, the way God wants to travel with Israel—that one is brother, sister, and mother to me! The "new family" Jesus thus creates surpasses the boundaries of clan and natural family. It is a redeemed togetherness of people with the most widely different backgrounds on a new basis given by God—entirely in service to the reign of God.

After Easter that new family is an established reality, because the events surrounding Jesus' death changed his disciples and even his own family. They began to understand. So the church begins as God's new creation, in which the natural family is integrated into the family of the *ekklēsia* so that it, too, can be transformed and redeemed.

Discipleship of Jesus is not meant to destroy the natural family but to integrate and build it into the new family, to heal and redeem it. Family needs redemption, like everything else in the world. It is not good in and of itself.

Luke's modest little note that Jesus' "brothers" were also part of the 120 who were gathered shows that Jesus' family repented after Easter and integrated itself into the new thing.

And even after all that, I have still not said the decisive thing. The essence of the assembly Luke describes must now, at last, be defined.

Community Cannot Be Made

Luke continues, then: all of them—the Twelve, the women, Mary, and Jesus' siblings—were "constantly devoting themselves to prayer." That is, they were praying for the Holy Spirit who was to descend on the assembly at Pentecost.

The fundamental manifestation of the church is thus not just the assembly, although *ekklēsia* does simply mean "assembly." There are countless assemblies throughout the world. The existential manifestation of the church is found in every assembly that is nothing but listening petition for the coming of the Spirit, because it knows that of itself it is completely helpless.

That is the difference between a genuine community assembly and the many gatherings in society: parliaments, councils, committees, commissions, and other bodies, no matter how bitterly necessary they all seem to be.

Among the church's most precious treasures is the knowledge that in itself it is unable to establish something that so much as resembles a community, even when it appears, from an outsider's perspective, to have gathered itself together. It is incapable of it, and if it nevertheless pretends to do so the end is always a no-win tangle of rivalries. Do we suppose Luke did not know that? In the sixth chapter of Acts he depicts a profound conflict over care for the widows of the Greek-speaking portion of the community in Jerusalem.

We cannot create community. The gathering of the *ekklēsia* thus has an ultimate, invisible center—beyond the Twelve—that sustains everything and that the assembly by itself cannot create. It is a gift. It is the Holy Spirit, the Spirit of Jesus Christ and the Father. Only through that center can it be of one mind, and that unanimity given by Jesus is then its whole strength.

Starting from Jerusalem

I have just attempted to interpret the three verses of Acts 1:12-14 and in the process to show what central statements about church and community this short piece of text contains. But I have still passed over something, because the text began, in verse 12, with the statement: "Then they returned to Jerusalem from the mount called Olivet, which is near Jerusalem, a Sabbath day's journey away."

What does Luke want to say here? Why does he speak of a "Sabbath day's journey"? As we know, a Jew must not travel a long distance on the sabbath. A "Sabbath day's journey" was about two thousand ells or 880 meters—just over half a mile—precisely the distance beyond the city walls that a pious Jew was permitted to travel. According to the scribes' interpretation of the Torah, anyone who did not pass beyond 880 meters from the city walls was still within the city.

Luke, then, by introducing the expression "Sabbath day's journey," is saying that in the beginning the disciples did not leave Jerusalem. They remained within the city even when they were on the Mount of Olives. Why is that so important to Luke? It cannot be about something purely superficial. Rather, his intent is theological. "Not leaving Jerusalem" (cf. v. 4) intends to say that Jerusalem—which, of course, means Israel—is the enduring place of the church's origin. The church must never forget that. Certainly it will very soon cross the boundaries of the city, beginning an incredible story of mission from Judea and Samaria to Rome (Acts 1:8), but its enduring point of origin is Jerusalem and therefore the people of God, Israel. The imagery says that the church may never distance itself from Jerusalem, that is, from the Old Testament people of God.

Luke elaborates the continuity between the time of Israel, the time of Jesus, and the time of the church in a whole variety of ways. One of his symbols of continuity is Jerusalem. I am convinced that it is primarily this insight into Lukan theology that enables us to see the history of the church in the right light. For when the church is in continuity with Israel, the fateful history of divisions did not begin with the separation between Rome and Constantinople in the year 1054, and certainly not only with Martin Luther and the Reformation. The first and fundamental division of the people of God was that between Jews and Christians. That was, so to speak, the primal division. It endures until today, and it is quite certainly the deeply hidden cause of all later divisions.

The church, just like Judaism itself, has suffered greatly from this first of all divisions. While it had been gathered as the eschatological Israel by the creation of the Twelve (and the New Testament communities never understood it in any other way) it hesitated to apply the honored name "Israel" to itself. That hesitation was justified and must be taken seriously in theological terms, because as the church developed after Israel it was not yet the whole Israel Jesus wanted. From that point of view the actual church is still not complete, despite everything with which it has been definitively endowed. It must remain in tension with the whole Israel.

The church should be aware of this impoverishment. Its affliction consists not only in the fact that Christians have repeatedly persecuted Israel and caused it immeasurable suffering. It lies also in the fact that the church itself, because of its prideful stance toward Judaism, has lost immeasurably: the obvious connection between faith and life, the coherence and visibility of its communities, the skepticism about any over-hasty spiritualizations, a realistic concept of redemption, the awareness of being a unique, irreplaceable people, the continual sanctification of everyday life.

We often confront the Torah and Israel's many laws without comprehending them at all. We imagine that we, as Christians, no longer need such things, but in doing so we overlook what Torah truly intends. The many prescriptions of Torah mean nothing other than that the whole day, from early morning until evening, as well as the whole week from its first day to the sabbath, are shaped and hallowed by God.

How much we could learn from faithful Israel! After all, our problem is precisely the fatal separation between the everyday and worship, between liturgy and life in the world. Torah overcame that separation. It places everything: profession, work, festival, worship, even the most ordinary, everyday things under the rule of God. That is its innermost meaning. We have so very much to learn from it!

The church is the eschatological Israel. It needs the experiences of Israel, from Abraham to John the Baptizer, and it must never forget that John Paul II again placed that truth before our eyes and that Benedict XVI followed him in that, tenaciously and with the utmost fidelity.

One of John Paul II's greatest and most unforgettable phrases was "purification of memory."[5] We have to recall what church really is. We have to grasp where we Christians have sinned. But we must also recognize what God has put in our hands. The church is the most beautiful and precious thing God has given us, together with his son Jesus Christ. That is what I have tried to show in this interpretation of Acts 1:12-14.

In retrospect we may say that pondering the image Luke painted in the tiniest space, in just three verses of Acts 1, tells us an astonishing amount about the nature of church and community. Let me only repeat the crucial points: the necessity of the apostolic office, the integration of office in the real life of the community, united and unified gathering, visibility of the communities, taking seriously the charism of women, overcoming clan-consciousness, unification of faith and life, linking to Israel—that is, to the experience of the many Jewish generations from Abraham until today.

There is much reason in all this—reason that is by no means a matter of course in the world of religions. It was developed in Israel, and it has had to be reclaimed in the church and its communities, often by hard struggle, until now. It is God's reason, which becomes apparent when God's people opens itself to God's will.

[5] Cf. "Homily of the Holy Father: Day of Pardon, Sunday, 12 March 2000," at https://www.vatican.va/content/john-paul-ii/en/homilies/2000/documents/hf_jp-ii_hom_20000312_pardon.html.

14

How Does the Church Resolve Its Conflicts?

Acts 1:12-14 is highly significant for the image of the church that Luke places before readers' eyes, but there are even more such texts in this second book of his. We may, in fact, say that the whole of the Acts of the Apostles is such a text. Luke tells an unbelievable story: that of the expansion of the church from Jerusalem through Judea, Samaria, and Syria, all the way to Rome (cf. Acts 1:8). By telling this story Luke shows how the church is led by God, what it is in terms of its origins, and what it should always be.

I am faced with the question of which, out of those many shorter narratives—all of them part of a single story—I should choose, beyond Acts 1:12-14. Because the concrete church has tumbled for centuries from one division to another and has been torn apart to its very depths, I will choose a text in which Luke shows how conflicts in the church can be resolved and imminent divisions healed. I am referring to Acts 15:1-35, the story of the so-called apostolic council.

This is the last community assembly Luke depicts in detail; for him it marks a turning point in the church's history. After that the narrative thread carries us away from Jerusalem until chapter 21. The great assembly in Acts 15 is occasioned by a quarrel that threatens to split the church. It is about whether the men among the Gentiles who are crowding into the church must undergo circumcision before being admitted and whether Gentiles as a whole are bound to keep the whole Torah—a question that, given the intensive missionary work of the community in Antioch, is becoming more and more urgent.

Before I engage in an interpretation of Acts 15:1-35 I must first say something about methodology. Here again, what interests me is not the historical question, as meaningful as it obviously is. I am concerned only with the lines of the Lukan presentation, and that requires a synchronic interpretation of the text, something that is proving very fruitful in contemporary exegesis. What does the text we have before us—completely independent of all historical (that is, diachronic) questions—mean to say by means of its strategies, particular emphases, and above all the extended incidents it describes? Here and elsewhere Luke means not only to show what once happened but also, and primarily, how past history can illuminate the problems of the church as its life continues.

Who Decides?

First: the name "apostolic council" does not describe the real subject of Acts 15:1-29, because it suggests that the apostles made a decision in isolation, in the manner of a classic council or even a conclave. What Luke describes is essentially more subtle.[1] Let us look closer!

Luke devotes an expansive narrative, beginning in Antioch, to the fundamental question in the earliest church: male circumcision or not, keeping the whole Torah or not? By this time there were Gentile Christians living in Antioch, and the men were not circumcised. Now Jewish Christians come from Judea and stir up controversy because they say: "Unless you are circumcised according to the custom of Moses, you cannot be saved" (Acts 15:1). We may add, "because without circumcision you are not part of the community of salvation that is Israel." Obviously this threat arouses not only agitation but theological strife. Luke speaks of the disturbance as *stasis*, "dissension" (implying "uproar"), as well as "debate." As a result the community sends a delegation to Jerusalem "to discuss this question with the apostles and the elders" (Acts 15:2). The most important members of the delegation are Paul and Barnabas.

[1] For what follows see especially the analysis by Linda M. Maloney, *"All That God Had Done With Them": The Narration of the Works of God in the Early Christian Community as Described in the Acts of the Apostles*, AUS 7, 91 (New York: Peter Lang, 1991), esp. 152–57.

Luke then describes how the delegation from Antioch is received by the community in Jerusalem—and not only received. The reception moves directly into a community gathering in which everyone listens to the delegates from Antioch:

> When they came to Jerusalem, they were welcomed by the church and the apostles and the elders, and they reported all that God had done with them. (Acts 15:4)

Resistance arises immediately—evidently from the group who had previously agitated in Antioch against freedom from male circumcision:

> But some believers who belonged to the [school[2]] of the Pharisees stood up and said, "It is necessary for them to be circumcised and ordered to keep the law of Moses." (Acts 15:5)

That brought into the open a problem that had long been simmering in the church—and the confrontation happens during an official assembly of the church at Jerusalem and in the presence of the apostles and elders. It is most certainly not a question of style, language, or local customs. For the Jewish Christians from the community of the Pharisees, who had started the quarrel, it was about the fundamental question whether the church is a new people of God that has separated from the people of God, Israel—that, indeed, has declared Israel to be dissolved and a thing of the past as far as the history of salvation is concerned—or whether the church remains with Israel and holds fast to the history that began with Abraham and led, at Sinai, to God's covenant with Israel and the gift of the Torah. That, at any rate, is how those Jewish Christians must have seen it. To state the question in terms of Romans 11:17-24: does the church remain bound to its sacred root, the olive tree that is Israel, or not? We should not regard the faithful Pharisees in this debate as hopelessly reactionary fundamentalists. This is about a foundational question for the church.

[2] AV, NRSV: sect; NABRE: party. With the translation *Schule* (school) for *hairesis* the author distances his reading from the pejorative connotations often attached to the term (but see Acts 26:5).—Trans.

How was this existential question for the Christian community decided, according to Luke? And how was the decision reached? What procedure did the Jerusalem church use? Luke writes: "The apostles and the elders met together to consider this matter" (Acts 15:6). Who dealt with the question? A special assembly apart from the rest of the community? A closed meeting of the leaders of church and congregation? Did the apostles and elders meet together behind closed doors? That is the opinion of some interpreters! At any rate speakers in this assembly included Peter and James, the brother of the Lord, as well as Barnabas and Paul. We hear nothing of others who spoke.

On the other hand, there were serious conflicts in this assembly of apostles and elders (Acts 15:7). So were the Jewish Christians from the company of the Pharisees, who had advanced the controversial question in the first place, perhaps present as well? Another indicator points in the same direction: in the course of the assembly, after Peter's speech, we read that "the whole [*plēthos*] kept silence" (Acts 15:12). How should we translate *pan to plēthos* here? "The whole crowd" or "the whole assembly" or "the whole community"? Translators differ,[3] but in any case at Acts 6:5 *pan to plēthos* was clearly the "whole community," and in the more immediate context—namely, at Acts 15:30—*plēthos* simply means the congregation at Antioch, which gathers. In addition, at the moment when James finishes his speech (I will return to Peter's and James's speeches later):

> Then the apostles and the elders, with the consent of the whole church, decided to choose men [*andras*] from among them and to send them to Antioch with Paul and Barnabas. They sent Judas called Barsabbas, and Silas, leaders among the brothers [and sisters] [*adelphoi*]. (Acts 15:22)

Here, then, the whole *ekklēsia* of Jerusalem participates in the decision to send a delegation to Antioch. Still, the letter to be sent, whose formulations are juridically of the highest importance for our question, seems to point in a different direction. It reads:

> The brothers [*adelphoi*],[4] both the apostles and the elders, to the brothers and sisters [*adelphoi*] of gentile origin in Antioch and Syria and Cilicia,

[3] AV: "all the multitude"; NABRE, NRSVue, "the whole assembly."

[4] NRSVue. Translators struggle here. NABRE has "brothers" for *adelphoi*, while NRSVue tries for inclusivity but is still unwilling to write "brothers and sisters" in reference to the "apostles and elders," though the word (*adelphoi*) is the same.—Trans.

> greetings. Since we have heard that certain persons who have gone out from us, though with no instructions from us, have said things to disturb you and have unsettled your minds, we have decided unanimously to choose men [*andras*] and send them to you, along with our beloved Barnabas and Paul, who have risked their lives for the sake of our Lord Jesus Christ. We have therefore sent Judas and Silas, who themselves will tell you the same things by word of mouth. For it has seemed good to the Holy Spirit and to us to impose on you no further burden than these essentials: that you abstain from what has been sacrificed to idols and from blood and from what is strangled and from sexual immorality. If you keep yourselves from these, you will do well. Farewell. (Acts 15:23-29)

Who are "we" in this letter? Apparently the apostles and elders, because they alone are named in the classical prescript of the letter, which does not read "the apostles and elders and the whole community at Jerusalem." On the other hand, the "we" in the middle of the letter clearly refers to the whole congregation, since it says "we have decided unanimously to choose men and send them to you, together with our beloved Barnabas and Paul" (Acts 15:25). That is about something that, according to verse 22, the apostles and elders had decided in agreement with the whole community. Thus "we" in the letter does not refer solely to the apostles and elders.

What should we think of this peculiar oscillation in the text between the entire local church in Jerusalem and a perhaps separate gathering of the apostles and elders? Was this unclear description simply the result of a mistake or carelessness on Luke's part? For such an accomplished stylist and master of the language as Luke—the letter contains a subtly constructed and positively classic periodic sentence—that would be utterly unlikely. There must be a different reason.

Luke wants to describe an assembly of the whole Jerusalem community, but at the same time he wants to emphasize the official function of the apostles and elders.[5] Hence the emphasis on their role in verses 6 and 23, and thus the stress on the role of the entire community in verses 4, 12, and 22. The final decision falls to the apostles and elders, but the whole community, or more precisely the whole local church of Jerusalem, participates in the decision, because in

[5] This is also the conclusion of Hans Hubert Klein, *Sie waren versammelt. Die Anfänge christlicher Versammlungen nach Apg 1–6*, FTS 72 (Münster: Aschendorff, 2015), 20–21.

Luke's view the local church is of decisive significance for the church as a whole.

So much for the question of who, in this instance, decides one of the most important questions in the church's history, although from Luke's point of view not nearly all participants in the decision are named. After all, at a crucial point in the letter to Antioch we find: "it has seemed good to the Holy Spirit and to us" (Acts 15:28). This infinitely refined formula says that for Luke, in cases where such a fundamental question is at issue, in instances when all the apostles and elders have gathered, in the event that the whole community is involved, and should it happen that the decision is being made in the mother community in Jerusalem, the one who really decides is the Holy Spirit—but together with the church. We must, of course, interpret the pointed "the Holy Spirit and us" in the sense of the classical formula: God acts in the world, but does so through people whose freedom and independence are not diminished.[6]

I have just listed a whole series of conditions that, according to Luke, must be fulfilled if the church is to unite in the Holy Spirit. But I omitted three other conditions. Those three are first revealed when we look more closely at the community that is making the decision. That brings me to the second part of my exegesis of the so-called apostolic council.

How Are Decisions Made?

The assembly proper begins with "much debate" (Acts 15:7). Luke gives no further information. Readers of Acts could imagine for themselves the arguments that were introduced and the agitation among the members of the assembly. The arguing ceases when Peter begins to speak. He is the first to do so because he is part of the group of the Twelve, whom Luke had portrayed in the first part of Acts as playing the crucial role in securing the continuity of the time of Jesus. Peter, in fact, is not merely part of the group of the Twelve. In both Lukan lists of the names of the Twelve (Luke 6:12-16; Acts 1:13; cf. Matt 10:2-4; Mark 3:16-19) he is named first, and he is also the most important actor in the first part of Acts.

[6] Cf. Gerhard Lohfink and Ludwig Weimer, *Die Lust an Gott und seiner Sache oder: Lassen sich Gnade und Freiheit, Glaube und Vernunft, Erlösung und Befreiung vereinbaren?*, 2nd ed. (Freiburg: Herder, 1982) (see above, chap. 12, n. 49).

Peter thus steps forth in the midst of the quarrel. The crucial point is formulated right away, in the first sentence of his speech: "My brothers [*andres adelphoi*], you know that in the early days God made a choice among you" (Acts 15:7). God has thus already acted directly and so has decided—and has done so through actual history. Of course, historical facts can have multiple meanings, but these are unambiguous. Peter reminds the assembly specifically of the conversion of the centurion Cornelius and his whole household, an episode Luke has already related at length in Acts 10. (It is one of the longest narratives in the two-volume Lukan corpus.) It was certainly a unique event, but according to Peter it had made God's will clear to him, since the Holy Spirit had fallen on Cornelius and his household just as had happened to the assembled Jews on the day of Pentecost. And anyone who believes and has received the Spirit is no longer unclean but clean (Acts 15:9). This direct decision by God means that it is simply the community's obligation to obey this divine choice.

When Peter ends his speech "the whole assembly" keeps silence (Acts 15:12). We should not skip over that little statement; it is of the utmost importance, and we should reflect on it again and again. When does it happen in our society that a whole crowd who are debating hard questions suddenly fall silent? The assembly's silence is a sign of the impact of what Peter has said, but it is also a silent assent to what appears to be the will of God.

After Peter's speech, Barnabas and Paul are also in a position to report to the assembly the signs and wonders God has worked among the Gentiles through their preaching. Their argumentation moves on the same level as Peter's: they point to what has already happened. God speaks through the events; all that is necessary is to look at them carefully and with the eyes of faith.

Then James, the brother of the Lord, begins to speak. He argues on a different level, but one that is equally important: James looks at the question in light of Sacred Scripture:

> My brothers, listen to me. Simeon has related how God first looked favorably on the gentiles, to take from among them a people for his name. This agrees with the words of the prophets, as it is written,
>
> "After this I will return,
> and I will rebuild the dwelling of David, which has fallen;
> from its ruins I will rebuild it, and I will set it up,
> so that all other peoples may seek the Lord—
> even all the gentiles over whom my name has been called.

> Thus says the Lord, who has been making these things known from long ago."
>
> Therefore I have reached the decision that we should not trouble those gentiles who are turning to God. (Acts 15:14-19)

This collection of quotations from the prophets is a combination of Amos 9:11-12 LXX and Isaiah 45:21. It is intended to show that, first of all, "the dwelling of David, which has fallen," that is, Israel, must be rebuilt. That has happened in the time since Easter, depicted in Acts 1–7, or at least it has begun to appear, and so the Gentiles may now come to it. The syntax is important here: Israel had to be restored "so that" (*hopōs*) the Gentiles might come to it.

James thus argues in terms of the pilgrimage of the nations promised in Scripture. The key point is that Israel itself must first become a shining city before the nations can make their way to it. For James, the brother of the Lord, that pilgrimage is already in progress and therefore no one may hinder the streaming of the Gentiles to eschatological Israel—but that would happen if male circumcision were demanded of them.[7]

James's speech brings about a definitive unity. In Luke's mind it was also helpful, to that end, that James follows his scriptural argument with four minimum requirements resting on Leviticus 17–18, where they are demanded of "resident aliens" in Israel (Lev 17:10, 12, 13; 18:26) and for that reason should also be obeyed by Gentile Christians: "to abstain only from things polluted by idols and from sexual immorality and from whatever has been strangled and from blood" (Acts 15:20). The point of these four requirements is to enable community among Jewish and Gentile Christians at table. The uncleannesses of Gentiles must no longer attach to Gentile Christians who gather with Jewish Christians for meals. Hence renunciation of "things polluted by idols," of "sexual immorality," of "whatever has been strangled," and "from blood," this last meaning the consumption of blood. "Strangled" refers to animals not ritually slain. "Sexual

[7] Even the Old Testament texts about the pilgrimage of nations to Zion are extremely open in this regard: the pagan peoples who go up will revere YHWH and serve the people of God. According to Zech 8:23 there will be a traveling company that includes Israel; Isa 56:6 says that they keep the sabbath and the covenant, pray in Jerusalem, and offer sacrifices there. None of the pilgrimage-of-nations texts speaks of a necessary male circumcision.

immorality" is about illegitimate incestuous marriages, which were a horror in Jewish eyes. "Things polluted by idols" refers to participation in heathen cultic meals or, for example, eating meat that had been slaughtered for pagan cultic offerings.[8]

We can see that male circumcision is no longer required; that was the radical part of this decision. It is replaced by baptism in water and the Holy Spirit as well as by the saving death of Jesus. Luke has already spoken of that elsewhere (cf. Acts 2:38; 3:18-19; 5:30-31).

Criteria

If we look back we will see that the telling of what has already happened is essential to the success of this great assembly at Jerusalem. The narration to the gathered community of the events of the most recent past lays the groundwork for the resolution of the disputed question. What has happened for the Gentiles is interpreted as the action of God:

> [They] listened to Barnabas and Paul as they told of all the signs and wonders that God had done through them among the gentiles. (Acts 15:12; cf. 14:27)

The past events are only recognizable as the acts of God, however, because they are considered in light of Sacred Scripture. What James develops is a firm historical theology based on biblical prophecy. That theology of history makes it possible to understand the very recent past and locate it within salvation history. Therefore the scriptural citation ends with a reference to the plan God "has been making . . . known from long ago."

Important, finally, is that all this takes place within the mother community at Jerusalem—where the witnesses live who were present from the very beginning (Acts 1:21-22)—and that the assembly is prepared to listen to the words of these witnesses. In short: what, according to Luke, is necessary in order for serious conflicts within the church to be resolved?

[8] More information on the question of "flesh offered to idols" can be found in chap. 11 of this book, "How Paul Talks to His Communities."

1. The parties to the conflict gather—and they do so in the place where the church's beginnings are still a living presence, the place of the assembled church's tradition.

2. The parties to the conflict gather around the apostles and elders, who embody and guarantee, in their persons and through their experiences, what was laid down for the church in Jesus' time.

3. The whole community takes part in the decision of the apostles and elders. Luke is very clear about precisely that. The ultimate responsibility of the apostles and elders is not thereby eliminated; according to Luke it is emphasized. But it is equally important to him to demonstrate the common responsibility of all.

4. The assembly looks to what God has done in the most recent past. It thus tests and interprets the immediate past in terms of God's actions. In doing this it has to listen to what qualified witnesses to the events such as Peter, Barnabas, and Paul have to say.

5. The assembly measures everything it has to decide against Sacred Scripture, that is, the canonized experiences of the people of God. To put it another way: the history of the people of God from the distant past must also be a criterion for its decision.

6. The assembly should listen with open ears to what others say. That listening always presumes an attentive silence.

7. The assembly is prepared to respond to those who, in their confusion and agitation, have entrusted themselves to it. In our case it is the Jewish Christians who do not see how they can properly keep table fellowship with "unclean" Gentile Christians. The four "conditions of James" are meant to give them time to grasp, slowly, that faith and the gift of the Holy Spirit have long since freed the Gentile Christians from all cultic impurity.

When all that happens, Luke tells us, the church assembly can open itself to the Holy Spirit, be of one mind, and resolve its conflicts.

You have probably sensed by now that the so-called apostolic council is something altogether unique, one in which the whole community at Jerusalem takes part as the entity that at that time embodied and solidified the church. If we were to make a reality of this text in all our assemblies, meetings, committees, commissions, and chapters today, and do so repeatedly, the church would look different. "Make a reality today" cannot mean, of course, that what Luke depicts is to be reproduced in every detail. We no longer live in the first century CE. The issue can only be whether we can translate what Luke depicts to the twenty-first century, meaningfully and appropriately, and make it a reality again and again.

One last thing: Acts 15 is not about some marginal issue. It concerns the crucial question for the church *as such*. As I have asked: is the church to separate from Israel, or does it remain part of the people chosen and led by God since Abraham, and to whom God remains faithful through all times?

The decision Luke presents is unambiguous: The church is not some "new" people of God, not some "new" Israel, not a new construction outside of and distant from Israel. In the church God has rebuilt the ruined dwelling of David. God has renewed Israel and it is now possible for the Gentile nations to stream to the holy and hallowed people of God in that pilgrimage for which the prophets hoped.[9]

So what it is all about, in the difficult decisions with which the church is confronted today, is to follow with the same clarity the great lines of Sacred Scripture, but also the experiences the church has had with the always-acting God in the course of its own history.

[9] And what about the Israel that does not believe in redemption through Jesus, the Messiah? Has it become superfluous? Luke also has a great deal to say about that, but the most thorough treatment and profound theological grounding are found in Paul's letter to the Romans, chaps. 9–11. See ch. 11 above.

15

How Does the Church Do Mission?

How missionary is an ordinary parish in Europe? To put it another way: What answer would we receive if we were to ask an average Roman Catholic churchgoer to tell us spontaneously how she or he responds to the word "mission"? What would we hear then?

The answers might be very different. In Germany, certainly, for a large number of church attendees the word "mission" still evokes activities in distant lands. The recently coined expression "New Evangelization" is something scarcely anyone would utter (with the exception, of course, of people in church employment). Regular Mass attendees are also certainly prepared to donate to the missions. The great missionary movement of the nineteenth century has still left fragments of memory in people's minds. At the same time people are also aware that certain religious orders or church offices are dedicated to mission. We take care of the problem by donating on "World Mission Day."

Nowadays engagement on behalf of suffering groups of the population, especially in Latin America, Africa, or places currently suffering crises are much more in the foreground. There is still very little awareness that a parish should be missionary within its own territory and surroundings.[1] How can that even happen? Should people stand on street corners like sectarians or go from house to house? Elders smile indulgently when young people from the parish invite passersby to "Nightfever" in the candlelit church, where a particular atmosphere is created in great detail. No one is against such actions,

[1] Note: I am talking about Roman Catholic parishes in Germany. Things are quite different in Protestant parishes of an evangelical bent.

but they think: does it have anything to do with mission? No, mission is something "others" or "those responsible" should do.

A Jewish Couple

Against this background it makes sense to take a closer look at another text from the Acts of the Apostles, namely, Acts 18:1-11, where we read:

> After this Paul left Athens and went to Corinth. There he found a Jew named Aquila from Pontus, who had recently come from Italy with his wife Priscilla, because [Emperor] Claudius had ordered all Jews to leave Rome. Paul went to see them, and, because he was of the same trade, he stayed with them, and they worked together—by trade they were tentmakers. (18:1-3)

It is quite useful to consider this couple, Prisca and Aquila, because in this way we can cast an eye on the early Christian mission and at the same time on the earliest Christian communities, which were so very different from our "comfortable congregations."

The couple, Prisca and Aquila, appear several times in the New Testament: not only in Acts 18 but also in Romans 16:3; 1 Corinthians 16:19; 2 Timothy 4:19. In the above passage Prisca is called by her pet name, "Priscilla," that is, "Little Prisca." She and Aquila were extraordinarily important to Paul's missionary work.

Our text shows that Paul met this Jewish-Christian couple in Corinth. What the text does *not* say is that these two were not brought to belief by Paul. They must have already been Christians, as 1 Corinthians 1:14-16 presupposes, before Paul met them. Aquila's calling[2] is that of tentmaker, and he has his own business establishment. At that time smaller tents could be made of linen, but larger ones were woven of goats' hair or were made of hides. For that reason tentmakers were also workers in leather. In all probability Aquila and Prisca's shop not only made tents but also manufactured leather from which tents, bags, sandals, belts, saddles, and bridles were crafted.

The information about the Roman emperor Claudius is confirmed by the historian Suetonius:[3] Claudius had driven some of the Jews out

[2] And Prisca's also, according to Acts 18:2-3.—Trans.

[3] Suetonius, *Claudius* 25.

of Rome, apparently because of constant disturbances brought on, there in the capital city, by quarrels between Jews and Jewish Christians. Prisca and Aquila were among those driven out and were now carrying on their business in Corinth. Thus they were already settled there when Paul met them. They took him into their family. At first Paul worked with them in the shop and at the same time made use of their house and business as the base for his missionary work (Acts 18:1-5).

After many months of fruitful laboring together in Corinth, the three moved to Ephesus—probably not least in order to enable Paul to establish a fixed base in Asia Minor (Acts 18:18-19). In Ephesus, too, Paul lived and worked in their house as needed; that house in Ephesus was also the gathering place for the community there, or at least a part of it. We know that from 1 Corinthians, which Paul wrote in Ephesus; in it he sends many greetings from "Aquila and Prisca, together with the church in their house" (1 Cor 16:19).

In Ephesus, at a time when Paul was absent, there arrived a highly gifted Jew from Alexandria named Apollos, and he met the couple. They took him into their house as well and introduced him to the Way that salvation history had followed (Acts 18:24-28).

Years later, when Paul wrote his letter to the Romans as he was preparing for his missionary journey to Spain, he asked the Roman community to give his greetings to Prisca and Aquila in particular:

> Greet Prisca and Aquila, my coworkers in Christ Jesus, who risked their necks for my life, to whom not only I give thanks but also all the churches of the gentiles. Greet also the church in their house. (Rom 16:3-5)

This request for greetings shows that in the meantime Prisca and Aquila had returned to Rome, where they had originally had their business. It may be that during the time when they had to leave Rome a non-Jewish artisan had kept their workshop going. And in Rome, just as in Corinth and Ephesus, there was a congregation that met in their house. It would have included their own extended family but also Roman Christians who gathered regularly in their spacious home.

How Congregations Were Then Formed

Thus the house of Prisca and Aquila offers us a vivid picture of the "new family" as Jesus had begun it. Here is a normal family that, however, lives not only for itself and its private interests but places its household totally at the service of the gospel. The couple's house becomes the base for Paul's mission—first in Greece, then in Asia Minor—and probably the resettlement in Rome was meant to create a base for Paul's planned mission to Spain.

At the same time the house of Aquila and Prisca became the core around which new communities crystallized and grew. There they found the necessary space for their gatherings—but not only the space; there was much more: a couple that placed themselves at the disposal of the communities with everything that was theirs. They instructed Apollos in the faith and undoubtedly many others besides. They stuck out their necks for Paul in Ephesus. All the Gentile Christian communities owed them gratitude, as Paul says.

From all this we can easily see that in the early stages of the church the creation of new communities always depended on whether there were families like that of Prisca and Aquila—families that were prepared to move to other cities for the sake of the gospel and there, together with their household, to become a center for a new community.

The principle of area-wide pastoral service at any price did not yet exist. There was no concept of "ministry" in the sense of an official, territory-based *cura animarum* before the early Middle Ages, and that idea had very little to do with what Paul wanted. His primary concern was building up living, compact communities, and those were not laid out on a map. They depended on persons: believers who placed their lives and property at the community's disposal. A considerable part of the Christian mission was conducted by way of families like that of Aquila and Prisca.

The Role of the "God-Fearers"

But back to the Acts of the Apostles! Once Luke has described the strong tie between Paul and the couple, Prisca and Aquila, he turns to Paul's mission in Corinth:

> Every Sabbath he would argue in the synagogue and would try to convince Jews and Greeks. When Silas and Timothy arrived from Macedonia, Paul was occupied with proclaiming the word, testifying to the Jews that the Messiah was Jesus. When they opposed and reviled

> him, in protest he shook the dust from his clothes and said to them, "Your blood be on your own heads! I am innocent. From now on I will go to the gentiles." (Acts 18:4-6)

The text means to say that in the synagogue Paul not only conversed with circumcised Jewish men but also with "God-fearers." When Luke speaks here of "Greeks" who are in the synagogue the reference can only be to "God-fearers." These were Gentiles who were fascinated by Judaism: its monotheism, its ethic, and its way of life. They participated in the life of Jewish communities, but they had not yet taken the last step, which for the men meant circumcision.

Evidently Paul had little success among the Jews in Corinth. When they began cursing Jesus he did as Jesus advised, shaking the dust from his clothes—a sign-action meant to say "I am separating myself from you, down to the tiniest fleck of dust, so that at the judgment I will not be condemned along with you." He cannot shake the dust from his "shoes" (cf. Mark 6:11) since he is remaining in Corinth; hence he shakes it from his clothes. With that sign-action he brought an end to his work of persuasion in the synagogue.

"From now on I will go to the gentiles" is not intended categorically; it is aimed at the conditions in Corinth, and the Gentiles are evidently God-fearers from the circle surrounding the synagogue, with whom Paul could expect much better chances than with Gentiles who had not had any contact with Judaism.

Spatially, too, Paul does not simply vanish from the synagogue community. Instead, he changes the place where he preaches—moving to the house of a God-fearer directly neighboring on the synagogue. That was a clear and unmistakable provocation! Paul was no coward. Luke writes:

> Then he left the synagogue and went to the house of a man named Titius Justus, a worshiper of God; his house was next door to the synagogue. Crispus, the official of the synagogue, became a believer in the Lord, together with all his household, and many of the Corinthians who heard Paul became believers and were baptized. One night the Lord said to Paul in a vision, "Do not be afraid, but speak and do not be silent, for I am with you, and no one will lay a hand on you to harm you, for there are many in this city who are my people." He stayed there a year and six months, teaching the word of God among them. (Acts 18:7-11)

The fact that Crispus, the synagogue official, came to belief in Christ together with his whole household was, of course, an extraordinary aid, because many Corinthians then joined him in adhering to the Jesus movement. Which "Corinthians" were they? Jews or Gentiles? Evidently not Jews, because they had previously hurled insults at Paul and would very soon "unite" in dragging him before the judgment seat of the proconsul, Gallio (Acts 18:12)! But not Gentiles either, because what was there about a synagogue official that could be interesting for a Corinthian Gentile?

Those Paul taught must have been God-fearers whom Paul had previously met and who were now deeply moved by the confession of faith on the part of the synagogue official. In other places also, Paul had his greatest missionary success exclusively among the God-fearers.[4] The circumcised Jewish men very often rejected him, and those who were simply pagans considered the preaching about Jesus a curiosity (Acts 17:18, 32). But among the God-fearers Paul found open ears, because they had already been introduced to Israel's Sacred Scriptures and the history of the people of God. This is especially clear in Acts 17:1-9. Paul speaks about Jesus as Messiah in the synagogue at Thessalonica on three sabbaths, and he finds listeners there. But who were they?

> Some of them were persuaded and joined Paul and Silas, as did a great many of the devout Greeks and not a few of the leading women. But the Jews became jealous, and with the help of some ruffians in the marketplaces they formed a mob and set the city in an uproar. (Acts 17:4-5)

Luke depicts the reaction of pure pagans a little later when he writes about Paul in Athens (Acts 17:16-34). Paul had almost no success is preaching to typical Athenians. Instead he encountered amusement, ridicule, or polite rejection: "We will hear you again about this" (Acts 17:32).

Paul's experiences in Corinth were similar to those in Thessalonica. The adherence of the synagogue official Crispus would evoke serious consequences, which Luke narrates in Acts 18:12-17. The night vision of Christ gives him courage to remain in Corinth all the same. The

[4] See in detail Marius Reiser, "Hat Paulus Heiden bekehrt?," *BZ* 39 (1995): 76–91 (see above, chap. 12, n. 11).

words that Christ speaks in the dream about the "many people," including the word *laos*, recall the people of God whom Jesus had newly gathered and who now included both Jews and Greeks.

The Role of "Houses"

Much more could be said about Paul's mission to the Jews and especially about his success among the God-fearers, but in this context I want to speak about something else. Acts 18:7-8 refers to the house of the God-fearer Titius Justus and that of the synagogue official Crispus; previously we heard about the house of the couple Prisca and Aquila. Of course, "house" always refers to the family occupying it, but not only that. In our context the word "house" implies a great deal more, and I want to comment on that.

It is amazing how many households are known to us by name, just in connection with Paul's apostolic work: for example, that of Lydia, the dealer in purple in Philippi (Acts 16:14-15); that of Jason in Thessalonica (Acts 17:5-9); that of Titius Justus (Acts 18:7) and that of Gaius in Corinth (Rom 16:23); that of Nympha in Laodicea (Col 4:15); that of Philemon and Apphia in Colossae (Phlm 1–2); and those of Prisca and Aquila in Corinth, Ephesus, and Rome (Acts 18:1-3; 1 Cor 16:19; Rom 16:3-5).

At that time in the early Christian era the life of the communities developed in those and many other houses. The natural family that was at the center of those homes opened and bound itself within a much broader context: the "new family" of the church—and still the church lived in and out of families like those I just listed.

In those houses catechumens were instructed, while traveling sisters and brothers in faith were welcome guests. There the community gathered for its meetings and to celebrate the Lord's Supper. Here unemployed Christians found work, and these houses were the places where most of the first contacts were made with people who wanted to get to know a Christian community. What they learned there was not just a set of abstract doctrines, but Christian life.

Within a pagan society such a Christian life had to present a contrast. In a thoroughly pagan society—like the one we are moving toward again at present—Christians had to behave differently from the rest of society in a great many ways. They were forced to swim against the tide, and that could not happen unless they lived in a social unity with one another. In his commentary on Philemon the New Testament scholar Peter Stuhlmacher rightly says:

> Paul himself had lived and taught in house communities, and he had founded some. For him it was not only the large assembly but also the house community that was the place where the sociological and ethnic-religious barriers between Jews and Gentiles, free and unfree, men and women, high and low, educated and uneducated that were especially significant in antiquity were broken and made insignificant in favor of and out of the one new bond between all people and Christ the Lord.[5]

One thing needs to be added: the houses in which Paul lived were often those of the first converts in any given city. That was the case with Lydia's house in Philippi, that of Jason in Thessalonica, probably also that of Gaius in Corinth, which is mentioned in Romans 16:23. It was also in the houses of the first converts that the community usually assembled. Besides, those houses embodied a piece of living community history that was present in every gathering—not just in the rooms, but above all in the persons who were there.

In this connection we should also consider the following: an ancient house cannot simply be equated with our houses today, which for the most part are merely dwellings. By contrast, in antiquity and for a long time afterward the house was a large and complex social unit—at least among the wealthy. Their houses contained not only their families in the narrower sense but also many other people who lived and worked there: the house was often a production site as well. Major production centers separate from houses were rare. This meant that in Christian houses such as, for example, those of Aquila and Prisca, faith and life, or faith and work, were utterly combined.

That, of course, was a major advantage in contrast to our current circumstances in which occupation, family, and Christian life are often widely separated. One of the greatest problems in our society is, in fact, its segregation into different spheres. Sociologists rightly say that modern life takes place in completely different worlds, that society is fragmented into partial realities or functional systems of equal weight. But let them say what they will in their specialized language; I am

[5] Peter Stuhlmacher, *Der Brief an Philemon*, 2nd ed., EKKNT 18 (Zürich: Benziger; Neukirchen-Vluyn: Neukirchener Verlag, 1981), 74 (see above, chap. 12, n. 16).

simply talking about the spheres within which we live and that are constantly drifting farther and farther apart. There is that of the school and education; there is that of job or profession and of business; there is that of free time on the weekend and on vacation.

But there are many other spheres of life: those of politics, the economy, scholarship, law, medicine, art, sport. Each has its own rules, its own vocabulary, its own behaviors, its own modes—and its own time. In this way faith has also become a subfield, limited to a small sector of life—and that in turn portends its slow wasting away or even its death, because genuine faith demands our whole life.

The people of ancient Israel knew that. Just as Jews do today, they recited the prayer "Hear, O Israel" every day. It begins:

> Hear, O Israel: The LORD is our God, the LORD alone. You shall love the LORD your God with all your heart and with all your soul and with all your might. (Deut 6:4-5)

That is: one's whole life belongs to God, from morning to evening, from January 1 to December 31, in the house and outside it. Obviously the same is true of Christian faith. It must shape one's whole life: it *is* a way of life.

But precisely this "wholeness" of a unified way of life is made extraordinarily difficult for us by the splintering of our society. The ancient "house" with its union of work and life had it much easier. But in addition it was true at that time that communities were much smaller and easier to conceive as wholes, which made being together a real possibility. And naturally it made mission much easier: one could invite "outsiders" into the "house," into an easily comprehended group of people, into a way of life that involved solidarity and mutual aid.

What Comes Next?

Now let me make a giant leap from the Christian community in Corinth to a present-day theologian, Cardinal Walter Kasper. In the ecclesiology he proposed in 2011 he introduces a vision of the future church.[6] He says that the concrete form of the future church cannot

[6] Walter Kasper, *Katholische Kirche: Wesen, Wirklichkeit, Sendumg* (Freiburg: Herder, 2011), 392–99. [English: *The Catholic Church: Nature, Reality and Mission*, trans. Thomas Hoebel (London: Bloomsbury T & T Clark, 2015), 289–95.]

be proposed on the basis of a shortage of priests and a lack of faith. That is: the future church must not be like a rolled-out lump of dough. Instead, it must have centers like those in the ancient church, which was much more strongly missionary than we are. The ancient and medieval church missionized out of central points: namely, diocesan centers, city churches, and monasteries. In this connection Kasper speaks of "centrally located churches" in which, especially on Sundays and feast days, a church life could be experienced that is not reduced and slowly dying but is blooming and strong and from which mission can shine forth anew.[7]

But will it not happen, then, that what lies outside these centers of faith will dry up and become a "pastoral desert"? To prevent that, Kasper writes, there must also be a variety of forms of community in addition to the centrally located churches. He speaks of household groups, basic communities, spiritual communities, Bible groups, prayer circles, catechumen groups, circles of families and friends. All these constellations could be "biotopes of faith in which Christian life is experienced and lived and where active participation in ecclesial life can be concretely practiced. They can then radiate the light and warmth of faith into the environment."[8] Then he points to the way of life of the New Testament house churches.

I cannot say whether Kasper is right in projecting the immediate future of the church in this way. I am not a pastoral theologian or a sociologist or a prophet. But however it may be, what Kasper proposes near the end of his book is now increasingly a matter for discussion. Therefore I wanted to present a concrete image of how things were in these small communities according to the Acts of the Apostles. Beyond that, I wanted to show something about the structures of the early church, but above all of its mission. At that time it was simply a matter of course that every community—indeed, every Christian—should live a missionary life as witness to the gospel. There is no other way to explain the extraordinarily swift spread of Christianity in its early days.

It was also part of that swift expansion, however, that the earliest church adopted the "community principle" from Israel. After all, the social form "community" or "congregation" originated in Judaism

[7] Kasper, *The Catholic Church*, 279–80.

[8] Kasper, *The Catholic Church*, 280.

and is part of its rational nature.[9] There was nothing like it in any other religion. "Community" enables visibility, comprehensibility, joining of lives, mutual aid, life with and for others, a common faith, and above all unforced and appropriate mission.

[9] For more on the life and shape of the synagogal communities see Gerhard Lohfink, *Does God Need the Church? On the Theology of the People of God*, trans. Linda M. Maloney (Collegeville, MN: Liturgical Press, 1999), 114–20.

16

The New Testament Basis for the Priestly Office

Jubilees, anniversaries: they must be observed. The year 2017 marked five hundred years since Martin Luther began, in Wittenberg, in the center of Germany, something that was to change the church—and not only church but society as well. In these days my bedtime reading is the renowned book by the historian Heinz Schilling: *Martin Luther: Rebel in an Age of Upheaval*.[1]

There is an immense amount of information in this book; moreover, it is thrillingly written. There are passages in it, however, that irritate me: for example, when Schilling repeatedly refers to the pre-Reformation church as a "papal church," a "priestly church," and a "monastic church,"[2] or when he speaks of the "Roman priestly caste."[3] Does he mean simply to give readers a taste of the deliberately abusive language of the antagonists at the time? Or is this his own judgment? That is not really clear.

Of course, Schilling rightly emphasizes the serious abuses in the church at that time and Rome's inability to reform them. Martin Luther suffered profoundly from those abuses. He wanted to purify the church and for that purpose he logically appealed to the New

[1] Heinz Schilling, *Martin Luther: Rebel in an Age of Upheaval*, trans. Rona Johnston (Oxford: Oxford University Press, 2017). Original: *Martin Luther: Rebell in einer Zeit des Umbruchs* (Munich: Beck, 3rd ed. 2014).

[2] E.g., in the English translation on pp. 62, 84–85, 124, 132, 162–63, 178, 186, 218–21, 240, 279, 312, 338, 361, 367–69, 394, 400, 434, 508, 526–27, 532, 539 [papal church]; 125, 539 [priestly church]. The English translator does not use the phrase "monastic church."

[3] E.g., on pp. 157, 311.

Testament. Thus the professor and reformer who wanted to restore the church became, relatively soon, a prophet and judge who condemned the Roman church as the work of the devil and tried to restore the original church—as he thought he found it in the New Testament.

Consulting the New Testament

Luther finds in the New Testament no priests, but—according to the letter to the Hebrews—only the one, unique priest Jesus Christ. He certainly does not find any ordination of priests. Therefore he battles not only against indulgences and the whole indulgence system but also against the priestly office as the church has understood it since the second century. For him the fact that all the baptized are priests, according to 1 Peter 2:9, is the basic grounding for any theology of orders—and that overthrow of all previous theology of office becomes the real mover of the Reformation. In his "Open Letter to the Christian Nobility of the German Nation"[4] Luther writes:

> It is pure invention that pope, bishops, priests and monks are to be called the "spiritual estate": princes, lords, artisans, and farmers the "temporal estate." That is indeed a fine bit of lying and hypocrisy. Yet no one should be frightened by it; and for this reason—viz., that all Christians are truly of the "spiritual estate,"[5] and there is among them no difference at all. . . . [This is] all because we have one baptism, one Gospel, one faith, and are all alike Christians; for baptism, Gospel and faith alone make us "spiritual" and a Christian people.
>
> But that a pope or a bishop anoints, confers tonsures; ordains, consecrates, or prescribes dress unlike that of the laity, this may make hypocrites and graven images, but it never makes a Christian or "spiritual" man. Through baptism all of us are consecrated to the priesthood, as St. Peter says in I Peter 2:9, "Ye are a royal priesthood, a priestly

[4] Martin Luther, "An Open Letter to the Christian Nobility of the German Nation Concerning the Reform of the Christian Estate, 1520," trans. C. M. Jacobs, in *Works of Martin Luther: With Introductions and Notes*, 2 (Philadelphia: Holman, 1915), at https://www.projectwittenberg.org/pub/resources/text/wittenberg/luther/web/nblty-03.html.

[5] On the point that, according to the New Testament, all Christians are *pneumatikoi* (spiritual, gifted with the Spirit), Luther is correct. Cf. 1 Cor 2:13; Gal 6:1.

> kingdom," and the book of Revelation says, "Thou hast made us by Thy blood to be priests and kings" (Rev. 5:10).

Conclusion: There is no longer any need for a priesthood appointed by God and having its own authority over the church. Every baptized person has a share in the fullness of the gifts God has given the church. Of course Martin Luther intended that there should be order and office in the church. He rejects a "church of the Spirit" like those that make their way in esoteric circles. But priests in the sense of the Roman church he likewise rejects.

He wants pastors who preach the gospel correctly and administer the biblically attested sacraments of baptism, confession, and the Lord's Supper in accordance with the gospel. He is convinced that only baptism, confession, and the Lord's Supper were instituted by Christ, and *not* the sacrament of orders. In principle, therefore, every Christian can administer the sacraments—that is, baptize and celebrate the Lord's Supper. Pastors exist only for the sake of order, and they are commissioned by the congregation to carry out the duties that are proper to all Christians. But in principle all the baptized have the same authority over word and sacrament on the basis of their common priesthood:

> Let everyone, therefore, who knows himself to be a Christian be assured of this, and apply it to himself,—that we are all priests, and there is no difference between us; that is to say, we have the same power (*potestas*) in respect to the Word and all the sacraments.[6]

Similarly in his sermons for the year 1524:

> When I call you a Christian I also at the same time call you a priest who can administer the sacrament, offer intercessions before God, and judge teaching.[7]

Anyone who is baptized and believes in the gospel, says Luther, therefore no longer needs a priest because she or he has received the

[6] *The Babylonian Captivity of the Church: A Prelude*, 7.15 (WA 6, 566): *Esto itaque certus est sese agnoscat quicunque se Christianum esse cognoverit, omnes nos aequaliter esse sacerdotes, hoc est eandem in verbo et sacramento quocunque habere potestatem.*

[7] WA 15, 720: *Si dico te Christianum, statim dico et sacerdotem, qui potest dare sacramentum, interpellare coram deo, et iudicare de doctrina.*

Holy Spirit and so is immediately present to God. The only mediator is Christ. Therefore: away with the pope and the priests, who have made themselves mediators and use their mediatorial office to make money, exercise power, and corrupt congregations!

As I have said: Martin Luther appeals to the New Testament for this, his basic reformational position. Wasn't he right? Don't the gospels themselves support him? After all, they do not speak of priests anywhere, except for the priests who serve in the temple. But those priests—according to the theology of the letter to the Hebrews—are members of a priesthood that has been abrogated forever through Jesus Christ, and more particularly through the sacrifice he offered, once for all, on the cross.

It is true that Jesus acknowledged the service of the priests of his time: for example, when he sends a leper he has healed to show himself to them so that his healing may be affirmed (Mark 1:44). But the disciples he gathers around him have nothing to do with the priests who serve in the temple, not in the least. Such a priest is called *hiereus* in the Greek Bible (Latin: *sacerdos*), and it is only since the third century that the church has applied the cultic title *hiereus/sacerdos*—first to bishops, and later also to the priests who are associated with the bishop.

There are still no cultic designations in the New Testament for the office of leadership in the congregations; significantly, there is only a terminology stemming from ordinary civil office. There are apostles,[8] *episkopoi*,[9] deacons,[10] presbyters,[11] leaders,[12] those who serve the community in other leadership roles.[13] These titles, without exception, come from the nonsacramental vocabulary. In Hellenism public officials or communal superintendents could be called "*episkopoi*," and "presbyters" are quite simply "elders." According to the book of Deuteronomy there were already "elders" in Israel at the time the covenant was made at Sinai (Deut 5:23) and, at the end of the wilderness wandering, at the making of the covenant in Moab (Deut 29:9; 31:9, 28). In Jesus' time, however, they existed mainly in the synagogue communities. Thus the "offices" or "services" referred to in the New Tes-

[8] Cf. here esp. the broader concept of apostolicity in Rom 16:7 and Acts 14:4.

[9] *Episkopoi*: Acts 20:28; Phil 1:1; 1 Tim 3:2; Titus 1:7.

[10] Deacons: Rom 16:1; Phil 1:1; 1 Tim 3:8-13.

[11] Presbyters: Acts 11:30; 14:23; 15:2, 4, 6, 22, 23; 16:4; 20:17; 21:18; 1 Tim 5:17, 19; Titus 1:5.

[12] Leaders (= those who are in charge): Rom 12:8; 1 Thess 5:12.

[13] "Forms of leadership": 1 Cor 12:28.

tament lack even the most distant relationship to the cult personnel in the temple.

Moreover, the priests and Levites who make their living from the temple do not come off very well in Jesus' view—not, at any rate, in the parable of the Good Samaritan (Luke 10:25-37). There both a priest and a Levite see the beaten man lying by the road, look away, and travel on. Does that not suggest that Jesus expected very little or nothing at all from these individuals in service to the renewal of Israel?

The church, with its efforts to find something like a priestly ordination in the New Testament, very quickly concentrated on the Last Supper, and particularly on Jesus' words: "Do this in remembrance of me" (Luke 22:19; 1 Cor 11:24, 25). The reference was certainly correct, but it lacks a basis. It would have been better to have looked first to a different text-complex and only later to Jesus' Last Supper.

The fundamental texts on which the church should have relied in support of priesthood are the appointment and sending of the twelve disciples in Mark 3:13-19; 6:6-13. I will look first at one of these passages—and from an absolutely historical point of view. I will ask, without ignoring Mark's depiction, about what Jesus himself did.

A second preliminary remark is necessary here. To begin with I will not ask about the innermost center of the priestly office in the sense of the church's tradition. That needs to come at the end of these reflections. My first interest, in principle, is in the institution of the office in the church. The principle is this: every church office rests on mission, sending. And the basis and original model of all mission is Jesus' sending of the Twelve.

Appointment and Sending of the Twelve

In 3:13-19 Mark, having said previously that Jesus gathered disciples, describes the appointment of the Twelve. First he tells about the calling of Simon and Andrew, James and John (1:16-20), then that of Levi (2:13-17): examples of how Jesus summons his followers. Mark has already said at 2:15 that there are "many" who are following Jesus. Then, in 3:13-14, Jesus chooses twelve from among those many followers. Mark writes:

> He went up the mountain and called to him those whom he wanted, and they came to him. And he created twelve to be with him and to be sent out to preach and to have authority to cast out demons. So

> he created the twelve: Simon (to whom he gave the name Peter), James son of Zebedee and John the brother of James (to whom he gave the name Boanerges, that is, Sons of Thunder), and Andrew, and Philip, and Bartholomew, and Matthew, and Thomas, and James son of Alphaeus, and Thaddeus, and Simon the Cananaean, and Judas Iscariot, who handed him over. (Mark 3:13-19)

In this scene Mark recalls a historical event that was of central importance for Jesus' work. A number of New Testament scholars have, indeed, disputed that and asserted that the role of the Twelve in the earliest community was projected back to the time of the earthly Jesus; there never was a choice and commissioning of twelve disciples before Easter. But that assertion is a nonstarter in face of the fact that, in all the lists naming the Twelve, Judas Iscariot is among them (Matt 10:4; Mark 3:19; Luke 6:16; Acts 1:13, 16–20).

It is altogether improbable that a fictional appointment by the earthly Jesus would have included, of all people, the disciple who handed Jesus over to the Jerusalem authorities. But still more important is the fact that the appointment of the Twelve fits so very well in the context of the preaching and practice of the historical Jesus.

Jesus must have chosen the Twelve out of a larger group of disciples and appointed them in the presence of the others (or even the people as a whole?). What he did was anything but an incidental or peripheral event. This was a prophetic sign-action whose meaning everyone in Israel could understand. Now everyone could see that Jesus was acting in and for the people of the twelve tribes. And since in Jesus' time the twelve tribes no longer existed as such—at most they numbered two and a half—it was clear that now Jesus is marking the beginning of an eschatological event: he intends to create the Israel that God, according to the prophetic promises, will restore in the end time.[14]

Note: a prophetic sign-action was more than just a didactic instrument used to help people grasp the point more easily. A prophetic sign-action was also more than a merely demonstrative expression of intent. There was something creative about it. It established reality, a new reality in word and sign, coming from God—and in that way it certainly was something very like what makes a sacrament.

[14] Cf. Isa 11:11, 16; 27:12-13; 35:8-10; 49:11; 60:4, 9; 66:20; Ezek 39:27-28; Mic 7:12.

We should note here that Mark says Jesus "created" the Twelve. In the Old Testament "create" could mean the installation of officials such as judges or priests, and Mark is speaking here of such a public and official action. But a good deal more is at play in Mark's text. Everyone familiar with the Bible would have heard in the background the fixed formula "God created" from the account in Genesis 1:7, 16, 21, 25, 27, 31; 2:2, 3 (LXX). The same language echoes in Deutero-Isaiah, who says more than once that God "created" a people (Isa 43:1, 7 LXX) and would "create" new things for them. Mark means to say that the promise in the book of Isaiah is coming to fulfillment with Jesus' installation of the Twelve. The new creation of Israel is beginning now. The Twelve are the beginning and center of growth for the eschatological people of God, and they are put in place in order to express Jesus' claim to the whole people of the twelve tribes. With the symbolic proclamation of this claim Jesus has already inaugurated the gathering and new creation of Israel. In that sense we may certainly say that the installation of the Twelve is a symbolic-sacramental event.

Mark, using a narrative technique he frequently employs (cf., e.g., 3:22-30 within 3:20-35), inserts other story material between the choice of the Twelve and their sending on mission. Only after Jesus has been rejected in his home village of Nazareth does Mark tell of the sending of the Twelve, thus continuing the sign-action of 3:3-19. What then happens is, so to speak, part 2: the Twelve are sent out—to Israel.

For what purpose are they sent? To preach to Israel? That by no means describes their purpose. They are sent by Jesus to proclaim the reign of God in Israel; they are its official witnesses. That is more than preaching. The Twelve are to announce the reign of God everywhere in Israel—that is, they are to make known that it is coming now. By proclaiming it they make it present.

That the Twelve do not primarily preach but instead proclaim the reign of God is clear from the fact that where they are not listened to they are to shake the dust from their feet and move on. They thus become witnesses to judgment on that place (Mark 6:11). That has little or no relation to the didactics, certainly not to the pedagogy, of preaching.

We can see that they are witnesses from the fact that they are sent in pairs (Mark 6:7). In Jewish legal practice the witness of a single person is insufficient; there must be at least two witnesses, and their testimony must agree. We can also see that they are *official* witnesses from the fact that they are sent by Jesus himself and endowed by him with *exousia*, full authority (Mark 6:7). The Twelve testify officially—I could also say "as officeholders"—to the arrival of the reign of God in Israel.

More precisely: they testify officially that the reign of God is now arriving in Israel, and that is visible in the fact that they drive out demons or, in our terms, that they heal people of the demonic social compulsions that individuals cannot overcome by their own power.[15] The apostles' expulsion of demons is happening in the *now*, and therefore the reign of God is coming *now*.

The appointment and sending of the Twelve reveals still more: what the Twelve do, that is, their reality-altering proclamation of the reign of God, is not a result of their own giftedness or that of the people of God concentrated in them. They have it solely and utterly from their commissioning by Jesus. He gives them the *exousia*, the authority to heal and drive out demons. In that authority they make Jesus directly present; they represent him. This representation is evident from the fact that they do precisely what Jesus does: they proclaim the reign of God, heal the sick, and drive out demonic spirits.

Conclusion: The sending of the Twelve, the official, ministerial character of their witness to the now-happening arrival of the reign of God, and the representational character of Jesus that comes with it form the basis for office in the church. Every church office is characterized by sending, by mission that comes through Jesus, and in fact—this is important—by sending to the people of God. Again: that, essentially, points only to the basis of all ecclesiastical office. I will speak later of what is specific to priesthood.

Interim Remarks on Method

I have begun with the historical Jesus or, more precisely, with the historical Jesus as he can be perceived in the Markan narrative. It is clear that, after Easter, the character of the Twelve as official witnesses was accommodated to the new circumstances and had to be developed accordingly. The Easter events most certainly played a crucial

[15] For more on Jesus' expulsion of demons see Lohfink, *Jesus of Nazareth: What He Wanted, Who He Was*, trans. Linda M. Maloney (Collegeville, MN: Liturgical Press, 2015), 143–45.

role in that development. Paul reports an appearance of the Risen One to the Twelve (1 Cor 15:5) that was evidently experienced as a continuation and strengthening of the sending of the Twelve during Jesus' lifetime. Thus their official ministerial witness endures. In the beginning the Twelve also play a crucial role within the earliest community in Jerusalem.

Still, one particular element comes more to the fore: they not only continue to preach the gospel in Israel, now proclaiming Christ as well. They also recognize themselves as the eschatological judges of Israel, because the day of the Human One's[16] return is imminent. The recognition of this judicial aspect of their office could well stem from Jesus himself (cf. Matt 19:28; Luke 22:30). Here again, the Twelve's office of witness is shown to be eschatological in character.

In the extreme end-time tension immediately after Easter the group of Twelve is reconstituted after the defection of Judas Iscariot by the addition of another of Jesus' disciples, one Matthias (Acts 1:15-26). As time passed, however, no further additions occurred because the outward form of the imminent expectation gradually altered, and external conditions also changed as the church rapidly expanded into Samaria and Syria. When James the son of Zebedee was executed by Herod (Acts 12:2) no further election to the Twelve followed.

I could go on in this way, attempting a historical reconstruction of the origins and development of offices in the nascent and early church. I would have to cover a very broad field, and one that would be hard to access because so much remains hypothetical. Apart from Paul's letters we have very few reliable sources for this earliest period of the church.

At any rate, I would have to speak of the communities of the Pauline mission. Did they already incorporate church offices in the later sense? Or were those communities organized charismatically? I would have to discuss the original diversifying of the concept of apostle, which would include men like Barnabas (Acts 14:14) or couples like Andronicus and Junia (Rom 16:7). I would have to talk of the role of prophets and itinerant preachers in the Syrian communities as reflected in the *Didachē* and the so-called Teaching of the Twelve Apostles, but probably also in the Gospel of Matthew. I would have

[16] From Daniel's *bar enosh*, which previously was translated "Son of Man." NABRE retains "son of man" (without caps); NRSV and NRSVue write "human being."—Trans.

to discuss the introduction of the office of "elders" in Jewish-Christian communities. Finally, I would have to speak of the theology of office in the seven letters of Ignatius of Antioch and in 1 Clement.

But I am not going to do all that now. Certainly the attempt to reconstruct the development of offices in the early church is necessary and meaningful. Many outstanding studies of the subject have already appeared. But those historical reconstructions do not touch on the central question, which is theological. Our understanding of office in the church cannot be established by historical reconstructions. It must first and primarily be determined from what Scripture says, based on the word of God itself. That is: it must be decided on the *theological* level, and concretely that means we must ask what the New Testament itself, in its definitive text, at the level of its own statement, has to say about office in the church.

Only in that way will we also do justice to the urgent questions Martin Luther posed. It is true that Luther, as a contemporary of the Humanists who wanted to get back to the earliest sources, was profoundly interested in historical-critical questions, and he also did historical research. We can see that from the fact that the original form of the church played a significant role in his argument with Rome.

But beyond all that, Luther plumbed the word of God with the utmost radicality. That, in fact, is his great merit. And the word of God is not what historians or specialists in religious studies reconstruct as historical sequences or historical variety. Rather, we have the word of God only on the statement-level of Scripture itself (presupposing that we read Scripture on the ground from which it emerged, namely, as the church's book).

Therefore in what follows I will not attempt a historical reconstruction of the development of offices in the church. Instead, I will examine two groups of texts in the New Testament to see how they depict office and its continuity. The first source is Luke's two-volume work and the second is the so-called Pastorals: 1 and 2 Timothy and Titus.

I have chosen these two text-complexes because, within the New Testament, they deliberately and explicitly go into the question of the continuity of the development of ecclesiastical office. Both the Lukan work and the Pastorals were created in a time when, after the death of the apostles, the church was threatened by a dangerous collapse of continuity. Both mean to show what it is that must combat that breach of continuity: what is "apostolic" in the church or, more precisely, the tie to the apostolic office of witness.

Incidentally—and I say this only parenthetically here—what I have just said about Luke and the Pastorals already applies to the Gospel of Mark. Current biblical scholarship has long recognized that the gospels do not simply intend to give us a historical account of Jesus, his disciples, and the reactions of his contemporaries. It is true that they also do that, but at the same time they intend to say what it all means for the contemporary church—to make the events of that time transparent to the church's present. That is true not only for Mark but also for Luke and Matthew. When Mark was writing his gospel, forty years after Jesus' death, he not only wanted to evoke long-ago events from Jesus' time; he also wanted to set before the eyes of his contemporary communities the enduring meaning of those past events. When he reports the selection and appointment of the Twelve he is at the same time saying that the Twelve are the enduring foundation for the eschatological people of God.

But this transparency of the gospel to the later church is not so immediately obvious in Mark as it is, for example, in Luke. Therefore I will now turn to Luke's two-volume work and afterward to the Pastorals.

Theology of Office in Luke–Acts

In Luke 6:12-16 and 9:1-6 the Gospel's author draws on his Markan model to describe the choice and sending of the Twelve, but he gives a much more significant theological profile to the former than Mark does. As in Mark's account, Jesus goes up a mountain, but he goes there to pray. He spends the whole night in prayer, asking that he may make the right choice. When day comes he calls his disciples to him and chooses the Twelve from among them. And Luke adds something to the scene, which he has made much more vivid than Mark's account: "twelve, whom he also named apostles" (Luke 6:13).[17] Thus for Luke the choice of the Twelve is of the utmost importance, and he also makes it clear right away that for him these are "the" apostles. The Twelve and the apostles are identical, according to Luke: he recognizes no apostles other than the group of the Twelve.[18]

[17] Some mss. of Mark contain Luke's redactional expansion at Mark 3:14; it was probably copied there from Luke.

[18] The sole exception is in Acts 14:4, 14, where Barnabas and Paul are called "apostles." Interpreters offer various explanations: (a) Luke is following an older

Within Luke's Gospel, then, the twelve apostles play an especially prominent role.[19] That is especially clear at the end of the Gospel. After their encounter with the Risen One the disciples who had traveled to Emmaus return immediately to Jerusalem, where they find the "eleven" gathered (Luke 24:33) and are told: "The Lord has risen indeed, and he has appeared to Simon!" (Luke 24:34).

This is followed by the Easter appearance to the eleven apostles and those who are with them. The Risen One names them "witnesses" to his suffering and resurrection (Luke 24:46-48). At the same time they are ordered to remain in the city.

That "staying in the city" is extraordinarily important for Luke's theology. As the forty days during which the Risen One remains with the apostles (Acts 1:3) are a temporal symbol for the continuity between Jesus' time and that of the church, so remaining in Jerusalem is a spatial symbol. That is why Luke could not tell about the appearances in Galilee (to Peter, for example). He could only allude to them in Luke 24:34.

Luke's second book, the so-called Acts of the Apostles, takes up and develops the conclusion of the Gospel. The apostles are named immediately, in the "Foreword," with the added note that Jesus "had chosen [them] through the Holy Spirit" (Acts 1:2).[20] They are again instructed to remain in Jerusalem and there await the coming of the Holy Spirit (1:4). After the forty days and Jesus' ascension Luke gives a list of the apostles (1:13-14), even though he had already done so in the first book. Then he relates the election of Matthias (1:15-26), thus making it clear that the apostles, in their full number, are qualified as "witnesses" (1:8) to everything Jesus did and taught (cf. 1:1)

---

source here; (b) at this point Luke regards Barnabas and Paul unspecifically as "those sent" by the community at Antioch; (c) Luke has not maintained his own nomenclature and is simply inconsistent.

[19] Cf., e.g., Luke 9:12; 11:49; 17:5; 22:14, with the corresponding sources.

[20] Many translators link "through the Holy Spirit" to *enteilamenos* [instructed], but that is certainly wrong. Cf. Gerhard Lohfink, *Die Himmelfahrt Jesu. Untersuchungen zu den Himmelfahrts- und Erhöhungstexten bei Lukas*, SANT 26 (Munich: Kösel, 1971), 221. [The translators mentioned include Jerome, and those of the AV, NRSV, NRSVue, NABRE, NIV, et al. Lohfink, in *Himmelfahrt*, links it to Luke 6:12-16, where Jesus spends the night in prayer before choosing the Twelve. His point is that the action Jesus does "through the Holy Spirit" is his choosing of the Twelve, not his instructing them—Trans.]

because they were with him "beginning from the baptism of John until the day when he was taken up" (1:22).

Then, in chapters 1–15, these apostles play a crucial role, either as a group or in the person of Peter and, to some extent, of John the son of Zebedee (3:1, 11; 4:13, 19; 8:14). Their last great and significant appearance within the narrative fabric of Acts is at the so-called apostolic council (Acts 15). In these fifteen chapters Luke tells how the Twelve interpreted the life of Jesus to Israel, how they attested to his resurrection, how they healed the sick (3:1-10), expelled demons (5:12-16), gathered those in Israel who were willing to change their lives, and resolved conflicts within the community.

It is in the context of such a conflict resolution, in Acts 6, that Luke tells of the apostles' installing other persons in office, namely, the "Seven." Historically these seven men obviously represent a collegial leadership group within the Greek-speaking portion of the original community, which probably assembled separately. But that was of no interest to Luke, or perhaps he did not even know about it. For him the choice of the Seven was an example of how the Twelve handed on some aspect of their own office: they wanted to devote themselves entirely "to prayer and to serving the word" (6:4), and the Seven should take over "wait[ing] on tables" and thus primarily serve the poor (6:1-3). In fact, Luke's account shows two of the Seven (Stephen and Philip) acting, like the apostles, as preachers of the gospel.

We should not underestimate the significance of the choice of the Seven, as Luke tells it, for the theology of office. Here he had material at hand with which he could show how the apostles delegated authority. At this point Luke again explicitly (and for the last time in his two-volume work) uses the concept of the Twelve (6:2). The Twelve call together the whole Jerusalem community (6:2); the necessity for delegation of office is explained to the community (6:2-4); the community agrees and chooses the Seven (6:5) and has them "stand before the apostles" (6:6). Then the apostles pray over those chosen and lay hands on them (6:6[21]). In this context Luke again gives a

[21] Various constructions are possible at this point. Either "they [all members of the community] brought them to the apostles; they [all members of the community] prayed and laid hands on them." Or, with a change of subject: "they [all members of the community] brought them to the apostles; they [the apostles] prayed and laid hands on them." Such changes of subject are possible in Greek literature, especially

complete list of their names, as he had done previously with the Twelve (6:5).

We may certainly suppose that at this point Luke was inserting a ritual of installation in office from his own time into his picture of the original Jerusalem community. That makes it all the more difficult to evaluate the whole process. Luke is showing how he imagined the handing-on of apostolic authority. To repeat: this, for Luke also, is not only about "table service." Philip very soon afterward begins preaching the gospel of the reign of God in the capital city of Samaria (8:12). He testifies to Christ (8:12), heals the sick, and expels demons (8:6-7). In other words, he does everything the apostles do.[22]

Somewhat offhandedly Luke lets us know that the Jerusalem community contained not only the twelve apostles and the Seven but also *presbyteroi*, elders. They appear for the first time at Acts 11:30 and are also mentioned at 15:2, 4, 6, 22, 23; 16:4; 21:18. Luke says nothing about their installation in office, though he probably presumes one because he has given an example of such a proceeding in the case of the Seven. It is only in the context of the missionary activity of Paul and Barnabas that Luke tells of the installation of elders. His intention here is to show, in principle and by example, how the witness of Paul and Barnabas was handed on to persons appointed in the individual local communities. "And after they had appointed elders for them in each church, [laying hands on them,] with prayer and fasting they entrusted them to the Lord in whom they had come to believe" (Acts 14:23).[23]

Does this show clearly that in Luke's two-volume work all installations in office must be performed by Jesus himself, or by the apostles, or even by official "witnesses"—that is, witnesses who had been appointed to their office as such by the Risen One himself?

---

when the new subject has been previously mentioned, as here. Ultimately, then, the decision must be based on internal evidence. At this point it is highly likely that Luke was thinking of Num 27:18-23 LXX, where Moses transfers his official authority to Joshua by laying hands on him. Previously he has "had him stand" before the whole community of Israel. As Moses ordains, so here the Twelve ordain, in the presence of and with the witness of the whole community. Also, the parallel in Acts 14:23 is more significant than Acts 13:3.

[22] Philip then (in Acts 8:26-38) teaches the gospel to a foreigner and baptizes him—before Peter does those things in Acts 10.—Trans.

[23] AV: "And when they had ordained them elders in every church, and had prayed with fasting, they commended them to the Lord, on whom they believed."

Perhaps. But perhaps not, because in Acts 13 we encounter a remarkable report that certainly must not be overlooked here:

> Now in the church at Antioch there were prophets and teachers: Barnabas, Simeon who was called Niger, Lucius of Cyrene, Manaen a childhood friend of Herod the ruler, and Saul. While they were worshiping the Lord and fasting, the Holy Spirit said, "Set apart for me Barnabas and Saul for the work to which I have called them." Then after fasting and praying they laid their hands on them and sent them off. (Acts 13:1-3)

The function of this passage is obvious. It introduces the great missionary work of Paul that is now to be narrated. Again we see an ordination taking place: after prayer, hands are laid on those to be sent out. But this time it is not, as in Acts 6:6, the apostles, or, as in 14:23, Paul and Barnabas who lay on hands: clearly here it is the whole community. The subject in verses 2 and 3 is, in both cases, the Christian community in Antioch.

If we view Acts 13:1-3 in isolation we have a precise model of church office as envisioned by the Reformation, in the most radical form imaginable: the community itself installs its officers after having struggled in prayer over the right choice. As a sign of its choice the community lays hands on the future officeholders. But the whole process takes place in and through the Holy Spirit. This means that it is the Holy Spirit who sends, but the Spirit does so through the acts of the community.

No one should object that this is not about ordaining leaders for the community in Antioch but about sending on mission. That is too superficial. After all, as regards the "prophets and teachers" who "were" in the community at Antioch (13:1) Luke says nothing at all about how they came to occupy their offices. Evidently Luke knew that the church incorporated a wide variety of offices and an equally wide spectrum of ways in which offices could "originate." Luke knew that there were Jewish-Christian communities with "elders" as their leaders and that in Gentile-Christian communities the corresponding offices of leadership were held by "bishops [*episkopoi*]," that is, "overseers" (cf. Acts 20:28; Phil 1:1). He knew that there were itinerant prophets who could also settle down and join themselves to a community (Acts 21:10-11), and he knew also that there were teachers who played an important role in proclamation and preaching (Acts 13:1).

Luke did not trouble himself to explicitly and directly derive all these offices bestowed by the imposition of hands from the office of the twelve apostles. What does interest him is that the commissioning must be done through the Holy Spirit, and those commissioned must be in communion with Jerusalem, the place where the Twelve are. In the case of Barnabas, Luke describes that connection explicitly: cf. Acts 4:36; 9:27, and especially 11:22-23. Here Barnabas is sent by the apostles from Jerusalem to Antioch, and indeed as official messenger and "filled with the Holy Spirit." But Luke also develops the link between Paul and the Jerusalem authorities quite extensively: Barnabas presents Paul to the apostles after his conversion, and Paul "went in and out among them in Jerusalem" (Acts 9:27-28).

With all that we have long since arrived at the Paul of Acts. As I have said, the "time of the apostles" extends, in Acts, to the end of chapter 15. Thereafter the narrative is devoted to the "time of Paul." That overlaps with the time of the apostles, because as early as Acts 7:58 Paul appears at the execution of Stephen and his conversion is related at length in chapter 9. But that "overlapping" is intentional, because here again Luke means to signal continuity. As Jesus' time and that of the apostles are partly simultaneous in the "forty days" of Acts 1, so there is a partial overlap between the time of the apostles and the time of Paul.

In Luke's work, however, Paul is not called to be an "apostle." Nothing must detract from the specific function of the Twelve. Paul appears as the "thirteenth witness" in addition to the apostles.[24] But Paul, like the Twelve,[25] is a genuine witness to Christ.[26] He proclaims the reign of God (20:25) and Jesus' resurrection (13:33); he heals and he expels demons as Jesus and the apostles did (14:3, 10; 16:18; 20:10), and he plays a decisive role in spreading the gospel. Luke devotes major space to the description of his work in Acts 13–28. All this makes it clear that in Acts it is the Twelve and Paul who are the authoritative witnesses to Jesus Christ and the gospel.

[24] Cf. Christian Burchard, *Der dreizehnte Zeuge: Traditions- u. kompositionsgeschichtliche Untersuchungen zu Lukas' Darstellung der Frühzeit des Paulus*, FRLANT 103 (Göttingen: Vandenhoeck & Ruprecht, 1970).

[25] For the Twelve as witnesses cf. Luke 24:48; Acts 1:8, 22; 2:32; 3:15; 5:32; 10:39; 13:31.

[26] The texts of Acts 22:15 and 26:16 are controlling here.

Acts 20 is, then, of prime significance for our subject. Paul is on his way to Jerusalem, where he will be greeted by the outrage of his Jewish opponents and will be imprisoned by the Roman authorities. While in Miletus he summons the elders of the Ephesian community and addresses them. This is a farewell speech—but not simply for the Ephesian elders. In Luke's intent Acts 20:18-35 is Paul's great farewell oration to the church. The crucial passage for our subject is Acts 20:28-31a:

> Keep watch over yourselves and over all the flock, of which the Holy Spirit has made you overseers, to shepherd the church of God that he obtained with the blood of his own Son. I know that after I have gone, savage wolves will come in among you, not sparing the flock. Some even from your own group will come distorting the truth in order to entice the disciples to follow them. Therefore be alert.

This text is revealing in many ways, and at the same time it serves well as a conclusion to our survey of the theology of office in Luke's two-volume work.

First of all, Luke shows Paul addressing the problems of his own present time: false teachers appear, and not only from without but above all from the communities themselves, that is, those in the area of the Pauline mission. As we can discern from another remark in this discourse to the church (i.e., 20:20: "I did not shrink from . . . proclaiming the message to you") these are primarily false teachers who are introducing new doctrines. Luke must have Gnostic teachers especially in mind, people who, in long esoteric speeches, depict the Risen One as showing a new way to salvation.

It is against these false teachers that the departing Paul speaks as he moves toward his death. Moreover: it is against false teachers of that kind that, essentially, Luke wrote his whole two-volume work. He wants to present Theophilus and the communities for whom he writes with the real facts and the true Christian teaching. Above all he wants to show them that the Christian message is anchored in the earthly Jesus and in the apostles who have preached that message truthfully. For that purpose he not only has to narrate in his first book what Jesus did and taught. He also has to show how the earthly Jesus himself sent forth the Twelve with that teaching and how, then, the Risen One affirmed the mission of the apostles.

But even that was not enough. Luke had to go beyond that, showing that this teaching was also truthfully transmitted even after the time of the apostles. For that purpose he has introduced the great figure of Paul, who, according to Luke's presentation, is not only the "thirteenth witness" but is truly one who has seen the Risen One and a person who went in and out among the apostles. And Paul himself had installed elders everywhere in his communities to secure the continuity of "apostolicity" to the church that existed in Luke's own time. The great farewell discourse in Miletus, which Luke quite deliberately stages at this point, presumes all that. It shows how important office in the church is for Luke. It holds a conspicuous place in the farewell speech to the elders from Ephesus. Still it is true that, to a certain degree, Luke leaves open the question of the concrete character of this office. At first, in 20:17, he refers to "elders" (*presbyteroi*), but he is not interested in the details of offices.

What does interest Luke is that all those who hold church office are installed by the Holy Spirit and are connected with the apostles or Paul. Every church office must be in relationship with Jerusalem, the place of the church's origin. What concerns Luke as regards the increasing numbers of false teachers is the threat to continuity between Jesus and the Jerusalem community—and, correspondingly, the continuity between the Jerusalem community and his own ecclesial present. For that, church office is of the highest importance. It must be grounded in Jesus. It must be affirmed by the Risen One. It must be set in place by the Holy Spirit. And it must be connected to the apostles. That is still not a *successio apostolica*[27] that insists on an unbroken chain of impositions of hands. But in outline, and in the sense of what *successio apostolica* really ought to mean, it is already present.

Theology of Office in the Pastorals

What has already appeared in Luke's work in outline comes fully into the light in the so-called Pastoral Epistles. I can give a briefer presentation here because in these three letters the development of offices has advanced a great deal and the intention to show continuity with the apostolic beginnings emerges more prominently than in

[27] *Successio apostolica* = continuing transfer of the apostles' missionary character.

Luke and Acts. For the Pastorals it is Paul, however, not the Twelve, who represents what is apostolic. I assume, with the great majority of scholars, that 1 and 2 Timothy and Titus do not come from Paul. There can be no reasonable doubt about that: not only is their style completely different, but so is their point of departure.

These three letters assume a situation similar to what lies behind the Lukan work: the threat of a breach of continuity with the apostolic time and seizure of authority by false teachers. Now, however, those teachers are clearly named: they are Gnostics:[28]

> Timothy, guard the deposit [*parathēkē*] entrusted to you. Avoid the profane chatter and contradictions of what is falsely called knowledge [*gnōsis*]; by professing it some have missed the mark as regards the faith. (1 Tim 6:20-21)

It is astonishing how often false teachers are referred to in the Pastorals, and yet the precise profile of what they are teaching remains obscure. Nevertheless, that need not occupy us here. What is clear is that the author of the Pastorals appeals to "sound teaching" against the positions of these opponents. There are three concepts that play a decisive role in that context: the "gospel," the "teaching" (*didaskalia*), and the "entrusted deposit" (*parathēkē*).

"Gospel" primarily means the gospel preached by Paul, the gospel of Jesus Christ the Savior; any number of confessional formulae are used for it.[29] "Sound teaching" is broader in scope. It consists primarily of ethical admonitions, especially principles for particular groups or orders of life: men, women, widows, young adults, the rich, enslaved persons, *episkopoi*, elders, deacons, and above all those who hold office (personified by Timothy). The "entrusted deposit" is the whole of what Paul has handed on to Timothy to be faithfully kept: the precious treasure of the faith. All this has been given in trust to Timothy and to Titus by Paul, and they are to hand it on faithfully. That is the best protection against false teaching.

[28] Here I assume that in ancient Judaism, as in ancient Christianity, there were countless types of *gnōsis*. It is not necessary in this context to give a more precise definition of the kind of *gnōsis* the Pastorals are opposing. What is crucial is that here the apostolic tradition is rightly brought to bear against false teaching.

[29] Cf. 1 Tim 2:5-6; 3:16; 2 Tim 2:11-13.

Thus in the Pastorals the defense against false teaching is above all the tradition faithfully preserved—the tradition that comes from Paul and extends by way of his pupils, above all Timothy and Titus, to the present time of the church. There have to be bearers of this tradition, however, or, more precisely, persons responsible for the faithful transmission of the gospel and the teaching. They, too, play an important role in the Pastorals, but they are viewed entirely as persons who serve the correct handing-on of the tradition.[30]

First of all, there is Paul himself. He appears not only in the three introductions to the letters—which follow the precise pattern of the genuine Pauline letters—as "apostle of Jesus Christ" or "servant of God and apostle of Jesus Christ." Throughout the bodies of the letters, too, a great deal of space is devoted to his life, his concrete circumstances, and his service to the gospel. Paul is extolled as "a herald and an apostle" (1 Tim 2:7), as "a teacher of the gentiles in faith and truth" (1 Tim 2:7), as "a herald and an apostle and a teacher" (2 Tim 1:11) who has "fought the good fight; . . . finished the race; . . . kept the faith" (2 Tim 4:7).

Besides Paul, the principal figures in the letters are, of course, Timothy and Titus. They are repeatedly addressed, for example, in this sort of pattern:

> I hope to come to you [Timothy] soon, but I am writing these instructions to you so that, if I am delayed, you may know how one ought to behave in the household of God, which is the church of the living God, the pillar and support of the truth. (1 Tim 3:14-15)

The fiction is that Paul himself will be coming but cannot do so at the moment. In reality he will "be delayed," that is, he will not return again. With the aid of this schema, which New Testament scholars call "the epiphany of the apostle,"[31] the Pastorals make it clear that Timothy and Titus have now taken the place of Paul.

[30] Cf. Gerhard Lohfink, "Die Normativität der Amtsvorstellungen in den Pastoralbriefen," *ThQ* 157 (1977): 93–106. In that essay, however, I undervalued the role of office and the *successio apostolica*.

[31] Cf. esp. Robert W. Funk, "The Apostolic Parousia—Form and Significance," in *Christian History and Interpretation: Studies Presented to John Knox*, ed. William R. Farmer, C. F. D. Moule, and R. R. Niebuhr (Cambridge: Cambridge University Press, 1967), 249–68. See also Gerhard Lohfink, "Paulinische Theologie in der Rezeption der Pas-

But as what? As a kind of bishops? Or perhaps as provincials or archbishops? We should not waste time on such anachronisms. In the sense of the Pastorals they fill the vacancy between Paul and the present time. I need to say that even more precisely: the Pastorals themselves, with their principal figures—Paul, Timothy, and Titus—fill the vacancy between the historical Paul and the ecclesial present of the letters' author.

We need to picture that concretely. The historical Paul had not returned from his journey to Jerusalem, and now his apostolic presence, his letters, and the messengers he sent are absent from the communities in his missionary field. There was no "hierarchy" of officeholders, not even a somehow orderly system of community leaders that was the same everywhere. His companions or disciples now filled the gap, first of all, with his letters, which had been preserved and collected. Then, quite soon, other letters written in his name were added. The apostle became *present* in these letters and thus filled the vacant space.

It is altogether possible that these three letters were meant to legitimate Paul's historical coworkers Timothy and Titus everywhere, but that cannot be said with certainty. What is certain is that both are intended as portrayals of the ideal officeholder of the postapostolic period.

Likewise, it is in any case certain that in the Pastorals the figures of Timothy and Titus are the bridge, the transition to the later officeholders who play a significant role in these three letters, and who evidently existed within the sphere of the Pauline mission at that time. There are overseers/*episkopoi* (1 Tim 3:1-7; Titus 1:7-9), elders (1 Tim 5:17-22; Titus 1:6), and deacons (1 Tim 3:8-13). Two things about them remain unclear. It is not certain whether there were individual overseers who were in charge of single communities, as bishops later were, or whether the Pastorals are speaking of episcopal *collegia*.[32]

toralbriefe," in *Paulus in den neutestamentlichen Spätschriften. Zur Paulusrezeption im Neuen Testament*, ed. Karl Kertelge, QD 89 (Freiburg: Herder, 1981), 70–121, at 114–19.

32 The bishop, as the church understands that figure today, does not appear in this form in the New Testament. The Pastorals come closest: cf. the "mirror for the *episkopos*" in 1 Tim 3:1-7. Still, the *episkopos* in this text is probably not a single figure but is part of a *collegium* of *episkopoi* within a single community, and it is not even clear whether he already presides at the Eucharist. Besides, the text says he should be a good "household manager" who brings up his children responsibly. One should be able to see in all this whether he is in a position to lead the *church* household well.

Similarly, the relationship between the overseer or overseers and the elders is not clear. Do the Pastorals already present us with the later division: bishops, priests, deacons? Or is the hierarchy of orders only emerging at the time of the Pastorals? We have to admit that the three letters give us no clear information in this regard, and from that we may conclude that they are evidently not interested in a precisely defined system of offices. What does interest them is above all that there should be offices in the communities and they should be occupied by qualified persons.

The real interest of the Pastorals is in the continuity between Paul and the current officials in the sphere of the Pauline mission. The agents of that continuity are Timothy and Titus, and primarily through the fact of the three letters themselves. Paul writes these letters to them (fictively, of course), and they hand on what is in the letters. Thereby they are already the bridge that secures continuity. Added to this, of course, is the chain of impositions of hands, which is carefully stated, first concerning Timothy:

> Do not neglect the gift that is in you, which was given to you through prophecy with the laying on of hands by the council of elders. (1 Tim 4:14)

This obviously refers to an installation in office, an ordination, and the grace given is that of office. We are, of course, puzzled that it is not Paul himself but a *presbyterium* that lays hands on Timothy. Was Paul simply present? Or did he himself lay hands on Timothy? If my interpretation of the fundamental intent of the Pastorals is correct, there is a felt need to put Paul more clearly in the picture. That happens in 2 Timothy 1:6-7:

> For this reason I remind you to rekindle the gift of God that is within you through the laying on of my hands, for God did not give us a spirit of cowardice but rather a spirit of power and of love and of self-discipline.

But the chain of succession in office must continue to the present. Only then is the bridge complete. The Pastorals note that also—now in the person of Titus:

> I left you behind in Crete for this reason, so that you should put in order what remained to be done and should appoint elders in every town, as I directed you. (Titus 1:5)

With that the arc of *successio apostolica* is drawn from Paul through Timothy and Titus and down to the present and future—and everywhere in the communities founded by Paul. The author of the Pastorals may have imagined the situation in the rest of the church similarly, but he did not need to say that.

To summarize: for the Pastorals, similarly to Luke's two-volume work, there is a problem of continuity, caused primarily by false teachers becoming rife in the church. This problem is resolved by recourse to what is apostolic: in Luke's work by resort to the Twelve, in the Pastorals by drawing on Paul. "Recourse" in both cases means concentration on the "teaching of the apostles" or, in the latter, "of the apostle." That requires offices in the church. Luke's work depicts office as guarantor of continuity in a variety of ways; in the Pastorals it is still clearer in the emphasis on the *successio apostolica*. How offices were individually shaped within this great arc of *successio apostolica* still remains open to a certain degree, both in Luke's work and in the Pastorals. But the necessity of office—and, in fact, an office instituted by the Holy Spirit and going back to the sending of the apostles (or the apostle) by Christ—is taken as a matter of course.

A Canon within the Canon?

Would not a narrowing of the gap between the confessions be possible on the basis of the theology of office that Luke and the Pastorals present—especially between Rome and Wittenberg—and, in fact, simply through a closer inspection of Sacred Scripture?

But things are not that simple. Let me illustrate with an example. On June 21, 1962, Ernst Käsemann gave a lecture in the Theological Working Group of the University of Tübingen, which involved both Roman Catholic and Protestant theology professors. His title was "Paul and Early Catholicism." In that lecture he spoke of fundamental differences within the New Testament itself as regards the understanding of office. On the one side there were

> the Lukan writings and the Pastorals, which offer instruction on community order in letter form in order thereby to be able to claim the authority of the apostle. Here, it seems to me, we find the monarchical bishop surrounded by presbyters, deacons, and other coworkers under vows. Office is conferred by ordination and, because established by students of the apostles, installing persons in an apostolic succession.[33]

As we can see, Käsemann goes beyond what I tried to show in the previous section, even finding the monarchical episcopate in the Pastorals. But he encounters the Catholic understanding of the church even in Luke's two volumes:

> The Lucan work as a whole is totally incomprehensible if it is not seen that only in the stream of apostolic tradition does one also belong to the one holy Church as the earthly realm of salvation.[34]

Certainly "the one, holy church" that is an "earthly realm of salvation" and to which one belongs only if one stands "in the stream of apostolic tradition" is apparently, for Käsemann, profoundly suspect. Where he encounters such a thing in the New Testament he calls it "early Catholicism," and he vehemently contrasts it with Paul's communities:

> Characteristically, the genuine letters of Paul mention neither ordination nor the presbytery, but leave the functions of the Church to charismatics and address every Christian as a charismatic. That is not to say that certain duties were not more or less firmly bound to persons suited for them. Nonetheless, in their positions these people counted as special representatives of the universal priesthood, to which baptism with the gift of the Spirit calls the Christian and for which the Spirit qualifies [her or him] ever anew. To put it pointedly, but without exaggeration, the Pauline church is composed of nothing but [laypersons], who nevertheless are all, within their possibilities, at the same time priests and officeholders, that is, instruments of the Spirit for the enactment of the Gospel in the everyday world.[35]

[33] See Ernst Käsemann, "Paul and Early Catholicism," in his *New Testament Questions of Today* (Minneapolis: Fortress Press, 1969), 236–51.

[34] Käsemann, "Paul and Early Catholicism," 247.

[35] Käsemann, "Paul and Early Catholicism," 245–46.

We can see immediately that the Pauline communities are here described as archetypes of Martin Luther's ecclesiology—and in contrast to them an early Catholicism is perceived even within the New Testament as flowing through an unbroken process into the Catholicism of the ancient church. Käsemann even indicates some understanding of the development of primitive Christianity into early Catholicism—how else was the primitive church to deal with the problems of its time: rampant enthusiasm[36] and the fading of imminent expectation of the end? But his heart is with Paul; no, more than that: Paul and his supposedly pure charismatic idea of office are for him the absolute measure by which all other theologies of office in the New Testament must be measured and, when necessary, judged.

With this, however, Käsemann dangerously relativized the canon of Sacred Scripture, something that was taken for granted by the church even in the first centuries. He says that quite clearly elsewhere: the New Testament canon cannot be a basis for the unity of the church because it contains divergent theologies and different ideas about office. The conclusion can only be

> that the canon is not simply to be identified with the Gospel and is only the Word of God in so far as it is and becomes the Gospel. Only within these limits is it the foundation of the unity of the Church. For the Gospel is the sole foundation of the one Church at all times and in all places.
>
> But the question "What is the Gospel?" cannot be settled by the historian according to the results of [her or his] investigations but only by the believer who is led by the Spirit and listens obediently to the Scripture. The unity of the Church is never immediately accessible; it exists only for faith.[37]

This means that while the New Testament canon may remain as it is, it must be measured against Paul's theology—and Paul's theology

[36] Käsemann speaks of the "ferment of enthusiasm in the churches." Cf. "Paul and Early Catholicism," 247.

[37] Ernst Käsemann, "Begründet der neutestamentliche Kanon die Einheit der Kirche?" in *Exegetische Versuche und Besinnungen* 1, 4th ed. (Göttingen: Vandenhoeck & Ruprecht, 1965), 214–23, at 223. See Ernst Käsemann, "The Canon of the New Testament and the Unity of the Church," in *Essays on New Testament Themes*, trans. W. J. Montague (London: SCM, 1964), 95–107, at 106.

by the gospel (ultimately, as Käsemann says, there are early Catholic tendencies even in Paul).[38] But what the gospel is—that is something that can only be experienced now and then, by believers.

I have quoted Ernst Käsemann at some length, but he is only an example because he is not alone. There are many other possibilities for evading the whole of the New Testament canon and establishing a "canon within the canon." For example, one might construct a church built entirely on the model of Acts 13:1-3, or on that of the Johannine writings, whose author, according to many scholars, represented a purely charismatic idea of community that would have had to defend itself against the grip of firmly established offices. There are many other possibilities as well, and they are used and brought to bear against the idea of office in the Roman Catholic Church.

But if we remain with the idea of the New Testament as a book that is not made up of different writings that can be played off against one another but is one book because the church has joined it together as a single text (also including the Old Testament), then we must apply the rules of interpretation that are proper to a unified text. It is true that the New Testament is not unified in the same sense as is, for example, a novel or a scholarly treatment. It was put together out of twenty-six or twenty-seven writings.[39] But this was not done in such a way that those different writings were simply tied together externally—much as, nowadays, the writings of different authors are brought together in a collected volume. In such a case each author represents only him- or herself and must be interpreted in isolation from the others.

That is not how it is with the New Testament. It is a deliberate composition[40] that begins with Jesus in the four gospels and ends with the Revelation to John. The letters, certainly, were in a different order than what we find in the editions we now have. Acts was directly linked to the "catholic" epistles, for good reason: Peter, John,

[38] Paul also "was a forerunner of early Catholicism," according to Käsemann, "Paul and Early Catholicism," 238.

[39] Only twenty-six if one counts the two-volume Lukan work as a single unit!

[40] In what follows I am indebted to David Trobisch, *Die Endredaktion des Neuen Testaments. Eine Untersuchung zur Entstehung der christlichen Bibel*, NTOA 31 (Fribourg: Universitätsverlag; Göttingen: Vandenhoeck & Ruprecht, 1996).

and James play important roles in Acts, and therefore the letters attributed to those three were tied directly to Acts.

It is obvious that what we have here is a deliberately sustained composition: it begins with the gospels as a reflection of the time of Jesus. It ends with Revelation and its look to the end of all history. The Acts of the Apostles continues with the letters corresponding to it. And to make this order possible in the first place, the second part of the Lukan two-volume work was separated from the first. So what we have is a consistent composition; behind it lies a clear principle of order and an authorial will. The latter, for example, includes the intention to place the writings of the three pillars of the first community—Peter, James, and John—alongside those of the apostle Paul and to give them equal weight.[41]

Obviously the church authors who established this book knew that it contained older and newer parts. The older ones were important for them because they led back to Jesus and Paul, but the newer ones were equally important because they dealt with problems of the developing church.

To play the older texts against the newer ones in interpreting this one book conceived as a unit is contrary to every rule of textual interpretation. The authorial intent was that the text should be viewed as a unit; therefore it is relevant in all its parts—even when, within the whole, different evaluations and perhaps even tensions and discrepancies appear. The authentic Paul is as important as the Pastorals, and the Pastorals are as weighty as Paul.

The concept of canon represented by Käsemann had nothing to do with the understanding that was taken for granted in the church over centuries, nor does it correspond to current textual hermeneutics, which tends to say that in a complete text the youngest layers are determinative for the interpretation. That is quite obvious in the case of juristic collections.

Beyond that, I ask myself whether Paul can be played off so sharply against Luke and the Pastorals. Certainly there are differences, but the image of charismatic Pauline communities drawn by Käsemann seems to lack Paul himself. After all, Paul appeals most emphatically to his apostolic office when writing to his communities. He had a

[41] Trobisch, *Endredaktion*, 122.

keen awareness of his apostolic authority. It was he, Paul, who laid the foundation in Corinth (1 Cor 3:6, 10). He intervenes when his communities fall short. He gives binding rules for the moral lives of individuals and for the common life of the communities.

An unprejudiced reading of the authentic letters of Paul reveals a "contrast" throughout between Paul and his communities that rests on his mission from Christ. Certainly Paul is thoroughly charismatic, but his apostolic office cannot be simply categorized among the charisms of the community[42] and is definitely not derived from them. When Paul insists on his apostolic office at the beginning of each letter, rigorously disrupting ancient epistolary style, he is appealing to a mission that simply cannot be compared to the charisms in his communities.

Likewise the *successio apostolica* that is established in the Pastorals has its basis in Paul himself—that is, when he writes to the community in Corinth:

> I appeal to you, then, be imitators of me. For this reason I sent you Timothy, who is my beloved and trustworthy child in the Lord, to remind you of my ways in Christ Jesus, as I teach them everywhere in every church. But some of you, thinking that I am not coming to you, have become arrogant. But I will come to you soon, if the Lord wills, and I will find out not the talk of these arrogant people but their power. For the [reign] of God depends not on talk but on power. What would you prefer? Am I to come to you with a stick or with love in a spirit of gentleness? (1 Cor 4:16-21)

Why is this text from the historical Paul so revealing? It presupposes that the apostle is absent. He is not with his community. Even though it is urgently necessary, he cannot directly present either his teaching or his apostolic existence to the Corinthian community. But Paul can still communicate his presence. For the moment he sends Timothy, who is his "beloved and trustworthy child in the Lord." Timothy, in the absence of Paul, is the living "reminder" of Paul and his teaching.

In principle this authentic Pauline text already implies the succession: one of Paul's coworkers conveys Paul's intentions, hands on his teaching, comes as a representative of the apostle, makes Paul's

[42] See also 1 Cor 12:28-30, where Paul clearly sets the triad "apostle, prophet, teacher" apart from the services mentioned afterward, both by the fact that he numbers them—"first, second, third"—and also by his shift from persons to functions.

apostolic "presence" possible. The Pastorals, then, in a situation when Paul was dead and could never come again, took up precisely that pattern and made it concrete. Thus the critical succession is already given in the historical Paul as a "hereditary endowment."

The "Service of Reconciliation"

Everything I have so far presented relates in its broader sense to the priestly office. The priest, too, is sent to the people of God, is a witness to the rule of God, is to preach the gospel of God's reign and to preserve the precious treasure of the apostolic tradition entrusted to the priest. But the priest's primary duty is what Paul in 2 Corinthians calls the "service of reconciliation." It is worthwhile to take a closer look at what Paul says about that service. He begins with a radical statement: the reconciliation to which he refers is not something within human abilities. It comes from the cross:

> For the love of Christ urges us on, because we are convinced that one has died for all; therefore all have died. And he died for all, so that those who live might live no longer for themselves but for the one who for their sake died and was raised. (2 Cor 5:14-15)

This, then, is about the death of Christ, who died "for all." That death on the cross took place out of "the love of Christ." His love is to encompass "all" and draw them into the sphere that Paul describes as "being in Christ." Here "for oneself" is no longer valid, but only "for others." This revolution in existence is so enormous that it is at the same time dying and rising. Precisely here, at this point, God transforms the world. Whoever is "in Christ" is a "new creation":

> So if anyone is in Christ, there is a new creation: everything old has passed away; look, new things have come into being! All this is from God, who reconciled us to [God's own self] through Christ and has given us the ministry of reconciliation; that is, in Christ God was reconciling the world to [God's self], not counting their trespasses against them, and entrusting the message of reconciliation to us. So we are ambassadors for Christ, since God is making [this] appeal through us: we entreat you on behalf of Christ: be reconciled to God. (2 Cor 5:17-20)

Paul speaks here of the service assigned to him as an apostle. We can simply say: he speaks of an office, because "service" is the New

Testament term for office.[43] It is the office of reconciliation. What is so remarkable about the whole passage is that Paul speaks of the decisive saving act of God in the death and resurrection of Jesus but at the same time and in the same breath of the creation of the office of reconciliation. Gisbert Greshake rightly says that "in the reconciling event of the cross of Christ, God has combined both in one: reconciling us with God in Christ and creating the office of reconciliation." The office is not added later in some way that is difficult to establish; rather, "it is established in and with the cross and resurrection."[44]

What is also important in this text is that Paul speaks of a "relationship" to the community. The "we" by which Paul designates himself refers to his own service.[45] It is to him, Paul, that the service of reconciliation has been assigned and entrusted. He himself admonishes the Christians in Corinth and begs them: "be reconciled to God." Thus Paul is an "ambassador for Christ," and it is "in place of Christ" that he asks. Christ is not simply identical with the community in Corinth, and likewise neither is Paul simply a part of the community when he pronounces the call to reconciliation to them. God (or: Christ) acts through the apostle. Christ speaks directly in Paul's appeal, "be reconciled to God," and Christ is present in it. As we have already seen in regard to the proclamation of the reign of God by the Twelve, so also here: in the action of the apostle the action of Christ is present. The apostle represents the action of Christ.

Likewise important in these texts, however, is the following: the "word of reconciliation" spoken of here must not be understood as preaching *about* reconciliation. It is an effective, salvation-giving word that promises, indeed creates, reconciliation with God. It is no accident that Paul can say, precisely in this context: "So if anyone is in Christ, there[46] is a new creation: everything old has passed away; look, new things have come into being!"

Now, with this understanding of the office of reconciliation instituted by God, rooted in the saving event of the cross and resurrection,

[43] The pertinent concepts such as *timē*, *telos*, *leitourgia*, and *archē* are avoided in the New Testament.

[44] Gisbert Greshake, *Priestersein. Zur Theologie und Spiritualität des priesterlichen Amtes* (Freiburg: Herder, 1982), 34.

[45] Paul refers to himself here in the plural. Cf. 2 Cor 3:1, 12; 4:1, 7-18.

[46] Greek: "he."

and to be affirmed in the effective words of reconciliation, we have come very close to what is meant by priestly service. That service is the proclamation of the gospel of the reign of God—but at the same time and above all pronouncing the word of reconciliation. If we seek further in this direction within the New Testament we inevitably come to the event of the Last Supper.

"Do This in Remembrance of Me"

What is happening here? Again, I will leave aside any and all historical questions and focus in purely theological terms on the story as presented in the Synoptic Gospels and the theology of Paul. Only that theological level is relevant to our question.

First of all: Jesus does not celebrate the evening Seder according to the usual custom, with his family or just any friends. He celebrates it with the Twelve. That is important to the evangelist Mark (14:17), but also to Matthew (26:20) and Luke (22:14). It is true that Luke speaks of the "apostles" who are with Jesus at table, but we already know that for Luke that means precisely the Twelve.

So: the principal content of the Seder is the solemn remembrance of God's great deed of salvation: recalling the night of the exodus from Egypt. The text presumes as a matter of course that Jesus celebrates that memorial with the twelve disciples, though it is not stated. Something else is more important.

During the meal Jesus takes the bread, speaks the thanksgiving over it, breaks it, and gives it to the Twelve. So far that is established ritual. It is the table prayer before the main course. What is special is that Jesus interprets the broken bread he gives to the Twelve with the words "This is my body" (Matt 26:26; Mark 14:22): the briefest interpretation possible! We can expand it: "I myself am this bread, with my whole history and life. My life will be broken like this bread. I give it to you so that you may have a share in me and my death."

So here again, as at the installation of the Twelve, we are dealing with a symbolic action! This one is, to begin with, a prophecy of death. Jesus indicates in the sign of the broken bread that he will die a violent death. Yet at the same time this sign-action is much more than a death prophecy because Jesus gives the Twelve a share in his existence, which will be handed over in death. His death has a depth dimension in which the Twelve—and thus Israel because, after all, they stand for Israel—are to have a share.

At this point Matthew and Mark still leave open the nature of this depth dimension; it will be revealed only with the interpretation of the cup of blessing: "This is my blood [the blood] of the covenant, which is poured out for many" (Mark 14:24). In the line of tradition Luke represents, the interpretive words over the cup of blessing are "This cup that is poured out for you is the new covenant in my blood" (Luke 22:20).

I will not go into detail about the biblical background of these interpretive words. In Matthew and Mark they allude directly to Exodus 24:4-11 and intend to say that the blood of Jesus shed on the cross renews and completes the covenant God formerly made with Israel at Sinai. Jesus' blood frees Israel from its guilt and makes atonement for it. Thus the new creation of Israel and, by way of Israel, salvation for the nations results from the death of Jesus. The branch of tradition represented by Luke and Paul points in the same direction; here, however, the new covenant in Jeremiah 31:31 is the background.

Crucial in our context is the command to repeat the action: "Do this in remembrance of me!" (Luke 22:19; 1 Cor 11:24, 25). "Do" here represents a fixed expression that has its parallels in the Old Testament ordering of the celebration of feasts that recall historical events.[47] It means "fulfill," "observe," "celebrate." The idea of "memorial" stems from the same field in the Old Testament. It is more than a mere "remembering." In the renewed observance or celebration of the meal, the death of Jesus and the atonement effected by his death are made present. There is a text in the Old Testament that best explains how profound such "remembering" is. It is Deuteronomy 5:2-4, which refers to the previous covenant at Horeb that Israel is now making present a generation later:

> The LORD our God made a covenant with us at Horeb. Not with our ancestors did the LORD make this covenant but with us, who are all of us here alive today. The LORD spoke with you face to face at the mountain, out of the fire.

At that moment the event at Horeb was many years in the past, but in the "today" of proclamation the covenant of Horeb becomes present to the later generation—and so completely present that the

[47] Cf., e.g., Exod 12:47; 13:5; Num 9:2-4; Deut 16:1, 10.

later generation itself stands at Horeb and hears God speak. It is precisely the same cultic making-present that Paul intends when, in explanation of "Do this in remembrance of me," he writes: "For as often as you eat this bread and drink the cup, you proclaim the Lord's death until he comes" (1 Cor 11:26).

Luke could not have understood the command to repeat the action any differently. But he adds that it is addressed explicitly to the twelve apostles for, as we have seen, in his account (like those of Mark and Matthew) it is only the twelve apostles who are with Jesus in the evening of the Seder, and for Luke that is not incidental. The Twelve represent Israel and, in this evening before Jesus' death, reconciliation and new creation are given to Israel in the persons of the Twelve. But at the same time reconciliation is given to the church—as the newly gathered Israel. It will again and again celebrate its "breaking of bread" as a cultic memorial of the Last Supper (Acts 2:46).

It is, of course, no accident that Luke positioned the command to repeat the action immediately after the words over the bread and only here. For him the "breaking of bread" (Acts 2:46) and the command "do this in remembrance of me" go together. But it is also true that for him the cultic making-present of the Lord's Supper and the office of the Twelve belong together. "Do this in remembrance of me" is, for Luke, an instruction to the Twelve, that is, to the holders of the apostolic office, and no one else. Certainly Luke did not make a big thing of the matter. Probably by his time it was already a matter of course that those who held office in the church would preside at the eucharistic celebration.

The fact that for Luke the themes of eucharistic celebration and church office are connected also reveals another phenomenon. He locates the disciples' "quarrel over rank" immediately after Jesus' words at the Last Supper and the naming of the betrayer. Mark and Matthew have it in a very different place (cf. Mark 10:41-45; Matt 20:24-28). Here it reveals a bitter contrast: Jesus' words at the Last Supper, his speaking about the surrender of his life, and immediately afterward the betrayal by Judas, who is one of the Twelve, and then the failure of the other eleven as they quarrel over rank and career:

> A dispute also arose among them as to which one of them was to be regarded as the greatest. But he said to them, "The kings of the gentiles lord it over them, and those in authority over them are called benefactors.

> But not so with you; rather, the greatest among you must become like the youngest and the leader like one who serves. For who is greater, the one who is at the table or the one who serves? Is it not the one at the table? But I am among you as one who serves." (Luke 22:24-27)

What Jesus says here is instruction regarding office, and since it is the Twelve who are with him, it is instruction about apostolic office. It is to be pure service, self-surrender to others, just as Jesus gives himself. The apostolic office must reveal Jesus' *diakonia* and make it present. Otherwise the apostolic witnesses to Jesus will be like the rulers of the Gentiles and the church will be like pagan society. So we are not imputing anything foreign to Luke when we take seriously the fact that for him apostolic office and presiding at the Eucharist are intimately connected.

Incidentally, we can observe a similar phenomenon in John's Gospel. The Fourth Evangelist does not present a Last Supper scene; he takes for granted that it is known. But in its place he shows us the scene of the footwashing and, connected with it, an instruction from Jesus to his disciples about the necessity of service (John 13:1-20). That here also the issue is profoundly related to office in the church is shown by the sentence that concludes the whole instruction: "Very truly, I tell you, whoever receives one whom I send receives me, and whoever receives me receives the one who sent me" (John 13:20).

"Once and for All"

Then is there in the New Testament a basis for the priestly office that swiftly took shape in the early church? I think so. That basis can scarcely be ignored. To this point I have omitted the letter to the Hebrews from my discussion, but now it must come to the fore.

Hebrews regards Christ as *the* priest in whose life and death all of Israel's previous priesthood has found its fulfillment. The center of the letter (4:14–10:18) is an exposition of this theme. I will quote only one passage that summarizes it all:

> For it was fitting that we should have such a high priest, holy, blameless, undefiled, separated from sinners, and exalted above the heavens. Unlike the other high priests, he has no need to offer sacrifices day after day, first for his own sins and then for those of the people; this he did once for all when he offered himself. (Heb 7:26-27)

One of the basic ideas of the letter to the Hebrews is that the Old Testament offerings had to be brought forward constantly, day after day and year after year. Thus they were unable to provide definitive salvation. Had they done so it would not have been necessary to repeat them. Christ, however, has presented the sacrifice of his life in full freedom and perfect self-surrender, once for all. The gift of his life embraces his whole existence, and that is no longer subject to time since as the one sacrificed he has been exalted to the eternal world of God. Hence Christ is the completion of all previous cultic sacrifices, and therefore he is the definitive, perfect high priest. So much—really in shorthand—for a central aspect of the letter to the Hebrews!

Does this theology help to advance our inquiry? Does it offer an additional argument to show that the priestly office finds its foundation in the New Testament? Can this theology show that there is evidence of a priestly office in the New Testament?

Hebrews appears to demonstrate precisely the opposite, because it says that with Jesus' sacrifice of his life all the temple offerings have come to an end. Jesus has presented the sacrifice that supersedes all previous sacrifices "once and for all." Therefore the Christ who, with the offering of his life, has been elevated into the world beyond is the genuine and true high priest in whom all priesthood has found its fulfillment.

The Reformation brought into the field precisely this basic thesis of Hebrews against the ecclesiastical office of the priest and the character of the Mass as sacrifice. It said, and quite a few Protestant theologians say to this day, that the theology of the letter to the Hebrews signifies an end to any kind of cult in the church.[48]

And there is more: toward the end of Hebrews its author gives a series of admonitions: "Let mutual affection continue"; "Do not neglect to show hospitality to strangers"; "Remember those who are in prison"; "Let marriage be held in honor by all"; "Keep your lives free from the love of money" (Heb 13:1-5). And in that context also:

[48] See Erich Gräßer, *An die Hebräer*, EKKNT 17/1 (Zürich: Benziger; Neukirchen-Vluyn: Neukirchener Verlag, 1990), 26; idem, *An die Hebräer*, EKKNT 17/3 (Zürich: Benziger; Neukirchen-Vluyn: Neukirchener Verlag, 1997), 376–90.

> Remember your leaders, those who spoke the word of God to you; consider the outcome of their way of life, and imitate their faith. Jesus Christ is the same yesterday and today and forever. (Heb 13:7-8)

Although here the author of Hebrews speaks of Christ and the community leaders in one breath, no connection is drawn between them. The author does not even think of deriving a priesthood of community leaders from Christ's high priesthood; he does not once speak of an installation of those community leaders by Christ, but only of their service to God's word.

And even more than that: shortly before this the author of Hebrews had contrasted the event at Sinai and the New Testament saving event on Zion, writing:

> But you have come to Mount Zion and to the city of the living God, the heavenly Jerusalem, and to innumerable angels in festal gathering, and to the assembly of the firstborn who are enrolled in heaven, and to God the judge of all, and to the spirits of the righteous made perfect, and to Jesus, the mediator of a new covenant, and to the sprinkled blood that speaks a better word than the blood of Abel. (Heb 12:22-24)

Is it not true that in this text, very much as Martin Luther said, there is only a single mediator, namely, Jesus Christ, and there can be no priests who appear as mediators? For do we not see here that the whole community—indeed, the whole church—comes to the *sanctissimum*, the heavenly sanctuary, which now stands open to all and evidently requires no more priestly mediators but only the one mediator to God, Jesus Christ?[49] The concept of "approaching," which derives from cultic contexts and originally referred to the priest's approaching the altar,[50] is central to Hebrews.[51] But in that letter it is, in fact, the whole community that comes to the altar.

[49] Cf. H.-F. Weiß, *Der Brief an die Hebräer*, KEK 13 (Göttingen: Vandenhoeck & Ruprecht, 1991), 402: "But what was once—according to the measure of the ancient 'previously enacted' cultic order—a privilege reserved to the priest designated for cultic service—has now become a 'basic right' of the whole Christian community."

[50] Cf., e.g., LXX Lev 9:7-8; 21:17; 22:3; Num 18:3.

[51] Cf. Heb 4:16; 7:25; 10:1, 22; 12:22.

It seems, then, that the letter to the Hebrews does not offer a foundation for an office of priesthood in the church but instead excludes it. But that is only a superficial reading. Hebrews does not exclude what would later develop as priestly service, but it does compel us to be precise about what, in terms of the New Testament, priesthood can be and what it cannot be.

First: we have to take seriously the statement of Hebrews that Jesus Christ has become the mediator of the New Covenant (8:6; 9:15; 12:24). There can be no other. Jesus Christ, as 1 Timothy says, is the one, only mediator (2:5). In the sense in which the text here defines "mediator," priests cannot be that. Still: like the Twelve, they can be sent by Jesus (Mark 6:7). Like Paul, they can be called. They can speak the word of reconciliation as those sent as "ambassadors for Christ" (2 Cor 5:20). And, as the Last Supper tradition formulates it, they can do what Christ did at his last meal and so make present "in remembrance" the event of that evening and thus the event of the cross (1 Cor 11:24-26). That is not mediatorship, but it does mean proclaiming the one and only mediator and so making him present.

Therefore: obviously the sense of Hebrews 12:22 is that the whole community, together with its leaders, approaches the Holy of Holies, that is, God and the eternal High Priest and the heavenly assembly. The pre–Vatican II Roman Catholic liturgy expressed that through the form of the long procession through the apse of the church, and through the fact that the priest did not turn his face to the community but throughout the worship service joined the community in looking to the east, toward Christ. That is not meant to criticize today's *versus populum*. That, too, has its own significance. I only mean to show that "you have come to Mount Zion" does not exclude the special character of the priest's service.

Further: since the death of Christ is all worship "outside the gate" and "outside the camp" (Heb 13:12, 13) abolished forever? It is true that Hebrews again and again addresses, in ever new ways, the fragility and limitations of the old sacrificial cult. The offerings of past times had to be continually repeated. They could not save. Christ's sacrifice, in contrast, is offered once for all; in it lies the ultimate redemption. In view of this sacrifice the earlier cult is "obsolete" (8:13) and "abrogat[ed]" (7:18), because Christ has perfected all things. "Perfection" in this context is a concept specific to Hebrews (7:11, 19; 10:14; 12:2).

But does this mean that all worship is now at an end? Certainly, for Christians the ancient, powerless cult is ended. But now the exalted Christ is revealed within the heavenly sanctuary as "the reflection of God's glory and the exact imprint of God's very being" (1:3). "All God's angels" pray to the one who has been exalted to God's right hand (1:6). The whole community "comes" (12:22) and so "through him" we "continually offer a sacrifice of praise to God" the Father (13:15). Thus the "sacrifice of praise" and gratitude (cf. 12:28) has replaced animal sacrifice. That is not altogether new. The Old Testament can speak in similar terms (cf., e.g., Pss 50:9-15; 51:17-19). What is new, however, is the sacrifice of Christ's life that puts everything else in "shadow" (Heb 10:1). So when the community comes to this one who has been sacrificed—does that mean that worship is finished? No! It is not finished; it is transformed, has reached its perfection, and by no means has a cultless era begun. After all, is the church's eucharistic prayer, which is the center of all priestly activity and is thanksgiving and praise altogether in the sense of the letter to the Hebrews, not worship?

Perhaps it is not yet clear to some exegetes who are heirs of the Reformation that the words of consecration in the Catholic celebrations of the Eucharist are not an isolated formula but are an integral part of the thanksgiving that is the eucharistic prayer. The making-present of the one, unique sacrifice takes place in the form of the church's great prayer of thanksgiving, and within that pure thanksgiving, after remembering the Last Supper, the congregation says:

> We proclaim your Death, O Lord,
> and profess your Resurrection,
> until you come again.

The making-present of Christ's sacrifice thus happens within the language of the thanksgiving and is itself proclamation. And we cannot call that worship? Obviously we can reject older terms of speech and speak of the absolute cultlessness in Hebrews because the new thing breaks the mold of the old. But then we have to be careful not to altogether eliminate the context, namely, the emergence of the new thing from the old.

My last and closing reflection within this section is still based on the letter to the Hebrews, but it also looks back to a fundamental principle that is presupposed by the whole New Testament as a matter of course. Thus in what follows I will list a number of New Testament positions in a kind of theological summary.

Nowhere in the New Testament is Christ seen as a solitary figure separated from the rest of humanity, a pure "for oneself." He is absolute "for others," and in a twofold sense: first, obviously in that he has given his whole life for Israel and for the world. But in a second sense he is also not "for himself," and that is my point here: namely, that beyond his historical uniqueness he is model, type, prefiguration.

This means that in him we have a model of what is meant to emerge in the church. In him is gathered together everything that is meant to unfold. In him has already happened what will ultimately be fulfilled in the church. He is the first of all future sisters and brothers. He is "the pioneer of their salvation" (Heb 2:10) and "the pioneer and perfecter of faith" (Heb 12:2). He is the model. He is the one who prepares the way on which he precedes all his followers. That is what model and prefiguration mean.

It follows that Christ, as the model he is, must build himself up and shape himself in the church. He is not identical with the church, but he must take shape in the church that is his body. And for that very reason his priesthood, of which Hebrews speaks in such lofty terms, must take form in the church.

The question whether Jesus himself ordained priests—maybe in the sense intended by the Council of Trent, through imposition of hands, anointing, giving of a book of the gospels, and, ideally, also a *Codex Iuris Canonici*—completely misses the reality of what church is.

The church is God's creation in the world, *creatura verbi*, and here as everywhere creation takes place through evolution, but evolution through the power of the Holy Spirit, a self-development and self-formation of the endowment God has placed in the church. The church is endowed once and forever with Jesus Christ. He is the head of the body, and the church, his body, is to be built up and grow into its head and the whole fullness of Christ. The letter to the Ephesians formulates that in positively programmatic fashion (Eph 4:7-16).

The crucial question, then, is how what has definitively entered history in Christ, what has become new creation within it, shall now—in many, many steps—be built up and shaped in the church and take on the right, Christ-shaped form. That is all that matters. This is one of the fundamental principles of the church: that in everything—and above all in its priests—it should grow toward Jesus Christ, its head.

Now, the New Testament says clearly and unmistakably that Jesus needs people who witness with their whole lives to what they have heard and seen and that those witnesses are sent to Israel and, through Israel, to the whole world:

> Whoever listens to you listens to me, and whoever rejects you rejects me, and whoever rejects me rejects the one who sent me. (Luke 10:16)
>
> Very truly, I tell you, whoever receives one whom I send receives me, and whoever receives me receives him who sent me. (John 13:20)
>
> As the Father has sent me, so I send you! (John 20:21)

We saw at the very beginning of these reflections that in the gospels this official, ministerial witness is represented by the "figure of the Twelve." It is no accident that at the very beginning of his public work Jesus gathered disciples around him and then chose twelve of them. Those twelve witnesses are to do everything Jesus does. They are to heal as Jesus does. They are to drive out demons as Jesus does. They are to publicly proclaim the reign of God as Jesus does. But that means that in everything they do they are to represent Jesus and make him present to Israel.

This witness-character of the Twelve is continued in the offices of the church. The community of bishops and the community of priests around their local bishop have emerged since the second century as the form of official, approved witness to Christ—and that happened in a very brief period of time and throughout the whole church. Vatican II summarized an ancient church tradition when it said that the priest is representative and likeness of Jesus Christ. The crucial formulation is that the priest acts "*in persona Christi capitis*—in the person of Christ, the head."[52]

That is a very fortunate formulation, and it is altogether biblical, since the truth that the disciples Jesus sends as official witnesses to all Israel are his representatives is expressed in the words of mission just quoted above.

Certainly all priests must be profoundly daunted by the statement that in their priestly function they act as models of Christ, for they are all too aware of their own sin and unbelief. Nevertheless: there

[52] Cf. *Presbyterorum Ordinis* 2; *Lumen Gentium* 10.

is no other possibility. Jesus needs people who, as we say, act and speak in his name. That is the only way. Personal presence is a crucial basic structure of the New Testament, no matter whether we search through the Gospels, Acts, or the epistolary literature.

I therefore take it as given that what the exalted Christ is—in the sense of Hebrews, what he is as eternal high priest—must be modeled and take form in the church. But we have seen again and again that Jesus sends representatives to the people Israel, and the Risen and Exalted One sends people to newly gathered Israel, the church. Therefore the event that is essential for Jesus Christ must be reflected in the church, must take shape in it.

In concluding, I want to return to the beginning once more. As we have seen, for Martin Luther the idea of the common priesthood of all believers played a decisive role in the resolution of the question of offices in the church. He was convinced that, according to 1 Peter 2:9, all the baptized are priests. Consequently, there is no further need for a special priesthood instituted by God and having its own authority in the church. Every baptized person has a share in the fullness of the gifts God has given to the church. But does 1 Peter 2:9 really convey what Luther reads out of it? That verse cites Exodus 19:5-6. There, in connection with the making of the covenant at Sinai, we read:

> Now, therefore, if you obey my voice and keep my covenant, you shall be my treasured possession out of all the peoples. Indeed, the whole earth is mine, but you shall be for me a priestly kingdom and a holy nation. (Exod 19:5-6)[53]

[53] In light of v. 5, v. 6 is about the relationship between Israel and the other peoples of the world. We can read the twofold statement as a parallel. In that case the same subject would be characterized twice: Israel has a priestly function toward the other nations whereby, as "holy," it is distinguished from them. Whether every individual Israelite has priestly character in relation to the others is not the question. The same is true for the other possible interpretation of the text, which is focused more precisely on the individual formulations. Verse 5, in Hebrew, uses a different word for "people" than does v. 6 (v. 5, *'am*, v. 6, *goy*). In later texts especially, *goy* describes other peoples, while Israel is called *'am*. But the distinction in word usage is not present here, for *goy* is used in this passage for Israel. Another word combination raises a different issue. We can read *malkuth*, "royal rule," in the sense of "government by a king,"

Does this text really mean to say that every individual member of the people of God is a priest? If we read carefully we see right away that here the people of God is being contrasted with all other peoples. The nations are indeed God's possession, but they are not God's "treasured possession." That is Israel alone. The people are all God's own possession, but the place from which what is priestly and holy is to shine forth over "the whole earth" is Israel. So this is always about Israel in relation to the other nations, not about individuals in Israel in relation to other individuals therein. It cannot be concluded from this that each individual in Israel is a priest for other Israelites. The meaning is rather that Israel as a whole has a priestly function in relation to the other nations: it is God's special possession because God has need of it for the sake of the other nations. That is the only reading that makes sense of this text and of Old Testament theology as a whole. Fundamentally it corresponds to the theology of the pilgrimage of the nations, in which Israel is to become a sign for the nations. The first letter of Peter also understood Exodus 19:5-6 in precisely that sense. It is speaking out of a new situation. Now people from among the nations have come rushing to Israel. Do they, too, now have a share in the function of Israel toward the nations? The author of the letter, applying the word from Sinai to them, writes:

> But you are a chosen people [*genos eklekton*], a royal priesthood [*basileion hierateuma*], a holy nation [*ethnos hagion*], God's own people [*laos eis peripoiēsin*], in order that you may proclaim the excellence of him who called you out of darkness into his marvelous light. Once you were not a people, but now you are God's people [*laos theou*]. (1 Pet 2:9-10)

Thus the Gentile Christians have become God's people: that is, they have made the pilgrimage of the nations to Zion. The motifs of dark-

---

together with *goy* as meaning "the population that is ruled." That combination appears a number of times in the Old Testament and always means "rule/government + those ruled/governed." Here it points to a particular historical situation. There was no kingship in Jerusalem after the return from exile; the priests ruled. Accordingly, the population of this "priestly state" acquired the quality of holiness. This was the case until the Maccabees restored the monarchy. Thus the text very precisely describes a contemporary structure in Israel, and at the same time it characterizes the relationship between Israel and the other nations. This people, as a people, has sacral functions in relation to all other nations of the world. In this reading of the text, too, there is no question of a priesthood of each individual Israelite in relation to other Israelites. (I am grateful to my brother Norbert for this explanation.)

ness and light are part of the vocabulary of the pilgrimage of nations (cf. Isa 60:1-3). Now, therefore, the Gentile Christians are living in Israel's light (cf. Luke 2:32) and now they themselves are able to proclaim "the mighty works of God." That is precisely the priestly task of the people of God, given at Sinai—the people of God as a whole. Neither Exodus 19:5-6 nor 1 Peter 2:9-10 can be used to reject offices or to prove that all members of the people of God have the "same power over the word of God and every sacrament."[54]

Throughout his life Martin Luther held to his basic conviction that all members of the people of God have the same power over the word of God and every sacrament. But at the same time, in view of the ecclesiastical chaos brought about by enthusiasts, he laid increasing emphasis on a solid ordering of church communities. Even more: he insisted on an even stronger basis for office "from above" and saw it as a representation of Christ. Ordination presumes calling, sending occurs through Christ, and the blessing for the exercise of office is conveyed by the Holy Spirit.[55] In this way the later Luther approached, after all, what the Catholic Church had long understood the sacrament of orders to be. Above all he came close to what happens in Mark 6, that is, in the mission of the Twelve.

Certainly there are still many misunderstandings that have to be eliminated, above all the profound error that priests in the Roman Catholic Church are sacrificing priests who continually bring more offerings, even after Jesus' sacrifice on the cross. According to Hebrews that is completely impossible, and no one should ever have interpreted the Catholic priestly office in that sense. The rhetoric of many post-Tridentine theologians in which the Eucharist is said to "repeat" or "renew" the sacrifice of the crucified Jesus is extremely liable to misunderstanding, if not simply false. The sacrifice of Jesus Christ is not repeated; the one and only sacrifice is made present.[56]

[54] WA 6, 566. Cf. Norbert Brox, *Der erste Petrusbrief*, 2nd ed., EKKNT 21 (Zürich: Benziger; Neukirchen-Vluyn: Neukirchener Verlag, 1986), 104–10.

[55] WA 38, 401–33.

[56] Cf. John Paul II's encyclical *Ecclesia de Eucharistia* 12: "The Mass makes present the sacrifice of the Cross; it does not add to that sacrifice nor does it multiply it. What is repeated is its *memorial* celebration, its 'commemorative representation' [*memorialis demonstratio*], which makes Christ's one, definitive redemptive sacrifice always present in time. The sacrificial nature of the Eucharistic mystery cannot therefore be understood as something separate, independent of the Cross or only indirectly referring to the sacrifice of Calvary." Text available at https://www.vatican.va/holy

The priest can only, always, as asserted by 1 Corinthians 11:25-26, proclaim the death of Jesus: that is, make present what happened once for all. Nor can priests accomplish this making-present by their own power or by the potential of the community as itself conveying the office. What the priest does comes entirely from Christ and is brought about by Christ, for that is precisely the essence of the sacrament. It is pure grace, given to the church. It points to Christ and makes him present. In just that way the authority of the priestly office is radically relativized.[57] It points away from itself toward Christ, the only one who sends and who remains the only one who acts.

On the wall of the sacristy of the Lutheran collegiate church in Tübingen there hangs a prayer that the pastor may speak silently before the worship service. I once copied it from there when I was invited to preach in that church. It comes from Martin Luther, and it reads:

> Lord God, dear Father in heaven, I am indeed unworthy of the office in which I am to proclaim your glory and to care for and serve the community. But because you have made me a shepherd and teacher of the Word, as the people have need also of teaching and instruction, be my help and let your holy angels be with me.
>
> Should it then be your pleasure to convey something to your glory and not to my own fame or that of other human beings, give me, out of your pure grace and mercy, a right understanding of your Word and much more, so that I may do it.

I spoke that prayer softly, as it stood—and I would not want a single line of it to be any different.

_father/special_features/encyclicals/documents/hf_jp-ii_enc_20030417_ecclesia_eucharistia_en.html.

[57] Formulated following Greshake, *Priestersein*, 29.

17

Marian Devotion: Superfluous or Essential?

There is a whole series of questions that Protestant Christians repeatedly pose to Catholic Christians. One of their most penetrating queries is: hasn't Catholic tradition added a whole lot of superfluous, even false and harmful, stuff to the faith of the New Testament? Everyone knows that there can be growths within an organism—tumors, lumps, and the most feared of all illnesses: cancer, the multiplication of malignant cells.

Dangerous Proliferation?

To put it another way: Hasn't the faith of the Catholic Church been overdeveloped? Isn't it true that for a long time the Catholic Church(es)' traditions have suffered from a dangerous multiplication of cells while the churches of the Reformation returned in the sixteenth century to the simplicity and clarity of the gospel?

Example: the newer Marian dogmas. Don't they—as many Protestants ask—exaggerate the New Testament's few simple statements about Mary beyond all measure? Still worse: Isn't it true that among Roman Catholics the simple Jewish girl called Miriam became a secret goddess? Hasn't the "Great Mother" of the religions—for example, Diana of Ephesus—tiptoed back in?

To put the whole thing another way: I have often been asked, even by Protestant friends, "Why should I call on Mary? I pray to God. I don't need any intermediary. I simply can't deal with these complicated Catholic ideas."

And isn't all that, aren't all these religious growths made utterly palpable in the dogma of the immaculate conception? Where in the New Testament, Protestant Christians ask, is there any mention of a preservation of Mary from original sin? Isn't that adding something inappropriate, and fundamentally superficial, to biblical faith?

In what follows I want to show that the Roman Catholic teaching about Mary adds nothing to biblical faith, but—to the contrary—it develops essential features of that faith, so that its teaching about Mary is not something excessive but rather essential. I will use the dogma of the immaculate conception as an illustration. I could just as easily use Mary's assumption into heaven.

Let me say at the outset: a tree that ceases to grow and puts forth no new shoots is dying. New branches in spring are not pernicious growths but signs of life. The tree is not dead. It is alive. It blooms and produces fruit. If a tree, or any living organism, would cease to change, it would already be dead.

Mary: Archetype of the Church

Inappropriate addition or essential development? That, then, is the question. And now let us take the first step. There is one basic premise required for a right understanding of Roman Catholic doctrine concerning Mary. Without it, it is impossible to understand Mariology and Marian piety; in the end both will be misunderstood as unbiblical excrescences. We can formulate this basic premise as follows.

In the New Testament, and likewise in subsequent centuries into the High Middle Ages, there was never simply the young woman called Miriam; she was always at the same time the epitome of the people of God and the archetype of the church. That is: she was not only an individual but simultaneously a symbol, an image representing a larger context within the sphere of faith.

This Mariological axiom was likewise true even in the New Testament itself. Let me use the Magnificat as an example.[1] The Magnificat,

[1] For the following interpretation of the Magnificat cf. esp. Norbert Lohfink, *Lobgesänge der Armen. Studien zum Magnifikat, den Hodajot von Qumran und einigen späten Psalmen*, SBS 143 (Stuttgart: Katholisches Bibelwerk, 1990), 13–22, as well as idem, "Psalmen im Neuen Testament. Die Lieder in der Kindheitsgeschichte bei Lukas," in Georg Braulik and Norbert Lohfink, *Liturgie und Bibel. Gesammelte Aufsätze*, ÖBS 28 (Frankfurt: Peter Lang, 2005), 461–80.

which Mary speaks in Luke 1 upon her encounter with her cousin Elizabeth, takes a very peculiar course. I do not know if you have ever noticed that. At the beginning, the Magnificat fits very well within the concrete situation in which Mary finds herself. Following what the angel had previously announced to her, Mary can rightly pray:

> My soul magnifies the Lord,
> and my spirit rejoices in God my Savior,
> for he has looked with favor on the lowly state of his servant.
> Surely from now on all generations will call me blessed,
> for the Mighty One has done great things for me,
> and holy is his name. (Luke 1:46-49)

All that fits superbly within the concrete situation of this young woman—more precisely, in the situation of this woman as Luke depicts her. But then it continues:

> He has shown strength with his arm;
> he has scattered the proud in the imagination of their hearts.
> He has brought down the powerful from their thrones
> and lifted up the lowly;
> he has filled the hungry with good things
> and sent the rich away empty.
> He has come to the aid of his child Israel,
> in remembrance of his mercy,
> according to the promise he made to our ancestors,
> to Abraham and to his descendants forever. (Luke 1:51-55)

It seems at first glance that there is a profound inconsistency in the text of the Magnificat. Why does Mary praise God for things God has not done at all for her? When did God scatter the proud in Mary's life? When in her lifetime had God brought down the powerful from their thrones, or in connection with her made the hungry full and sent the rich away empty? Isn't there some kind of break in the Magnificat here?

The answer can only be: no, not at all! There would only be a break in the Magnificat, a profound inconsistency, if Mary were speaking here simply as a private person. But that is not what she is doing. There is no rupture between the action of God in Mary and God's actions in the past for Israel, because in the Magnificat Mary is speaking not only as a private person but as the spokeswoman, the representative of Israel. Therefore the deeds of God in Israel and those done for Mary flow seamlessly into one another. Let us look more closely. In verse 51 we read: "He has shown strength with his arm; he has scattered the proud in the imagination of their hearts." What did faithful Jews think when they heard that? Most certainly they thought first of the pride of Pharaoh and the destruction of the Egyptians at the Sea of Reeds and thus above all of the rescue of Israel from Egypt. The "Song of Moses" (Exod 15:1-18) echoes here; it, too, speaks of "God's right hand" that smashes the Egyptians (15:6, 12). Then, in verse 52, the Magnificat says: "He has brought down the powerful from their thrones and lifted up the lowly." Here again the background is the conflict with the Pharaoh and so the exodus from Egypt. That is all part of Israel's fundamental confession of faith.

Then, in verse 53, we read: "he has filled the hungry with good things." When did God do that? Well, when God led the people through the wilderness and fed them with manna. Finally, verse 54: "He has come to the aid of his child Israel, in remembrance of his mercy." What is the allusion at this point in the Magnificat? The background, in light of the theology of the Servant, is quite clearly Isaiah 41:8-9 and thus Israel's being brought back from Babylon into its homeland.

Thus in her song of praise Mary summarizes Israel's whole history, and at the end, in verses 54-55, she finally speaks about herself. The miracle God has now done in her is thus, for Mary, the culmination of all God's miracles for God's people Israel—since Abraham. In Mary the whole history of Israel is gathered up, and now, through God's mercy, it produces the Messiah. But if, in her, God has finally and irrevocably accepted Israel, then Mary stands for Israel, and she is Israel's representative, the image of faithful Israel: she is the embodiment of the people of God.

If Mary were simply an individual historical figure who was looking at her life in isolation, the Magnificat would be incomprehensible. But that is not how Luke sees Mary. For him she is more than an individual, isolated person who experiences strange things. She speaks the Magnificat as representative of God's people Israel, just as she has already said yes on behalf of all Israel. Because she summarizes God's deeds on behalf of Israel she can, without any transition, speak first of herself and then of God's actions in and on behalf of God's people. Thus there is no break in the Magnificat's text as such. It is completely unified—but only if one understands that here Mary is depicted as the figure of Israel.

The Equation of Mary with the Church

This deeper meaning of Mary—that she is the image of Israel and of the newly gathered people of God, the church—was always present to the great theologians of subsequent centuries. Rather than citing all the texts that could be brought forward here—from Irenaeus to Vatican II—I will offer only two examples.[2] The medieval theologian Rupert of Deutz (†1129) wrote in his commentary on John's Gospel:

> Where the mother of Jesus is, that is, where the mother church is . . . the true faith in the incarnation of Christ is proclaimed.

Thus Rupert of Deutz presents an equation: mother of Jesus = Mother Church. The two parts of the equation are interchangeable. This comparison, "Mary = church," was a matter of course for the church fathers and the medieval theologians. The Cistercian monk Isaac of Stella (†1178) even formulated a rule for interpreting this telescoping of church and Mary:

> In the inspired Scriptures what is said in a universal sense of the virgin mother, the Church, is understood in an individual sense of the Virgin Mary, and what is said in a particular sense of the virgin mother Mary is rightly understood in a general sense of the virgin mother, the Church. When either is spoken of, the meaning can be understood of both, almost without qualification.

Both of those are very unusual statements. I think it is clear what this means in practice. All dogmatic statements about Mary are at the same time statements about the church and about believing and hopeful Israel. All the hymns we sing about Mary are simultaneously hymns about the church and about believing and hopeful Israel. The same is true of every sculpture and painting in which Mary's beauty is depicted. They, too, are supported—whether the artists knew it or

[2] For the text references and further examples see Gerhard Lohfink and Ludwig Weimer, *Maria – nicht ohne Israel. Eine neue Sicht der Lehre von der Unbefleckten Empfängnis*, 2nd ed. (Freiburg: Herder, 2012), 267–69.

not—by the theological axiom: what is said of Mary is likewise said of the church and of believing and hoping Israel. One must know this fundamental axiom if one wants to have even a remote understanding of Roman Catholic Mariology and Marian devotion.

Election for the Sake of Others

Now for a second step. When Pope Pius IX on December 8, 1854, after a worldwide survey of Roman Catholic bishops and theological faculties, solemnly proclaimed the dogma of the immaculate conception, the crucial passage read:

> We declare, pronounce, and define that the doctrine which holds that the most Blessed Virgin Mary, in the first instance of her conception, by a singular grace and privilege granted by Almighty God, in view of the merits of Jesus Christ, the Savior of the human race, was preserved free from all stain of original sin, is a doctrine revealed by God and therefore to be believed firmly and constantly by all the faithful.[3]

The word "privilege" is, for many, the most offensive part of this dogmatic formulation. We are very much disturbed when others are "privileged." We don't like it; we find it suspect. And therefore many people also dislike this kind of Mariology-of-privilege, which appears to make Mary an absolutely exceptional figure.

Still, the matter looks different when we keep in mind the basic axiom of Mariology: Mary is the epitome of the church and of faithful Israel. In that case the statement about Mary's privilege is above all about a privilege of the people of God, of Israel.

Then the question arises: has God privileged Israel? The answer can only be: obviously! The privileging of Israel is a fundamental statement of the Bible. God has chosen Israel from among all the nations and made them God's own people—certainly not because God despised the other nations but because God needed Israel. God chose Israel precisely for the sake of the other nations and placed on its shoulders the burden of election. Behind God's love for Israel stands, immovably, God's love for the whole world. At the same time this love of God for Israel is unfathomable and underivable—as is every genuine love. Therefore we read in Jeremiah 31:

[3] Pope Pius IX, *Ineffabilis Deus*.

> I have loved you with an everlasting love; therefore I have continued my faithfulness to you. Again I will build you, and you shall be built, O virgin Israel! (Jer 31:3-4)

On that basis we must read all statements about the privileging of Mary with new eyes. Mary represents believing and hoping Israel, and therefore her so-called privileging is primarily a statement about the election of the people of God. But it is not an election in the sense of partisan preference; rather, it is an election for the sake of others. We may indeed sense that if we read every statement about Mary simultaneously as a statement about Israel and the church, then the doctrine of Mary's privilege immediately takes on a profound biblical sense. I would, however, prefer always to speak of "election" rather than "privileging." "Election" is good biblical language, while the word "privileging" leaves a bad aftertaste.

Sanctified in Word and Sacrament

A third step: is there a biblical foundation for Mary's holiness and freedom from original sin? Certainly. Deuteronomy 7 reads:

> [Y]ou are a people holy to the LORD your God; the LORD your God has chosen you out of all the peoples on earth to be his people, his treasured possession. It was not because you were more numerous than any other people that the LORD set his heart on you and chose you, for you were the fewest of all peoples. It was because the LORD loved you and kept the oath that he swore to your ancestors that the LORD has brought you out with a mighty hand and redeemed you from the house of slavery, from the hand of Pharaoh king of Egypt. (Deut 7:6-8)

This text makes clear what is meant by speaking of a "holy" people or "holy" church: not individual achievement, not personal effort, but an unearned holiness that is pure gift and comes from God's fidelity and love. It is in precisely the same sense that the Old Testament calls Israel a holy people and the New Testament calls the church holy and whole. I will quote here one of the crucial New Testament texts for the church's holiness. It is from Ephesians 5:

> Husbands, love your wives, just as Christ loved the church and gave himself up for her in order to make her holy by cleansing her with the washing of water by the word, so as to present the church to himself

> in splendor, without a spot or wrinkle or anything of the kind, so that she may be holy and without blemish. (Eph 5:25-27)

Theologians from the patristic period repeatedly, with reference to this text, called the church a virgin and bride of Christ, made "pure," "holy," and "unblemished" through him. "Unblemished" in Latin is *immaculatus*. Long before there was any such thing as a doctrine about Mary, the church fathers called the church *ecclesia immaculata*, because in the sacrament of baptism it is purified and made holy.

Holy, Because Hallowed

Note: I have said, calling on Ephesians to back me up, that the church is holy because its "children" are cleansed and hallowed in the sacrament of baptism. It is not holy in and of itself. It is not so because of its own strength and powers. In itself it is a church of sinners in which there remains endless misery, stupidity, and guilt.

The church is holy only because it is sanctified, again and again, in word and sacrament: because Christ, with his life, has opened for it a space of freedom from the power of sin. This understanding of the church's holiness was also expressed, very early on, in the creed: "I believe in the one, holy, catholic, and apostolic church." The church is holy from the beginning because it is made holy by Christ and because it has received the gift of Christ's Spirit.

Now you understand why Catholic tradition must also say of Mary that she was, from the first moment of her existence, holy and unharmed by the powers of sin: because everything said about Mary is always also said of the church. Because the church is holy, the same must be said of Mary, the prototype of the church. So nothing has been added, there is no rank growth of the tradition; rather, all is a development of statements in the New Testament—Ephesians, for example—consistent and highly proper, the result of insight and under the precondition that Mary is the epitome of the people of God. But, as we have seen, that insight already existed in Luke's work.

The Real Mary

Now we must take a fourth and last step, and I will begin it with an immediate objection. The church is the *immaculata*, and therefore

Mary is also the *immaculata*—fine! But that conclusion can apply to Mary only to the extent that she is the epitome of the church, the figure and symbol of the church.

But is that true of the real Mary, of the Jewish girl Miriam, of the individual? Hasn't the church overstepped itself here when it concludes from the freedom of the church from original sin to the same freedom on the part of the historical Mary?

Let me pose a counter-question: can something be true of a symbol that is not true of the real person who has become image and symbol? That would be perverse. The church has never made such a separation. For the church, Mary was always inseparably a real person and an epitome in one.

Theology has always had a consequential argument for the freedom of the real person from original sin. According to the account in Luke 1, Mary answers the angel's announcement by saying: "Here am I, the servant of the Lord; let it be with me according to your word" (Luke 1:38). We need not regard the whole scene as a historical report, and we do not have to fix on "let it be with me according to your word" as applying to a historical point in time. But in any case we must take this statement seriously as an existential statement about Mary. Otherwise we would be doubting the truth of the Bible. Mary must have been a pure, unfettered, unreserved *yes* with her whole existence. She must have made herself a lifelong "servant" of God. Mary wed herself to the will of God, even when that will remained obscure to her, even when it became a sword for her, one that pierced her soul (Luke 2:35). Hans Urs von Balthasar rightly said of Mary: "if Mary's Yes had contained even the shadow of a demurral, of a 'so far and no farther' . . . the child could not have taken possession of the whole of human nature."[4]

Our Own Yes

In this context let us make clear what our own yes normally looks like. We should read the "annunciation scene" in contrast to how we

[4] Hans Urs von Balthasar, "Maria in der kirchlichen Lehre und Frömmigkeit," in Josef Ratzinger and Hans Urs von Balthasar, *Maria. Kirche im Ursprung*, 5th ed. (Einsiedeln: Johannes Verlag; Freiburg: Herder, 2005), 87–111, at 93. [English: *Mary, the Church at the Source*, trans. Adrian Walker (San Francisco: Ignatius, 2005), 105.]

ourselves all too often deal with the will of God as soon as it appears to us: either we act as if it were not at all clear to us what God wills, saying, "Well, if I knew what God wants from me, obviously I would do it." But often that is pure escapism. Usually we have a pretty accurate idea. But we don't want to do it.

Or else we say: "Yes, I want to do what God asks of me. But does it have to be today? I need time." That, too, is escapism. Augustine, in his *Confessions*, gave a masterful description of how horribly this "putting-off of repentance" had crippled him for quite a long time. It was the crippling of a person who is called, who has understood, and who still does not want to. Augustine describes his putting-off of real repentance as follows:

> "Presently, lo, presently"; "Leave me a little while." But "presently, presently," had no present; and my "leave me a little while" went on for a long while. . . .
> For I said mentally, "Lo, let it be done now, let it be done now." And as I spoke, I all but came to a resolve. I all but did it, yet I did it not. (*Confessions* 8.5.12; 11.25)

It can also happen that we actually begin to do the will of God, but we have reserves, places where we do not let God in. Certainly: God should be the master of our lives—but not in everything. If we compare our life to a house, we do actually open the door to God; we do not leave God standing outside in the cold air. We certainly invite God in, offer a seat, enter into conversation.

But do we let God into the whole house? Into every room? Aren't there some spaces where we by no means welcome God in? Where we certainly cannot let God in because we haven't tidied up there or, to put it more precisely, because it is pure chaos? And aren't there also some very dark basement rooms, that is, reservations, caveats, places where we serve our own will and don't let even God meddle with us? There are spaces within the house of our life whose doors remain sealed. We want those places for ourselves alone. The ultimate result is that we are torn between two masters: God and ourselves.

That is the bitter reality that makes us suffer from our own selves and makes our lives so miserable. It is only in the face of this division in our own lives that we can clearly understand what it means when Luke says of Mary that she spoke a pure, unqualified yes and made herself God's "serving-maid."

Freedom from the River of Refusals

Indeed, a pure, undivided yes presupposes freedom from original sin, freedom from this stream of resistance and indifference that runs throughout history. For we must regard original sin as a terrific potential for evil that estranges us from God, darkens the world's spirit, and robs human beings of their freedom. If Mary said her yes in complete freedom—and otherwise God could not have become a human being—she cannot have been a part of the river of evil that is original sin.

Certainly we should not imagine this as if God had performed a kind of special action to snatch Mary from original sin's potential for evil. The struggle for freedom from original sin, that is, from the powers of evil that had grown as a result of many individual sins throughout history, took place in Israel, beginning with Abraham. Mary's purity and the absolute integrity of Jesus were prepared and fought for through a centuries-long, arduous, and painful history.

Mary is truly the *immaculata*, but that freedom from the world's potential for evil did not come to her through a spectacular divine intervention that snatched Mary from the darkness of sin. That freedom was acquired through many generations in Israel—not, of course, without the untiring grace of God. Mary's freedom and clarity could never have existed without the surrender of many generations before her to the will of God.

Here we can see again that all statements about Mary are at the same time statements about the believing people of God who were struggling to bring about God's will.

Also a Dogma about Israel

Now, in conclusion, let me look back once again. It has probably become clear that we cannot speak about Mary without continually speaking about the church. But we most certainly can only speak of Mary when we also speak of Israel. The dogma of the immaculate conception is also a dogma about Israel.

We must not be content with saying that Mary was showered with grace in a special act of God and thus preserved from all earthly guilt. As correct as that way of speaking may be from a certain point of view, it separates Mary from her roots. Mary's freedom from original sin was fought for in Israel in a long history of struggle. It emerged, in the course of Israel's history, that the world contains not only potentials for evil and contexts of guilt but saving events and a history of freedom. Grace presupposes not only nature but also history.

Torah repeatedly insists on the holiness of the people of God. "You shall be holy, for I the LORD your God am holy" (Lev 19:2, and frequently). Torah faith regarded it as the duty of the chosen people to live holy lives and to hallow the world. The exodus from Egypt was to lead the people into a holy land and make possible a holy—that is, a just—society that brings about God's social order as reality. When it is said of Mary that her existence was altogether holy and spotless from the beginning, that means nothing other than that Israel's long struggle was not in vain. The holiness God longs to see in the world became reality in Mary: not separated from Israel but together with it, and not separated from Christ but joined with him.

The Reality of Redemption

Hence our Protestant brothers' and sisters' question should not be: Can we really believe that such great things may be said of Mary? It should instead be: Do we believe that God has really given the world this freedom from evil? Do we believe that God's grace was victorious? Do we believe that the promised redemption is already present, already happening?

All Christians, of course, believe that redemption in Christ is already present. But do they also believe that it has been in preparation since Abraham, that it has shone forth in Israel again and again, then became full reality in Christ, and that since then in the church, because of Christ, it has become a place of salvation and freedom in the world? Mary represents this space of freedom and salvation bestowed. Believing in Mary's freedom from original sin means believing that the redemption God has given the world through Christ is real, that it exists not just in the mind of God but has really come into this world through Christ, in Mary, and in the people Mary represents: the church, the eschatological Israel.

Basically, what we say about Mary decides the question whether we really believe in genuine redemption here in this world, true redemption that can be seen: visible, tactile, and in our midst in its rational nature. For Mary is one of us. No, this is not about proliferation, not about excess, but about the essence of Christianity.

May We Pray to Mary?

Finally, please permit me a remark on Roman Catholic veneration of Mary. I have said that Mary is one of us. She is, so to speak, family: part of the family of believers, the "family of God." But in a family people look to one another, rejoice together, talk together, ask each other for help, and cry out when in crisis. That is the most normal thing in the world.

This reflection does not change in the least the truth that we worship God alone and lay all honor, praise, and ultimately all our needs at the feet of God. But we are not alone in doing so. We do it together with Mary, and we do it in a profound gratitude that God has given us this sister and mother. Mary is not a mediator. She is our dear mother with whom we stand together before God.

18

Foreign, Hunted, and Shunned

The world has always been in motion. There have always been migrations. There have always been migrants, refugees, people persecuted and expelled. For a long time now people have been fleeing from Africa and Asia to European lands because they can no longer live in their homelands. But the year 2015 became, in this sense, a fateful one for Europe. It was as if floodgates had opened. Misery and want were suddenly tangible: in the needs of people who were inadequately clothed, hungry, had traveled on dangerous routes and wanted, finally, to live in peace and security.

Not only Germany but nearly all European countries are increasingly faced with the question of how to deal with this flood of refugees. Reactions are widely different. They extend from distress, fear, distancing, and defensiveness to solidarity, readiness to help, and the firm desire to receive the strangers. Christians who act on behalf of refugees often hear quoted, precisely in this context, words that Jesus speaks in his role as world judge:

> I was hungry and you gave me food,
> I was thirsty and you gave me something to drink,
> I was a stranger and you welcomed me,
> I was naked and you gave me clothing,
> I was sick and you took care of me,
> I was in prison and you visited me. (Matt 25:35-36)

Many Christians have heard these words with new ears. Suddenly they are no longer long-ago sayings, words spoken two thousand years ago. It is as if they were said today. But what, more exactly, do they say? What is their background? To whom are they addressed, and what is their purpose? In what follows I will try to uncover that background.

A Text to be Learned

First: these statements are found in Matthew's Gospel, in the last major speech Jesus gives there, which is about the end time. It begins with chapter 24 and ends with the conclusion of chapter 25. This speech is given exclusively to Jesus' disciples (Matt 24:1, 3, 9), and it concludes with a depiction of the Last Judgment (Matt 25:31-46). The passion account begins immediately afterward. The consequence is that the passage about judgment receives heavy emphasis and at the same time represents a conclusion. But its weight comes not only from the fact that it stands at the end of Matthew's extensive speech composition[1] and before the account of Jesus' passion. That emphasis also results from the spectacular scenery projected in it:

> When the [Human One[2]] comes in his glory and all the angels with him, then he will sit on the throne of his glory. All the nations will be gathered before him, and he will separate people one from another as a shepherd separates the sheep from the goats,[3] and he will put the sheep at his right hand and the goats at the left. Then the king will say to those at his right hand, "Come, you who are blessed by my Father, inherit the kingdom prepared for you from the foundation of the world, for I was hungry . . ." (Matt 25:31-35)

Here begins the great speech of the world's judge, and it is interrupted only by the questions of the blessed and those of the condemned. At first neither group can comprehend that their actions were done to the world judge.

Everyone who hears or reads this text notices the repetitions. The section in 25:34-46 has two parts: the first deals with the people on the right, who are blessed; the second is about the people on the left,

[1] Matthew 5:1–7:29; 9:35–11:1; 13:1-53; 18:1-35; 24:1–25:46.

[2] *Bar enosh*, literally "Son of Humanity," usually translated "Son of Man," as (without caps) in NABRE; NRSV and NRSVue: "human being." (See chap. 16, n. 16 above.)

[3] The correct translation of Greek *eriphos*, or *eriphion*, is debated. Possibilities are "ram," "goat," "billy goat," "kid." I decline to enter here into a discussion of the agricultural background. The crucial point is that a strict separation is made.

who are condemned. The positive first part corresponds to the negative second part. So: positive side and negative side. That is simple and powerful.

Still, the two parts of the speech composition are further subdivided: those on the right respond with questions, because they have not understood. Those on the left also respond in the same way, and in both cases everything is repeated. In this way the six-part series I have cited[4] appears four times as a whole, even though it is progressively tightened.

Why did Matthew do it this way? Why these repetitions? Quite simply because it gives the judgment dialogue immense force and monumental character. But the repetitions have an additional purpose: the words are intended to be striking and to impress themselves in people's memory. They must never be forgotten, and the church *has* never forgotten them. As early as the third century it put together, out of Matthew's text, the "seven corporal works of mercy," adding a seventh to the six given here:

> Feed the hungry,
> Give drink to the thirsty,
> Clothe the naked,
> Shelter the homeless,
> Visit the sick,
> Free the prisoners,
> Bury the dead.

This sequence of works of mercy, of love, has had an extraordinary impact in the church throughout its history: it has produced countless hospitals, nursing homes, hospices, hostels, homeless shelters, burial societies, orders dedicated to the freeing of prisoners. If I tried to tell the history of these Christian institutions I would never finish.

I would have to begin with the collection that Paul gathered from the congregations of his mission field for the suffering community in Jerusalem, and I would have to end with the wells that Christian charitable organizations such as Bread for the World are now digging so that

[4] Listing of individual works of love on behalf of the poor was widespread in the ancient Near East, the Old Testament, and Judaism—especially in connection with judgment of the dead. Cf. the summary in Johannes Friedrich, *Gott im Bruder? Eine methodenkritische Untersuchung von Redaktion, Überlieferung und Traditionen in Mt 25,31-46*, Calwer theologische Monographien 7 (Stuttgart: Calwer, 1977), 164–72.

people in developing countries may have clean water. All that is (not only, but also) a consequence of the judgment discourse in Matthew 25. It is good that Matthew made his text so clear, so easy to understand, and so precise: as a result, the church has never forgotten it.

Yes/No, Either/Or

In fact, Matthew did that again and again in his Gospel: the compositions are both clear and impressive. They make this Gospel a vivid, living thing. What is special about it is that its statements are clear as glass. Nothing is fuzzy or whitewashed. It is all "yes, yes," "no, no," "either/or"! "Don't just talk: act! Not tomorrow: now!" Matthew is always clear, and that is what gives his compositions such power.

We can also observe, with regard to Matthew, that this evangelist is no theoretician. He cares nothing for abstract systems. He builds no speculative cathedrals. Don't misunderstand me! The church needs theory. It needs the effort to conceptualize. It needs great theological systems. Where would we be without Paul, Augustine, Thomas Aquinas, or Francisco Suarez?

But Matthew is not part of that series. He makes no finely chiseled distinctions. He does not deal in abstractions. He does not build systems. For him it is all about real action. In this he is not only a disciple of Jesus but also a good Jew. What good are the loveliest truths if they are not put into action? When the gospel is lived, truth will also appear.

That is evident, for example, in the greatest and most powerful speech composition in Matthew's Gospel,[5] the Sermon on the Mount. Matthew shows Jesus saying, at the end of that great discourse:

> Everyone, then, who hears these words of mine and acts on them will be like a wise person who built a house on rock. . . . And everyone who hears these words of mine and does not act on them will be like a foolish person who built a house on sand. (Matt 7:24, 26)

Shortly before this are these words, hard and clear:

> Not everyone who says to me, "Lord, Lord," will enter the [reign of God], but only the one who does the will of my Father in heaven. (Matt 7:21)

[5] Certainly Matthew's Sermon on the Mount draws on a previous stage in Q.

In the judgment discourse of 25:31-46 Matthew also formulates entirely in terms of *doing*. Help the hungry, so that they may at last be filled. Give water to the thirsty. Receive strangers. Give clothes to those who are freezing. Care for the sick. Bring help to those in prison. And then come the incredible words: "Truly I tell you, just as you did it to one of the least of these brothers and sisters of mine, you did it to me" (Matt 25:40).

That is service to the poor, christologically grounded—and yet it is pure practice, simple action. In the poor countries with their gigantic shanty towns and *favelas* this requires no translation. It is all literally true. In our privileged situation in the West we have to translate it. Here it is often paralleled with the "spiritual works of mercy," but it remains just as real: in everyone we encounter and who is in need, Christ stands before us. That could mean, for example, that Christ encounters us in everyone who is lonely, sorrowing, despairing, embittered, confused, those for whom we have to give up our time: in short, in everyone we look in the face and whom we can help—for they are all Christ's "least sisters and brothers."

In the last few years that has all become physically, materially, and indeed offensively real for us. Refugees from Syria, Iraq, and Afghanistan stand before us with empty hands, needing a roof over their heads, food and clothing, language instruction, medical aid, jobs. When we come to the aid of such people, even if we are not at all aware of the Christological background of our actions, if we simply help as need demands, we are already among those to whom Christ will say: "Come, you who are blessed by my Father!"

That is what is so infinitely comforting in Matthew's great judgment speech, but at the same time it is what is so profoundly frightening—namely, when, in light of this text, I have to recognize myself as one who, because of my refusal to act in the crisis surrounding me, would have to stand at the left hand of the judge and not the right: that is, among those who are not blessed but have condemnation spoken over them!

Who Are the Persecuted?

What have I just done? I have tried, quite incidentally, to offer a glimpse into the unique character of Matthew's Gospel. I have sought to point at least briefly to the compositional art of Matthew, his decisiveness and clarity, the weight that practical action has for him. But now, at last, I need to come to the thing that matters to me most.

Indeed I have, all this time, been interpreting Matthew 25:31-46 as has been done everywhere since the beginning of the nineteenth century.[6] I have explained it as if it were a matter of course, the way it is understood today in countless sermons, catecheses, and speeches—as if this text were about all those in need, all the hungry, all the suffering of this earth. That reading is popular with people today. It meets us halfway and speaks to us. It matches our modern humanism and our longing for an undogmatic and practical Christianity. But it also corresponds, primarily, to our openness to the *ethos* of other religions, no matter which worldview or confession one accepts: we are to help our fellow human beings who are in need, and we are thereby justified. There are very few texts in the Gospels that seem so immediately plausible and are so beloved as this one—but only as long as it is interpreted to refer to all the poor and suffering of this world.

But I do not want to conceal from you that there is a very different way of looking at this text, one that for a long time now has been spreading among biblical scholars. Many students of the New Testament have recently come to regard the text from a completely different angle. In my opinion this newer path to interpretation, which in essence was also that of the ancient church and the church of the Middle Ages, touches the original meaning of the Matthean text.

What I said before has not simply become obsolete. It is certainly a possible application of Matthew 25:31-46 to modernity. We must take such updatings seriously. But what Matthew himself meant and what Jesus himself most probably meant[7] was something else, with an entirely different point of view.

So what does this new interpretation look like? We arrive at it when we ask: who, in fact, are the people Jesus calls the "least" in this Matthean text (25:45), or "the least of these brothers and sisters of mine"

[6] Cf. the excellent overview of the history of the influence of Matt 25:31-46 in Ulrich Luz, *Das Evangelium nach Matthäus,* EKKNT 1,4 (Zürich: Benziger; Neukirchen: Neukirchener Verlag, 2002), 521–30. [English: *Matthew 21–28,* trans. James E. Crouch, Hermeneia (Minneapolis: Fortress Press, 2005), 263–84.]

[7] For methodological reasons I will not enter here into the question of what parts of Matt 25:31-46 are Jesus (or Jesuanic) material. That would require a more extended discussion and ultimately the decision is difficult. I am only concerned with the level of statement in Matthew.

(25:40)? Who are they? Are they really everyone in the world who is hungry, thirsty, homeless, naked, sick, and imprisoned? Who are the "least," the "humble"—the sisters and brothers who are especially close to Jesus and for whom he is more concerned than for any others, even though everyone is in his heart?

Four Observations

First of all: In Matthew 25:40 Matthew speaks of the poor and suffering as his "brothers and sisters." But the fact is that wherever in Matthew's Gospel the words "brothers" and "sisters" appear they refer either to his "brothers in the flesh" or his "sisters and brothers in the community" or "disciples." See in this regard especially Matthew 12:49, 50; 18:15, 35; 23:8. Never—let me emphasize—*never* do these words have the universal sense of "human sisters and brothers" or of the suffering or poor throughout the world.[8] Especially important in this context is the appearance of the Risen One to the women at the end of Matthew's Gospel. There the Risen One says: "Do not be afraid; go and tell my brothers and sisters to go to Galilee; there they will see me" (Matt 28:10).

Obviously this does not refer to Jesus' brothers in the flesh, but neither is it about "fellow human beings" in a vague sense, and certainly not "all the people of this earth." The reference is clearly to Jesus' disciples (cf. Matt 28:16). Should they not also be those referred

[8] Friedrich, *Gott im Bruder?*, 233–39, reaches a different conclusion. For Friedrich *adelphos* in Matthew cannot mean only "physical sibling" or "sibling in faith" but also "fellow human being" in a general sense. He finds that universal meaning especially in authentic words of Jesus such as Matt 5:22, 23, 24; 7:3, 4. But why, in those passages, would the historical Jesus not have appealed to his Jewish audience on behalf of their Jewish siblings-in-faith in Israel? Friedrich (like many others) refers especially to the opening to love of enemies in Matt 5:43-48 and sees love of enemies as "an innovation in contrast to Judaism" (p. 236). But love of enemies is already found in the Old Testament—directly in Exod 23:4-5, indirectly in Lev 19:17-18. And the category of unrestrictedness does not describe what Jesus meant by *agapē*. Did Jesus really speak universally, in the sense of "all people"? Rather, he addresses himself decisively to Israel. Everything he says in universal terms relates to the idea of the pilgrimage of nations to Israel and is not about Israel itself. For the whole subject see Gerhard Lohfink, *No Irrelevant Jesus*, trans. Linda M. Maloney (Collegeville, MN: Liturgical Press, 2014), 64–74. See also Eberhard Schockenhoff, *Die Bergpredigt. Aufruf zum Christsein* (Freiburg: Herder, 2014).

to in the judgment speech—and in the very precise sense that whoever helps Jesus' disciples thereby helps Jesus himself?[9]

Second observation: Evidently Jesus could refer to his disciples as the "little ones," that is, the "least" (cf. Mark 9:42 // Matt 18:6, 10, 14). It is possible that Jesus' opponents used such words to ridicule and demean his disciples: "Those are the little ones, the least of all; they have no idea what the law says!" Jesus could have taken up that kind of contemptuous speech and turned it into something positive. But however that may be, Matthew 10:42 says, on the basis of Mark 9:41:

> [W]hoever gives even a cup of cold water to one of these little ones [*mikrōn*] in the name of a disciple—truly I tell you, none of these will lose their reward.

This text is very weighty in regard to our question, for the "least" (*elachistos*) can, in Greek, be the superlative of "little" (*mikros*). Thus Matthew 10:42 is shown to be a key text for Matthew 25:45. In both cases the subject is "little ones" who are identified in 10:42 as Jesus' disciples. Readers of Matthew's Gospel who have previously read 10:42 could therefore only understand the "least" in 25:45 to be Jesus' disciples.

A third observation: Shortly before this text in Matthew 10:42 that is so important in our context we read: "Whoever welcomes you, welcomes me" (Matt 10:40). The meaning is: "Whoever welcomes you, the disciples I have sent out, shelters you overnight and receives what you preach: such a one is welcoming me." The basic structure here corresponds very closely to the statement: "whatever you have done for the least of my sisters and brothers, you have done for me." The issue, then, is that Jesus' disciples should receive help. Whoever helps and receives them also receives Christ.

A fourth observation: In Jewish reference "the nations" or "the peoples" are normally Gentiles. Is Matthew following that usage in 25:32? At any rate the plural *ethnē* (= peoples, nations) means Gentiles everywhere else in his book[10] (cf. 6:32; 10:5, 18; 20:19, 25; 24:9, 14; 28:19). But what is crucial in our context is that in the passages I have listed the Gentile peoples are *contrasted with the disciples*. Thus when

[9] At least at the level of the Matthean redaction Friedrich, *Gott im Bruder?* agrees.

[10] Here I will not consider the quotations in 4:15; 12:18, 21, although they also speak of the Gentiles.

the judgment speech begins by saying that "all nations" will be summoned for judgment, the reference is to the Gentile nations in contrast to the disciples of Jesus.[11] In this judgment scene the Gentiles are measured according to their behavior toward Jesus' disciples.

All these observations show that the "least sisters and brothers" of Jesus in Matthew are not the poor and miserable of this earth but the disciples Jesus sent out, who are hungry at night, have no roof over their heads, are in need, are often rejected and persecuted. Matthew describes that in the great mission discourse of 9:35–11:1. The disciples who are sent are not received everywhere (10:14). They fall among "wolves" (10:16); they are handed over to judgment (10:17, 19); they are flogged in the synagogues (10:17) and brought before governors and kings (10:18), even betrayed by their own relatives (10:21), and are hated by everyone (10:22). Thus the judgment dialogue in Matthew 25 is based on Jesus' own sending of his disciples.

It is clear that in this way two strata of time overlap. On the one hand there is the sending of missionaries that Jesus performed: he sent out disciples two by two and they were to proclaim the reign of God everywhere in Israel (cf. Mark 6:6-13; Luke 10:1-16). But at the same time Matthew had in mind the fate of the itinerant Christian missionaries who, after Easter, preached the gospel at first in Israel and then in Gentile lands (cf., e.g., Acts 13:1-3). Probably, though, he meant not only messengers of the faith sent by Christian communities but, beyond them, all Christians who are persecuted and in need.

The "Least" of Jesus' Sisters and Brothers

Who, then, are "the least of my sisters and brothers" in Matthew 25:31-46? How, more precisely, did Matthew picture things when he was writing his Gospel, some time after the year 70? Here is what I think.

When the day of the world's judgment comes the gospel will already have been preached among all the Gentile peoples (Matt 24:14;

[11] Whether, contrary to common Jewish usage, Matthew in 25:32 includes Israel among the *ethnē* is something that can remain open. It could be favored by the fact that in Matt 10:16, 17, 21 people from Israel also encounter the disciples in a hostile manner. At any rate it does not include the disciples and the Christian communities.

28:19). Then Gentiles have had the Christian witnesses among them; these have been poor and oppressed, often coming to them persecuted and in need. And they have had in their midst Christian communities whose very existence witnessed to Jesus Christ.

> *The criterion for the Gentiles at the world judgment will be how they have behaved toward Christian messengers of the faith and Christian communities.*

If they have helped them, even with as small a thing as a cup of fresh water (Matt 10:42), they have thereby helped Jesus' cause and have a share in the reign of God. If they have not helped them, they are not part of the reign of God and will be judged.

Thus in Matthew 25 the Human One identifies with his disciples, his followers, his communities of disciples. As much as Christ is on the side of all the poor, the most important thing in the world, for him, is the existence of his people, because it is only through that people that the poor of the earth can really be helped. That is a fundamental idea of biblical theology. Therefore in the judgment on the nations what is important is how they have behaved toward the Christian messengers of the faith and toward Christian communities.

This interpretation can offer very solid and—it seems to me—irrefutable arguments for itself, but it does not exactly encounter general approval. Although it is acquiring more and more adherents among exegetical scholars, many find it abhorrent. Even the New Testament exegete Johannes Weiß (1863–1914) called such an interpretation an expression of "intolerable Christian arrogance"[12] while others branded it as positively sectarian. Johann Gnilka has joined that chorus and writes, in his commentary on Matthew: "This view [seems] not very Christian and not very Matthean: Christians as the privileged of this earth!"[13]

But in the context of the Bible as a whole an interpretation in terms of the persecuted disciples is not at all unusual—moreover, it is good Matthew: Israel, or the church, is God's instrument for the healing

[12] Cf. Luz, *Matthew 21–28*, 280n152.

[13] Joachim Gnilka, *Das Matthäusevangelium* II. Teil, HThKNT (Freiburg: Herder, 1988), 375.

of the world, and those who come to the aid of Jesus' disciples come to the aid of Jesus himself (Matt 10:40-42).[14]

We should also insist that not necessarily *everything* is demanded of the Gentiles who come into contact with Christians. What is asked of them in the first place is humanity toward these Christians. Sometimes even a cup of water is enough. Infinitely more is demanded of the Christians themselves: not only a cup of water, but their whole existence, their whole lives, complete trust, and a clear confession of Christ.

And obviously the disciples themselves are also subject to the judgment of the Human One. They cannot escape it, if only because they bear the name "Christian." That Christians will also be judged is something Matthew has already said quite clearly and to a drastic degree that is positively terrifying, in the three parables of the faithful and unfaithful slaves (24:45-51), the wise and foolish bridesmaids (25:1-13), and the money given in trust (25:14-30). In all three parables, as in the judgment discourse in Matthew 25, there is both a right and a left side: that is, generous reward or bitter destruction.

But here, at *this* point, at the end of the great eschatological discourse, the subject is no longer judgment on the disciples and Christian communities; here it is about the fate of the Gentile nations. Matthew describes the criterion by which the Gentiles who have not grasped the full message will be judged.

The objection raised against this interpretation is that it makes the whole Matthean depiction of the world judgment nothing but a "consolation" for Jesus' disciples. They are not at all affected by it; they are outside, separate. We could only see them in the text as "the least" of Jesus' brothers—so the judgment would pass them by. Exactly! The judgment speech is indeed a word of consolation for the "least sisters and brothers." But that insight is entirely in line with Matthew's view, because the great mission discourse in Matthew 10 closes precisely with consolation to the disciples being sent out: "Whoever welcomes you welcomes me" (10:40).

[14] See also Luz, *Matthew 21–28*, 280: "Are the 'lowliest brothers' a special group within the Christian community? In the text 'lowly' is contrasted with the 'great' heavenly King and World Judge. The term emphasizes rhetorically the gigantic distance between the needy and the World Judge and has the effect of emphasizing the surprising miracle of his identification with them."

The judgment speech in Matthew 25:31-46, as interpreted here, however, is not only altogether in line with Matthew 10:40. It also follows a pattern that is very biblical. It is especially well developed in Psalms 9/10, whose theme is the poor who seek their rights from God. They are called "needy,"[15] "afflicted,"[16] "oppressed,"[17] and "helpless."[18] For that very reason God does not abandon them; God comes to their aid and gives them justice (9:5). God is seated on the throne (9:5) and gathers "the peoples/all nations" in the divine presence (9:9, 18). As judge and "king" (10:16) God speaks a destroying judgment on the Gentile nations and those in Israel who united with the pagan peoples against the poor.

The commonalities with Matthew 25 are striking: It is not only that "all nations" are gathered before the king's throne. What is important in our context is that in Psalms 9/10 the poor and oppressed (like Jesus' "least sisters and brothers" in Matthew 25) have nothing to answer to the judge for; they do not appear as accused persons before the judgment on the "enemies" (9:7). We have to imagine them as accusers (cf. 9:14; 10:1-11), but that is simply assumed. What is said directly is that God appears as royal judge and does justice for the poor and oppressed. Then comes the decisive point: the fact that God creates justice for them in this judgment gives the poor "consolation and hope" (10:17; 9:19). Psalms 9/10 thus show that it is in no way absurd to see Matthew 25:31-46 as a speech of consolation for Jesus' persecuted disciples.

And We?

Let's not pretend: the misery described in Matthew 25 is, today also, the misery of many Christians in any number of countries. In these years, in these months, in these weeks Christians, women and men, are discriminated against because of their faith, have obstacles placed in the way of their observance of that faith, are pursued, tortured, killed simply because they are Christians, disciples of Jesus. They are truly "the poor," "the suffering," and "the weak."

15 "Needy": Pss 9:13, 19; 10:2, 9, 12, 17.

16 "Afflicted": Ps 9:19.

17 "Oppressed": Pss 9:10; 10:18.

18 "Helpless": Ps 10:8, 10, 14.

Others have to hide, dare not speak about their faith, are verbally abused as idolators, live in constant fear, consider desperately how they might flee—out of all the many countries in which they are currently persecuted. In all the history of the church there have never been so many persecuted and murdered Christians as in our days. Matthew 25 has acquired a fearful pertinence.

And with that we can turn the judgment speech in Matthew 25 against ourselves: if we do not help these persecuted and oppressed people, these poor and distressed, our Christian sisters and brothers—if we do not shelter them and care for them, if we are indifferent to them, if we do not protest and cry out publicly whenever Christian churches are burned and Christians murdered—then we are the same as the Gentiles in Matthew 25 who are judged because they have neglected to help the "least sisters and brothers."

Here at the end let me look back once more over the whole subject, above all the awkward question of the addressees. Everything I have said here is primarily about Christians because, as we saw at the beginning, Matthew's whole judgment speech in 24:1–25:46 is addressed to Jesus' disciples. It is true that, for Matthew, Jesus' disciples are primarily those who followed the earthly Jesus, who traveled with him throughout Israel, whom he sent to all Israel, and whom, at the end of the Gospel, he as the Risen One sends to all nations. But those disciples are representative of all Christians.[19] Matthew already sees in the disciples whom Jesus gathered about him in Israel at that time the beginning of the post-Easter Jesus communities. What Jesus says to the disciples thus applies equally to all who will confess him after Easter. If we take seriously the fact that the whole eschatological discourse is addressed to Jesus' disciples in this sense, the depiction of the world judgment in 25:31-46 can initially be nothing but a *speech of consolation* for Jesus' disciples, that is, for persecuted Christians.[20]

[19] For this question see esp. Jürgen Roloff, *Die Kirche im Neuen Testament*, NTD Ergänzungsreihe 10 (Göttingen: Vandenhoeck & Ruprecht, 1993), 154–55.

[20] There are elements of consolation also at earlier points in the eschatological discourse. Cf. 24:13, 22, 31, 33.

And yet it goes far beyond being mere consolation, because much more is demanded of Jesus' disciples than of the Gentiles, who are addressed by the world judge in the judgment speech regarding their attitude toward Christians. If the Gentiles are measured, before the judgment seat, by whether they have come to the aid of Jesus' poor, abandoned, and persecuted disciples, that applies all the more to the Christians as regards their own sisters and brothers in need. Of them is asked the self-surrendering sibling love Matthew demands, for example, in the Sermon on the Mount (Matt 5:43-48).

Is it not true that what is required of every Christian is also demanded of the state? Must Christian politicians fight to make all borders open in principle, so that all migrants and refugees from economic crisis, who often likewise suffer great need, may be received, that housing may be found for them, and security within society be provided?

Here a distinction is required. It is not for nothing that I have emphasized, again and again, that the whole eschatological discourse is addressed to Jesus' disciples and therefore to Christians. But that also means that it is not addressed to the state, which must stand by its own laws, the justice that (hopefully!) it has established by wise assessment and in harmony with human rights. Beyond that, it must adhere to legislation it has created in cooperation with other states in order to resolve the problem of refugees and asylum seekers. Laws and regulations of this type seek to establish a balance. They try to make their own land open for the persecuted and provide protection for refugees from war until they can return home without danger.[21] But the laws of the state must at the same time provide for order and stability in the land and take responsibility to see that the social fabric is not endangered. Creating this balance is, at present, a task seemingly beyond human capacity. It can be mastered only with patience and calm reason.

Christians can motivate their political leaders; they can stimulate them and above all help them, but they must not burden them with the qualitatively so very different standards of the gospel, and they may not demand of them that they apply the texts of the Gospels in the sense they have for the direct addressees of those texts. Even in

[21] Thus the constitution of the Federal Republic of Germany contains Article 16: "Those subjected to political persecution have the right to asylum."

the most difficult questions regarding refugees, what Jesus once said in such clear and powerful words remains true: "Give therefore to Caesar the things that are Caesar's and to God the things that are God's" (Matt 22:21).

The state must care, in rational ways, for order, justice, legal certainty, and equality, and Christians must help it to do its duty. But their true and most important task is to apply themselves with their whole existence on behalf of the gospel and the building up of communities who live it. Such communities will then also be an effective aid on behalf of strangers, refugees, and the persecuted. Making and preserving that distinction—between the things that belong to the state and the much, much greater cause of the gospel—that is truly a major element in the rationality of Christian faith.

Acknowledgments

My thanks are due especially to Professor Dr. Ludwig Weimer. For many years he has helped to shape the theology of the Katholische Integrierte Gemeinde with his profound knowledge of the Bible and of the history of philosophy and theology. I have learned much from his knowledge and his passion for the rationality of faith.

As always, I thank my brother Norbert for our ongoing conversations about theology and the church, which of course have made their way into this book as well. I have likewise spoken with Professor Dr. Marius Reiser about many of its questions and have always profited from our conversations. I again thank Hans Pachner for his efforts in collecting necessary literature. Herr Dr. Bruno Steimer of Herder urged me to write the book and accompanied it most ably. Frau Antje Bitterlich reviewed all the biblical passages and improved my orthography. I thank her especially for her hard work and her joy in theology.

Last but not least, of course, my very special and heartfelt thanks to my tested and theologically learned translator, Dr. Linda M. Maloney, who makes my books accessible to so many readers in the United States and far beyond.

Index of Biblical Passages